JONATHAN EDWARDS

OLA ELIZABETH WINSLOW

JONATHAN

EDWARDS

1703-1758

COLLIER BOOKS
NEW YORK, N.Y.

To
HARRY EDWIN MILNES
MINISTER

ACKNOWLEDGMENT

THIS BOOK would not have been possible except for the hospitality and kindness shown by the various custodians of the Edwards memorials and of the many other materials pertinent to this chapter in American religious history. It is a pleasure to acknowledge my debt to all those who have so graciously given permission for the examination and use of these materials.

My largest debt is to the Library of Yale University, where most of the Edwards manuscripts are to be found. I wish particularly to record my gratitude to Mr. Andrew Keogh, former Librarian, to the members of the Library Committee, and to Miss Anne S. Pratt and Miss Emily Hall of the Library Staff. I owe a large debt also to the Trustees of Andover-Harvard Theological Seminary, and to the Rev. Owen H. Gates, Librarian, for making available the rich storehouse of manuscript materials collected by Mr. Sereno E. Dwight, descendant and early biographer of Jonathan Edwards. I wish to thank also Mr. J. L. Harrison, of Forbes Library, Northampton, Massachusetts, for the use of the Judd MSS., the Minutes of the Hampshire Association, and various other materials pertaining to Northampton local history; Mr. Lawrence Heyl of Princeton University Library, for the privilege of examining the books which once belonged to Jonathan Edwards and to his son; and Sir William Foster, of London, for access to the Records of the Coopers' Company at Coopers' Hall.

It is a pleasure also to recall and to acknowledge the many courtesies shown me at the Library of Congress, the Massachusetts Historical Society, the New York Historical Society, the New York Public Library, the American Antiquarian Society, the Boston Athenaeum, the Congregational libraries of Boston and of London, the British Museum, the Library of Lambeth Palace, and the various other libraries to which this search has led, not forgetting the day-to-day services of the Library of Goucher College and, during the present summer, the Library of the University of Maine. The interest shown in this study by those from whom it has been necessary to ask many favors has been more valuable and more encouraging than any mere statement of indebtedness can possibly suggest. The warmth and friendliness of this interest have

7

brought continuing reassurance that perhaps another biography of Jonathan Edwards may not be amiss.

Within the limits of a single volume it has not been possible, in addition to his life story, to do more than indicate the chronology and general import of his ideas, particularly with respect to his changing fortunes. The sweep and complexity of these ideas, their roots, their relation to the thought of his own day, and their impact on the thought of the men who came after him make quite another story, and a long one. That also is a story which wants retelling.

O. E. W.

ORONO, MAINE
August 14, 1939

CONTENTS

Princeton

JONATHAN EDWARDS

Prologue

THERE IS A COMMON SAYING that the life of a philosopher does not matter. Only his thought is important. At first glance, the life of Jonathan Edwards seems to provide confirmation for this somewhat too easy assumption, and to provide it in a peculiarly ironic example. Certainly the story of his fifty-four years leaves one with a disturbing sense of futility in human endeavor. The cause he sponsored, even within the limits of his own life, proved to be a lost cause. Viewed in perspective, it was already a lost cause a generation before he was born; yet, like his fathers before him, he gave his life to the hope, and died, not knowing. The defeats and humiliations of his personal career have long since passed into American legend, to lend color to the story of an age as well as to the story of a man. The annals of American genius could ill afford to lose the chapter recounting the tale of this philosopher in exile, applying his great powers of mind to the mastery of a clumsy dialect, in order that the Housatunnocks might, on occasion, be warned in their own tongue as to the dangers of excessive rum. Philosophy and metaphysics and the great *History of Redemption* waited on such admonishings and waited too long, for death lurked only around the next turning.

But greatness has many patterns—and which of them is not ironic? Of these none is more familiar than the pattern of a career in eclipse, a leader forgotten in the on-going life of the generation he has helped to liberate, a thinker denied the garnering of his own harvest. Rediscovered to fame, Jonathan Edwards has become picturesque in his rejection and loneliness. The paradox no longer reproaches. After nearly two centuries, it has ceased to be important.

The facts of his life are few, but revealing. As a panorama of incident, all is in the open, and clear to the naked eye. His movements, his relations with men, his participation in the life of his time show few hidden corners and no unwelcome secrets. Such slight enlargement of the tale as is still possible after many generations does not change the verdict. His personal story bears inspection. Yet this almost year-by-year record of fact offers an uncommonly slender clue to that which has caused Jonathan Edwards to become a name. New England religious history does not explain him. Northampton

13

local color does not explain him. The theological system which he defended does not and cannot explain him. The heart of his mystery yields to no inquiry which concerns line and color and a dated sequence of events. For him as for other religionists in other times and countries, the traceable outline of external events is of distinctly secondary importance; the inner curve of spiritual experience is all-important. Religion was his starting point and his goal. It was also his element. In it he breathed and thought and came to life as a leader of men. After the saints in heaven "have had the pleasure of beholding the face of God millions of ages, it will not grow a dull story; the relish of this delight will be as exquisite as ever",[1] he could write, and mean it. If he had a secret, it somehow concerned his own capacity for such delight, while he still had his feet on New England earth.

Obviously the life story of such a man can be written only by himself, and Jonathan Edwards busied his pen with other matters. A sentence from the rough draft of one of his own letters, written late in life to one who, as he thought, had deeply wronged him, supplies a teasing suggestion as to the *Apologia pro Vita Sua* which he might have written, but did not.

"If you had the History of my Life from the Beginning", he wrote, "'tis probable the very things which now appear mysterious to you would be explained."[2]

What was in his mind? Certainly not the history of his life as the churchly records tell it, or as his thousand sermons and many volumes of fine-spun argument tell it. Toward that luminous spiritual history he might have written but did not, he left a few pages, themselves luminous, but far too few. From the hints these pages supply, and from the several recorded occasions on which, under stress of earnestness, of personal sorrow, or of outer tumult, the surfaces of his life were rent asunder, allowing mind and spirit to lie revealed, one catches glimpses of the hidden resources underneath this record of defeat and frustration. The mystery of such a life, no matter who lived it, is a perennial challenge, and a challenge which becomes even more insistent when that life happens to have been lived by a philosopher whose thought has had a shaping part in times beyond his own.

Chapter 1

The Edwards Family

IT WOULD be easier to derive Jonathan Edwards from his posterity than from his ancestors. Compared with his illustrious descendants who have been called upon to close more than one argument in heredity, his known forbears, once they have been stripped of their posthumous glories, stand forth as men and women of homespun talents, righteous in their way of life, useful in their day and generation, but distinctly of the rank and file. Their story read for itself yields little which suggests even dimly that the forces were gathering to produce an intellectual giant. No one of these practical-minded men and women knew the compulsion of great powers or the loneliness of those who may not walk the common way. No one of them had wrestled with the angels. In terms of genius Jonathan Edwards was the first of his race.

His known heritage extends through four generations, divided equally between clergy and laity. Only one minister had preceded him in the American line—his own father, Timothy Edwards of East Windsor, Connecticut. His grandfather, Richard Edwards of Hartford, was a prosperous merchant-cooper, concerning himself with the very tangible realities of barrels, warehouses, and shipping. His great-grandfather, also of Hartford, was a cooper of more humble sort, making with his own hands the barrels which bore his mark. If the English chapter of the Edwards ancestry were more fully known, it is probable that these two generations in the warehouse and shop would appear sharply out of line with earlier family tradition. "Richard Edwards, Minister of the Gospel in London", with whom the English record begins and ends, may not have been the first of the line to wear the cloth. It was his untimely death in the never-to-be-forgotten plague year 1625 and the immediate marriage of his widow Anne Edwards to James Coles,* cooper, that turned the family fortunes into a new channel. Emigration to America followed, and thereafter the urgencies of frontier life sent William Edwards, son of Richard, to the cooper's bench

* Also written Cole.

instead of to college. In time he inherited his stepfather's tools and taught his only son Richard how to use them. Richard Edwards of Hartford, one generation more safe from frontier perils, in his turn prospered, read books, and sent his son Timothy to Harvard College. After that there were to be no more barrels. In two generations of pioneer living the Edwards name had acquired the dignity of lands, substantial wealth, and such social standing as these involved in a new society. In addition it had regained the ministerial prestige which Anne Edwards forfeited when in 1625 she married the tradesman James Coles.

In bare outline this four-generation story is almost typical for New England clergymen of the mid-eighteenth century. The English forbears of these men had usually been ministers —most of them belonging to the more radical Dissenting wing. Migration to the New World had more often than not broken the pulpit succession. Sons of clergymen had turned laymen, worked with their hands, built houses, kept shops, but remembered their heritage. In the third or fourth generation prosperity with its consequent leisure had again meant education, and education had again meant the ministry. The intervening chapters from English to American pulpit had been a story of courage and resourcefulness tested and strengthened in a thousand ways by necessity and hardship, and of piety challenged by sterner emergencies than might have been imagined by Separatists of the Stuart or Cromwellian regimes. Jonathan Edwards had lost nothing by the generations spent in the cooper's shop, as he would have been the first to acknowledge. His Hartford grandfather and great-grandfather had written a record of hardy pioneering, of godliness, of tenacity to principle, and of fearlessness in action which laid durable foundations for the achievements of the mind and spirit that were to be his quite different portion. His father's Harvard degree relieved him of any necessity to choose a profession, made the pulpit his stage and theology his natural idiom of thought. Otherwise his ancestral heritage, so far as it is known, fails to explain him.

His unknown English background, for this very reason, has been the object of unusually eager and persistent search in the hope that genius if not to be explained may at least be rationalized through connection with distinguished names. This part of the story, however, has always remained a lost chapter except for the brief statement of Samuel Hopkins, first biographer and personal friend of Jonathan Edwards.

For months at a time Samuel Hopkins had been a member of the Edwards household, and he was presumably recording what passed as current family tradition when he wrote:

"Mr. Wm. Edwards's father was the Rev. Mr. Rich. Edwards, Minister, of the Gospel in *London*. He lived in Queen Elizabeth's Day, and his Wife Mrs. Anne Edwards, assisted in making a Ruff for the Queen. After the Death of Mr. Edwards she married to one Mr. James Cole. She with her second Husband and her Son Wm. Edwards, came into *America,* and all died at *Hartford* in *Connecticut.*" [1]

The irrelevant detail of the royal ruff would seem to be a false clue, although no modern biographer would be disposed like Ebenezer Hazard to label it an "uncouth excrescence".[2] To have been repeated in the Edwards circle it must have been respected as sober truth; and it may indeed be such, particularly if pushed back one generation. Samuel Hopkins in his emphasis on the time of Elizabeth would seem to be confusing the traditions of two generations. Otherwise Anne Edwards, who lived until 1680, was making ruffs at a tender age for such employments. Fictional or not, however, this pleasant shred of romance does not invalidate the truth of the statement concerning "Richard Edwards, Minister", who at last becomes an established fact in the christening record of his son William. This record, so long sought by builders of the Edwards family tree, appears on the parish register of St. Botolph's Church, Aldgate, London. The entry reads:

Nouember Anno Domini 1618,
William Edwardes sonne to Richard Edwardes, Minister,
& Anne his wife,
Christned on Sunday the first day of the Moneth.[3]

That this was William Edwards of Hartford is established beyond doubt by two legacies left to him years later by residents of St. Botolph's parish, Aldgate: one from Julian Munter, his maternal grandmother, "unto my grandsonne William Edwards the sonne of Richard Edwards deceased",[4] and the other from her husband Henry Munter, "unto William Edwards sonne of the said Anne Cole by her former husband Richard Edwardes".[5] A surviving Boston record of 1647 showing that William Edwards of Hartford authorized the collection of one of these legacies[6] makes the identification certain.

The clue to St. Botolph's parish, however, does not lead to illustrious names or to such ministerial services as shed luster on family annals. Richard Edwards, father of William, was not a man of consequence in the London ministry of his day. At the time of the St. Botolph's entry he seems not to have been invested with a regular church living. Shortly thereafter he appears as a schoolmaster in charge of the elementary education of about a hundred boys in the Ratcliffe Free School, maintained by the Coopers' Company of London in Stepney parish. For this humbler post he was probably indebted to his father-in-law Henry Munter, a cooper, prominent in the affairs of the Coopers' Company and, at the time of this appointment, one of its wardens.

Records of the Coopers' Company give no hint of the earlier career of Richard Edwards but merely set him down as Master of Arts. He applied for the Ratcliffe position on May 18, 1620, was appointed on July 24th of the same year, and served until his death from the plague, August 31, 1625.[7] Record of his death also appears on the register of St. Dunstan's Church, Stepney parish, of which Ratcliffe was at that time a part. The record reads,

> [August 31, 1625]
> plague   Richard Edwardes Scholemaister of
>   Ratcliffe ffreeschoole the same day.

Nine days later, September 9, 1625, the Consistory Court of London granted administration of his goods to Anne Edwards, his widow,[8] who three months later married James Coles, cooper. Record of this marriage, which caused a detour in the Edwards fortunes for two generations and meanwhile brought the family to America, is preserved in the Register of St. Dunstan's Church, Stepney parish, under date of December 6, 1625, as follows:

> James Cole of the pish of Whitechappell Cooper
> & Anne Edwards of Ratcliff widow maried by licence
> out of the office of the ffaculties the 6th day.[9]

Thereafter the path of Anne Edwards and her son William leads straight to Hartford, Connecticut, and to the pioneer chapter in the Edwards annals.

As for Richard Edwards, schoolmaster, the story is almost a complete blank. There is no portrait, no scrap of handwriting, no personal tradition by which he may be brought to life after more than three hundred years. He remains little more than a name on the records of the Coopers' Company and on the tablet at the present Ratcliffe School, listing headmasters in former times. All early records and memorials of the school, which might have filled out his story, perished long since in the fires which partially destroyed the institution several times during the seventeenth and eighteenth centuries. As to what manner of man he was, and what heritage of personal traits he left to his pioneer son William Edwards, there is no hint.

Even the outer shell of his life during his five-year mastership is pieced together with some difficulty from scant contemporary allusion to the Free School of the coopers, which in the 1620's had already been in existence for almost a century.[10] In Richard Edwards' own generation the village of Ratcliffe, in which it stood, had changed rapidly. Although still London's "farthest east", a place of ships and sailors, this once scattered settlement had become a center of bustling activity. Once known as the home of distinguished seamen, it was now also the notorious haunt of rogues, knaves, thieves, and vagabonds, with the rougher element in boisterous majority. The schoolhouse no longer stood alone as in John Stow's boyhood, "a Faire Free School", but was now jostled on every side by the "strong houses" of shipwrights and the smaller houses of mariners and sailors. As schoolmaster, Richard Edwards would have been one of a diminishing company of gentlemen, most of whom were associated with ships and shipbuilding. When he walked the narrow, crowded streets he would have been a man apart—a man of the cloth —for the mastership of the Free School, since it involved the reading of prayers in the chapel, was open only to a clergyman, and accordingly it carried with it the dignity and social prestige of a Church of England living.

In addition to his responsibility for the instruction of the hundred boys entrusted to him, their governance and daily well-being, he was also charged with the entire management of an adjoining almshouse, which by the bequest of Lady Avice, the founder of the Free School, provided for certain "Bedemen and bede Women from Families of Coopers and from the parish of Ratcliffe". From such memoranda of the Master's duties as have been preserved [11] it appears that the Ratcliffe Free School was in effect a small parish, calling not only for a schoolmaster's knowledge of grammar, Latin, and the three R's but for experienced leadership in various practical matters as well.

Obviously, in partial qualification for such an appointment, Richard Edwards was a university man and an ordained minister. Whether he was also a seasoned schoolmaster is not clear, but the fact that his license to teach was not issued until after he had assumed charge of the Ratcliffe school [12] suggests that he had not previously held a teaching post within the jurisdiction of London. He may even have turned schoolmaster in 1620 more from necessity than from choice, since at the time he had a wife and child to support and was apparently unplaced. If he were still young enough to have been a university student during the preceding decade, as his wife's age suggests, he may well have been Richard Edwards of Salop and of St. John's College, Oxford, who obtained his B.A. in 1606/7 and his M.A. in 1617.[13] If so, he may also have been the Richard Edwards of Salop and of St. John's College, Oxford, who according to the *Liber Ordinationum* of St. Paul's Cathedral, London, was ordained deacon by the Archbishop of London March 4, 1610, and presbyter June 3 of the same year; but until sustaining records concerning these two possible identifications come to light his career must be limited to his five-year service in the Ratcliffe school.

In the story of the four Edwards generations the significance of this earliest known representative begins and ends with the one word "Minister" on his son's baptismal record in St. Botolph's Church. Richard Edwards of Ratcliffe has been hard to find because he played an obscure rôle in a bustling, dangerous time. Something in him, however, or in those who came before him, marked him for choice of the contemplative life. For this reason, obscure though he was, he makes a logical beginning for the ancestral tale of a great religionist and theologian. Jonathan Edwards belongs thereby —as far back as the record goes—to intellectual interests and to what he called "the things of religion". It is a fitting derivation and removes any enigma suggested by his later heritage in the trades.

For Anne, wife to Richard Edwards, no clue remains, beyond the fact that she was the daughter of Julian Munter, wife to Henry Munter, cooper, of St. Botolph's parish. Even her maiden name is lost.[14] Whether by her marriage to James Coles, cooper, she returned to the station to which she was born or departed from it, is unknown, but on either track her second marriage was natural enough, in view of her step-father's relation to the fraternity of the coopers and her own former residence in Ratcliffe. Had Richard Edwards lived, her son William would probably have followed his father's example—gone to college and become a Church of England clergyman. Instead, he learned to make barrels. Also, thanks to James Coles, he became a Dissenter, and later an American.

The clue to this chapter may be easily followed through a sheaf of letters copied into a *Letter-Book* [15] by Nehemiah Wallington, a friend of James Coles. It appears from these letters that financial difficulty provided the immediate motive for leaving England. In 1634, nine years after his marriage to Anne Edwards, James Cole met with reverses, fell into debt, and fled from London to escape imprisonment.

"I do desier to have the biggest child with me",[16] he wrote back to his wife. William Edwards, then in his sixteenth year, took the shilling proffered by a neighbor and joined his step-father in this self-imposed exile, sharing both his hardships and his fears of prison until emigration to America opened the way to a new life. Meanwhile, throughout the nine years of his boyhood he had presumably been under strict tutelage in Dissenting doctrine, for James Coles was an ardent, even militant opponent of ritualistic worship. Frightened and giving thanks for a penny, he could forget his own woes if on Sunday he might worship in a church "where there is neither Crosses nor Surplus, nor kneeling at the Sacrament nor the booke of common prayer nor any o thes behaviours but reading the word Singing of psalms prayr before and after Sarmon with Catichisme which I did thinke it had not bine in any Congregation in this Kingdom if I had not seene it". In the same letter, written to Henry Munter from Warwick, he added, "If I could haue peace I should content my selfe with poore meanes so I might inioy such Christian Liberty".[17] Coming to America meant both peace and liberty, and in due time he came.

The circumstances under which he obtained license to sail, the ship in which he took passage, and the date of his arrival in America have not come to light. He was still in England on June 6, 1635.[18] Four years later he was listed in the records of Hartford, Connecticut, as one of the proprietors of the town and the owner of ten acres of land.[19] Although the intermediate steps lack documentation there would seem to be little reason to doubt the traditions of the Cole family that, together with his wife Anne, her son William Edwards, and his own children James, Abigaile, and Timothy,[20] he arrived in America during the latter part of the year 1635, possibly tarried briefly at Mt. Wollaston (now Braintree) or at Cambridge, and in the spring of 1636 joined the party of Thomas Hooker, migrated to the Connecticut valley, and settled in Hartford.[21] Here he lived for the remainder of his life, prospering sufficiently not only to regain the dignity of solvency but from time to time to make small purchases of land, and shortly before his death in 1652 to build himself a "new dwelling-house" in Hartford.[22] It would probably have surprised him to know that in after years his name was to be honored by a place on the Hartford monument erected in honor of the original settlers of the town.

His wife survived him by twenty-seven years and apparently found his cooper's legacy of three annual pounds sufficient for her needs. By the terms of his will she was also provided with an upper room in the "new dwelling-house", wood for her fire, fruit or herbs from the orchard and garden, use of the well, and, if she desired, the privilege of keeping a cow, a hog, or poultry.[23] Such a pattern of life would have seemed strange indeed to Anne Edwards in the Ratcliffe days, but like other pioneer women she had long since shaped her desires to a quite different standard. No hint of her personal quality remains except the picture suggested by one item in the inventory of her effects taken down at the time of her death February 20, 1679/80. Among her meager possessions therein listed are "1 silver spoon and a thimble one New serge gowne a muffe and gay Apron".[24] The gay apron invites speculation concerning one who was perhaps gently born, who lived for more than forty years as a first-generation pioneer in a strange land, and who at the time the serge gown was new must have been more than eighty years old.

To his "well beloved sonne William Edwardes", James Coles left half of his cooper's tools in perpetuation of a way of life already established beyond change through years of close association and joint labor. Thanks to the Plague Year 1625, William Edwards had become a small-town tradesman and the founder of a proud family in the New World.

The family record for the first three American generations is a tale to be read on the pages of the town books of Hartford and in various church records of East Windsor, Connecticut. Except for Jonathan Edwards' sake there would be little reason to recall any of it. It is a tale more typical than individual, illuminating at many points the movement of colonial life from rigor to measurable comfort, from uncertainty to confidence, and illustrating a brand of piety as practical as business and as incorruptible as the seasons. As the story of individual lives it lacks epic proportions, but it would furnish stirring chapters in that epic of colonial village life which in pioneer days no one had time to write, and in later times no one has had the imagination to conceive.

William Edwards, cooper—first of the American line—was, as one might expect, a man of distinctly modest attainments. According to the books he was not made freeman until his fortieth year, and thereafter performed no community services more important than viewing the town chimneys and correcting disorders in the time of public worship. His holdings in land were meager; he owned his dwelling house with the cooper's shop beside it, and various strips of meadow land —all of them small. Except for an occasional apprentice he kept his trade within the capacity of his own hands. Honest and upright himself, he was quick to invoke the law against his erring neighbors, once bringing upon himself the censure of the court for his vehemence. Nor was his own conduct blameless according to the code of the hour. Thanks to a fellow Christian's watchful eye, his personal record was twice blotted: once the constables caught him "smoaking in the street contra to law", and once he (or some other "William Edwards") drank more at a funeral than could escape a fine. Otherwise his record is clear. He did not "detain a horse", give short weight, sell cider to the Indians, leave the highway out of repair, take hogs out of the pound unlawfully, work on Sunday, break a fence, or commit any of the other offenses against churchly decorum or village citizenship so frequently on the town books. Within the specifications of some seventy items—brief, impersonal memoranda of his Hartford life [25]—William Edwards would seem to have been a plain man of relatively small importance, yet a man who had his edges of individuality, a citizen before whom his fellow townsmen walked carefully, and a workman whose cooper's mark was a guarantee. Within the specifications of this same record he may even have been a man of bold distinction, no officeholder, but a potent voice at the town councils. If this latter verdict be true, however, the evidence is not on the books.

He married Agnes Spencer, widow of his fellow townsman William Spencer. If (as some have supposed) in Agnes Spencer lies the secret of the Edwards genius, that secret still eludes search; for in extant memorials she is even more vague than Anne Coles. Traditionally, she is thought to have been connected with an English family of importance, but no clue survives save the legend that one of her brothers was mayor of Exeter and another of Barnstaple. In the search this clue proves insubstantial, yielding conjectures but no proof.[26] Her heritage, her background, even her name, remain unknown. She became the wife of William Edwards at some time between 1642 and 1645; the precise date is not recorded.[27] If by this marriage she lost some of the local prestige she had enjoyed previously as the wife of a Representative to the General Court, she probably conferred, at least temporarily, a corresponding dignity upon the house beside the cooper's shop.

One child was born of this second marriage, a son, named Richard for his paternal grandfather. About this Richard Edwards there is no vagueness. He comes into the family story with a clear-cut definiteness both of objective fact and of personal character. Born in Hartford in 1647, he lived there for all his seventy-one years—long enough to see the town change from a frontier settlement to a prosperous commercial center; long enough also to see his famous grandson a student at Yale College. He may even have made one of the important relationships in Jonathan Edwards' life up to his fifteenth year, for Hartford was within easy horseback distance of East Windsor, and the Edwards family were great travelers.

It would be pleasant to imagine in the light of his grandson's propensities that this Richard Edwards, born to the cooper's bench as he was, availed himself in his school days of a new schoolmaster's ability to teach Hartford boys Latin and Greek as well as the three R's; but there is no evidence that he was one of those who yearned for such extras. In his mature life he owned nine or ten books, enough to justify his son Timothy's statement that in addition to the Bible "Other Good books were in ye Season thereof Much Read in his house",[28] but not enough to establish a claim to bookish tastes. Richard Edwards was essentially a man of business— energetic, careful in details, tireless and, for his day, highly successful. His wealth came chiefly through merchandising, yet throughout his life he maintained, in addition, a cooper's shop, working regularly at the bench himself. Success came early. By his thirty-seventh year he had outgrown his first warehouse and was applying to the town for permission to build another, measuring to be sure only sixteen by twenty feet, but in that day of small things large enough to make him the envy of his less successful competitors. His holdings in land, cattle, oxen, horses, and farm equipment were also more extensive than those of most of his fellow townsmen, and his house in Hartford was the seat of a man of considerable wealth for his time and station. At the time of his death in 1718 his estate was valued at some twelve hundred pounds with recorded gifts to his children more than equaling that amount, for in his son's word, "no Lover of filthy Lucre he, when he had it and Occasion call'd for it, Money went easily from him".[29] His Hartford home, to judge from the itemized inventory of its furnishings, was comfortable but not luxurious. "In yᵉ New Room att yᵉ East End of yᵉ House" there was nothing which according to the standards of his day could be called elegant, not even the one "pare off brass fac'd And Irons" valued at eighteen shillings.[30]

As might be expected his community services and his local honors were both more numerous and more important than those of his father. Made freeman at twenty-one, he became successively chimney viewer, town surveyor, constable, selectman, and also on several occasions representative to act on behalf of the town. After he was sixty years old he was admitted to the bar, and still later he received an appointment as "Queen's Attorney".[31] This list of recorded dignities sorts well with the description of his appearance set down by his son Timothy:

"A stalwart man of noble stature and comely countenance, erect, robust and nimble to an unusual degree, good in argument, pleasant in consultation and well furnished for society." [32]

The further phrase "not Given to excessive Laughter" places him firmly in the Edwards tradition of later generations. So also his abhorrence of deceit, his warmth of spirit (though controlled), his excellent spirit of government, his "uncommon sense of the vanity of the World", his "not insensible spirit" which caused him to weep easily over "things of a spiritual nature". He was uncompromising in his loyalty to the meetinghouse, once suffering keen remorse at the memory of having nodded during a sermon. "Not that he was ever that I know of Given to Sleep at meeting", wrote his son by way of complete exoneration. Most of all, perhaps, he was in the family tradition for his habit of plain dealing with other men concerning their faults. When Timothy Edwards wrote,

> "In that thing I have hardly ever (if ever) known the
> Like of him",

he was unaware that men were later to say the same of him and of his son after him. Deliberate in action, Richard Edwards was one who "knew and observed his stops, weighed things", was not easily discouraged, or soon "Daunted in his Lawfull and Just undertakings by Great words, or by the Frowns and big Looks of Men".[33]

This resolution in action and indifference to hostile criticism found their most spectacular illustration in his divorce proceedings which astounded Hartford in the 1690's. Through this action, unique for its day, Richard Edwards stood alone against the law, the ministry, the social standards of his time, and by sheer persistence and the weight of his own adamantine convictions forced an eventual victory. It is a most revealing story set down in his own words in the statement entitled:

> "A True Abreviate of the Case of Richard Edwards
> Respecting Elizabeth His Late wife".[34]

The tragic fact was that Elizabeth Tuttle, who had been his wife for twenty-four years and had borne him six children, was not of sound mind and had not been at the time of her marriage in 1667.[35] Three months later she named under oath before two magistrates the father of her unborn child, but even then Richard Edwards did not put her away. In accordance with the law of the time he appeared before the proper authorities, paid the accustomed fine, but held his peace. His father's action against the man named was withdrawn (possibly at Richard Edwards' desire), the child was taken into the home of Elizabeth Tuttle's father [36] in New Haven, and Richard Edwards went about his daily business as usual. For twenty-four years he continued to live with her in spite of periodic repetitions of infidelity for which he "did never yet forgive her", of perversity "too grievous to forgitt and too mutch here to Relate", even threats of physical violence, until there came a day when he could bear no more. He filed petition for divorce on scriptural grounds October 9, 1690, and was refused. In the following spring he renewed his plea and was again refused. Unwilling to accept the negative decision, he asked that a committee of ministers be appointed to review the case. The committee was appointed, the case reviewed, and the divorce granted October 8, 1691.[37] At the time of this action Richard Edwards was forty-four years old. One year later he married Mary Talcott, daughter of Lieutenant John Talcott, one of the original settlers of Hartford, [38] and for twenty-seven more years continued to challenge his critics by his silence and dignity.

In the Edwards annals the case of Richard Edwards versus Elizabeth Tuttle, both in the fact and in the manner, is deeply significant. Such action was almost without parallel in seventeenth century America. When the question of divorce came up in church councils some compromise was usually effected, so that at least in the letter the seventh commandment could be saved. There are records of insane women removed from their homes, but without the granting of divorce to the husband. In his clear-cut demand that the letter of the law be broken that the spirit might be kept, Richard Edwards was generations ahead of his time. Also the restraint with which he set down the cause for his action, and his unwillingness to detail in writing the specifications of his wife's "folly" because these things were more proper for his own lamentation than for public discourse—these are typical Edwards attitudes. It is impossible to read this episode as an ancestral tale without thinking of striking parallels in Jonathan Edwards' later dealings with his Northampton detractors. He had the same sense of inexorable justice, the same ability to detach himself from that which concerned him intimately, and the same unassailable dignity. In a matter of conscience he too could walk alone, even though it meant walking straight to his own ruin. In many such ways he seems more the son of Richard Edwards, his grandfather, than of his own father.

The divorce episode is also significant because of its acknowledged cause. Through Elizabeth Tuttle the taint of insanity entered the Edwards inheritance. In other members of her immediate generation it went as far as violence. Fourteen years before the divorce action her brother Benjamin Tuttle had killed their sister Sarah Slosson with an axe, and had confessed his crime and died for it as though he had been fully responsible.[39] Another of her sisters had killed her own son. In the Edwards line there were no such tragedies, but for several generations after Elizabeth Tuttle became part of the story an erratic strain persisted, sufficiently pronounced to be easily traced. It reappeared in Martha, youngest daughter of Timothy Edwards, and in two of her daughters, Martha and Hannah; in Pierrepont, son of Jonathan Edwards; in Aaron Burr, his grandson; in another grandson, the son of his daughter Mary Dwight, and in various others. An overdelicate, oversensitive, highly nervous organization also persisted for several generations. What relation, if any, this unbalanced strain had to the genius of Jonathan Edwards is still an unsettled question. The temptation to explain his powers by the unknown and mysterious elements in his heritage has been doubly strong because the known and logical have yielded so little which accounts satisfactorily for them. Suffice it to say the Tuttle episode is on the record, inviting speculations from those qualified to offer them. Meanwhile, no one who studies the life of Jonathan Edwards deeply can miss the certainty that genius in him, whatever its hereditary basis, was built into the firm structure of an essentially sound and healthy personality. Not at any time in his stormy career is there the slightest hint of either mental or emotional instability.

Nor did his father Timothy Edwards, first and only son of Richard Edwards and Elizabeth Tuttle, bear the taint. Timothy Edwards lacked many things, but sanity, complete and unmistakable, was not among them. There is not one erratic or even baffling detail anywhere in his whole record. Throughout his eighty-nine years he had his feet firmly on the Connecticut earth, and rarely if ever did anything which would not have been definitely predictable. Not by any stretch of the imagination could his processes be called intricate or even faintly devious. He lived by logic and was consistent to the inch-mark—monotonously so. His story is all in one key, and except for the fact that his East Windsor parish was the background of his son's life, his sixty-four-year pastorate in that remote village would have no interest for later generations. The fact that he was a minister and that through him the Edwards family was again identified with the professions is more important to his son's story than any other detail on his record. Whether the decision to leave the trades was his own or his father's for him is not clear, but the fact that as a boy he was placed under the tutelage of the Rev. Pelatiah

Glover of Springfield, who received students in divinity, would indicate that the decision was made early.

How long he lived in the home of Mr. Glover before he matriculated at Harvard College, or whether he ever pursued his studies in residence at all, is a matter of some uncertainty. On the records of the college it appears only that he was listed in the steward's book as of the class of 1691,[40] although he did not receive his degree until July 4, 1694, when his B.A. was conferred in the morning and his M.A., in the afternoon. This unusual procedure has always been starred in the Edwards annals as indicating something of special merit in the public exercises performed by the young candidate on this occasion, and possibly with good reason, although the further fact that his name appears once in the *Severe Punishments* column with an "ominous mark" beside it suggests that tutelage under the Rev. Mr. Glover may, after all, have been a rustication. Insufficiency of the record protects young Timothy from certainty in this matter, however, and makes it still possible to assume a Commencement performance of some distinction. In the light of his whole career this would not be surprising. Meticulous precision and thoroughness were his household gods, and to be anything less than letter-perfect was to have failed, no matter how simple or how difficult the task. When he memorized his Sunday sermons he did so without the loss of a sentence; when he measured corn on Monday he did it to the half-pint, "made the negro sweep it up very clean", and then measured the sweepings. So his mind and conscience worked.

He went to East Windsor (now South Windsor) in 1694, fresh from his Harvard studies in divinity. At that time the little town across the river had no meetinghouse, no parsonage, not even an organized congregation.[41] He remainded for life. During the years his one extra-village honor of consequence was an invitation to preach the Election Sermon in Hartford in 1732.[42] According to custom the sermon was ordered printed. It was his only publication. Otherwise he belonged to the village, preaching and ministering to the hundred families of his farmer-neighbors, among whom he was greatly respected though hardly beloved. His people thought him more deeply learned, a more eloquent and animated preacher than his quiet-voiced son. His brother ministers considered him progressive, and to some extent they were right. Within the limits of his time and geography he well deserved the eulogium "Successful Minister of the Gospel", carved deep in the flat stone under which he sleeps in peaceful South Windsor churchyard.⁴³ Successful but not great. His thought was neither profound nor original. He kept well within the channels marked out by other men and was content to do so. Industrious and painstaking beyond most, versatile, possessed of a tireless energy and enormous zest for living, Timothy Edwards would have stood out in a group of men of similar interests in any age; but the fire of genius was not in him. He was a pedestrian.

At the same time there were many resemblances between father and son. Both men centered their lives in the "things of religion"; both lived by line and precept and were incapable of compromise in thought or action. Both took infinite pains, and yet with a difference as subtle as genius itself. Timothy Edwards often took pains with things that did not matter. He made endless lists of what other men had said, and then with elaborate care and the eager excitement of an explorer he sorted, arranged, and classified these same items. His logic was the logic of ordered arrangement and had little to do with innerness of meaning. Categories delighted him. His tribute to his own father Richard Edwards ends with a list of seventeen mercies attending the manner of his death, separates his dying words into thirty-five items, works out six ways in which he glorified God at his death, and proceeds to supply numbered particulars under each. It is an amazing document illustrating Timothy Edwards' intellectual processes completely. He had too much intellectual energy for his supply of originality. He tried too hard. In an effort to do complete, encyclopedic justice to his father's character he painted over the canvas so many times that he blurred the likeness. His orderliness instead of clarifying his thought merely ended with itself. When his son took infinite pains, as was his wont likewise, he also respected categories and set down his thought in neat columns; but he did not stop there. The end of the list, at his best, was only the beginning of his thought. Orderliness was his servant, not his master. In all but the scaffolding of their intellectual exercises father and son were precise opposites.

Genius aside, however, comparison of the two men shows many correspondences and deep mutual sympathies, born in part of temperament but more of common interests and the sustained comradeship of a lifetime. Even after Jonathan Edwards had a home and a parish of his own, son visited father and father visited son with regularity and frequency, making the long horseback journeys in all seasons and all weathers. Until the Stockbridge era, never more than a few weeks elapsed between visits. They died less than two months apart. For Jonathan Edwards the association had been literally lifelong, a fact which accounts to the letter for many of his ministerial attitudes and opinions and, more fundamentally, for the set of values which gave religion first place in his life. As lifelong monitor and guide Timothy Edwards is the answer to much which concerned the framework of his son's life and thought; but as to the enigma of his genius he supplies scarcely a hint.

His wife Esther Edwards has sometimes been a court of last resort, on the assumption that great powers must against all odds be derivative. The argument that from her came the lion's share of her son's intellectual endowments may indeed have some warrant, despite the warmth with which her claims have sometimes been urged. She was Esther Stoddard,[44] daughter of the much esteemed, much opposed, and much beloved Solomon Stoddard (with whom Jonathan Edwards was later to be colleague pastor) and of Esther Warham Mather, daughter of John Warham, first minister to Connecticut colony. Partly because she could boast connection with such impressive churchly names, partly because she lived to be ninety-eight years old in the village to which she had come as a bride, and partly because she was the mother of a great man and lived long enough to be honored for it, Esther Edwards became even during her lifetime the center of a body of tradition suitable to the ancestor of a theologian. At the distance of almost two hundred years it is difficult to separate legend from fact. The tradition has been fed by the fame of the man it was intended to explain.

It is true, however, that her heritage, both personal and ecclesiastical, is more impressive than that of anyone in the Edwards line up to her time. The Stoddards, like the Edwardses, had come to America as laymen, had acquired wealth in the first generation through Anthony Stoddard, a merchant, and social prestige through Mary Downing, niece of Governor Winthrop and half-sister of Sir George Downing, Baronet,[45] whom he had married. Ecclesiastical prestige had come in the second generation, through Solomon Stoddard, who at the time of Jonathan Edwards' birth was making the Stoddard name a sword in the American meetinghouse, and a half-century later, though dead, was to triumph over his more famous grandson in the Northampton pulpit, which both had occupied. Esther Edwards was his daughter.

She had grown up in the shadow of her mother's very imposing reputation: so imposing that few churchmen of Connecticut colony at the end of the seventeenth century would have been able to recall a time when the name of Esther Warham Mather Stoddard had not been a synonym for forceful godliness, intellectual vigor—especially in argument—and indomitable strength of purpose. In New England church history there was no more honored trio of great names than the three she bore, and she not only had lived up to the obligations they imposed but had added a considerable store on her own account. It was she of whom Samuel Sewall wrote, when he saw her in her seventy-fourth year, "Lame of the Sciatica, and yet spins at the Linen-wheel".[46] It would have taken more than sciatica to halt Esther Warham Mather Stoddard, who at that writing had twenty-two years yet to spin and read pious books.

To what degree Esther Edwards exhibited her mother's qualities in her own right is not clear, for the legends concerning the two women fall together at many points. Both were remembered for their dignity, their uncommon piety, their wide acquaintance with theological writers, and their intellectual superiority to their husbands. In surviving Edwards memorials, however, the practical gifts of Esther, wife of Timothy, have larger place than any unusual intellectual powers she may have possessed, although both may have been her generous portion. One gets the impression also, from her husband's many tributes of affection, his tender solicitude, and his allusions to the beauty of their life together, that she possessed sweetness as well as strength. Esther Warham by comparison seems austere, even forbidding. She would have called forth tributes of another kind, even from those who loved her most.

To Jonathan Edwards as a child, his famous grandmother was an important fact. The emanations from Esther Warham's piety, and the weight of ecclesiastical authority which attached through her to the great names she bore, were shaping influences, and are difficult to measure. When he preached her funeral sermon in 1736, after she had sat under his own ministry for ten years, he took for his text

"And their works do follow them".[47]

Even then he was probably still unaware that this Scripture had been a fulfilled prophecy in his own life since his earliest childhood. That in addition his intellectual powers owed much to the Stoddard inheritance is a fair enough conclusion, difficult as it would be to prove. Certainly as the son of Timothy and Esther Edwards and the grandson of Solomon and Esther Stoddard his bookish interests, his choice of the ministry as a profession, and perhaps much besides were as inevitably foreordained as his six-foot, one-inch stature and his physical comeliness.

In a sense also, one might say his predilection for religion, his ability to endure hardness, his capacity for self-discipline and single-minded endeavor were alike antenatal. In this he was not unique. Many third- and fourth-generation Americans built their lives on similar foundations. More than one gifted young New Englander, born at the dawn of the new century, might have brought from family annals a record startlingly like this ancestral tale of Richard and Anne, William and Agnes, Richard and Elizabeth, Timothy and Esther Edwards. All but one of these men and women, like the villagers with whom they shared their lives, had been disciplined by pioneer rigors to a sharp sense of everyday reality. All of them in their several ways recognized a more compelling loyalty to things unseen than to the world which lay about their feet. Of two of them, Richard Edwards of Hartford, godly merchant—fearless before magistrates yet weeping easily in meeting—and Esther Warham Mather Stoddard, notable mother in Israel, one might wish portraits. These two more than the others, at least on the written records, look the ancestral part they unconsciously played; but if the family records were more ample, portraits might possibly begin with still earlier generations.

With or without portraits, however, the family history of a man of parts raises more questions than it answers. Jonathan Edwards was more than the abundant total of the abilities and capacities of his forebears. The delicately adjusted balance in him between the intellectual and the spiritual, the dynamic quality behind his intellectual and spiritual powers, and the intense innermost loyalties of his nature have no parallels in his known heritage. Genius by any definition would not require that they should. Rather by some strange alchemy of opposites, some blending of the soundness and perhaps also the unsoundness which lay back of him, he was born an alien unto his own. At least so it seems. Perhaps one looks for the wrong signs. Perhaps the marks of genius in their more remote origins are less impressive than one expects. Was genius in him no more than the ability to recognize his own dearest desires unmistakably and to focus them to an unerring goal? Was it only that he possessed a greater sensitivity than other men, so that his intellectual and emotional perceptions took an imprint more deeply individual? Even so the fact remains that he stands alone in the record of the Edwards generations, and with him the family history went swiftly into a new chapter.

Chapter 2

A Frontier Childhood

JONATHAN EDWARDS was born in the East Windsor parsonage on October 5, 1703. This was precisely nine years after Timothy Edwards had come with his bride, Esther Stoddard, to the newly gathered congregation across the river. He was now thirty-four years old and his wife was thirty-one. Four daughters had already been born into their home and six more were to follow. Jonathan was their first and only son. Was he named Jonathan for what the name means, "Gift of Jehovah", for some English ancestor now lost to view, or for the Welsh theologian and controversialist, Jonathan Edwards of Jesus College, Oxford, whose *Preservative Against Socinianism* [1] had been completed and published earlier in the year 1703? Any one of these reasons might have seemed the best reason to Timothy Edwards.

One cannot but remember that three months earlier, in a Lincolnshire parsonage on the Isle of Axholme, another son had been born to another minister and his godly, strong-minded wife. The two great religionists were never to meet, or even to know why such a meeting would have seemed significant to historians of another century. On two continents John Wesley and Jonathan Edwards were to go their separate and quite different ways, changing the meaning of religion for many thousands, and with it also the cultural pattern of their generation.

In 1703 the East Windsor parish was still a young enterprise, full of promise. During the nine years he had been among them as their pastor, Timothy Edwards had definitely succeeded. The bitter controversy incident to the separation of his small flock from the parent congregation across the river had gradually slipped into the background and, in spite of occasional reminders that the new parish was made up of both factions in the dispute, withdrawal had abundantly justified itself in the growth and contentment of the new congregation. To go safely to meeting on their own side after years of perilous canoe crossings in all weathers was blessing untold. Month by month new families had come to reside on their fertile holdings across the river and the six-year-old meetinghouse was already too small. The new parish was now a separate township with full power to order its own affairs. This too was a great blessing. For the most part the pews liked the minister, and though no revival had yet come to bless his labors among them they believed God was merely testing their faith; and they waited confidently.

By 1703 life in this far-flung settlement had taken on a fairly settled character and was growing steadily safer year by year in spite of periodic alarms and very real dangers. When Jonathan Edwards was four months old the ever present Indian peril came close to the parsonage in the murder at Deerfield, Massachusetts, of Eunice Williams, half-sister of Esther Edwards. Two of Mrs. Williams' children were also killed, her husband and four more children carried into captivity.[2] The news brought deep personal grief; it was also a grim reminder of the time when churchgoing Windsor had been fined for not carrying muskets to meeting, according to order. Indians were not very numerous in Connecticut by this time, and they were for the most part friendly; but there was still cause for fear. Not for another generation could a child grow up without the memory of a thousand cautions as to what was by no means a phantom danger.[3] From all perils within and perils without, the village must be sufficient unto itself, for this part of the "Lord's Waste" was still a remote frontier. Except for Timothy Edwards and a few other great ones of the village, who occasionally took horse and rode away to Boston, the town limits were the very boundaries of life. One was born, had children, and died without ever going so far as Hartford—two centuries later, only twenty minutes away. As for the vast worries of the land of their grandfathers—Whigs and Tories battling over the nature of the monarchy at home, the War of the Spanish Succession raging abroad, and a stupid queen on the throne— these things were no longer the realities of life. Connecticut colony, East Windsor in particular, was all the world.

Agricultural pursuits made up the background of village life and, as in all country parishes of the day, the minister was perforce a farmer among farmers. He divided his time between his study and his acreage, directing the spring plowing or taking a hand at skinning a cow quite as naturally as he expounded the Scriptures or conducted a funeral. The isolation of East Windsor made the separation between parsonage and parish, sacred and secular, even less sharp than would have been true of Hartford or Northampton. In consequence,

Timothy Edwards, for all his austere dignity, was not a man apart from his people. They cut and carted his wood as part of his "rate", made his children's shoes, brought him sugar and mutton and spice as they happened to have abundance, and advised him when to cut the hay. He gave them credit in his *Rate Books* [4] for their services and donations, and in his turn taught their children for pay, bought their cider, distilled it into brandy and sold it back to them again, and engaged in many other sorts of barter convenient to both parties. He was their pastor whom they respected, to a degree feared, and sometimes opposed bitterly; but he was also their neighbor whom they knew in his second-best clothes. On Sundays and Thursdays he preached and assumed the full dignity of his priestly office; on other days he was one of themselves, taking part with them in the exchange of commodities and services by which this isolated little community maintained its independent life.

According to family tradition he was irked by these weekday details and inclined to delegate responsibility for them to his capable wife. Possibly, for he had been town-bred and as a boarding pupil in Mr. Glover's home had escaped chores at an early age; but as an East Windsor husbandman he could not have claimed immunity from farm tasks. The Edwards acres were fairly extensive: there were fields to be fertilized, crops to be harvested, woods to be cut down and put under cultivation, stock to be cared for, hides to be tanned, extra acres to be rented for pasture, and numerous routine chores to be performed daily. Some supervision of all these multiple concerns fell to him as head of the house, no matter how distasteful it may have been. Besides, there is plenty of evidence that he knew the details first-hand and had some share in the actual labors which came with the seasons.

By his son in his own country parish days, these tasks would be assumed far more naturally. Born part villager, part farmer, he would be able throughout life to accept the routine of field and barnyard as a necessary, normal part of life, to be performed without protest or apology. The difference between father and son in this as in so many other directions was a difference of emphasis. Jonathan Edwards hewed his life to the line of his main interest, consciously subordinating those things which he considered lesser; Timothy Edwards often became confused under tasks hostile to his main interest, scattered his energies in a fretful and futile busyness, and was at times defeated by the very details he hated. Both men handled minutiae with a conscience; only the son chose to split hairs in an argument, not to measure corn to the half-pint.

Jonathan Edwards grew up in the house built as the gift of Richard Edwards of Hartford at the time of Timothy's settlement in East Windsor. It stood on the east side of the present highway, about a quarter of a mile from the old burying-ground. As described by Sereno E. Dwight,[5] who saw it in 1803, and by John Stoughton,[6] who added memories of the oldest settlers in the mid-century, the house conformed to the general plan of substantial middle-class dwellings of the 1690's. It was a severely plain, two-story structure of moderate size, built low to the ground and with the second story projecting slightly beyond the first. A single chimney separated the two first-floor rooms, one of which was the kitchen-living-room—possibly also a bedroom as the family increased—the other, called by Timothy Edwards the "parlour", was really the schoolroom. In this room, which was equipped on three sides with benches fastened to the wall, Jonathan Edwards and his ten sisters, together with the village boys who aspired to college and some who did not, received their elementary education. Like other Connecticut houses of the period the parsonage grew with the family, various lean-tos being added, and also an eight- or nine-foot projection at the middle front, spoken of as the "porch" but really a vestibule.[7]

Tradition has built this house of somewhat better materials, more ample proportions, and more expensive appointments than the other houses in East Windsor. Possibly, although its alleged "elegant ornaments" would hardly seem consistent with the character of the donor, Richard Edwards. More probably like the Grant Mansion [8] built in the same decade, it merely introduced architectural improvements hitherto unknown along the "Street". Any house built in the 1690's would naturally have been superior to the log houses of the first residents. Extant expense accounts show the parsonage to have been built of hewn lumber, probably brought by sledge from the nearest mill at Scantic, and of bricks carted from Podunk.[9] The labor of building was the donation of the parishioners, who put a year of their spare time into the task. How well they did their work became a village legend to be repeated confidently generations afterward when the house was being torn down.[10] During all its one hundred and eighteen years, said the great-grandchildren of the pioneer builders, this house had but one covering of shingles—those originally nailed in place by the brethren. Such statements are best left unchallenged, if only to perpetuate the picture of deacons in their old clothes, armed with hammer and saw to a godly end.

In this frontier parish and in this house, its recognized center, Jonathan Edwards lived for the first thirteen years of his life. In many ways he was fortunate, not only for what he missed but for what he gained by such isolation. No wonder the beauty and majesty of nature stamped themselves unforgettably on his early thought. In such a setting nature would have been the most important daily fact to a sensitive child. With a horizon in all four directions he could hardly have escaped impressions of a spacious world: a world of meadows, unending forests, the river; a world of ever changing beauty, not a world of man's making. Even today, standing on the slight eminence which marks the site of the Edwards parsonage, the virgin forests gone and the meadows turned into tobacco fields, one still has a sense of spaciousness and isolation amounting almost to loneliness. Before 1716 isolation meant also helplessness, for danger lurked beyond the dark line of the forest, and miles beyond there were still no habitations.

From the "Street" running in front of the house he could see to the west, beyond the meadows and beyond the river, the turret of the Windsor meetinghouse—larger than his father's—and the more numerous dwellings of the parent settlement. Trips to Windsor in the homemade canoes, so much feared by the older folk, would have been events in his boyhood. In the foreground, a little to the right of the parsonage and just across the ravine from his father's meetinghouse, stood the small fort or Palisado built a generation earlier as a place of rendezvous in time of Indian attacks, but in his boyhood used for more peaceful purposes. Even so, to every boy in the village, acquainted with the tales of earlier raids, a blast on the infrequent Palisado trumpet would have sounded a hope of high adventure for his generation also.

Scattered along the "Street" beyond the meetinghouse and beyond his own home were the houses of the other families of the parish, fewer than one hundred in all. They stood scarcely closer together than the farmhouses along the present highway, on which life now goes so rapidly by; for East Windsor was not a huddled village. Each house was built on its own acres; and the tracts, small for farms, were large for town plots. The house nearest the Edwards home was that of Captain Thomas Stoughton who, in the year the parsonage was built, married Abigail, sister of Timothy Edwards. In the Stoughton home there were also eleven children, with ages corresponding almost exactly to those of the Edwards eleven. Seven of these were boys—three older, three younger, and one almost the exact age of Jonathan Edwards—so that the companionship with boys which he missed in his own home he had with his seven boy cousins next door. The assumption that, as the only son in his father's house, he had to endure being petted by his ten sisters and made to share their girl games is absurd. In addition to the Stoughtons similar hosts could have been mustered from almost every one of the hundred houses in the village, for in spite of the "throat distemper", upsetting canoes, and home remedies East Windsor, as well as the rest of colonial New England, was full of children.

At the rear of the house, toward the east, there was scarcely a suggestion of man and his concerns. The land slopes gently down to a brook on the Edwards side, then up a hill—at that time densely wooded. Somewhere along this brook Jonathan Edwards built the booth in which he and his boy companions used to meditate and pray. These were the fields in which "multitudes of times" he had "beheld with wonderment and pleasure" the spiders marching in the air from one tree to another, "their little shining webbs and Glistening Strings of a Great Length and at such a height as that one would think they were tack'd to the Sky by one end were it not that they were moving and floating".[11] One may be sure he had also watched other living and growing things with the same philosophic eye. He may even have committed his observations to paper frequently, for the spider essay, so often cause for the marvel of posterity, can hardly have been his only excursion into a realm so minutely known and so confidently possessed. When he wrote of spiders, he wrote not of something which transiently caught his eye but of a world which belonged to him by right of long and deep intimacy.

Inevitably in his speculations about the universe he shared the belief of his contemporaries that the processes of nature went on by personal manipulation of the Almighty and therefore had a logical relation to the shortcomings of man; but having accepted this major tenet his mind went freely on to other queries. Although when he wrote of the rainbow [12] he was probably still young enough to believe that the ends of it stood in basins of gold, his orthodoxy had been corrupted by no such pleasant fables. But to believe instead that it was the symbol of God's covenant with Noah did not paralyze his boyish inventiveness when it came to making a little rainbow of his own. There were several ways. He could take water in his mouth, stand between the sun and "something that looks a little Darkish", spurt the water into the air, and make a rainbow as complete and perfect as any ever seen in the heavens. He could get the same result by dashing up drops of water from a puddle with a stick. Unfortunately (and unforgivably) he had been deprived of a visit to the sawmill at Scantic; but he had heard his "Countrymen that are Used to sawmills" say that rainbows could be seen in the violent concussion of the mill waters. It is pleasant to imagine the picture of this serious-faced and persistent small boy catechizing his sawmill countrymen for purposes of his own philosophic speculation. In the spider essay he accepted the current notion that spiders are the most despisable of the insect kind. They are the "corrupting nauseousness of the air", and yet this assumption, borrowed from his elders, did not vitiate his own clear-sighted observation as to the spider's ballooning habits, or his inspired guess (for a twelve-year-old) as to the liquid character of the unspun web.

In an eager desire to discover the child as father of the man, this unit of boyish composition, possibly written even earlier than his twelfth year,[13] has been dignified more than once into a truly remarkable piece of scientific observation for its day and assumed to contain proofs that Jonathan Edwards had potentialities for a career in science as great as, if not greater than, in theology. Such enthusiasm is pardonable, and the conjecture is perhaps warranted. Argument spends itself vainly on such matters. The fact is that Jonathan Edwards' observation of flying spiders is accurate so far as it goes, even when tested by the findings of mature observers in a later day. As the findings of a boy who had no training in scientific observation, no microscope, no body of specialized knowledge by which to test his own observations or his conclusions from them, this juvenile effort is indeed arresting. It might do credit, in the observation alone, to an amateur twice his age.

The deductions leading from his observations are even more arresting: the basis for classification, the theory of equilibrium by which he explains the spider's navigation of the air, the character of the web, even his naïve justification of nature in providing creatures with just such equipment. That he took great pains with the essay is apparent, especially in the extant manuscript which was probably a first draft. The erasures and substitutions suggest that he had set himself to deserve a hearing from his learned correspondent, not realizing that the boyish letter accompanying his effort would easily have gained the hospitality of one not interested in spiders.

"Forgive me, sir, [he wrote] that I Do not Conceal my name, and Communicate this to you by a mediator. If you think the Observations Childish, and besides the Rules of Decorum,—with Greatness and Goodness overlook it in a Child & Conceal Sir, Although these things appear very Certain to me, yet Sir, I submit it all to your better Judgment & Deeper insight. . . . Pardon if I thought it might at Least Give you Occasion to make better observations, on these wondrous animals, that should [be] worthy of Communicating to the Learned world, respecting these wondrous animals, from whose Glistening Webs so much of the wisdom of the Creatour shines. Pardon Sir

"your most Obedient humble servant,

"JONATHAN EDWARDS" [14]

As to spiders, how many kinds were there? Why did they always fly in a southeasterly direction? How was it possible for them to navigate the air? Determined to satisfy his curiosity as to the "manner of their Doing of it", he became, as he said, "very conversant with Spiders", spending in their interest days in the woods—exploring rotten logs, tracking them down, classifying them, and trying to understand how they stretched their webs from tree to tree. Like any other wide-awake boy he was sufficiently inventive to devise ways and means of finding out what he wanted to know; but unlike most boys his age he was unable to rest until he had finished what he had begun. After he had evolved a satisfactory technique of observation, he "Repeated the triall Over and Over again till I was fully satisfied of his way of working". When presently he saw the second string issuing from the tail of the spider he held on his stick, he concluded that he had "found out the Whole mystery". Stick in hand, he gave demonstrations to his companions of the spider's habit of "mounting into the air", discussed his theory with others and no doubt set his sisters and the Stoughton cousins to watching spiders and reporting their observations. One hopes also that he hoarded a collection of specimens on the parsonage window sill.

Years later when he preached on the spider as one of the four things on earth which are exceeding small and yet exceeding wise, how did he remember this boyish attempt to solve the spider's mystery for itself, not as the prop to doctrine? [15] Perhaps he did not remember it at all, for long before that time the door to this early world was shut, and he had lost the key.

Whatever its precise date, this precocious essay, as perhaps the earliest of his voluminous writings, is of unquestioned biographical importance. More than precocity is involved. The quality of mind revealed in these boyish observations and deductions would be equally significant whether he was eleven or thirteen when he wrote them down. The essay is a chapter in his mental development, a glimpse into the world he lived in, a world of speculative thought reached through objective fact. It is illuminating also as a personal document out of his East Windsor boyhood, testifying to long afternoons in the meadow when as a little boy he lay on his back, apparently idle, but his mind and eye intent on the life of the fields. There was no reason two and a half centuries ago for any East Windsor neighbor to set down a description of Jonathan Edwards as a child; but if his portrait were to be imagined in characteristic pose, the open fields should be the background, the figure that of a healthy boy dressed in sturdy homespun, sitting alone, doing nothing with his hands, but mentally as active as though bent over his books. Aged eleven or twelve he was no daydreamer, or even Boy of Winander, taking sensitive pleasure in bird calls and cloud movements or in listening to the rhythms of Nature, heard and unheard; he was already a thinker, pushing his natural boy's curiosity about the universe as far as infinity. On such days his East Windsor boyhood was indeed "fair seed-time" for the soul of a philosopher.

In the light of his mature development one need scarcely wonder why he did not continue to devote his great powers of mind to scientific thought. The answer is that science would not have satisfied him. The physical universe was to him only the skeleton of reality, and scientific investigation was the means of stripping off only the outer layers of the mystery. From the utmost bounds of material science other speculative minds likewise have been teased along until they have leaped from the known and measurable to the intangible and infinite. To such minds only the ultimate questions as to the whence and whither of being seem worth the asking. Even as a boy, Jonathan Edwards was one of this company. Why a world at all? he was saying. "What need was there that any thing should be?" [16] To Pascal, Newton, Swedenborg, and other giants in scientific reasoning his intellectual history would be an open book. These men also turned from physical science to religion; but they turned late in life after they had made contributions which changed the direction of scientific thought in their day. Jonathan Edwards turned away before he had made more than a bare beginning, but he obeyed the same impulse.

Had he been the son of Josiah Franklin he might have carried his boyish observations further; but as the son of Timothy Edwards he was not allowed to grow up in the meadow watching spiders, unsupervised. Like Aunt Mary Emerson's famous nephew he was "born to be educated", and indications are that the process began as early as speech. The setting was favorable. Whether Timothy Edwards had begun to prepare boys for Harvard College as early as Jonathan's infancy is not clear, but there were already four other Edwardses needing his services, and the "parlour" was in daily use. Under a discipline more rigorous than obtained in any "dame school" of the period, Jonathan Edwards laid substantial foundations for his ministerial career from the time he could first read. He began with the "Tongues".

Some few hints of the pedagogical process survive in several letters written by Timothy Edwards to his wife, when she was obliged during his absence on military duty in the fall of 1711 [17] to take over his schoolroom duties. He admonished her not to let Jonathan, aged seven, lose the Latin he had already learned by heart, suggesting that she have him "say pretty often" to the girls from the Latin *Accidence* and both sides of "propria Quae moribus", and also that he help his younger sisters to read as far as he had learned. More than economy of effort for the teacher was back of this law of the Edwards schoolroom, by which the older child taught the younger. Timothy Edwards knew that, by the time the young Latinist had said "pretty often" to one group and heard "pretty often" the "sayings" of another group, he would have the Latin *Accidence* and both sides of "propria Quae moribus" for life; and to learn them less permanently was not to learn them at all.

His parent-teacher could hardly have been one whose teaching brought joy of the vision or made discipline seem more than an end in itself; but by his tireless persistence, which brooked no indolence and no half-knowledge, Timothy Edwards fortified his son for life against textual errors, major and minor, and made thoroughness one of the Ten Commandments. Unlike the tutor of Cotton Mather he did not encourage his pupils to compose poems of devotion in the tongues they were to master. He preferred that they be letter-perfect in their verbs. Jonathan Edwards accepted his father's standard when he was too young to question it, and several years later, when the unlucky "Stiles" who was also a "parlour" product could not tell the "Preteritum of Requiesco" in a Yale examination, Jonathan shared his father's humiliation. The fact that Stiles committed no error in Tully's Orations, which "he had never Construed before he came to Newhaven, nor in any other Book, whether Latin, Greek or Hebrew",[18] would seem to a modern college board examiner something of an extenuating circumstance, if indeed he could believe the sight of his eyes; but not to Timothy Edwards. No wonder Harvard and Yale were glad to accept his pupils. The lesson of strict accuracy was perhaps the most valuable lesson which Jonathan Edwards learned in the East Windsor schoolroom, along with his own unforgettable preterits.

Parental discipline was not limited to schoolroom exercises. The other minutiae of daily life were likewise under a supervision all but omniscient though never harsh, and filial obedience was the first law of the household. Timothy Edwards' elaborate catalogues of instruction, written on march and sent back to his partner in authority, re-create more fully than it has been elsewhere preserved the panorama of parsonage life as it was lived under the watchful eyes of the head of the house. These letters are therefore an important part of Jonathan Edwards' childhood story. Written in homesick mood, they constitute a kind of last will and testament of affection to those Timothy Edwards had left behind and might not see again. In the light of his phrase "If I Live to come home," his exaggerated worries become understandable. As he called up the familiar round, his homesickness took the form of an imagined disaster for each child of the flock. In his absence something might go wrong. Hence the pyramid of hypothetical woes and multiple cautions which, taken out of their emotional context, appear almost ludicrous.

The letter of August 7th is the richest in household detail. It is also a strange medley and a revealing glimpse into a man's mind.

"Tuesday
"Newhaven Aug/ 7th/ 1711

"My Dear

"This comes to express my Dearest Love to thee, and to Informe Thee y^t I am (Through the goodness of God) yet in Good health, & do expect to Go towards Albany in a few days; ye Govn:^{or} Intends ye part at Least of ye Regiments Shall March to morrow, & talks of Going himself on Friday next at furthest.

"I desire thee to take care y^t Jonathan dont Loose w^t he hath Learned but y^t as he hath got ye accidence, & above two sides of *propria Quae moribus* by heart so y^t he keep what he hath got, I would therefore have him Say pretty often to ye Girls; I would also have ye Girls keep what they have Learnt of ye Grammar, & Get by heart as far as Jonathan hath Learnt: he can help them to Read as far as he hath Learnt: and would have both him and them keep their writing, and therefore write much oftener than they Did when I was at home. I have left Paper enough for them which they may use to ye End, only I would have you reserve enough for your own use in writing Letters &c.

"I hope thou wilt take Special care of Jonathan y^t he dont Learn to be rude & naught &c. of wch thee and I have Lately Discoursed. I wouldnt have thee venture him to ride out into ye woods with Tim.

"I hope God will help thee to be very carefull y^t no harm happen to ye little Children by Scalding wort, whey, water, or by Standing too nigh to Tim when he is cutting wood: and prithee take what care thou canst about Mary's neck, which was too much neglected when I was at home, & Let her also sometimes read over what She hath Learnt in the Grammar y^t she Maynt Loose it: and Let a new rope be speedily put upon ye well pole, if it be not done already: And Let Esther & Betty Take their powders as Soon as the Dog Days are Over, & if they dont help Esther, talk further with ye Doct^r: about her for I wouldnt have her be neglected: Something also Should be done for Anne who as thou knowest is weakly: & Take Care of thy Self, and Dont Suckle little Jerusha too Long.

"My horse Got a bad wound her in Broth^r: Mathers Pasture, I would have due Care taken y^t he May be well lookt to, and thoroughly cured, If he Should be Neglected, or Ridden much before he be pretty well, It may be of very Ill consequence.

"I herewith Sent you a Bill of 40^{sh}, because I would not have thee want mony in My Absence; this & ye other I Left with thee thou knowest are Loose papers, & if they be not carefully Laid up they may Soon be Lost. ye Lord Jesus Christ be with thy Spirit my Dear, & Incourage thee to hope and trust in him, & discover his Love to thy Soul to whom I commit thee & all thine and mine, to whom Remember my Love, & also to Mercy Brooks & Tim: Demming & tell him y^t I shall much Rejoice If I Live to come home to know y^t he hath been a Good Boy, & tell my Children y^t I would have Them to pray dayly for their Father, and for their own Souls, and above all things to Remember their Creator and Seek after ye Lord Jesus Christ now in ye Days of their youth. God be with & bless you all.

> "I am my Dear, ever Thine in y^e
> "Dearest Love and affection
> > "TIM^o: EDWARDS.

"If any of ye children should at any time Go over ye River to meeting I would have them be exceeding carefull, how y^y Sit or Stand in ye boat Least they should fall into ye River.*

"I like thy letter so well my dear both as to ye hand, and ye framing of it, y^t I Desire more of y^m one at Albany would be exceeding wellcome to me towards which place I am going to-morrow.

"Let care be taken y^t ye cattle dont get into ye orchard & wrong ye trees.

"& y^t ye barn ben't left open to ye Cattle, thy^r Dung be carried out & Laid in ye orchard where there is most need before winter, & y^t ye flax be not spoiled.

"The fleet sailed Last Monday was Sev'n night (consisting of 100 Sail of all Sorts, & as is computed here of about 20 men of war. this I had from ye post last Friday evry Sev'n night: Col: Whiting also sent it to ye Govn:^r in a Letter, as I have been told.

"Let Mary write pretty often as well as the Rest of ye Girls &c." [19]

If the legend of Esther Edwards' strong-mindedness be true, these marginal additions must have somewhat mitigated her joy in the pleasure her letter had given. For one of her instincts and her breeding to be reminded of what she could not possibly forget—her children's safety, and, on one later occasion, her manners [20]—would seem to have been a severe strain on her Christian forbearance.

In these multiple admonitions Timothy Edwards sat for his own mental portrait. Like his son he had the kind of mind which visualizes its concepts, an excellent kind of mind to possess if one would be a preacher of the Last Judgment, but requiring sterner terrors than scalding whey, flying chips, and neglected medicine to summon its powers appropriately. The son's resources of imagination were, by contrast, reserved for the agonized suspense of the final day and the subsequent

---

* These last instructions are written in the margins.

tortures of the damned, not unleashed to conjure up minor injuries to the children around the kitchen stove. As he lays bare his characteristic ways of thought in these intimate letters Timothy Edwards shows himself to be a man careful and troubled about many things, one who forgot nothing and yet assumed that everyone else forgot everything continually, one who busied himself unnecessarily with the obligations of others and half enjoyed the self-imposed burden of details innumerable. In all these counsels, which by long habit he usually delivered in the negative, there is not the slightest hint of a peevish or unpleasant spirit. He merely could not help thinking for everyone else and compiling ubiquitous lists of tasks to be done, with all conceivable hazards present to his mind at every turn.

Instead of quieting childish fears he raised them, as though parental guidance consisted in advance notice of potential disaster. A letter written to his daughter Mary when she was attending school in Hatfield,[21] begins with cautions against wet feet and going "too thin to meeting", proceeds through warnings against losing her good name (especially since she is a woman), and ends with an injunction to remember she has an immortal soul lodged in a frail mortal body. This letter might well stand as a father's legacy to his daughter in the days when one was permitted to live in order to get ready to die.

Such counsels were by no means unique. Children of Jonathan Edwards' generation, who were not sons and daughters of ministers, were made to live in the ever present consciousness of death. Every Sunday might be the last. Every parting was for eternity. Newspaper accounts of accident were invariably framed to suggest that no one dare boast himself of tomorrow. It was as though life were indeed lived in the formula of the Middle Ages: "What is this our life but a march toward death?" Children might as well learn it early as late. The chance legend

REMEMBER YOU WAS BORN TO DIE

surviving as a child's copy on the flyleaf of an old almanac,[22] and painstakingly scrawled nine times down the page, was no morbid reflection. It was merely the inevitable truth brought home afresh with each new onslaught of pestilence or other disaster, born of isolation and man's impotence.

Jonathan Edwards like other children of his day grew up

with this as a settled conviction, although his own childhood was singularly protected from loss of those near him. Almost phenomenally the Edwards family circle remained unbroken for thirty-five years, and when Sister Jerusha died in 1729, aged twenty, Jonathan Edwards was a man grown and had been away from East Windsor for thirteen years. This unusual record, be it said in all fairness, may have owed something to Timothy Edwards' tiresome vigilance, and that vigilance in turn may have owed something to the supposed mythology of his own boyhood, reputed to have been a succession of remarkable deliverances from drownings, freezings, scaldings, killing of playmates, and swallowing of peach stones. If these tales be not the sheerest invention memory doubtless aided imagination whenever he saw his own children set foot in a rocking boat or ride away on horseback.

The potential naughtiness of Jonathan, mentioned in the Albany letter, may have been only another parental chimera, although allusion to the late conference on the subject suggests that, thanks to Tim the chore boy, Jonathan, aged seven, may have manifested symptoms of taint. One hopes so, since his story includes all too few hints of a childlike childhood. East Windsor would have had its corrupting influences of course, like all towns small and large; but by comparison with less remote communities these would certainly have been less numerous. Samuel Hopkins, born in 1721, made the astonishing statement that up to his fifteenth year he had never heard a profane word from any of the children with whom he grew up in Waterbury, Connecticut.[23] The answer is of course that he had not been listening for profanity. His ears were stopped against all sinful matter because his head was full of something else. Jonathan Edwards at no time in his life was given to such impressive personal statements, but he too had been protected in childhood by the strength of his impulses in the opposite direction. From his birth he had lived in an atmosphere of respect for all things holy and had deep concern for the exercises of piety after the earlier American pattern. Until he rationalized and justified these attitudes by his own thought he accepted them as unquestioningly as he accepted the sunrise and the seasons.

It is in the light of such boyhood training that his later guidance of the Northampton boys and girls must be judged. Playing leapfrog in the parsonage yard while they waited their turn to be reproved by the minister was a gigantic impropriety in comparison with his own boyhood standard. Had he or any one of the Stoughton boys felt inclinations toward such blasphemous behavior they would not have dared indulge them in the very shadow of the meetinghouse turret. Satan would have been too much pleased.

Of Jonathan Edwards' earliest religious experiences there is no contemporary record; only his own later allusion to his first "awakening" which, as he wrote, took place "some years before I went to college",[24] and the well-known detail of the booth in the swamp, belonging to the same period. This may have been at any time from his eighth to his tenth year, for Timothy Edwards was having annual revivals during that period. Looked back upon, this first awakening did not seem to him a profound experience. It was rather a greatly quickened delight in the outward duties of religion which he had been performing all his life, but in which he now took intense new pleasure. The building of the booth in the swamp was a group response to the same quickening of religious interest and is not so strange as it has sometimes seemed to later generations. In part a boy enterprise, interesting in the doing, and in part imitation of adult action during a revival season, it probably surprised none of the parents whose sons were associated in the scheme. In a sense the boys who went to the booth to pray and to talk about their own salvation were playing at religion, as children of a later generation played at vast Tory and Continental hatreds, and reënacted the drama of adult action. The significant detail in this episode for the understanding of Jonathan Edwards is that praying with his companions did not satisfy him. Even as a child he felt religion as too personal an experience to be shared so intimately; hence, unknown to his companions, he had his own place of secret prayer deeper in the woods. This was years before his mind acknowledged that religion must be an individual experience, else it was nothing; but even as a child he felt it so, and in this solitary quest was responding to the deepest instinct of his nature. Going back and forth to the meetinghouse, keeping the Sabbath as the son of Timothy Edwards was expected to keep it—these things were not enough. Religion was more than the mere observances of it. What it was, he could not have said, except that his mind was "deeply engaged in it" and no other delights were comparable.

There is not the slightest suggestion that either at this time or at any time later in his life he courted austerity for its own sake, or that in his solitary devotions he sought deliberately to mortify the flesh in order to develop the spirit. Always his mind was on the end, not the means, and the discipline itself was of so little importance that he was usually oblivious of it. Moreover, at this time, going to the woods to pray was something of a practical necessity in a household so numerous that privacy was all but impossible at any hour in the twenty-four. In addition to the Edwards flock guests were frequent, sometimes staying for weeks and paying board as was the custom. Some of Timothy Edwards' pupils from other towns also lived at the parsonage. One wonders how or where. Certainly there must have been times when, between parental supervision, sisterly criticism, and the presence of perhaps twenty persons under one sloping roof, those "little nervous strings" which, according to Jonathan Edwards' boyhood reasoning, proceed from the "soul in the brain" [25] must at least have been "jarred" by these external things. For one to whom solitude was an unquestioned necessity, to be obliged— not only in his boyhood but throughout his life—to live in houses which were more like hostelries than private dwellings seems unkindness indeed.

Particularly in connection with these earliest religious experiences one would like to know more than the records tell of his relation to his mother Esther Edwards. No letters to her or from her are extant for any time in his life. She takes on individuality only in his father's numerous epistles filled with everyday details testifying to her resourcefulness in the minor crises of frontier life, and to her unsparing vigilance as she nursed one after another of them through serious illnesses. "We find your absence, (especially So Long) makes a great empty place in the house", he wrote on one occasion.[26] One might think it would. She was the shadow of a great rock to them all. Did she, in addition to her practical gifts, her intellectual vigor and zeal in good works, have also an understanding of her son's deeply spiritual nature, his sensitive approach to religious experience? There is no recorded answer to these questions. An unauthenticated tradition that during one of her husband's revivals she made public profession of conversion would certainly suggest, if true, that she had not only the courage of her convictions in a difficult test but also a capacity for religious emotion which might have given her a sympathetic understanding of his young ecstasies; but, if so, the evidence does not appear. He spoke freely of his experiences to his father, but there is no record that he confided them also to his mother. She lives only in the filial idiom "Remember my Duty to my honored Mother" unfailingly included in his letters to his father.

The fact that Sister Jerusha, six years younger than Jonathan, was also given to solitary walks and prolonged devotions, with corresponding abhorrence of "froth and levity in conversation" and delight in weighty discourses, particularly books of divinity, may mean that she was consciously or unconsciously imitating him, or more probably that something in their joint heritage prompted these similar yearnings and in a sense unfitted them both to live in the world as they found it. In Jerusha there is no hint of mystical raptures. She was merely engaging in devotions, with more than a hint of childish asceticism in the manner of them. It was her custom on Saturday nights to stay up later than the rest of the family, in preparation for the Sabbath, and in the morning to walk alone to the house of God in solemn meditation. When she returned from the afternoon service, if the weather were not too severely cold, she diligently improved the remainder of the holy day in an unheated upper room, as the saying was, "filling in all the chinks of the Lord's day with useful thoughts". When she attended any merry meeting of young people she took no part in the merriment, but instead sat on "one side of ye Company with some person who would entertain her upon some sollid and profitable subject". Not that she was an "enemy to something of innocent Jesting", her sisters protested; she merely chose to use her wit as sauce, thinking it "very improper food, for ye soul".[27]

Even after allowance is made for sisterly overstatement, this picture of Jerusha Edwards with her beautiful countenance, her blameless life, and "Quiet Virtue" has its ludicrous side, even for a minister's daughter in a godly age. Her extravagant pieties, however modestly she attempted to hide them, must have made her something of a village oddity and none too welcome at the merry meetings she rebuked by her soberness. She judged by a standard too high for weekday living, yet thought it her duty, for the good of others, to speak her criticism frankly. When on one occasion she so far overshot the mark as to attempt to improve the virtue of her sweetheart and "preserve him against ye infection of vice" by telling him what was wrong with his behaviour, the sally cost her a budding romance. But she had done her duty as she saw it and in the sequel bore herself like a true Edwards, her calm unruffled by the ferment of gossip which ensued. So great was her personal triumph (so said her sisters) that she took no pains to contradict the story that he had jilted her but went serenely to meeting, all eyes upon her. Such was the Edwards code.

With all his flat-footed good sense Timothy Edwards applauded these unyouthful rigidities. He was, in fact, responsible for most of them. Jerusha was the eloquent embodiment of the Christian virtues he preached; only, being her father's child, she had taken them somewhat too literally. Had she lived, her wit might have helped her to attain a better balance, but she was denied the chance. Even before her death she seems to have been all but canonized in the Edwards household where she lived with her sisters "in love, not unlike to y^t which is in ye heavenly regions".

Had Jerusha been nearer to him in age Jonathan Edwards might have found much in common with her; but when he left home for college she was a child of six, who he was to know later only in brief vacations. It was to his practical sister Mary, two years older than himself, that he turned for companionship through all his young life. When she went away to school in Hatfield he sent her the family news; and when later he went away to Yale College she did the same for him. These letters tell a story of affectionate comradeship and mutual dependence pleasant to read. It was to Mary that his first extant letter, written when he was twelve years old, was sent. In the news of the revival with which he begins, he talks more like a deacon than a twelve-year-old boy; but with his own awakening behind him he was already on the side of the pulpit and yearning toward the unconverted. By his twelfth year, also, he had learned the formalities of polite correspondence, and out of respect for a missive which must be carried by hand (sometimes by several hands) he did not fill his pages with light matter but appropriately subordinated the trivialities of chickenpox and toothache to lists of the newly converted and the newly dead. He wrote in a neat hand and made the customary epistolary flourishes. The letter reveals much as to his childhood background of thought and his standards of value.

"Windsor May 10 1716.

"Dear Sister

"Through the Wonderfull Mercy and Good[ne]ss of God there hath in this Place Been a very Remarkable stirring and pouring out of the Spirrit of God, And Likewise now is But I think i have Reason to think it is in Some Mesure Diminished but I hope not much. About thirteen Have been joyned to the Church in an estate of full Comunion These are those which by Enquiry I Find you have not heard of that have joyn'd to the Church, viz; John Huntington, Sarah Loomas the Daughter of Thomas Loomas, and Esther Elsworth. And their are five that are Propounded which Are not added to the Church, namely, John Loomas, John Rockell's wife, Serg.t Thomas Elsworth's wife, Isaac Bissels wife, and Mary Osband I think there Comes Commonly a Momdays above thirty Persons to Speak with Father about the Condition of their Souls.

"It is a time of Generall Health here in this Place. There Has five Persons Died in this Place Since you have been gone, viz. Old Goodwife Rockwell, Old Goodwife Grant, and Benjamin Bancroft who was Drowned in a Boat many Rods from Shore wherein were four young women and many others of the other Sex, which were verry Remarkably Saved, and the two others which Died I suppose you have heard of, Margaret peck of the New Town who was once margaret Stiles hath Lost a Sucking Babe who died very Suddenly and was buried in this Place.

"Abigail Hannah and Lucy have had the Chicken Pox and are recovered and jerusha has it now but is almost well I myself Sometimes am much Troubled with the tooth ack but these two or three Last Days I have not Been troubled with it but verry little so far as i know the whole famaly is well except Jerusha.

"Sister i am glad to hear of your welfare So often as i do I should be glad to hear from you by a Letter and therein how it is with you as to your Crookedness.

"Your Loving Brother Jonathan E.

"Father and Mother Remember their Love
unto you. Likewise do all my Sisters and Mercy and tim

To Mrs
Mary Edwards
At The House of mr
Samuel Portrige
At Hadly   These
Q 8 C

It is plain to see that already the meetinghouse had first place in all his boyhood plan of life. It was his one extra-mural interest, his larger world. He saw the whole drama of village life from the angle of the parsonage and the pulpit.

East Windsor was a parish, a little corner of the Lord's vineyard, not a center of secular interests. What he knew of the world outside the town limits came chiefly from visiting clergymen who brought news of the Lord's work in other corners of the same vineyard. The ministerial language of the hour was as natural an idiom to him as the language he spoke in the schoolroom. Likewise the pulpit controversies of the hour: the Halfway Covenant and Grandfather Stoddard's bitterly opposed amendment thereto, the old and the new way of singing in the churches—all this was familiar territory in his thought.

When East Windsor had its own village quarrel over where to set the new meetinghouse, it is safe to imagine that he listened to the long and bitter arguments detailed in nightly sessions at the parsonage, had his own opinion on the subject, discussed it with his father and was respectfully heard, and that when the church finally voted to rebuild on the old site (the usual decision after the peace of a village had been sadly frayed) he was one of those present at the demolition of the old structure and thereafter watched week by week the new meetinghouse take shape under parish labor. It would have been an absorbing drama more intensely personal to him than to the other village boys, a major event from which to date his own smaller concerns. Before the still greater village excitement of "dignifying the seats" came to pass he was a student at Weathersfield and for the first time in his life met with new scenes, new thoughts, and new ways of thinking them.

Childhood ended for Jonathan Edwards just before his thirteenth birthday. He had recited his last lesson in the "parlour" and was now ready for college. These first thirteen years had determined many things: his sober view of life, his reflective bent, his refinement of self-discipline, his pursuit of religion as the unquestioned goal of life. To some extent his mind was already his servant; he could think for himself. He had learned the benediction of solitude amid the quiet beauty of woods and fields. His calling was a straight path before him. The foundations of a deep understanding sympathy had been laid with the man who was to mean more to him throughout his life than any other human being he was ever to know—Timothy Edwards, his own father. Poles apart in temperament, in natural endowment, and in ways of thought, father and son were to enjoy for life a rare fellowship.

Outwardly, there would not be much change in the look of life. College would mean no quadrangles, no spires and deep-toned bells. Matriculation day to Jonathan Edwards meant merely exchanging a schoolroom in one Connecticut farmhouse for a similar room in another, slightly more pretentious. He was not even to be taught by strangers. His own cousin Elisha Williams, nine years his senior, was to be his tutor. In such terms the distance between life as it had been and life as it was to be does not seem very great; but to Jonathan Edwards, as to any child standing on the threshold of independence, it was a chasm. In the fall of 1716, just before his thirteenth birthday, he took horse and rode away to Yale College, leaving his childhood behind him.

Chapter 3

An Embattled Education

In THE fall of 1716, Yale College was still in the throes of being born. It was now fifteen years since that memorable September afternoon when, according to tradition and probably also according to fact, a little group of the brethren had laid their contributions on Samuel Russell's table in Branford with the words, "I give these Books for the founding a College in this Colony".[1] Long before that day the Connecticut ministry had known it was high time they had a "Fountain" of their own. They had seen afresh time after time the necessity of providing training in traditional orthodoxy close at home. Harvard College was too far away. Besides, Harvard was becoming unfortunately liberal. Pure doctrine to the northward was being corrupted by dangerous new ideas. New England was forgetting her heritage, and the founding of the Brattle Street Church [2] was the sign. Let it also be a warning. Before it was too late, the pulpits of Connecticut must be buttressed impregnably against false doctrine and all the innovations in church polity which followed in its wake. A "Fountain" for the sons of the colony within their own borders was the best guarantee of such safety. To this end and with the far future in their eye ten ministers of the colony, led by James Pierrepont of New Haven, had laid their gifts on the parsonage table in Branford. The volumes thus honored made something less than a five-foot shelf, and if the theology in them was already outmoded and therefore doomed, the farsightedness back of the gift was well worthy of pioneer churchmen, if not of minor statesmen.

The granting of a charter in the following year (1702) turned the ten brethren into trustees, and their dream into the Collegiate School. The Connecticut ministry rejoiced. Before the year was out one student had enrolled and one degree had been conferred. Thereafter in each succeeding October a new freshman class had matriculated, and in each September Rector Pierson had conferred more degrees in appropriate Latin. But for all this, after fifteen years, the new college was still a very small affair. It had as yet no buildings, no corporate unity, hardly even a name. The term Collegiate School had merely been a convenient label.

The roots of the trouble went back to the very beginning of the new enterprise. With all their foresight the trustees had neglected one important matter. They had failed to give the college a geography. As a result, in 1716 the students were still scattered: some at Saybrook, some at Weathersfield, some at New Haven. So far as nurture in orthodoxy went, having three logs instead of one made little difference. The tutors taught and the students learned, but since no college liveth to itself the rival villages aspired and laid their plans accordingly. Saybrook, Weathersfield, New Haven, and Hartford each entertained hopes of becoming the permanent seat of the college, and delay turned hopes into campaigns to that end. By not daring to brave the consequences of a choice in the beginning the trustees had merely stored up more bitter trouble for themselves. After fifteen years of rivalry between the seacoast brethren led by New Haven, and their more interior neighbors led by Hartford, the unwisdom of further delay was apparent to all; so also was the peril of finality. The quarrel had split the Connecticut ministry into two camps and become an open sore in the colony. The Collegiate School was in a "broken and tottering State".[3] Meanwhile the students fell off and the cause languished.

In 1716 a piece of good fortune hastened the decision. During the preceding year the college had acquired two collections of books: one assembled by Jeremy Dummer, London agent for Massachusetts Colony, and the other by Sir John Davie (shortly before, plain John Davie, Connecticut husbandman). The books had arrived. Possessions called for a building; a building called for a site. In their perturbation and anxiety, the trustees hardly realized that these new acquisitions, which added more than a thousand volumes to the original forty, conferred a distinction on the new "Fountain" for which Harvard College might well have envied her puny rival. Nowhere in America was there in 1716 so sizable a collection of "modern" books. But innocent of the treasures they possessed, and also of the heresies shut up in some of these dull bindings, the trustees merely stored the heavy boxes in Saybrook, appointed a custodian, and sat down to their long postponed decision.

They were agreed that the five hundred pounds appropriated by the Connecticut General Assembly should be spent in the erection of a suitable building in which to house both books and students, but where? Saybrook had the books for the moment and counted this an additional advantage toward her claim; Weathersfield had the most students and the most popular tutor; Hartford had two irreconcilable and apparently unbeatable trustees; New Haven had the most money and a plot of land. Tension increased as debate lengthened, until on November 17, 1716, the trustees thought to end both by a majority vote in favor of New Haven. As a matter of fact, they had merely sent the struggle into a new chapter; and before it was ended the florid remark of Cotton Mather, himself the "godfather to the beloved infant", that the babe was "in danger of being strangled in the birth by a dissension . . . as to where it shall be nourished in the wilderness",[4] was not nearly so extravagant as it sounds to later generations.

In October, 1716, in the midst of the first excitement of victory for New Haven, a new freshman class of ten boys matriculated. Jonathan Edwards was one of them. It was a poor time for the things of the mind and spirit. He had begun his adult mental life in an atmosphere of strife and bitterness, and while he lived he was never to be free from either. In the woods and meadows of East Windsor he had left behind the only outward peace he was ever to know. The story of this long-drawn-out inter-village quarrel was already thoroughly familiar to him. He had heard it discussed all his life, chiefly from the Hartford angle. The old story became current news, however, when on matriculation day together with his nine fellow freshmen he found himself suddenly transplanted to the arena of conflict. To the boys as to their ministerial elders, this was no mere village contest for material advantage and wordly honor. It was a kind of godly crusade in which they now took front-rank positions. This new realization conferred upon them a vast importance. Aged twelve to fourteen, they had come down from their respective meetinghouse galleries to be actors in a great drama at a great moment. No wonder they took themselves as seriously as their subsequent behavior suggests. Possibly in the light of two centuries and more of Yale College history, no pioneer class had a better right.

Record of their movements for the next four years is not complete, but in outline their story can be pieced together. It appears that they first assembled at New Haven and began their studies under the newly appointed tutor, Samuel Johnson, later to be the first president of King's College (now Columbia University). Exactly what happened is not entirely clear, but a few weeks after matriculation, the whole class left New Haven and went to Weathersfield, where they placed

themselves under Elisha Williams, not yet a regularly appointed tutor of the college. Jonathan Edwards went with
them. Dislike of Tutor Johnson was in part the cause for this
action, but possibly not the whole cause. More probably they
were tools of the Hartford faction, and took the liberty with
full parental approval. Fathers and sons alike may have assumed that until the new college house was built, choice of
residence was still free, but in any case removal to Weathersfield was interpreted as a blow to the New Haven majority.

This change of geography would have been agreeable to
Timothy Edwards, since in Weathersfield his son was only ten
miles from home and had as his tutor a relative [5] who might
naturally be expected to take special interest in young Jonathan, his precocious cousin. Elisha Williams was a brilliant
and magnetic young man, a native of Massachusetts, who
numbered John Cotton and Simon Bradstreet among his ancestors and attempted to live up to their importance and dignity. He was well-to-do, a graduate of Harvard College, and
at the age of twenty-one had already travelled considerably,
owned a farm, and had made an entry into politics as Clerk of
the Lower House of the Connecticut General Assembly. To
his thirteen-year-old country cousin he may well have seemed,
by virtue of all this, an impressive person. Certainly he was a
stimulating teacher. In the light of the harvest of discord and
dire personal trouble Jonathan Edwards was later to reap
through this association, one might well wish his choice of
freshman residence had been Saybrook or New Haven, but
for the time being all was serene. As a freshman he may even
have lived at the Williams farmhouse, since no college quar-
ters were provided in Weathersfield and the boys were obliged
to board around in the village, with relatives or strangers according to their fortunes.

Once initiated in their new routine of study, Jonathan
Edwards and his nine mates were, for the nonce, absorbed in
their own very new affairs. The foreground was crowded with
all the daily minutiae of study and recitation; life was cloistered and discipline, though not rigorous, was fairly exacting.
From sunrise prayers to the nine o'clock bedtime the hours
were checked off in scheduled precision. Friday evening to
Monday morning was one long Sabbath, filled with sermons
and prayers and private devotions. Outwardly, life seemed
peaceful to monotony, and yet Weathersfield was too close to
Hartford for the boys to miss the occasional rumblings of
trouble to come. Trustees Woodbridge and Buckingham were

active in opposition to the New Haven majority, and though the college house was slowly taking shape under the carpenter's hammer Hartford had not yet relinquished hope of becoming the seat of the college. Repeatedly, emissaries from New Haven came to urge the Weathersfield group to return to Tutor Johnson, and on each such occasion the boys were obliged to justify afresh their determination to stay with Tutor Williams. If their young peace was untroubled by this conflict of loyalties, their sense of importance grew lustily under each new sally from the opposing camp. Meanwhile Saybrook built fainter hopes around the Lynde house wherein the precious books, still unpacked, remained useless merchandise.

On ceremonial days and especially at commencement time, disaffection became more pronounced, until in September, 1718, it suddenly took on sensational news value. The Weathersfield students not only refused to attend the New Haven commencement, but held a rival commencement of their own. Graduates performed public exercises and were given certificates by authority of the Hartford trustees. This action appeared more belligerent than similar action of the preceding year, because the 1718 commencement in New Haven was the occasion of an elaborate ceremony in public recognition of the gift of Governor Yale and the naming of the college in his honor. The Governor of Connecticut colony and other dignitaries were present, the Governor "graced the solemnity with an elegant Latin Oration", an elaborate memorial to the new benefactor was read, and in conclusion the members of the college and their distinguished guests formed a procession and marched to the new "College House". For more than a third of the college to absent themselves wilfully on so important an occasion amounted to open mutiny; and the fact that trustees rather than students were responsible made matters still worse. A letter from Timothy Woodbridge, one of the Hartford trustees, to Benjamin Colman of Boston reveals that a request had been sent by the Hartford faction to President Leverett of Harvard, asking that the Weathersfield group might be transferred to Cambridge, and upon satisfactory examination, receive a Harvard degree. "They will be Subject to all y° Rules of y° Colledge & they are persons of a good Conversation",[6] he added. But evasion of the General Assembly order that they proceed to New Haven for the completion of their education was not so easy. The fiat had gone forth.

Shortly afterward, when the precious Saybrook library was also ordered to New Haven, some overzealous Saybrook citizens, thinking to oppose force with force, fell upon the caravan in an unguarded moment, and overturned some of the oxcarts. In the ensuing "Tumult and Confusion, about 250 of the most valuable Books, and sundry Papers of Importance were conveyed away by unknown Hands, and never could be found again".[7] With this sensational episode, militant measures between the seacoast brethren and the Hartford faction ceased. Officially, New Haven had won, and the books were safely stored under the roof of the new "College House" which faced the village green. The battle, however, was by no means over. The resulting "Anarchy and Confusion" were still to deal with, and peace was still far distant. Years afterward, the reverberations of this neighborhood strife could still be heard, all of it so strangely out of line with the soundness and far-reaching vision in which the college had been conceived. But in the battling years the battling brethren thought otherwise.

When the students reassembled in October, 1718, Jonathan Edwards, along with the other boys of the Weathersfield group, obeyed the General Assembly order and came to New Haven, taking up his residence in the new building. But not for long. After one month all but one student had returned to Weathersfield and Tutor Williams. Jonathan Edwards was not that one. The group remained with Williams for another six months until illness forced his withdrawal and the consequent closing of the Weathersfield branch of the tripartite college. After June, 1719, all students were in residence in New Haven and subsequently remained one company. Meanwhile, Timothy Cutler, aged thirty-five, a graduate of Harvard College, had been appointed Rector. One can hardly blame the students for their previous disregard of the Assembly orders, in view of the rival commencements, the overturned oxcarts and all the confusion of the prolonged tumult. When men of seasoned judgment could promote their cause by such means, the loyalties of boys from sixteen to twenty must have been sadly tangled.

What part Jonathan Edwards may have had in these minor insurrections is not recorded. Perhaps not the part of a leader, since belligerency at any age was not his natural rôle. Certainly it is unthinkable that during the brief stay of the Weathersfield boys in New Haven in 1718 he could have deserved any share in the verdict that they were so immoral in their conversations as to make themselves "odious to the people of the town." It would be easier, and perhaps nearer to the truth, to imagine him as the scribe who drew up the mandate of grievances against Tutors Johnson and Browne, and thus in student eyes justified secession of the group to Tutor Williams. The only statement in his own hand relative to this secession occurs in a letter to his sister Mary, dated March 26, 1719, two months later. He wrote from Weathersfield:

"[I th]ink it [is] Fit that I should give you an account of something of My Condition relating to the School. I suppose you are Fully acquainted with our coming away from New Haven and the Circumstances thereof since which time wee have been in a more prosperous Condition (As I think) than ever, But the Council and Trustees having lately had a meeting at New-haven concerning it they have Removed that which was the cause of our coming away viz; Mr. Johnson from the Place of a Tutor, and have Put In Mr Cutler Pastor of Canterbury President who (as we hear) Intends verry speedily to be Resident at Yale College So that All the scholars belonging to our School Expect to Return there as soon as Our Vacancy after the Election Is over".[8]

A letter from Timothy Edwards to his daughter Mary testifies to Jonathan's "Good name at Weathersfield [both] as to his Carriage and his Learning"[9] during this same period. Another written to Timothy Edwards during the following session by Rector Cutler includes congratulations upon Jonathan's "promising Abilitys and Advances in Learning".[10]

The other letters and memorials from his college days tell a similar story. There are a few hints that exile from all his childhood associations cost him some quite natural pangs of loneliness, but on the whole he bore his transplanting with fortitude and acquitted himself from the start as a potential valedictorian. While plots and counterplots engaged his elders, he steered a straight course, with the result that by his junior year the direction of his loyalties was clearly established; he was absorbed in his studies and rapidly finding his own world. In 1718 the real drama of college life for him was not the rival commencements, the Saybrook scuffle over the books, or even the secession from New Haven. His drama was being enacted on the pages of Locke's *Essay on the Human Understanding*.[11] Here was one who spoke the language for which he had been listening. It was neither the language of scientific observation nor that of theological dogma, but the pure serene of abstract speculation. Reality; what is it? Human knowledge; what are its bounds and limits? Perfect knowledge; what are the conditions of its possibility? Under the spell of this new teacher, his thought took wider range. He discovered powers he had not known he possessed and was free with a freedom never before experiencd. He fell upon the new treasures as upon "miser's gold". All this was happening while the village quarrel was at its height. The suggested picture is deeply prophetic.

Not only as a fifteen-year-old boy, delicate of feature, quiet of manner, was he to sit apart, rapt in solitary study, while small battles raged about him. Throughout his life, even when he was the center of the storm, he was to be detached in his own spirit, free—a citizen of other realms.

Prior to his junior year, his studies had been largely disciplinary. He had been set to the task of fundamentals, particularly the tool subjects preliminary to the study of divinity. In the first year he had studied arithmetic, algebra, and the "Tongues" (Latin, Greek, Hebrew); in the second, geometry, rhetoric, and logic, of which logic was chief. Except for logic, these studies were largely continuations of those already begun in the schoolroom at East Windsor. They were lessons to be learned and recited. Excellence still meant unfaltering accuracy with tables, conjugations, paradigms. The weekly reciting of the *Assembly's Catechism* in Latin, of Ames' *Medulla* and his *Theological Theses and Cases,* much of the formal study of the Bible and the later repeating of sermons, were also memory exercises chiefly. For excellence in all such he had been meticulously trained; but merely saying lessons was not enough. Even as a child he had been eager to be on, to use the tools while he was learning to handle them. Now after two more years of memorizing and reciting he was ready for something beyond mere learning by rote; he was ready to be confronted with ideas. Of all the areas of thought into which he might have been plunged, aged fourteen to sixteen, philosophy was perhaps the most fortunate. It opened a new world and made syllogistic reasoning of the copybook variety come alive in strange ways.

Record of this new stimulus survives in several brief pieces of his own composition and in two series of topical jottings: [12] one entitled "The Mind" and the other designated by his first editor as "Notes on Natural Science", all of which appear to date from his college years. The importance of these first excursions into the realm in which he was to do his great work needs no new emphasis. These college essays both reveal and predict. They are glimpses behind the scenes; documents in the awakening of a mind. It would not require the round handwriting of his early years to prove that these are young efforts. Youth is written all over them. They are the conscious efforts of a mind engaged in conscious thought and enjoying the experience. Compared with early attempts of other brilliant young novices to move about in the realm of abstract ideas, these pieces are arresting in that they neither begin nor end in platitudes, and do not consist in mere paraphrases and rearrangements of themselves. As a young philosopher Jonathan Edwards started out with a proposition that is really a question, and then step by step pursued the answer, apparently following his own thought rather than directing it, and as it were, feeling his way along a new and unfamiliar path. His reasoning in the section of "The Mind" labelled Existence illustrates this exactly. He wrote:

"It is now agreed upon by every knowing philosopher, that Colours are not really in the things, no more than Pain is in a needle; but strictly no where else but in the mind.

"But yet I think that Colour may have an existence out of the mind, with equal reason as anything in Body has any existence out of the mind, beside the very substance of the body itself, which is nothing but the Divine power, or rather the Constant Exertion of it.

"For what idea is that, which we call by the name of Body? I find Colour has the chief share in it. . . . And if that, which we principally mean by the thing itself, cannot be said to be in the thing itself, I think nothing can be.

"If Colour exists not out of the mind, then nothing belonging to Body, exists out of the mind but Resistance, which is Solidity, and the termination of this Resistance, with its relations, which is Figure, and the communication of this Resistance, from space to space, which is Motion; though the latter are nothing but modes of the former. Therefore, there is nothing out of the mind but Resistance. And not that neither, when nothing is actually resisted. Then, there is nothing but the Power of Resistance. . . .

"And how is there any Resistance, except it be in some mind, in idea? What is it that is resisted? It is not Colour. And what else is it? It is ridiculous to say, that Resistance is resisted. . . .

"But now it is easy to conceive of Resistance, as a mode of an idea. It is easy to conceive of such a power, or constant manner of stopping or resisting a colour. The idea may be resisted, it may move, and stop and rebound; but how a mere power, which is nothing real, can move and stop, is inconceivable, and it is impossible to say a word about it without contradiction.

"The world is therefore an ideal one; and the Law of creating, and the succession of these ideas is constant and regular." [13]

It would be of great interest and considerable importance to know whether Jonathan Edwards had hit upon his philosophic idealism, as forecast in this little unit of his thought and in the more familiar "Of Being", by merely giving free rein to his own questionings, or whether he knew, either directly or indirectly, of George Berkeley's earlier thought in the same direction. This enigma in American philosophy is not likely, however, to be solved conclusively. The facts are that although Berkeley's *Essay Toward a New Theory of Vision* had been published in 1709, and his *Treatise Concerning Human Knowledge* in 1710, neither volume was in the Yale College Library during Jonathan Edwards' undergraduate residence. There is also nothing to indicate that either Rector Culter or Tutors Williams and Johnson knew of their existence. In Samuel Johnson's *Catalogue of Books,* read after leaving Yale College, Berkeley's works do not appear until 1728/9. In Jonathan Edwards' *Catalogue,* the entry is undated, but the fact that both books appear on the page immediately preceding the entry of Berkeley's *Alciphron,* first published in 1732, and the fact that the third edition of this later work included also the *Theory of Vision,* and that the *Treatise Concerning Human Knowledge* was reissued in 1734, suggest that he may have been reading both of them for the first time in these later editions,[14] fifteen years after he had anticipated their conclusions. Even so, the case for his originality is not thereby proved. Some hint of the direction of Berkeley's thought might very easily have found its way to America, if not to New Haven, before 1716. The idea was in the air and might have come on more than one current. In fact, it would seem strange if some English correspondent of Cutler or Williams had not mentioned this new hypothesis. A mere hint would have been sufficient to a boy capable of thinking the thoughts and raising the questions in these college pieces.

Even without it, no one need be greatly puzzled. The history of thought presents enough examples of new ideas finding simultaneous expression through spokesmen who have never conferred or read each other's books for anyone who knows the mind of Jonathan Edwards in its early development to expect him, aged possibly fifteen, to have been just such a spokesman. What more likely source of ideas never before thought in the world than a brilliant young mind, as yet unclogged and unintimidated by vast knowledge? George Berkeley himself had revealed just such a mind when in his college days he recorded in his *Commonplace Book* the nucleus for all his future thought. Jonathan Edwards did it again. Possibly during the Weathersfield days, he set down his early speculations in unpunctuated sequence, and then spent the rest of his thinking days trying to get to the bottom of the issues he had raised. Not one of the nine foolscap pages of "The Mind" but presents, sometimes in the precise language, problems he was to wrestle with forty years hence:

"12. Whether any difference between the Will and Inclination".
"16. Concerning Liberty, wherein it consists".
"45. Whether it be possible for a man to love any thing better than himself".

If it is a thinker's good fortune to chart his main course early, Jonathan Edwards was indeed fortunate.

The jottings in the series labelled "Notes on Natural Science" show by contrast topics and ideas which seldom reappear in his later pages. The habits of mind, however, which are revealed in this projected attempt to explain the whole physical universe in terms of law suggest that had he chosen to apply himself to answering the queries he raised, he might soon have discovered that thunder, however "wonderful" and "inexplicable", is not a meteor; that the "effluvia" thrown off the tails of comets does not "feed the Sun with matter"; that mountains are possibly not all "pitched over to the westward". He might even have made progress toward the "Definition of the Atom".[15] He is not merely recording his textbook knowledge on these subjects; he is raising objections to current theories, asking questions and suggesting methods of observation and critical procedure. The insistent demand of his mind to get behind and underneath the phenomena he is observing, his feeling for classification, and his desire to bring larger and larger areas under orderly control are suggested in almost every one of these brief summaries set down for later consideration. In his "The Mind" there is one autobiographical detail of importance in this connection. It occurs under the caption *Logick*.

"One reason why, at first, before I knew other Logick, I used to be mightily pleased with the study of the Old Logick, was, because it was very pleasant to see my thoughts, that before lay in my mind jumbled without any distinction, ranged into order and distributed into classes and subdivisions, so that I could tell where they all belonged, and run them up to their general heads".[16]

Evidence of this pleasure is on every page of these college jottings, and in every finished treatise of his mature years.

Many of these new ideas were no doubt suggested to him through the addition to his course of study of physics and "natural philosophy" in the third year, and ethics and divinity in the fourth. Meanwhile he continued the study of mathematics and logic, only with less of routine recitation, more of public disputation, his training during his junior and senior years being more definitely shaped to a pulpit career. That he should continue to excel in his studies and be well pleasing to the rector and tutors was to be expected, and when at his graduation he was chosen for the honor of the Latin oration [17] it is not likely that anyone was surprised. He was then almost sixteen years old. As to what he would do next, there had never been a question. That decision had been made at his birth. In further preparation for the career to which he was destined, he remained at the college for two more years, continuing his studies in divinity, as was the custom for ministerial candidates. During this period he was freer to concentrate his attention on those subjects which delighted him most, and to indulge himself in what he called the lawful admixture of those "less Principal studies" toward which throughout his life his mind was continually attracted.

In the thought of his fellow students during all this period, he was primarily the student, a solitary boy, grave of countenance, austere in self-discipline, committed beyond temptation to the one purpose of learning, and to that end making every hour count.

"I am sensible of the Preciousness of my time",[18] he reported. That was of course partly his father's fault, partly the fault of a still earlier generation, but Jonathan Edwards suffered no less keenly in his day because he was not entirely to blame. His studious habits, his solitary bent, his extreme gravity, were all against him in the intimately shared life of a small college. Such a boy cannot hope to be popular; he is fortunate if he is not persecuted. There is no evidence that Jonathan Edwards was actively disliked by his mates, only that his unsocial habits cost him some peace.

Not in Weathersfield apparently, where the student group was small, fourteen boys at most. The arrangement whereby they had boarded out in the town, assembling for instruction only, had meant relatively few problems of personal adjustment. It was not until his senior year in New Haven that he was initiated into group living. During this time his position as college butler, a distinct honor for an undergraduate, was unfortunate in that it took him out of the student ranks and elevated him a little above the other boys. All his life he was to be one standing before many; never one of a group sitting side by side in friendly equality and comradeship. Mealtime would have been his best chance to meet his mates on grounds common to boyhood. Instead, he stood at one end of the hall serving plates and filling mugs, apportioning the midday beef, mutton, or veal in equal chunks and ladling out the accompanying sauce in due proportion. No doubt he did it all with complete abstraction and seriousness. It seems a strange rôle for one who was later to regard a normal appetite as unlawful temptation to sin, and its natural satisfaction an obstacle to mental exercise. But at this stage he was still a fairly healthy boy, eating what was set before him instead of selecting only those foods which would digest quickly and thus rob him of less time for study and contemplation. As he looked back upon this college period later, he saw himself still unredeemed; but one may be sure that to his less redeemed mates, he already belonged to a realm most of them had never entered.

No lifelong friendship dates from his college days. There is no record even of transient intimacies. Except for the fact that he roomed with his young uncle, Daniel Edwards, son of Richard Edwards of Hartford—a quite conventional arrangement—there is no suggestion of shared experiences. He was solitary both by temperament and by deliberate choice, and no doubt something of an oddity as well. To some extent his superior mental gifts might have compensated for his personal quirks, but more probably they merely exaggerated his woes and helped to make him still more of a defenceless target.

The "quarrels" which he reported to his father belonged to his years as a graduate student. At this time he was rooming with his cousin Elisha Mix, a freshman who objected to performing the usual services required of freshmen by their student superiors. Whether Cousin Mix was merely registering a democratic protest against such a system, whether Jonathan Edwards overdid his graduate privileges and demanded too much, or whether the cousin-roommate relationship proved too great a strain for both boys is not clear; at any rate there was trouble. The circumstances appear to have been utterly trivial, too much so to come into a life story at all, except as they gave opportunity for an Edwards trait to manifest itself in a typical example. Instead of settling his differences with

Cousin Elisha out of court, or else agreeing not to settle them but to change his arrangements, Jonathan Edwards wrote a detailed account of the grievance to his father and presumably also to Uncle Mix. Timothy Edwards straightway took action. He wrote to Uncle Mix, not only upholding his son's seventeen-year-old rights as against Elisha Mix's thirteen-year-old resentment of them, but also making his letter the occasion of several personal criticisms of his own against the Mix family, and promising, when he had more time, to write again

"Concerning Some things that I have Observed in you and met with from you, that have been not very pleasing, but to speak ye very truth, Considerably ungratefull & Grievous to me and I am easily persuaded were not Justifiable in you; but how Long it will be first I cannot tell".[19]

At present he was too busy to take time to enumerate them. In the same letter he called "Sister Micks" to account because before "three Young Women, two of them being strangers", she has talked against Jonathan in a way which "tended not a Little to diminish him and blemish his name" and was most unbecoming in his "Mother's Own Sister".

Such was the Edwards way of settling trouble. The result, as one might imagine, was not the restoration of harmony in the Yale dormitory, or in either of the parsonages involved. Before all had been said on both sides a trivial misunderstanding between two boys in their teens had been made the occasion of a sizable quarrel, adding another family of the blood to the Edwards list of enemies. Most of the serious troubles of Jonathan Edwards' mature life were complicated by family estrangements, some of which would seem to have been avoidable. One is reminded again and again of William Edwards of Hartford, making such clamors against his neighbor as led the court to administer a rebuke in the interest of community peace. The trait which made it necessary to see a grievance through to the end, despite the consequences, had persisted. Back of it was a sense of justice to the letter, a pastoral urge toward the reproof and correction of others, and a lamentable lack of any sense of humor. Jonathan Edwards came naturally enough by all these traits, and often walked a thorny path in consequence. Had he been willing to let his less circumspect contempories go their way while he went his, they might not have minded his superior righteousness; they might secretly have admired him for it. Instead, even when the circumstances did not concern him personally, he felt impelled be times to "tell others wherein he thought them somewhat to blame". The inevitable sequel inevitably followed. Throughout his life he showed the same curious blindness, making no allowance for human resentment of criticism, and continuing to act as though it did not exist.

From his father he received criticism respectfully, as in the schoolroom days in East Windsor. He even invited it. Aged eighteen, capable of solving "theorems in divinity", of filling vacant pulpits on occasional Sabbaths, and of expressing such ideas on the mind, the soul, and the nature of reality as are still taken account of in histories of thought, he was writing filial thanks for advice about being more social, reporting that he was much "improved" with respect to the visiting of friends, and promising to do still better in future. He might have written such a letter, aged ten. Unfortunately, parental advice could not help him. Solitariness was determined by his very nature. He could resolve to pay the calls, but there was nothing to say after he arrived. He lacked the kind of imagination by which he might have found the connection with other men's ways of thought. The entry in his *Diary* October 7, 1723, "Have lately erred, in not allowing time enough for conversation," tells all one needs to know as to the reason for the social failures he regretted so keenly.

As a boy among boys, he showed no understanding of the prankishness of youth, and no inclination whatever toward mischief. If there had been any reality back of his father's phrase, "the naughtiness of Jonathan" (aged seven), the offending Adam of such desires had been rooted out long before his college days. He was committed for life to the very strait and narrow way. Aged fourteen, he would join in a student secession on the grounds that the rector could not govern and the tutors were not well furnished with knowledge; but not at any age would he have subscribed his hand and seal to the fifteen shilling bond and protest, drawn up by the disgruntled boarders in the new "College House" who threatened to eat no more of the college fare unless the quality improved. His advice on this occasion to young Stiles (his father's protégé), who had joined the hungry malcontents, sounds like the advice of a grandfather. "Stiles to my Grief", he wrote, has done this thing, adding that the uproar had been out of proportion to the grievance. At this time he was probably feeling his graduate dignities a little consciously, and he was also probably right in his verdict; but at any age, in any issue which involved insubordination, Jonathan Edwards would have been on the side of the grandfathers.

The letter to Timothy Edwards detailing this episode is one of the most revealing of his young letters as to the quality of the father-son relationship. It is also enlightening as to the early scene at Yale College. For these reasons, although it has already been printed numerous times, it deserves yet another hearing:

Yale Coll. Mar 1st 1721

"Honoured Sir

"It was not with a little Joy; and Satisfaction that I reciev'd your Letter of ye 21st of Feb. by Mr. Grant, And with a Great Deal Of thankfulness from the Bottom of My Heart for your Wholsom advice, and Counsel, and the abundance of Fatherlike tenderness therein expressed. As Concerning the Complaint of the Scholars about their Commons; the Manner of it I Believe was no less Surprising to me: than to you: It was on this wise, Every Undergraduate, one and all, that had Anything to Do with Colledge Commons, all on a sudden, Before Mr. Cutler, or (I Believe) any Body Knew yt they were Discontented, entered into a Bond of 15s never to have any More Commons of the steward, wherupon they all forewarn'd him never to Provide more for them, telling him If he Did they would not pay him for it, Mr. Brown Notwithstanding Ordered Commons to be provided, and set upon the table as it used to be, and Accordingly it was, But there was no body to eat it:

"Mr. Cutler as soon as he was apprized of this Cabal sent On the same Day for Mr Andrew, and Mr Russel, who Came On the next, and with the Rector ordered all to appear Before them; Where the Rector Manifested himself exceedingly Vex'd, and Displeased at the Act, which so affrighted the Scholars that they Unanimously agreed to Come into Commons again. I believe the Scholars that were in this Agreement have so lost Mr Cutler's favour that they scarce ever will Regain it. Stiles to my Grief and I Believe much more to his was one that set his hand to this Bond; He Did it By the Strong instigations of Others who Persuaded him to it; neither had he a minutes time to Consider before his hand was Down: as Soon as I Understood him to be One of them, I told him yt I thought he had done Exceedingly Unadvisedly, & I told him also what I thought the Ill Consequences of it would be, and quickly made him sorry that he did not take my advice in the matter, I am apt to think that this thing will be the Greatest Obstacle of any to Stile's being Butler. I must needs say for my Own part, that although the Commons at some-times have not been sufficient as to quality, yet I think there has been very little Occasion for such an Insurrection as this. Although these Disturbances were so speedily Quash'd, Yet they Are succeeded By Much Worse and Greater, and I believe Greater than Ever were in the Colledge before, they are Occasion'd By the Discovery Of some Monstrous impieties, And Acts of Immorality Lately Committed. In the Colledge, Particularly stealing of Hens, Geese, turkies, piggs, Meat, Wood &c,— Unseasonable Nightwalking, Breaking People's windows, playing at Cards, Cursing, Swearing, and Damning, and Using all manner of Ill Language, which never were at such a pitch in the Colledge as they Now are; The Rector has Called a meeting of the trustees On this Occasion, they are expected here to Day tis thought the Upshot will be the Expulsion of some, and the Publick Admonition of Others: Through the goodness of God I am perfectly free of all their janglings. My Condition att the Colledge at present is every way Comfortable: I live in very Good Amity And Agreement with my Chambermate. there has no new quarrels Broke Out betwixt me and any of the Scholars, though they still Persist in their former Combination, but I Am not Without Hopes that it will be abolish'd by this meeting Of the Trustees. I have Not as yet wrote to Uncle Mix, Because I Heard he was Coming Down, But he Delaying His Coming I shall Do it speedily. I am at present in perfect h[ealth], and it is a time of health through out the Colledge and Town. I am about taking the remainder of my lignum vita. I am much Reformed with Respect to Visiting of Friends, and Intend to do more att it for the future than in time past. I think I shall not have Occasion for the Coat you Mentioned in your letter till I come home. I Recieved a Letter from my Sister Mary the Week before last and have heard of her Welfare this week By a Man that Came Directly from thence. I Pray you in your Next Letter to Send me your advice whither or no I had Best Come home in May, or tarry Till June. Please to Give my humble Duty to My Mother, hearty love to sisters, and Mercy, and still to be mindfull before the throne of Grace for me, who am,

"Stiles presents	"Honoured Sir
his Duty to your	"Your
Self with my	"Most Dutyfull
Mother and Service	"Son
to My Sisters"	"JONATHAN E.[20]"

Jonathan Edwards' allusion in this letter to the monstrous impieties and acts of immorality recently discovered in the college, and the announcement that through the goodness of God he was free of "their janglings," may sound to twentieth century ears like smug self-righteousness. In word certainly, but hardly in spirit if one may judge by the whole context of his thought and action. As boy or man he was incapable of self-righteousness. In this instance he meant exactly what he said; no more, no less. He was free of "their janglings" and glad of it. The boys who stole hens, geese, pigs, etc., night-walked, broke windows, played cards, indulged in cursing, swearing, and damning (whatever the fine-spun distinctions) were not hoodlums or near-hoodlums; they also were country-bred, the sons of ministers and on their way to being ministers themselves. Between parsonages they were not wicked; only bored. The restraints of their own home training and the strictness of the college regimen might forgivably have produced excesses less mild than these. The restraints of Jonathan Edwards' training protected him from joining his comrades because he was already self-pledged to a way of life which sanctioned restraint. Even when righteousness meant being in bed by eleven he obeyed an inner, not an outer, restraint. Perfection was in his eye and he was his own monitor.

If his standards of judgment seem unique, one has only to turn the pages of journals and diaries of other pious minis-terial candidates to find ample parallels, and to remember that in terms of college discipline these were still the days in which the ultimate punishment for the expelled culprit was to have his unworthy name torn from his own Bible by the president of the college.[21] Considered in the white light of such standards, "card-playing" and "ill language" take on a midnight hue. To Jonathan Edwards these misdemeanors were more than infringements of the college rules. Through them he came to his first realization of the sinfulness of his fellow men, and naturally the shock was proportionate to the parental zeal which hitherto had protected him so naïvely. The greater shock of the still more grievous unrighteousness beyond the college precincts was still to come, but he would be ready for it when it came. The college years had con-firmed him in the rightness of his father's standards of value. These were now his own standards as well.

This was not all. Intellectually, Yale College had been to him a process of self-realization. He had found his own world: a world not of men but of ideas. Companionship with boys his own age had not, as we say, socialized him. To the end of his life he was not socialized. This first experience in group living had served to isolate him still more in a world to which he could never belong. In partial compensation, it had given him the key to his own realm, the realm of Locke, of Newton, and of all those to whom reality is primarily of the mind and spirit.

Chapter 4

"A New Sense of Things"

LOGICALLY, one might suppose the greatest event of his college life to have been an intellectual experience, but such was not the case. The greatest event in these six years of study, as well as the central fact in his whole life and the key to all his thought, was what he called his conversion. To view his life from the outside, one might suppose that religion had always been the controlling impulse of his life, and that in his twelve-year-old freshmanhood he was already a dedicated spirit. Jonathan Edwards, however, made finer distinctions.

According to his own statement, written long afterward, this momentous experience took place in the early part of his second year of graduate study, when he was seventeen years old. Although he called it by the usual name, conversion, it did not come according to the usual ministerial specifications. No revival was in progress. He experienced no conviction for sin, no sudden ecstasy of forgiveness. He could not tell the moment at which the new life had begun. He was merely brought, as he said in his *Personal Narrative,* to "new Dispositions" and a "new Sense of Things".[1] For him the whole of life was altered; the divine glory was everywhere; and with a finality of assurance he knew that religion was henceforth to be the main business of his life.

A long struggle had preceded, beginning in a period of illness and continuing through many months. It was not primarily an experience of terror, in spite of the impression that at times God was shaking him over the pit of hell; rather it was an earnestness of seeking, agonizing in its intensity. In vain he left off what he called his evil ways, battled all inclination to what he called sin, laid himself under vows to God and gave himself night and day to the exercises of piety. Still peace would not come. When after weeks of alternate hope and despair, the struggle ended, he could not describe the experience in the fact, only in the result. Turmoil was past; peace had come. All at once he had entered a realm he had never known, and was experiencing transports of joy as strange as beautiful colors to one born blind. The divine excellency encompassed him; he was part and parcel of God.

The importance of this experience goes far beyond the changes it wrought in his personal life, for it became the cornerstone of his whole structure of thought, determining the basis not only of his revival preaching, but also of his religious philosophy. He first endeavored to search out the innerness of the experience and to understand it himself; then he endeavored to translate it into doctrine. The task was lifelong. One might almost say that out of a personal, emotional experience of his seventeenth year he built a theological system.

Unfortunately he did not write down the story until years later when he was more than twice as old, had had revivals in his own parish and witnessed scores of conversions. During the intervening years he had satisfied himself that religion was of the emotions, and that conversion had a rational and scriptural place in the scheme of redemption. One would greatly prefer to have had the story while the experience was freshly personal, not recollected in tranquillity after mind had brought feeling under control. Even so, he tells it with a glow and beauty of style seldom matched in his other writings. The loss of the original manuscript for this piece is a great misfortune. One would like to have so important a chapter in his inner life preserved to the letter in his own idiom, not "improved" by later hands.

Carefully he distinguished between this college experience and his earlier religious delights. The booth in the swamp, the secret prayer in the woods, the many religious duties in which as a boy he had taken such intense pleasure, now appeared to him merely the outward expressions of piety, not religion at all. As he now saw it, the delight had faded; secret devotions had ceased to be a joy, because he had never been admitted to the kingdom at all. No wonder, as he now believed, he had fallen into sin. It did not occur to him, as he recalled this sequence of declining ardors and all the suffering it had caused him, that during his college years his intellectual horizon had been greatly broadened and his mind filled with a thousand new excitements. He made no allowance for his own development or for the fact that as a child he had demanded a concreteness of expression which as a college student he no longer required. He had lost the joy because he had outgrown the medium through which it had formerly been expressed. Unknown to himself, the experience of struggle and search was itself abundant proof that religion was still, as it had always been, the first concern of his life. Within the old husk a new growth had been taking shape, and when the time was ripe it broke through its coverings and came forth.

The answer to this new search was an intuitive certainty. As Jonathan Edwards tells his own story, he first experienced this "sweet delight in God and divine things" when, as he read from Paul's Epistle to Timothy, he came upon the words,

Now unto the King eternal, immortal, invisible, the only wise God, be honour and glory for ever and ever. Amen.*

As he read, there came into his soul and was diffused through it a sense of the Divine Being different from anything he had ever experienced. Never had any words of Scripture seemed to him like these words. As he sang them over to himself, he longed to enjoy that Being of whose majesty he had caught a glimpse, "to be wrapt up to him in Heaven, and be as it were swallowed up in him for ever!" From about this time he began to have new apprehensions and ideas of Christ and the work of redemption through him. "An inward, sweet Sense of these Things" came at times into his heart and led his soul away into pleasant places. Particularly as he meditated on the loveliness and beauty of Jesus, he experienced

"a calm, sweet Abstraction of Soul from all the Concerns of this World; and a kind of Vision, or fix'd Ideas and Imaginations, of being alone in the Mountains, or some solitary Wilderness, far from all Mankind, sweetly conversing with Christ, and wrapt and swallowed up in GOD. The Sense I had of divine Things, would often of a sudden as it were, kindle up a sweet burning in my Heart; an ardor of my Soul, that I know not how to express".[2]

Almost without change of a word, this might be a page out of Jakob Böhme, Brother John of Parma, or some other initiate who, feeling the burden of the inexpressible, has sought relief in words.

"Mysticism" is a dangerous word, and there are many kinds of mystics, but for want of a more precise term one may say that in this college experience Jonathan Edwards joined this strangely diverse company, and that henceforth he spoke their language to the letter.

To him as to other mystics the excellency of God took

* I *Tim.* 1:17.

shape through the manifestations of nature: sun, stars, clouds, and blue sky. He saw the sweet glory of God in the moon and heard his voice in the thunder. Holiness took visible shape; the soul appeared as a "Field or Garden of God, with all manner of pleasant Flowers; . . . enjoying a sweet Calm, and the gently vivifying Beams of the Sun".[3]

To Richard Rolle, the Hermit of Hampole, the divine glory came as exquisite harmony, a music above all earthly music, releasing him to raptures of which no language could give account. The music and the rapture were one; both were incommunicable. The heavenly harmony not only enveloped him; he was part of it, and in this fullness of joy his soul rested.[4]

To Æ, a poet of different heritage, both racial and temporal, a "lost child of the stars" as he called himself, the vision appeared also in sound, fading away in the music of bells, and vanishing into the "wondrous underland" beneath the solid hillside on which he lay. Then the heart of the hills was opened to him and he knew "there was no hill for those who were there"; the Golden Age was all about him, and he knew "it was we who had been blind to it but that it had never passed away from the world".[5] To William Blake the vision came in color and movement. Truth took the likeness of angels, and long after they had passed he could paint them in "strong, level flight."

The parallels between such experiences go deeper than language or imagery, deeper even than the form of the illumination itself. The mystic's own nature, his gifts, and his training shape the vision and determine the language through which the joy finds expression. Being no poet, Jonathan Edwards could not detach his thought from the concrete image and take the symbol without the fact. Nature was analogy to him, as it was later to Bryant and Emerson. Natural facts were but shadows of spiritual truths, and yet the fact would not away. When he saw the soul of a Christian as a little white flower, low to the ground, diffusing sweet fragrance as it opened its heart to the sun, he could not, like Jakob Böhme, forget the analogy and, taking the flower alone, look into the very heart of things.

Neither was he musician or painter. He was the literal-minded son of New England and of Timothy Edwards. Hundreds of doctrinal sermons echoed in his ears. He was shackled hand and foot to a theological heritage, and must either explain what had happened in terms of theology or not explain it at all. For one of his age he had done a deal of thinking; he may even have thought himself boldly independent in some directions, but there were fundamentals which were not open to question, as is true for any thinker in any age. To one of his training, in 1721, not only had God made the world according to Genesis, but the outline of biblical events was inseparable from doctrine.

> In Adam's fall
> We sinned all,

and from the consequences of this sin there was no escape except by virtue of divine grace. The plan of salvation was all settled. It embraced the whole of human history from the creation to the Last Judgment, and was in God's hands only. One accepted the unalterable premise and built whatever individual superstructure his vision had revealed upon this foundation and this foundation alone. In catching a mystic's glimpse of the divine glory, Jonathan Edwards touched hands with men across many centuries; in finding the meaning back of the vision, he was a man of his time speaking in the current theological idiom. If only he might have freed himself from his studies in divinity long enough to look at his own experience of conversion directly, or if his conversion had come first, many things might have been different. Instead, he rationalized the experience in terms of New England Calvinism as he had inherited it. Whereas once he had demanded to know by what right God chose whom he would to everlasting life and rejected whom he would to everlasting torment, he now saw in the divine sovereignty the *raison d'être* for the new faith that was in him. Having experienced this revelation of the divine within himself, he could no longer question; he rejoiced in the very sovereignty which had once offended him. The doctrine became "exceeding pleasant, bright, and sweet". Intellectual assent followed the emotional experience. In his own word, he was convinced as well as satisfied, and his mind rested in the assurance of God's justice and reasonableness. Throughout his life he did not retreat from this position.

As a young thinker, he was probably fortunate in being able to reconcile the familiar theology with the new vision. Certainly he was more comfortable. As he grew older, theology still offered no contradiction to experience. The story of his intellectual life is not, as some have supposed, the story of a man who denied his young raptures, repudiated his visions, and became a cold logician, proving salvation by line and rule only. Calvinism did not for him destroy mysticism. Theology did not deny ecstasy. It merely provided an explanation and made a place for visions in the orthodox scheme of things, as was all-important in 1721. Had he been a complete mystic, instead of a theologian with mystical leanings, no explanation would have been required. The vision itself would have been its own answer to all questionings. But mind in Jonathan Edwards was too strong and logic too insistent for that. To see and to feel were not enough; he must also explain. The penalty was to be shut out from the innermost circle; he could never attain to the perfect beatific vision.

The test of visions is of course their translation into life. Not do they fade, or do they come again, but can one who has seen the glory keep his loyalty to this perfection too high for earth, once the sight of it has passed? That test Jonathan Edwards met. He had his dark hours, he swerved from the path and was sometimes outdone by the confusions around him; but, from his moment of revelation forward, his feet were in the way and he knew his goal. As he saw it, he had made a late start. Life, whatever its length, would not be long enough for the grace of God to work its way with him.

Soon after he first began to experience these new raptures, he went to East Windsor and gave an account of "what had passed" to his father, being as he said "pretty much affected by the Discourse we had together". Much of this recital must have seemed strange language to Timothy Edwards, for ecstasy was neither in his vocabulary nor in his life; but the tribute his son paid him by these confidences was tribute indeed. "And when the Discourse was ended" Jonathan Edwards wrote:

"I walked abroad alone, in a solitary Place in my Father's Pasture, for Contemplation. And as I was walking there, and looked up on the Sky and Clouds, there came into my Mind a sweet Sense of the glorious *Majesty* and *Grace* of GOD, that I know not how to express. I seemed to see them both in a sweet Conjunction: Majesty and Meekness joined together: it was a sweet, and gentle, and holy Majesty; and also a majestick Meekness; an awful Sweetness; a high, and great, and holy Gentleness".[6]

These experiences continued during the remaining year and

a half, as he went on to complete his studies in divinity. He had an increasing sense of divine things and more and more of what he called time after time "that inward Sweetness":

"The Appearance of every thing was altered: there seem'd to be, as it were, a calm, sweet Cast, or Appearance of divine Glory, in almost every Thing".[7]

He spent much time alone, walking the woods, delighting in this view of God's excellency, wisdom, purity, and love, of which all nature was the reflection. These were the months in which, as he wrote:

"I often used to sit & view the Moon, for a long time; and so in the Day-time, spent much time in viewing the Clouds & Sky, to behold the sweet Glory Of GOD in these Things: in the mean Time, singing forth, with a low Voice, my Contemplations of the Creator & Redeemer. And scarce any Thing, among all the Works of Nature, was so sweet to me as Thunder and Lightning. Formerly, nothing had been so terrible to me. I used to be a Person uncommonly terrified with Thunder: and it used to strike me with Terror, when I saw a Thunder-storm rising. But now, on the contrary, it rejoyced me. I felt GOD at the first Appearance of a Thunder-storm. And used to take the Opportunity at such Times, to fix my self to view the Clouds, and see the Lightnings play, and hear the majestick & awful Voice of God's Thunder; which often times was exceeding entertaining, leading me to sweet Contemplations of my great and glorious GOD. And while I viewed, used to spend my Time, as it always seem'd natural to me, to sing or chant forth my Meditations; to speak my Thoughts in Soliloquies, and speak with a singing Voice".[8]

It is a pleasant picture, too much obscured in the thought of later generations by the picture of the cloistered student, unwilling to waste a minute from study. Both are true. As life pressed in upon him and the making of many books became increasingly important, there was less time for the woods, as in most adult lives. Maturity also took toll, and raptures presently became more bearable; but to the end of his life his personal experience of religion was an emotional experience, similar in kind to the ecstasies of his student days.

During the months to which the first chapters of this new experience belonged, Yale College was anything but a peaceful setting. Rector Cutler and Tutors Johnson and Browne were not walking the path marked out for them, and when in the fall of 1722 they openly embraced Episcopacy the whole of

New England, and Yale College in special, were rocked to their foundations. As President Woolsey remarked on the occasion of the one hundred and fiftieth anniversary of the founding of the college, "I suppose that greater alarm would scarcely be awakened now if the theological faculty of the college were to declare for the Church of Rome, avow their belief in transubstantiation, and pray to the Virgin Mary".[9] The irony of this 1722 dereliction was all the more bitter to swallow, because the famous Dummer Library [10] had caused the undoing of its guardians. So long as four villages had been battling to possess the books, they had remained safe in their packing boxes, their contents corrupting no one; but, transferred to New Haven, the boxes had been opened and the books read for the first time. Not by undergraduates, but by Rector Cutler and his tutors, Johnson and Browne. For the custodians of orthodoxy, to whom the nurture of Connecticut's future ministry had been entrusted, to prove faithless was black enough, but for them to have drawn the poison from the precious books was almost too much. The trustees were humiliated as well as aghast at the enormity of it all.

No one was less to blame than the culprits themselves. Heresy had crept upon them unawares, and had been stoutly challenged for many months. They had not read the books with intent to disbelieve; rather to know. When Timothy Cutler had accepted the rectorship in 1719, he had presumably done so in good faith, although it is more than likely that the books had been a strong inducement. He had brought to his new duties a more hospitable attitude toward liberal views than would have pleased the trustees had they been able to read his mind at the time of his appointment. Samuel Johnson also, even in his fledgling days, was too much of a scholar to take the color of the orthodox Yale environment as a matter of course. He too had an inquiring mind. For more than two years these men had been quietly and very earnestly seeking to know the truth concerning a few troublesome doubts of their own.

Not doctrine but church polity had been the subject of their inquiry, and when they opened the Dummer boxes, to their surprise they found not one answer but two. Jeremy Dummer had had no intention of advancing the cause of Episcopacy in America; he could scarcely even have been aware of the intensity of feeling among the Connecticut clergy against it. In the 1720's Church of England missionaries were quite as unwelcome in Connecticut as Quakers had been in seventeenth century Massachusetts. As Messrs. Cutler and Johnson and Browne and their four ministerial friends read the Dummer books, they wondered why such hostility. As the readings and discussions continued, the entire group was gradually convinced, against its training and desire, that by the authority of Scripture, the Established Church and not New England Dissent was the lineal descendant of the Apostolic Church. But to be convinced was not to be at peace, since their Presbyterian ordination was thereby invalid and they were all usurpers in the house of God. There was nothing to do but to acknowledge their shift of loyalties, and as speedily as possible make amends for their long mistake. Samuel Johnson wrote in his *Journal* that he was willing to face any humiliation lest he continue to be "a stumbling block to others", adding, "There may be more souls damnified for want of Episcopal government in the country . . . than by making this appearance".[11] It was in this spirit that the heretics faced the censure and ejection which their boldness invited.

About the time they were ready to admit their change of view openly, trustee suspicion had begun to be aroused. The meetings in the library had been too frequent. No sooner had Rector Cutler uplifted his hands and dismissed the 1722 commencement audience with the words "And let all the people say Amen", than the trustees, speechless with consternation, went into secret session. On the following day, September 13th, they summoned Rector Cutler, Tutors Johnson and Browne, and their four ministerial companions in heresy— John Hart, Samuel Whittelsey, James Wetmore, Jared Eliot —gave them a hearing in the college library, and demanded a declaration of their changed views in writing. It was willingly given. The trustees, still more aghast, urged them to reconsider their action. When they refused to do this, a public debate was arranged, at which Governor Saltonstall was named Moderator. The debate was held October 16, 1722. Under fire, three of the group recanted, Hart, Whittelsey, and Eliot; Wetmore wavered; Cutler, Johnson, and Browne remained unshaken. The culprits were better furnished in argument than their trustee opponents, but that the decision would be adverse was foreordained. Having acted as prosecution, jury, and judge, the trustees announced as their verdict that "in faithfulness to the Trust reposed in them", they forthwith did excuse Rector Cutler and Tutors Johnson and Browne from all further service in the college.[12]

In the small world of New Haven, still a village of fewer

than one thousand inhabitants, this ultimatum took on the solemn dignity of a papal decree. The entire colony was plunged in deep gloom and the Connecticut clergy chagrined. It was the darkest of all dark hours, bringing to an ignominious close the only period of prosperity and semiharmony the new college had yet enjoyed. "We need pity, prayer and counsel", wrote Joseph Webb, one of the trustees, to Cotton Mather, and was hardly comforted by the reply he received.

No direct allusion to this unhapppy turn of college events survives in Jonathan Edwards' own papers, but the omission is understandable. During the preliminary chapters, while trustee suspicions were merely being whispered, he was absorbed in his new religious experiences; shortly before the dismissal of the rector and tutors, he had gone to New York to assume his first pastorate. He did not escape the result, however, of the sharp, timely emphasis on orthodoxy which resulted from the Inquisition in the college library. It is doubtful whether any event of his student years, aside from his conversion, was more determining in the history of his lifelong attitude toward orthodoxy than this early necessity to take a stand on the issues involved in the arraignment of these leaders. Trustee action had defined these issues anew: orthodoxy consisted in complete acceptance of the Saybrook Platform; heresy consisted in any variation therefrom, particularly in the direction of Arminian doctrine and prelatical church government as opposed to Congregationalism. In future all rectors and tutors would be obliged by trustee requirement to declare their orthodoxy in terms of these specifications, and upon the slightest suspicion of deviation therefrom they could be subjected to an examination. Had he been asked, *in absentia,* to give assent to these trustee regulations, he would have done so unquestioningly. He had once praised Rector Cutler for his good governance of unruly undergraduates, but doctrinal malfeasance was a different matter. By both precept and example, he was predisposed to subscribe to the Saybrook Platform and the Congregational way before he was asked. Furthermore, by this necessity to recognize his own allegiance, he was confirmed unaware in a grudging hospitality toward new views of old doctrine.

It might so easily have been different. He was only seven years younger than Samuel Johnson, the most gifted of the skeptics. His maturity, his intellectual acumen, his ability to hold his own in argument with men his seniors in age and experience, and also the fact that for two years he had enjoyed the privilege of reading the Dummer books, should have made him one of the group in the library. Instead, he had been discussing theology with Pastor Noyes, minister of the Old Church on the green. A year and a half later, when he accepted a Yale tutorship under the newly straitened requirements, the die was cast. For two more very important years in his intellectual development he lived in an atmosphere abnormally sensitive to the slightest breath of heresy, according to trustee definition, walked an orthodox chalk line in all his thinking, took the responsibility for buttressing younger minds against any skeptical leanings, and consciously strove to remove the blot from the college escutcheon. What is more important to an understanding of his later career than even the strengthening of his own allegiance to "sound doctrine" is that these experiences also developed in him a protective attitude toward the cause he espoused, with the result that henceforth throughout his life he did not so much proclaim the doctrine as defend it.

The New York pastorate which immediately preceded his tutorship had no relation to these doctrinal battles. This eight-month period was an opportunity for spiritual refreshment and further cultivation of the inner life, and at the same time a sharp break with all he had hitherto known. He ministered to a small Scotch Presbyterian congregation to which he was called in August, 1722. The personal circumstances which lay back of this call and acceptance are not known, but they need not have been of any special significance. Connecticut colony had been very friendly to the struggling Scotch Presbyterians in New York, and for that reason alone the call might naturally have come to a candidate from Yale College. Jonathan Edwards had completed his theological studies and was open to appointment. He was eighteen years old.

New York in 1722 was not yet a city of

"stretch'd wharves, docks, manufactures, deposits of produce";

but it offered wider horizons, a chance to be jolted out of village patterns of thought and to come at life from new angles. During the six years Jonathan Edwards had been away from East Windsor, he had to some extent freed himself from provincialism in his thinking; but as to the world of men and affairs, America's dawning sense of nationality, her new dreams of commerce, and the graciousness of life in the larger centers of population, he knew almost nothing. East Windsor was a parish; New Haven was a "nursery" for those who would spend their lives in other parishes. Secular interests had been almost nonexistent in his life; they continued to be non-existent in New York. He met no one of distinction. He kept closely to the meetinghouse circle, finding only what he had already known and, in effect, turning an urban parish into a village the size of East Windsor.

The church he came to serve was an offshoot from the first Presbyterian church in New York, situated on Wall Street near Broadway.[13] The seceding group met in a building on William Street between Liberty and Wall. Since their basis of withdrawal had been personal disagreement with the minister of the Wall Street church, James Anderson, the roots of per-manence were not in the new venture. The parent church, organized only two years previously through contributions from the presbytery of Scotland and from Connecticut, could ill afford to lose the seceders, who were likewise in no position to maintain themselves. Both societies were struggling. The seceders were financed temporarily by several individuals among them, who had assumed rent for the building they were occupying and for the salary of a pastor, but they were not incorporated as a church body.

The only record of Jonathan Edwards' sojourn among these people exists in his *Personal Narrative* and in a few ser-mons which probably date from this period. His new sense of divine things continued to have first place in his thought. He gave his days and nights to seeking after holiness, with more diligence, he says, than he ever pursued anything in his life, even with more earnestness than he had sought grace before he had it. Days spent in prayer, in meditation, and in solitary walks in the woods left no time or thought for the larger world around him. The foreground was to him totally unim-portant. He had no zest for exploration and no curiosity about men and their doings. New York as a place of ships, a new speech, and more crowded ways of life, was a blank in com-parison with the divine beauty of holiness on which his mind and heart were fixed. When he read the papers it was not to understand the world in which he was living, but to see whether he could find some news favorable to the increase of religion in far places. If so, his soul "eagerly catched at it", was animated and refreshed.

He touched the reality of earth at one point, however; he found a friend, John Smith, a member of his congregation and of the household in which he lived. This was not a friendship which brought new interests. John Smith, whose name is unfortunate for searching, seems to have been a currier,[14] employed about the docks near which the little church was located. He was apparently a simple person who supplied no new stimulus whatever, the only basis for companionship between the two boys being their pleasure in reading their Bibles, walking in the woods, and talking together about the "things of religion"; but this was quite enough. For Jonathan Edwards the sharing of such joys was a completely new experience. It was also of more than transient importance. Twenty years later he was still receiving letters from "my dear friend Mr. John Smith of York".

His congregation was apparently well pleased with his youthful sermons on the glory of the saints in light and their songs of rejoicing around the throne; but as a church they had no resources and no future. Soon after they had called Jonathan Edwards to minister to them, they realized that they could not hope to keep him. Their only chance of survival was union with some more prosperous congregation, but the fact that they postponed decision in the matter lest it "Issue in our deprivation of the much Respected Mr Edwards",[15] attests their satisfaction in his ministry. When of his own accord he decided to accept another call, they assumed his choice to be a leading of God for the solution of their own dilemma.

The new call came from Bolton, Connecticut. Negotiations had been in progress during most of the New York residence, but Jonathan Edwards had been slow in making up his mind. It was not until April, 1723, after "a most bitter parting with Madam Smith and her son", that he sailed away to New England.

"My Heart seemed to sink within me", he wrote, "at leaving the Family and City where I had enjoyed so many sweet and pleasant Days." [16] Doubtless he had made a wise choice. There was no longer any place for him in the pulpit he had occupied, and as he had made no effort whatever to be a part of the religious life of the city beyond the little circle by the docks, there was no hope of another New York call. Perhaps that too was just as well. By temperament, he was as much unfitted to accommodate himself to the currents of New York life ecclesiastically as socially. The New York pulpit did not speak his language, and the New York pew would not have understood it. In returning to New England village life he was returning to an atmosphere far more congenial to his own ways of thought and life. It was also an atmosphere destined to be less hospitable to original thinking, when that thinking should set itself to challenge approved doctrine or practice.

But the eight months had been by no means wasted. New York had been to him a sojourn in Arabia, or on the shores of Walden Pond. He had transacted a little very important business with his own spirit, and was returning to the workaday world with his own thought clarified and his sense of personal religious truth greatly enriched. His mind had lain fallow while he had increased in spiritual stature and in personal experience of "divine things".

He spent the summer in East Windsor, continuing his studies and renewing his boyhood associations after a seven-year absence. He may also have spent some time in Weathersfield, studying with Elisha Williams, his former tutor. Early in November the Bolton arrangements were complete. He had finished his candidacy and received the formal call. Salary and wood and pasture land and a homestead had been provided, to the satisfaction of both parties. He sealed the bargain by signing his name in the town book, as follows:

"Nov. 11, 1723. Upon the terms that Are here Recorded I do consent to be the settled Pastor of the Town of Bolton".[17]

His release came immediately after this formal acceptance. Had he settled in Bolton, he would have had a chance to make his own traditions, for the congregation was newly gathered. He might also have been buried for life. Something saved him; exactly what is not clear. The offer of the Yale tutorship was the obvious reason. There may have been other reasons. Timothy Edwards was at work on his son's career, and he may have been thinking Solomon Stoddard would soon be needing an Elisha.

The pleasant conjecture that Sarah Pierrepont may have been the real reason has at least the support of the New Haven geography. If she were the magnet, however, it was because he had heard she was "beloved of that Great Being who made and rules the world", and hardly cared for anything "except to meditate on Him",[18] not that as yet Jonathan Edwards had any claim to a share in her meditations. Nothing in his view of life in 1723 would have permitted him to make such a decision for personal reasons. He had gone so far, however, as to discover the delight of walking in the woods and talking of divine things with a congenial spirit, and the report that Sarah Pierrepont was given to doing likewise may have been enough to set his imagination to work. Later, after he had returned to New Haven, it is highly probable that she was one of those "distractions" which perplexed his thought and gave him more experience of his own heart than he had ever had before.

These were difficult decisions, leading him to acknowledge afresh his life purposes and ambitions in various ways. While he had been making up his mind where to choose, he had also been sealing a contract with himself. In January, 1723, while he was preaching in New York, he had made a dedication of himself to God for life and had written down his pledge:

43. *"Resolved,* Never, hence-forward, till I die, to act as if I were any way my own, but entirely and altogether God's, agreeable to what is to be found in Saturday, Jan. 12th. *Jan.* 12, 1723".

Under the same date he wrote:

44. *"Resolved,* That no other end but religion, shall have any influence at all on any of my actions; and that no action shall be, in the least circumstance, any otherwise than the religious end will carry it. *Jan.* 12, 1723".[19]

These were only formal acknowledgments of what had already taken place more than a year before, when he had experienced what he called his conversion.

Most of his other famous *Resolutions* belong to this same period, the spring and summer of 1723. In fact, they are in no way unique, but merely follow a convention of the time. Young men of serious purpose were accustomed to setting down their life intentions similiarly in numbered items and making no secret of having done so. For the more practical items in Jonathan Edwards' list there are numerous parallels in the journals and personal papers of his contemporaries. Philip Doddridge, for one, as student, tutor, and later as pastor, put himself in chains to a schematized pattern of living which had nothing whatever to do with inner values. Under the caption "Rules for the Direction of my conduct while a student", he committed himself to such purposes as the following:

4. "Never let me trifle with a book with which I may have no present concern".

5. "Never let me lose one Minute of Time, nor incur unnecessary expenses, that I may have the more to spend for God".

8. "Let me never delay any thing, unless I can prove that another time will be more fit than the present, or that some other more important duty requires my attendance".

13. "Let me consecrate my sleep and all my recreations to God, and seek them for His sake".[20]

Other young men, who did not become famous preachers, consecrated themselves similarly, often in almost the same words.

Courtesy, thrift, punctuality, early rising are more frequent in such lists than the intangibles. Even the items which concern religion usually go no further than religious gestures to be observed, often with corresponding penalties to be exacted if one failed to live up to his own standard. Daily chapters to be read, services to be attended on the Sabbath, prayers to be offered at stated times, specified sins to be avoided, as though religion consisted in looking at a Bible verse immediately before one's eyes closed at night, and then breathing a prayer with one's first morning breath, keeping awake in meeting, and eschewing forever all words easily classified as profane. If the sin were not concrete, it was usually made so in the penalty. In comparison with all such pious declarations, the *Resolutions* of Jonathan Edwards, for all their asceticism, belong in another realm. Not devotional gestures at all, but immeasurable values were his concern. Even as a child he would have been incapable of counting his prayers or penalizing himself by weight and measure. Before he had gone much further in adult living, he probably put away these resolves of his twentieth year, along with other childish things. They had become their own incentive for continuance and he needed no further spur.

He was appointed Tutor in Yale College on May 21, 1724, and served until he accepted the call to Northampton two years later. According to his own record the period of tutorship was a time of great mental and spiritual stress. He had exchanged a life of comparative freedom in the pursuits most congenial to him for an ordered program of activity and heavy responsibility. There had been no resident rector since Timothy Cutler was "excused". Consequently, in addition to their pedagogical duties the tutors were obliged to deal with many practical administrative matters. In 1724 the college numbered forty students, and in the following year, sixty. As senior tutor, Sir Edwards took the heavier load, and was virtually in charge of the college. The atmosphere was still troubled; the trustees, still suspicious. Students had grown lax in discipline. Contempt of tutors, intemperance, public disturbances such as hallooing, firing guns, unseasonable ringing of the college bell, called for frequent rebuke and punishment. Except for "offences very criminal", when two trustees must be called in, Sir Edwards and Sir Treat handled all such cases. Day by day, they were also charged with a list of minor chores, wearying to contemplate.

Various trustee records attest their faithfulness and efficiency. On September 29, 1725, there is record of a vote that the tutors

"for their Extraordinary Services of the Year past, & their Trouble & Pains in sorting the Books & fixing Catalogues to ye Boxes have five Pounds each added to their salary".[21]

One wonders whether a letter of Jeremy Dummer to Timothy Woodbridge, paying compliment both to the Latin and the penmanship of a diploma awarded to one "Dr. Turner", was not also a compliment to Sir Edwards. Dummer wrote that it was "drawn up in a true Roman diction, & both for language and sentiments exceed any thing I ever yet saw from My Own Alma Mater".[22] It was also "sent in a fine hand & so handsomely ornamented with flourishes".

Jonathan Edwards' orderly habits of work and his flair for detail fitted him admirably for his new duties and honors, young though he was for the responsibilities involved. He was not expected to branch out in new directions. Tutorship in those years meant strict maintenance of the *status quo*. He had been well schooled in conformity, and toed the mark to the satisfaction of all, giving generous measure of conscientious service, but at great cost, as he felt, to his continued growth in grace. The first entries in his *Diary* after he was settled in his new duties indicate clouds on the spiritual horizon. He wrote:

"*Saturday night,* June 6 [1724].

"This Week has been a very remarkable Week with me, with Respect to Despondencies, Fears, Perplexities, Multitudes of Cares, and Distraction of Mind: it being the Week I came hither to New-Haven, in order to entrance upon the Office of

Tutor of the College. I have now, abundant Reason to be convinced, of the Troublesomeness and Vexation of the World, and that it will never be another Kind of World".[23]

His dejection is understandable. The break with his former life had been too abrupt. Now that his days were mortgaged to scheduled tasks, there was no time to walk in the fields and chant his meditations. His religious transports ceased. Characteristically, he thought himself to blame. In humility he put himself under sterner rigors of self-discipline, denied himself food and sleep, and became more relentless in self-examination. Presently, the inevitable sequel followed, and in September, 1725, when he had been Tutor a little more than a year, he became severely ill and nearly lost his life.[24] This three-month illness appears to have weakened his constitution seriously. Never robust, although fairly strong and healthy up to this time, he was thereafter to suffer long illnesses during nearly every year of his life. His recurrent attacks of fever, his necessary care in diet, his long absences from pulpit duties are often mentioned in the family correspondence, although seldom by himself. As he grew older and held himself more rigorously to a cloistered life and longer hours of study, his health grew increasingly precarious. Asceticism became both a cause and a result of his frailty. Lack of vitality, weakness, and pain also explain much as to his somber view of life. Had he known in his adult years the measure of well-being which as a country boy grown man he had a right to expect, he might not have relinquished so willingly whole areas of human experience as having little interest in them.

After a long convalescence in East Windsor during the spring and early summer of 1726, he returned to the Yale tutorship and remained until the close of the session in September of that year. Meanwhile, the Northampton congregation had been casting about for a likely successor to the aging Solomon Stoddard. When Jonathan Edwards accepted the invitation of the town and became a candidate for the position, it is not likely that anyone in East Windsor or New Haven was greatly surprised.

His formal education and years of apprenticeship were now over. In most ways he had had all a gifted young American of his day could ask. There had been ten years of independence: six of them years of training, almost three years of practical experience in his chosen fields, and one year of forced inactivity. He had had encouragements and honors, and almost complete freedom to follow his own bent. He had been unhurried in his choice of a pastorate. Among the possible pulpits to which he might have aspired Northampton was most desirable, being ecclesiastically second only to Boston. To be chosen colleague pastor with one of the most successful ministers in New England church history was in line with the honor of the Latin oration and the Yale tutorship. To his contemporaries, particularly those of his father's generation, it must have seemed that the stage could hardly have been more favorably set for the lifework of Solomon Stoddard's grandson.

In retrospect, his preparation shows one serious omission. For one of his powers of mind it seems great pity that in his formative years he had had so little chance to cross intellectual swords with promising men of other interests and training. Jonathan Edwards and Benjamin Franklin might have had nothing to say to each other had they sat opposite, on occasion, but each might well have learned something from the mere meeting. Within his own realm of religious interest, some early temptation to skepticism might have encouraged Jonathan Edwards to try a new path instead of merely justifying the beaten track. Especially if he were to reshape and revitalize traditional beliefs so that men who were not theologians would listen, he needed more than anything else to know something of life outside the parsonage and the meetinghouse.

So we think, who esteem breadth an advantage, and in this case are probably wrong. Single-mindedness, not breadth, was to be Jonathan Edwards' distinction, and this had far more to do with the demands of his own nature than with any influence acting on him from the outside. The jostling of other interests would only have annoyed him. In his seventy *Resolutions* and his notes on "The Mind" he had already set the marks and limits of his own world. Perhaps he was wiser than he knew, perhaps only fortunate, when he chose as a setting for his life work a parsonage with Mt. Tom in his view instead of the Hudson River.

Chapter 5

Ministerial Legacy—1727

HE SIGNED his name in the Northampton Town Book on February 15, 1727. This was five months after he had presented himself as a candidate.[1] The congregation had heard him favorably, and after less than three months' trial had invited him to settle in the parish. In the expectation of his day, acceptance of this invitation meant that he had cast in his lot with the Northampton church for life. Prior to this time, many things important in the living of his life had been determined. By this decision, many more were determined. Among them, any chance that for him the traditions of the East Windsor parsonage and a provincial college would ever be successfully challenged by any other pattern of life was practically ended. His boyish ambition to meet and exchange ideas with men of intellect in Europe would never be realized. Instead, he would meet and exchange ideas with the straitened brethren of the Hampshire Association, a body of rural ministers from neighboring parishes. Once he had taken his place among divines so seasoned and change-resistant, he was destined almost inevitably to keep within the ministerial pattern as it had been reverenced in America from John Cotton's day forward.

He was also destined to a life of battle. Any young man coming to an American pulpit in 1727 was almost certain to be a protester, either against the old order within the church or against the new order without. For in the course of a century a strangely ironic drama had been enacted around the meetinghouse. Designed by those who first built it to be the cornerstone of the American state, by 1727 it had become the seat of a diminishing authority, and was attacked on every side by the secular forces of progress and swift change.

Such a sequel might easily have been predicted. It would have come to pass even though church membership and a certificate of baptism had been required of everyone who set foot on American soil. Before the "plantation religious" had even begun to take shape for the first-generation Separatists who had dreamed it to be possible, their children had accepted freedom from a ritualistic worship, not knowing what it had cost, and were pledging their loyalities to their own dreams, not to the never-to-be-realized Utopias of their parents. After three more generations all paths still led to the meetinghouse, but it had long been taken for granted. Too long. The controversies of active Dissent had grown vague and unimportant in comparison with planting new acres, building new houses, and in a multitude of new ways, making each village more nearly sufficient unto itself. Life in America in 1727 challenged the grandsons and great-grandsons of the first settlers at a thousand new gateways, and the present, not the past, was all-important.

In the course of the years also, the worshipping nucleus of colonial America had been outnumbered many times by those to whom the privileges of Dissenting worship meant little or nothing. These non-church members had also bred sons and daughters whose "godless" ways of living had considerably leavened the traditions of the "godly" with whom they had grown up side by side. Every town in America showed this cleavage, with growing numbers ever on the side of the "godless".

The clergy had a name for all this. They called it "decline of religion" as, looking backward, they made heavy lamentation for the godless present. They had begun their condemnations while the first settlers were still alive. As early as 1650 it was "too plain to be denied" that there was "a dying spirit in New England to the ways of God". Lament had become more petulant through the seventies and eighties, as the sons and grandsons of the first generation went their still stranger ways, until by the time Jonathan Edwards was born in 1703 true Christians were only a precious remnant; only a few pillars were left, there was a "decay upon the very vitals of religion", and the glory of the New England churches would be vanished in a generation. It was even now on the wing. Venerable divines paused on the verge of the grave to give dying testimony to this sad change. In 1701 John Higginson, looking back seventy years, and William Hubbard "above sixty", had no word of hope.[2] They had lived to see the children of New England throw away the precious legacy of their fathers and "vomit up their spiritual milk with scoffs". In the same year Increase Mather, thinking he was not much longer for this sinful world (and hoping he was not), began to give thought to his last words. He made them a dirge for this sad declension.[3] As the new century dawned, he could count on his fingers those whose righteousness caused God to hold back a well deserved destruction. Other divines likewise went to their own coronation feeling that they left behind them a lost cause.

In the outworn phrases of these men, Jonathan Edwards' father had been one of the few recruits from this lost and undone "Rising Generation" that had forgot its errand into the wilderness, and taking ease and security in sin, was pursuing a worldly interest with its whole heart, making a few shillings and saving them, but losing its soul. He was one of the lonely remnant for whom the Fountain (Harvard College) had not failed. If America were yet to be saved, it would be because dying patriarchs could cast their mantles on such as he.

"What is the Cause that the former Days were better than these", was Cotton Mather's text for his sermon *The Good Old Way*, preached in 1706. Anyone in the pews could have supplied the well worn answer. How had the power of godliness once flourished and how had it now fallen into decay! Religion was now religion in name only and everything was less than it had been in the golden age of the first generation. By means of pulpit eloquence the golden age became ever more golden. Never had the Babylonian dust been so successfully shaken off the feet of any generation; never had there been an outgoing of any nation like unto that which came in the first ships to America, and—to the glory of God be it spoken—perhaps never before had there been "such a Body of pious People together on the Face of the Earth" as the first settlers of New England.[4] Any boy or girl belonging to the "godly" portion of any village congregation would have known by heart John Norton's famous eulogy of the "plantation religious" upon whose forehead was written "the Profession of the Purity of Doctrine, Worship and Discipline".[5] As American history lengthened, and eloquence fed on eloquence, its righteous beginnings became ever more fabulous. The piety of the earliest generation was ennobled into a myth, as the brethren spoke in reverent hyperbole, unconscious that their hero-tale was shaped by a nascent patriotism, which only their grandchildren would dare to call by its proper name.

It was the clergy themselves who were blind and deaf. While American life was in swift flux, and the interests of the village were multiplying until the meetinghouse could no longer hold them together in unity, they continued to behave as though all things were static, as of the year 1620, and would be world without end. While they reminisced vaguely and sentimentally of an impossible golden age which had never existed, American life on scores of new paths went swiftly by them. New England had begun to dream of broader lands to the west and south, and of rewards of industry somewhat larger than the needs of the coming winter. There was a wider gulf between the associations of the sixth day and the seventh. Life had grown less solemn as it had become less precarious, inevitably. The pews were restive because they needed a new idiom of religious expression for a new day; but instead of helping them to bridge the gap between the meetinghouse and the enlarging life outside of it, the clergy continued to look backward, saying, "Let us return to what was". That a "Congregational church discipline is not suited to a worldly interest", was as true in 1720 as it had been a hundred years earlier, but its spirit might have been preserved in a new idiom, had the clergy been less literal-minded, more able to distinguish between husk and kernel.

Particularly on formal occasions, such as ordination days, commencement days, election days, preachers used their opportunity to lament the sad decay and to urge reform. It was an old story, dull at the edges. Titles of election-day sermons, chosen at random over a period of a hundred years, suggest the negative accent of these preachments. Negation had almost crystallized into a formula, and before the preacher announced his theme the congregation knew what to expect. It would be something like the following:

1700, Samuel Willard, *The Perils of the Times Displayed.*
1711, Stephen Buckingham, *The Unreasonableness and Danger of a People's Renouncing Their Subjection to God.*
1720, Stephen Hosmer, *A People's Living in Appearance and Dying in Reality, Considered.*
1730, William Russell, *The Decay of Love to God in Churches, Offensive and Dangerous.*
1733, Samuel Wigglesworth, *An Essay for Reviving Religion.*

Out of twenty such titles, not three were born of a hopeful vision. Each year new calamities provided fresh illustration of God's disfavor: the prevalence of the "throat distemper", the death of a clergyman, "a blast upon the wheat", the burning of a boat in Boston harbor. In such ways God was still speaking to a people who had forgotten His ways. Sins were named aloud, particularly drunkenness. Rarely did an election-day preacher fail to call Giles Firmin to witness that it had not always been so. His famous tribute to New England was as meaningless as it was familiar:

"I have lived in a Country seven Years, and all that Time I never heard one prophane Oath, and all that Time I never did see a Man drunk in that Land. Where was that Country? It was New-England"![6]

Through too frequent repetition condemnation failed to condemn. Young people went away from the very Assembly to sit out the remainder of the afternoon in the tavern, now a place of rendezvous in every village. Smoking in the street was no longer a family disgrace, and if a church member were caught taking his ease and chatting with his friends under his own apple tree in time of divine service, the statute might still put him in the stocks for "ye horrible neglect and contempt of Gods Ordnances", but the week would not be long enough to give all offenders a due sitting.

From time to time there was legislative response to the clergy's impassioned tirades against this "Deluge of Debauchery". Ordinances and laws were passed to regulate men's morals and insure a return to piety. In 1711 the General Assembly of Connecticut passed resolutions "against the prevailing of a worldly and covetous spirit; against intemperance in the use of lawful things; particularly against excess in drinking". Again in 1714 they recommended to the "Reverend Elders of the General Association that the state of religion be strictly enquired into".[7] Similar measures were taken in other colonies. In 1732 the Massachusetts House of Representatives voted in the interest of reform that the Cambridge Platform of 1648 be printed at the public charge and placed in the hands of elders and deacons for use in the churches. New synods were called to make effective what earlier synods had enacted, as though by such means religion could again be given first place in men's thought. Individual churches took action to "restore" the earlier practices, in the hope that the tides of evil might be checked by such futilities as requiring the "male youth" to assemble in one place after Sabbath exercise, and the "female youth" in another, to be examined by the elders on the morning sermon. It seems a strange blindness. A new generation was not interested in synods, nor were elders and deacons any longer the great ones of the village. More would be required than little pamphlets on swearing, Sabbath breaking, and the dire sin of schism to hold the male and the female youth to the ways of their fathers. It was all old wine in very old bottles indeed.

From the pulpit, religion was preached not as an inner satisfaction of the spirit but as a code of abstinence from such defilements as husking bees, journeys, and unsuitable discourse on the Sabbath, bonfires and fireworks on Lecture Thursday. Unaware of their inconsistency, preachers inveighed heavily against the doctrine of "good Works" and then proceeded to make a formula for American godliness in terms of the 1620's. They were guilty of exactly what they denounced. Emptiness begot emptiness, and yet the echoes of echoes droned on. With extreme diligence the older ministry saw to it that those who were ordained to follow them were rigorously schooled in the old tradition, with the result that their young-old successors continued to preach to ears still more deaf to such iteration, until nothing but a Great Awakening could again make religion a concern of first magnitude in men's thought, and then for a day only.

There is also another side to the picture. Diaries of non-ministerial visitors, the files of early newspapers, and court records provide only occasional evidence for the "avalanche of debauchery" denounced in election sermons.

"The strictest kept that ever I yet saw anywhere",

wrote Joseph Bennett, an English visitor, of the Boston Sabbath, as late as 1740. He repeated almost verbatim the famous Firmin observation concerning drunkenness, observing:

"It is a rare thing to meet with any drunken people, or to hear an oath sworn, in their Streets".[8]

"Tedious Courts at Plymouth and Barnstable. . . . Not a single criminal at either Court",

wrote Paul Dudley in the same year.[9] Obviously the clergy were denouncing an attitude rather than overt acts of lawlessness; obviously also, the non-ministerial observers were applying a different measuring rod from that of the clergy. The truth as to actual conditions probably lay, as usual, somewhere between the two views.

In the Halfway Covenant the clergy made one notable concession to the changing emphasis of American life and thereby retained a partial hold on their more worldly members for another generation. This plan, first proposed in the Synod of 1662 and eventually ratified by most of the New England churches, provided for the baptism of children of church members who could give no evidence of their own conversion, and for the admission of these children to full church membership upon their adult ratification of the baptismal covenant. If they chose not to ratify it, only one membership privilege was denied; they might not partake of the sacrament of the Lord's Supper.[10] This privilege was reserved for those who could give evidence of personal conversion, but since in seventeenth century America even nominal church membership carried with it marked social advantage, the more worldly members of the flock seized eagerly upon these halfway privileges. To be shut out from the Lord's Supper seemed at first a small price to pay for village prestige and for the privilege of presenting their own infants for baptism.

But before these same infants had grown up, surviving proponents of this compromise measure saw their sad mistake. They had unwittingly fired the first gun in a veritable Hundred Years War and at the same time had weakened their own defences past any subsequent mending. Perhaps they had no choice. Perhaps it was a case of compromise or else another separatist movement. At any rate they chose compromise and chose it to their own dire hurt. Increase Mather, limited as he was in his view and sour in his spirit, was right when he saw the rocks ahead. In the years before God hastened him out of the world he did what he could, but in vain.

The Synod of 1662 had forgotten history. In the church of the founders the main source of strength had been the absence of nominal Christians. There had been no division between those who were of the fellowship and those who merely conformed to the ordinances outwardly. Now every congregation had to carry its dead weight of halfway members who had not "owned the covenant" and whose hearts were not in the Lord's work. The unity of the flock was henceforth broken, and with unity went not only power in group action but also part of the very *raison d'être* of the meetinghouse as the fathers had conceived it. The modification of this original purpose to fit the needs of a new day was something of which the Synod of 1662 had not dreamed.

The founding of the Brattle Street Church in 1699, and the election of John Leverett instead of Cotton Mather as president of Harvard College in 1707, were expressions of the new liberalizing tendency from within. This was as much as Boston and Cambridge could accomplish in one generation. Another generation must work out the consequences of this defiance of church councils and this rebuke to the personal despotism of the Mathers in ecclesiastical affairs. It remained also for the liberalizing spirit to attack doctrine itself, but that day was far distant at the beginning of the new century.

When Jonathan Edwards was born in 1703, the patriarchs of Plymouth and Massachusetts Bay were all dead, and their legacy of lament for the decline of religion had long since lost its power to make the pews uneasy. The apostasy of New England had been written into the record and no longer required proof. He grew up with the settled conviction that nothing but a great "outpouring" would be trustworthy evidence that the anger of God had been turned away from this American corner of His vineyard, so peculiarly dear to Him. This was the pulpit speaking. Had the pews also been articulate, they would have said, "Stop scolding; show us a new vision", but neither he nor his brethren would have heard.

The history of the Northampton church he came to serve in 1727 stretched back far enough to epitomize most of the wars of the Lord on the American continent. As between conservative and liberal elements it inclined to the liberals. Gathered in 1661 under Eleazar Mather, brother of Increase, and a champion of the old order, it had been conceived in the strict tradition of John Cotton's day, but too late for the pattern to leave its print indelibly.[11] In the very next year, 1662, had come the Halfway compromise, by which the old order was doomed. Had Eleazar Mather lived, this compromise might have been long protested, but when he died in 1669—aged only thirty-two, but "remarkably ripe for heaven"—he had been immediately succeeded by Solomon Stoddard, a stout Liberal, equal to winning the wars he started. The Northampton church had been one of the first to ratify the new membership basis, and had therefore been a divided company from the beginning of his pastorate. The Covenant members enjoyed both sacraments. The non-Covenant members brought their infants for baptism, but on Communion Sunday, the most sacred of all days, were shut out from the Lord's table. As the baptized infants grew up, many of them like their parents, could give no evidence of "experimental piety" and were likewise shut out. The privilege grew in importance as it was denied, and when presently a line drawn through the congregation on Communion Sunday showed a hopeful majority on the side of the unprivileged, a new compromise was in order.

This innovation was the contribution of Solomon Stoddard to American church history. He laid his plans well. Upon being formally settled in the parish in 1672, he promptly married the widow of his predecessor, built himself solidly into the traditions of Northampton life, and made himself greatly beloved by his flock. In 1700, after his reputation as an eminent Christian and a highly successful pastor had gone well beyond the village limits, he astounded the whole of New England by proposing that the "unregenerate" be allowed to come to the Lord's table along with the converted members, provided only that they were not "scandalous" in their way of life. It was a staggering blow to the defenders of primitive purity in the churches. Battle was once more sharply drawn between the old and the new order, Increase Mather again defending the old, this time against his own brother-in-law.

All New England was alert to the fray. Ministers took sides; non-covenant members saw their opportunity and made the most of it. Solomon Stoddard's vigorous and rational treatises in support of his position were widely read,[12] and after New England had withstood the first shock it appeared that he had proclaimed his innovation in a propitious hour. Eventually, he carried most of New England with him. His arguments were practical rather than doctrinal. Let the unregenerate come to the Lord's table, he argued: it may help them. The Sacrament is a means of grace: let it be so used. The Mathers, whose approach was theoretical, were horrified. Their argument in brief ran thus: How dare the unregenerate approach the Table? Bold guests without a wedding garment —more bold than welcome; intruders, in fact. The Church is a Garden enclosed, a Spring shut up, a Fountain sealed. Mr. Stoddard lays it open to the whole world.[13] His position is unscriptural.

To the Northampton parish "Mr. Stoddard's Way", as his amendment came to be known throughout New England, had come as no surprise. He had been practicing it for years, had taken his flock into his confidence at the time he first proclaimed his view publicly, and accordingly had had their loyal support throughout the entire uproar. As parish after parish voted to adopt this proposal, the Northampton congregation enjoyed the distinction of having been pioneers in a successful enterprise. Many of them did not follow the arguments of their learned pastor, but they enjoyed the prestige he had brought them, and many of them on Communion Sunday profited by his liberality of view.

Seen in perspective, his victory was ironic in the extreme. In 1700, when he first proposed his scheme, New England Dissent was less than a century old. The original church members had withdrawn from a church which admitted the unregenerate; before the last one of these original members had died the church was again polluted. It would not have taken a sage to predict that a generation still further on, ministers would be wondering what to do when the "unregenerate" fell into scandalous disorders and refused to submit to pastoral reproof. But in the thick of battle Solomon Stoddard and his brother ministers did not think of these things. It was reward enough to have unity in the flock and surcease from nagging by the unprivileged. Certainly in Northampton there was no immediate evidence that a mistake had been made. The church prospered; revivals came; a new generation forgot that the Lord's Supper had ever been denied to anyone of the communion.

In 1727 battle was not imminent on any front. During the long truce since "Mr. Stoddard's Way" had passed into history, individual congregations had concerned themselves with smaller matters: the authority of consociations and the minutiae of ritualistic change. The most spirited quarrels had been intramural: where to set the new meetinghouse and whether to sing the New Way or the Old Way being chief among them. The answer to the first had been purely local; the second had somewhat wider implications.

By the Old Way each male worshipper sang without reference to the time and pitch of all the others. The women remained silent. By the New Way, or Singing by Rule, the entire congregation arrived at the same point in the hymn at approximately the same time and in approximately the same key. On this issue almost every parish in the land had been locked in more or less deadly strife at some time during the 1720's. The conservatives held that to exchange the old jargon for musical law and order was mightily to displease the Almighty. To follow rules in singing was to make the psalm purely perfunctory and hence to rob it of all flavor of personal devotion. What matter if a tune sung in one parish bore no resemblance to the same tune sung in another? The progressive wing was even more militant. In spite of the fact that music had been a subject of study at Harvard in the early years, the arguments of these advocates of the New Way had all the zest of a first discovery. Music has rules, they announced naïvely. It is all so easy, anyone can learn. Those who know how can begin anywhere in the psalm, wrote Thomas Clap [14] by way of winning over the opposition.

But the incredible discords which had hitherto passed as congregational singing did not willingly yield to any such revelations. The battle was on, and while it lasted minister and congregation forgot the praise in the manner of it. The logic of the opponents is easy to understand. Their disapproval was Dissent in one more application. From singing by rule it would be only one more step to praying by rule and "then comes Popery". But this time Dissent was impotent. The secret was out, and with it a new diversion for leisure hours. Itinerant music teachers saw their opportunity and seized it. From parish to parish they went, leaving schism in their wake. Singing schools sprang up in rapid succession in village after village, inviting to still further conflict. Should the children of the "godly" be allowed to attend, or should they not? Ministers and parents disagreed, and what might have been a new means of capturing the ever lukewarm "young people" became the means of estranging them still further as, regardless of pastoral counsel and possible frowns of God, they enrolled in the singing classes.

Ministerial diaries are full of the monstrous quarrel. Both sides sought scriptural warrant for their position, and in true Yankee fashion they sought it to the letter. The nadir of literalness was reached by the Reverend Hugh Adams of Dover, whose predilection for the New Way led him in strange paths. Having first seen to it that his congregation sang "more decently and in order" by obeying the rules, he sought to test the Almighty's approval in the matter by scriptural analogy. Taking example from Jehoshaphat's appointment of singers to go before his army in chorus, he did likewise when a timely Indian raid provided the opportunity, and by way of good measure he also armed his own two little boys with cow horns (horn of silver and brass being "out of reach of my procurement"), and instructed them to march around the parsonage, blowing with all their might. God honored the cow horns; the parsonage was saved, and by this *reductio ad absurdum* [15] the logic of the Reverend Hugh

Adams, A.B. of Harvard College, caused him to pity the congregations which had returned a negative vote in the singing crisis—an extreme, but by no means lonely example of ecclesiastical argument given village application in the 1720's.

In Northampton, under the sound guidance of Solomon Stoddard and the example of Boston, the congregation made the shift from the Old to the New Way without loss of their dignities. Even this mild flurry was over when the town took action toward the selection of a colleague pastor. The call had no reference to parish discord. A distinguished pastorate was drawing to a close, and the time had come to look ahead. Few in the congregation could remember the time when Solomon Stoddard had not stood in the pulpit. He had preached and ministered to them for fifty-five years, and his successor was not to be lightly chosen. The Committee, acting for the town, had made diligent search; and when the town, after due deliberation, acted on their report, it was with deep assurance as to the wisdom of their choice. The record on the Town Book, under date of November 21, 1726, is as follows:

"The Town taking into Consideration a vote passed by the Town August 29th last past for the Invitation of the reverend Mr Jonathan Edwards to Assist our Reverend Pastor Mr Stoddard in the work of the Ministry, in order to a Settlement & from what Experience we have had of him by his preaching & conversation as also from his Character from other places.

"The Question was put whether it was the mind of the Town that the Committee Should invite the reverend Mr Jonathan Edwards to Settle amongst them in the work of the Ministry and in Convenient Time to take office Amongst them, & it passed in the Affirmative by a very great Majority.

"Attest Ebenezer Pumroy Moderator"

Except for the fact that he was continuing a family succession which might entail troublesome loyalties, he began with almost everything in his favor.

As he took his ordination vows he had no thought of rewriting parish history. He had read Solomon Stoddard's books as a college student, and if he had any doubts as to the validity of the arguments in favor of admitting the unconverted to the Lord's Supper the time had not yet come to express them. For two more years he was to sit beside his grandfather in the pulpit, preach only once each Sunday, and take over parish responsibilities gradually as Solomon Stoddard was obliged to lay them down. As the two men sat side by side on Sunday morning, one eighty-four, the other twenty-three, both tall, dignified, and commanding, the congregation could hardly have missed the significance of the chapter which they were writing. A new era had come, and this serious-faced, quiet-mannered young Elisha looked the part he was to play. Not a man to know quickly and perhaps not a man to love, but an ornament to the pulpit and a worthy successor. In a cramped, unsteady hand Solomon Stoddard wrote the beginning of the new era in the record of the First Church of Northampton.

22 Febr: 1726/7
Mr. Jonathan Edwards was ordained a Pastour of the Church at Northampton.

The new pastor had entered upon graver responsibilities than he knew, not only because of the peculiar heritage which must be respected in this communion, but because of the changed place of religion in the life of the average American of 1727. His father, in 1694, had faced a far easier task.

Chapter 6

The Parish Round

In the 1720's Northampton still belonged to that vague territory known to the Boston newspapers as "our western frontiers". An aerial view of the town would have shown the square boxlike meetinghouse (to all but New England eyes looking more like a fort than a church) standing at the very center, on top of Meetinghouse Hill. Around the hill the weather-beaten houses of the townsmen crowded close on all sides, about two hundred in all. Some were built of logs; some, of rough lumber; all were unpainted. Here and there a larger house, set more to itself, showed that the town numbered a few greater ones.

Beyond the houses and completely encircling what had been the original settlement, were the old fortifications: the trenches, earthworks, and spike fences (overgrown now in many places, but their outline still plainly visible). Farther out, and extending up the rough slopes of Mt. Tom and Rocky Hill, were the sheep pastures, cleared of underbrush and marked off in irregular plots with hurdle fences. An occasional shepherd moved about among the flocks. Along the river were the fertile fields, explaining why a settlement had been made in this lonely spot, which was really no more than a clearing between the woods and the river. Roads were merely paths, made for horseback travel only, and lost to view at the edge of the clearing. On all sides deep forests blotted out the horizon. Only the river led out. A town built here must be sufficient unto itself, and what concerned one would concern all.

By 1727, when Jonathan Edwards came, life had become fairly safe in spite of remoteness. The burning of Deerfield by the Indians in 1704 had been the last horror of that sort, but the portholes in the meetinghouse and in the fortified houses around it still reminded residents who had reason to be reminded that such dangers had once been very real. Even yet, it was wise to take precautions. Occasionally a child wandered too far and was carried off. A man went into the woods to look for his cow, and was found scalped or never heard of again. Wolves were a continual menace to the flocks; sometimes to the children. But for the most part one thought little of these things. By 1727 Northampton was frontier chiefly in its isolation, and in that isolation the meetinghouse was the central fact, as in the earliest days.[1] Town and parish were still one; so much so that not even the tavern keeper could be quite indifferent to the minister and his preëminence in town affairs.

Aged twenty-three, Jonathan Edwards was able to assume this central position in town life without either false modesty or undue self-importance, for he had grown up with the idea that the ministry, as the highest of all callings, conferred honors and prerogatives that were commensurate. Like any other member of the pulpit fraternity in his day, he expected from his parish not only a comfortable maintenance and leisure for study, but also such honor and reverence as befitted the spokesman of God. Not to expect deference would have been to degrade the office. According to the traditional logic of ordination sermons, when a minister assumed the charge of souls, he assumed a burden too great for the shoulders of angels.[2] It followed therefore that he was a man of special privilege. If freedom of speech be a citizen's privilege, the brethren argued, how much more is it a minister's? If abuse of a man's natural parents puts him under a curse, how much more the abuse of his spiritual father? Nothing in Jonathan Edwards' experience as a minister's son, or as a student in divinity at Yale College, had ever called such assumptions into question. As a fledgling minister in 1727 he had still to learn, and so did his people, that such high notions were subject to change, and quickly. The minister too might become but a man.

But not yet. Formalities past, Northampton received him with traditional deference and went immediately to work on his first wood supply. In making the terms of settlement the town had moved with much deliberation, since local precedents for such action were practically nonexistent, except in the memories of the oldest inhabitants. By the terms finally agreed upon and voted separately in six carefully worded items,[3] he was to have three hundred pounds for the purchase of a homestead, and more if necessary; one hundred pounds a year salary, and more if the value of money declined, or if his family increased; ten acres of pasture land "against Slow-bridge", and forty acres up the river. One month after his ordination the sum for settlement was increased eighty pounds, and three years later when Solomon Stoddard died a hundred pounds was added to the salary. According to contemporary standards for rural parishes, these sums represent a fair, even a generous, arrangement, or, in the language of the Town Record, a

"Support Suitable & well adapted to that honourable office".

With the three hundred pounds allotted for settlement, Jonathan Edwards immediately bought the homestead on King Street in which he was to live for the next twenty-three years of his life.

No account of his formal ordination or its attendant festivities has come to light, but since there had been no celebration of this sort for fifty-five years, one may suppose Northampton did justice to the occasion. Certainly many neighboring ministers would have been present at the ordination sermon, partly out of respect for their venerable colleague, partly out of curiosity over his successor. Following the sermon there would have been a ball (of the churchly sort), feasting, and much gaiety, unless out of consideration for Solomon Stoddard such rejoicings were deemed inappropriate. This gala part of the program may have been considerably curtailed, possibly even postponed until it could be made a housewarming in honor of the bride who came five months later.

She was Sarah Pierrepont of New Haven,[4] daughter of James Pierrepont, first minister in the town, and according to tradition, the original mover in the founding of Yale College. Her mother also came of a notable ministerial line, being the granddaughter of Thomas Hooker, eminent divine and leader of the 1630 migration to the Connecticut valley. He had founded the town of Hartford, probably bringing with him William Edwards, cooper, first of the Edwards line in America. In the New England of his day Jonathan Edwards could not have joined his name to two more illustrious ministerial names than Pierrepont and Hooker. The prestige of both families was far superior to that of his own.

In her own right also Sarah Pierrepont brought abundance of gifts to her new station. By all accounts she possessed unusual beauty and comeliness, was far more at ease in conversation than her scholarly-looking husband, and for all her solitary walks and her piety, was noted for her charm, her flashing wit, and a gay repartee of which her English cousin, Lady Mary Wortley Montague, might have been justly envious. With just a little more encouragement to the laughter that was in her, just a little less godly conversation, and as much secret prayer, Sarah Pierrepont might have changed the definition of "religion" for those of the parish who were not inclined to solitary meditation alone. Instead, she regarded piety as the goal of life and, like her husband, pursued the "things of religion" with a single-mindedness of endeavor which set her apart even from those of her own age. At the time of her marriage she was only seventeen years old.

But she was no novice in parish affairs. In coming to Northampton she did not step outside the pattern of life to which she had been born. She merely exchanged one parsonage and the elevated seat in one meetinghouse for another of each. This was her chief, perhaps her only, disqualification for the new life she was to lead. The concerns of the new parsonage swallowed her up too early and too completely for her ever to see her own part in village life with that detachment which the case demanded—particularly later when the battles raged. Outwardly, she had lost more than she gained by her new bargain. In leaving her father's home on the New Haven Green she gave up a life of comfort and an atmosphere friendly to cultured pursuits for residence in a community but sparsely settled with intellectuals, and for a life outwardly plain, even to ruggedness. But only outwardly. Life in the Edwards home in Northampton and later in the wilderness of Stockbridge was lived in the aristocratic tradition. That was one reason why the storms broke over it so persistently, for the air of country parishes in the mid-century was none too friendly to aristocracy of the Edwards-Pierrepont stamp. For a man of Jonathan Edwards' temperament and his intellectual gifts, the frontier was not his rightful place. He should have gone to Boston. But one cannot write biography as it should have been written. Aged twenty-three, he used what wisdom he had, and with his seventeen-year-old bride set up his home on King Street, where it quickly became the center of a country parish of some two hundred families.

The marriage had taken place in New Haven on July 20, 1727, five months after his ordination. One would like to think that on the following Sunday, according to the custom of colonial New England, the bride walked to her elevated seat in the Northampton meetinghouse in all her wedding array. If so (there is little reason to doubt it), one hopes also that on that particular morning the usual catechizing of the young people as to the Text, the Doctrine, the Improvement, the Application of the morning sermon was omitted.

There had not been a bride in the Northampton parsonage for fifty-seven years, and as Esther Warham Mather had merely changed masters one might as well say, not since the church was founded in 1661. Accordingly, to Covenant and non-Covenant members alike, the coming of beautiful Sarah Pierrepont would have been an event to be starred in all the parish almanacs.

One would like to know more about the companionship of these two young Christians, so obviously drawn to each other by their intense awareness of spiritual reality. Because religion awakened and satisfied the deepest desires of their natures, their absorption in it, instead of dwarfing their love for each other, increased and intensified it. In the dimly etched lines of their personal story one finds hints of a deeply shared experience of spiritual things, as well as a rare companionship and rich happiness. Rather too much emphasis has been placed through the years upon Sarah Edwards as the efficient, capable wife who protected her husband from the encroachments of practical responsibility, as though she were a veritable Martha in the household. She was a Martha truly enough, as the mistress of a frontier parsonage and the mother of eleven children had need to be, but to honor her for her practicality alone is to honor her for only half of herself. She was also a woman of intellectual power and deep spirituality and, like her husband, was capable of religious transports. The balance in her nature, as in his, between the sense of fact and a capacity for emotional religion made her a fortunate choice as a life companion. So also her social gifts, which had no counterpart in him and must therefore have enlarged his thought in new directions. There is no indication that prior to his marriage his knowledge of women had ranged far beyond the limits of his own home circle. His mother had always stood before him as a pattern of solid godliness; his sister Jerusha was a gentle saint who withdrew into her own solitude; Mary was an everyday companion who shared his intimate boyhood confidences. Gaiety and charm in a woman would have been a new experience, although not nearly so important in the living of his life as the sympathetic understanding Sarah Pierrepont was able to bring to that which concerned him most; namely, religion.

Posterity knows her by two records: her lover's boyish tribute to her Christian graces, written when she was perhaps a child of twelve or thirteen, and her portrait painted some years later,[5] when she was in her early thirties. These two records deserve to stand together. The little paragraph of her lover's self-revelation, preserved by some happy chance and printed times without number, probably belongs to the time of the New York pastorate, when Jonathan Edwards was about eighteen years old. It is quite clearly the first chapter in a transcendental romance.

"They say [he wrote] there is a young lady in [New Haven] who is beloved of that Great Being, who made and rules the world, and that there are certain seasons in which this Great Being, in some way or other invisible, comes to her and fills her mind with exceeding sweet delight, and that she hardly cares for anything, except to meditate on him—that she expects after a while to be received up where he is, to be raised up out of the world and caught up into heaven; being assured that he loves her too well to let her remain at a distance from him always. There she is to dwell with him, and to be ravished with his love and delight forever. Therefore, if you present all the world before her, with the richest of its treasures, she disregards it and cares not for it, and is unmindful of any pain or affliction. She has a strange sweetness in her mind, and singular purity in her affections; is most just and conscientious in all her conduct; and you could not persuade her to do anything wrong or sinful, if you would give her all the world, lest she should offend this Great Being. She is of a wonderful sweetness, calmness and universal benevolence of mind; especially after this Great God has manifested himself to her mind. She will sometimes go about from place to place, singing sweetly; and seems to be always full of joy and pleasure; and no one knows for what. She loves to be alone, walking in the fields and groves, and seems to have some one invisible always conversing with her".[6]

The sequel, as a personal story, belonged to the lovers alone, but it seems to have been a story that the years did not make less beautiful.

To the face in the portrait maturity has brought dignity with a hint of imperiousness. There is still beauty, still sweetness, but the dominant impression is of vitality and force rather than charm. Hers is not the face of a saint abstracted from reality, but of a woman who spoke with calm assurance and authority. Had her portrait been painted again, toward the end of her forty-eight years, after pioneer hardship and the battles around the parsonage had taken costly toll, it would have shown her still more determined, though not ungentle. In her view of life one did not bear resentment; by afflictions of both flesh and spirit one grew in grace. But in 1727 her sorrows were all before her, and her woman's record still unwritten.

The parish welcome over, life in the parsonage quickly settled into a routine. There was much work to be done. For more than ten years age had been crippling Solomon Stoddard's energies, causing many things to slip. The young people had grown disorderly in meeting; children had not been catechized often enough; family prayer had been neglected. The religious duties of the pew needed sharp new emphasis and more diligent supervision. Jonathan Edwards went immediately to work, giving energetic attention to these intramural concerns. Month by month he assumed more of the parish responsibility, so that two years later when his grandfather died there was scarcely a break between the two eras.

Solomon Stoddard's death, February 11, 1729, brought emphatically to the attention of the New England clergy at large the name and qualifications of the young preacher who now stood in his place. One week afterward, Jonathan Edwards' sermon in honor of his grandfather [7] probably brought to Northampton most of the ministers within easy horseback distance. It would have been an impressive occasion of which neither the congregation nor the visiting clergy could have missed the significance. As for Jonathan Edwards himself, it meant a new challenge to his powers and a new consecration.

Aged twenty-six, he was now in charge of the most important parish in western Massachusetts. His congregation numbered over six hundred. During his two years as colleague pastor he had won the esteem and respect of the people, and to some extent their affection. They liked his quiet eloquence, and they liked his sound doctrine. They also liked him and his beautiful young wife. By all indications he would spend his life on King Street. When late in the same year, 1729, he fell seriously ill and was absent from his pulpit for many weeks, his people showed their concern and friendliness in many ways, building him "a Good Large Barn" during the time he was "Laid aside by his weakness from his work". His father, in reporting this kindness, added that by Benjamin Pierrepont's report

"ye people of Northampton seem to have a great Love and respect for him, and that they take Great Content in his Ministry".[8]

Before the shadows fell he was to have ten more years of harmony and quiet happiness.

His life during these years, before he became greatly involved in ministerial concerns outside his own parish, was a life of intense application to study as well as to parish routine. These were the years in which he borrowed books, bought books, read avidly, made elaborate notebooks, accumulated, arranged, and sorted the stores of knowledge upon which he based his mature writings. During these years also he found the special subjects, biblical and theological, which were to occupy his thought during his later years. Most of this study had very little to do with the sermons he was preaching. In his study he lived a life beyond the confines of the pulpit and the parish. He was free and a citizen of the world.

The direction of his studies, and to some extent their chronology, is apparent from his many extant notebooks. These show him to have been first and last a religionist, singleminded in his allegiance and yet, within the limits of his special interest, surprisingly catholic in his choices. Considered as a lifelong panorama of private study, the hundreds of jottings concerning books to be read, inquired after, subjects to be investigated, together with his ponderous collections of "Instances", his outlines, and thousands of notes, show that in the search for his particular kind of truth his mind went everywhere. There is hardly a page of his now famous *Catalogue* [9] which does not represent some ranging from the beaten track of pulpit interest; but always he ranged as the scholar in religion, never as the layman adventuring among ideas. The weakness of his scholarship is that he usually had a hypothesis to prove, was committed beforehand to the conclusion, and zealously accumulated materials to that end. By so doing he missed much which would sometimes have established his conclusions more firmly, and sometimes have overthrown them.

As a preacher and theologian he read exactly what a man of his time and training might have been expected to read. Records of the bookish interests of other clergymen in his day show dozens of the same titles read during the same years, but few ministers in either England or America could have matched him in the breadth, the thoroughness, or the amazing industry of his application. Books were hard to get in a country parish, but he searched them out tirelessly, writing scores of letters in their pursuit, and importing at considerable expense those he could neither buy nor borrow in America. In the narrow field of his special studies, not even remoteness of Northampton and Stockbridge could make him provincial.

His *Catalogue,* a homemade notebook of forty-three pages, bound in heavy brown paper, is in many ways the most interesting of all his manuscript remains. In this notebook he entered the titles of the books he was reading or wanted to read, adding notes and comments of various sorts. In its beginning it probably dates from the Yale tutorship days, and may have been begun in emulation of Samuel Johnson, the earlier tutor, who kept a notebook for exactly the same purpose. So did other young students. The particular interest of Jonathan Edwards' *Catalogue* is that he continued to make occasional use of it throughout his life, the last dated entry being made a little more than two months before his death. For this reason it supplies illuminating suggestions toward a history of his intellectual life.

The earliest pages have the interest of beginnings only. He was merely bringing together a fairly comprehensive and stereotyped list of standard books a young man of his pretensions should know. The same titles occur on various other student lists. In the later entries, often widely spaced in time, he made more discriminating selection, often with direct reference to his own special studies. There are enough dated items to give valuable hints toward the chronology of these studies, and occasionally to throw light on some disputed point of indebtedness. When, for example, Arthur Collier's *Clavis Universalis,* claimed by one of Jonathan Edwards' critics as the source of his idealistic philosophy in the college essays,[10] is found, not among the entries of the college years at all, but more than thirty-five years later, the supposed proofs of early indebtedness may be seriously questioned.

Quite as important as these more than six hundred titles themselves, with their suggested balance between the factual and the speculative, between books which were tools and books which were not, are the accompanying jottings, the quoted excerpts, the stated sources of his bookish information, the reminders to himself to search further. There is scarcely a page which does not throw some light on Jonathan Edwards the student, pen and paper at his elbow, reading one book that he might learn of another which he might read, and in his correspondence or conversation with other ministers invariably getting around to the subject of books. These jottings were intended for his own use solely; therein lies their value as clues to his thought and the method of it. For example, an entry on the first page predicts his lifelong hospitality to panoramic surveys of large subjects. Under the caption "Books to be enquired for" are the following:

"the best Geography
"the best history of the World
"the best Exposition of the Apocalypse
"the best General Ecclesiastical history from [Christ] to the Present time
"the best Upon the types of the Scripture
"which Are the most usefull & necessary of the Fathers
"the best Chronology
"the best historical Dictionary of the Nature of Boyle's Dictionary
"the best that speaks of the Ecclesiastical learning of the Jews
"the best History of Lives of Philosophers".

Almost any other page would tell as much, beyond the interest of the titles themselves. Again and again there is the alert response to a new body of truth, and usually it is a timely response. Contemporaneously with the Boston lectures of Ebenezer Kinnersley in 1751-52, concerning his experiments with the Leyden jar, this item appears in the *Catalogue.*

"To Enquire after some Philosophical Treatise of the Nature of Electricity the best that is extant."

Various entries concerning books on astronomy likewise follow a current emphasis. His mind reached out eagerly in many new directions, and yet his interests were not scattered. He kept consistently to what was grist for the mill of a religionist with a philosophical bent. Within that area he took a wide course and travelled far, but he never lost sight of his own goal. When he chose a book on science, it was not one which concerned the minutiae of nature, but rather the plan of the universe. Astronomy might help to answer his own questions as to the meaning of existence. Other outlying fields similarly were investigated for their contributions to his own field, not for themselves.

Quite naturally, during the earlier years of his ministry his studies ranged more widely than was possible after he began to write panoramic surveys of his own; but even in these early years his major interests were already established. This dog-eared *Catalogue* and the other homemade notebooks tell the story. When he filled them with his thousand jottings he did more than make notations for future reference. He also wrote the history of his own developing mind.

Twice a year he went to the meetings of the Hampshire Association to discuss parish problems with his brother ministers of the county. He was present at the organization meeting in 1731, and thereafter seldom missed a session. His recorded share in these biennial deliberations was relatively large; large enough certainly to contradict the notion that he was either unfitted for participation in a group enterprise or averse to such. Perhaps his largest service to the group was in connection with the Association Library, for which he prepared the original list of titles and thereafter acted as librarian for his part of the county. The volumes assigned to him and housed at the parsonage made a welcome extension to his own private shelves.

Records of these Association meetings from year to year [11] throw light on ministerial thought and practice in various ways, most of them disappointing. What stimulus to the mind of a young philosopher, for example, in such topics assigned for discussion as:

"Whether it be Lawfull to eat Blood?"

"What is the sin against the Holy Ghost?"

"In what Ways may Satan Transform himself Into an Angel of Light?"

"In what Sence Are We to Understand That Expression in ye Apostles Creed. He Descended into Hell?"

"What is the True Notion of a Lie?'"

"Whether it is absolutely forbidden to a Christian to marry with a Heathen?"

"Is the Institution of Deacons of Divine Origin?"

To discuss such questions young men of the cloth rode a hundred miles or more on horseback; and they presumably went home edified, Jonathan Edwards among them.

Record of Association action in cases of discipline also illuminates his own parish story, particularly through the oft repeated suggestions that pulpit authority was slipping. At the organization meeting in October, 1731, a subject for discussion had been:

"What is the Duty of Ministers, when any under their Jurisdiction and Government refuse to come to them when sent for upon account of misbehaviour?"

This question was destined to become progressively more

urgent throughout the next decade. Meanwhile, the Hampshire County ministry continued to deal out penalties according to the earlier interpretation of their prerogatives, as follows:

Should a woman who stole a silver snuffbox five or six years ago, and had sought to bring suspicion on another, now

"for the glory of God, and the peace of her Conscience, . . . make a public Confession of those her Crimes?" [Voted in the affirmative.]

"Should a woman who refused to name the father of her child be accepted by the church and allowed to present her child for baptism, supposing her Repentance in other Regards be visibly Sincere." [Voted in the affirmative after action had been delayed for six months.]

It is somewhat difficult, even for the historically minded, to visualize this assembly of ministers and other similar bodies, giving solemn audience to the dissatisfied members of their various communions who presented their grievances against one another for final arbitration. Particularly in these numerous cases of "defamation", it is surprising that a latent sense of humor did not sometimes cancel both the charge and the hearing, or, if the charge were sustained, that the public forgiveness to which both pastor and congregation must be witness could be carried through with fitting decorum. How did Deacon Stearns of Stoughton, for example, negotiate with appropriate soberness his public plea for forgiveness from his neighbor and fellow worshipper John Upham, whom he had previously called "an old one-eyed hypocrite and a lying old sinner"? [12] Or how did the congregation in decency suppress their pleasure in this Sunday morning drama? The frequency of such cases on the records probably provides the answer.

Through their action in these cases of discipline, often trivial in the circumstances and often not, the Hampshire Association and other ministerial groups, which had met in the beginning for informal counsels only, gradually took on the character of minor ecclesiastical courts and thus established troublesome precedents looking toward the superior authority of church councils as opposed to the power of individual congregations—the point around which so many battles of the mid-century were to be waged. During the years before Jonathan Edwards himself was to suffer at the hands of such a church council, he and his brother ministers of the Hampshire Association were helping to bring about just such an assumption of group authority which, more often than not, was opposed to congregational desire.

Action of this body also helps to clarify many other ministerial attitudes and practices. For example, Jonathan Edwards' alleged neglect of pastoral visiting, usually charged to his own zeal for private study, may easily bear a relation to Association action taken at the initial meeting, October, 1731. On this occasion the ministers present went on record as believing that the catechizing of children, one of the principal reasons for pastoral visiting, belonged in the home and should be kept there. An occasional visit from the minister might serve as a reminder, but the parents were responsible. This was exactly in line with Jonathan Edwards' lifelong practice. He was frequently in the homes of his people, but he went in response to special needs, not as a routine exercise. When he assumed the rôle of examiner, as he repeatedly did, to test the thoroughness of parental tutelage, he did so not by a house-to-house canvass, but in children's meetings; and thus conducted the business with greater dispatch as well as greater dignity.

Other ministers thought differently. Thomas Clap of Windham, a young man of exactly the same age and training, interpreted his pastoral obligation to mean not only visiting his seven hundred and twenty-two members, catechizing the children, but taking down the names, ages, and personal qualities of each in systematic array. He hoped that by making this individual case record for each soul under this charge he might "bear the names and circumstances of each on his breast at all times",[13] and especially when he approached the throne of grace. Jonathan Edwards reserved his skill in analysis, his penchant for categorical minutiae for other matters.

Record of his catechizing of the Northampton children survives among his papers in the form of lists of questions propounded in children's meetings designed for the purpose. In one notebook there is a list of one hundred and thirty-nine numbered questions to each of which a boy's name is attached. Answers are fortunately appended; else as an adult information quiz inflicted on a modern ministerial convention, these questions might cause distinct embarrassment. Not so to Northampton twelve-year-olds of the 1730's. A few samples taken at random may serve to illuminate the sacred pedagogy of the hour.

1. "Which of the Kings of Israel & Judah was it that Reigned longest?" (John Baker)

6. "How many Altars were in use in the Tabernacle?" (Eleazar Burt)

11. "Which of the three sons of Noah did the Egyptians come from?" (Timothy Wright)

14. "How many cities of Refuge were there in Israel?" (Noah Baker)

15. "How many Kings Reigned in Judah after the Captivity of the ten tribes?" (Amos Negro)

18. "What King was it that first Built the city of Samaria?" (Elisha Pomeroy)

— "How many years before Jacob was born did Shem die?" (Unassigned)[14]

An explanatory note states that each question was to be used several times, once for the literal answer, once for what the event typified, once for the commandment that was broken in the event, and last, as the basis for an exercise in reasoning. This was not instruction for which Jonathan Edwards received pay. It was part of his pastoral duty, as he conceived it. The care with which the questions are framed, the theory of instruction they represent, and the kind of training toward which they are directed, suggest in a single instance the integrity with which Jonathan Edwards performed his pastoral round. The value of such knowledge to the small Wrights, Pomeroys, Bakers and Burts, to say nothing of Amos, Negro, may be opaque enough to modern parent-teachers, but it was clear as sunlight to Jonathan Edwards. Unfortunately, he did not, after the modern pedagogical manner, plot the curve of juvenile delinquency respecting these questions; but that he took his catechizing duties seriously, in spite of his attitude toward pastoral calls, there can be no doubt.

In another manuscript notebook there is a list of fifty-three questions intended for young converts, likewise testifying to painstaking care, to the end that the young convert might know the doctrine, remote as it seems from vital religious experience in any age or idiom. It was also remote for Jonathan Edwards. Religion for him had nothing to do with the lifeless answers to such lifeless questions as

"How far the verity of the Godhead may be argued from the manner of the Creation?"

or

"What will be the Order of Events & proceedings of the Day of Judgment?"[15]

Such bloodless erudition was merely part of the orthodox young convert's orthodox bulwark against error. Therefore a place must be made for it in the pastoral calendar.

Other parish labors take on the concreteness of individual ministration through chance memoranda belonging to the Sunday morning service. Scattered through the sermon booklets are occasional leaves showing requests for prayers, thanksgivings for deliverance, personal appeals in a variety of distresses, bringing with them certain overtones of parish life. Almost a complete roll of the membership could be compiled from the names which appear on these sheets, for requests of Stoddards and Strongs and Pomeroys appeared along with those of more humble parishioners.

"Hannah Strong Being Sick: She with Her Parents: Desieres the prayers of this Congregation for her that God wood fit Her for his Soueren will & Pleasure."

"Ebenezr Clark Junr and his wife Desire ye prayers of ye Congregation that God would Sanctefi to them the Death of their new born Child: they Desire that this with former bereavements may work for their everlasting good."

"Ebenezer Miller and his children desire the prayers of Gods peopel for his wife and their mother that is bereved of her understanding that god would restore her understanding to her a gain if it be his will if other wayes fit them for his holy will."

"Elkanah Burt Desireth that gods name might Be praised in this Congregation for his Grate goodness to him in his Jurnuing into a foran Land. that his Life was preserued from the Dangers of the Deeps and from the Sword, of the Enemy from Death when infected with that mortal Distemper; that he is Returned home in Safety. his Parents desire the Same."

Often more eloquent than the request itself are the scrawled signatures of all members of the family which gave it scriptural validity. The awkward phrasing, bad spelling, and cramped handwriting in most of these petitions from the pew force the suggestion that the rank and file of Jonathan Edwards' congregation asked little of his great powers. Yet he preached to them one and all as though they were his peers.

Time was to him the most precious of commodities, yet in the line of pastoral duty there were no marks or limits to his generosity. He could spend half of his morning composing a methodical fourteen-page answer to Deborah Hatheway of

Suffield, who had requested "Mr. Edwards" to tell her *Some Directions how to Conduct [Her] Self in her Christian Course*.[16] He had time to prove to a boy of thirteen that a piece of matter two inches square is eight times as large as a piece one-inch square. The demonstration was made with pieces of wood cut by Jonathan Edwards, first into one- and two-inch cubes, and then into smaller and smaller pieces to be handled and measured by the incredulous child.[17] The picture is pleasant and thoroughly characteristic. More than one child of the parish might have recalled a similar proof of pastoral patience in the unfolding of truth.

Such a detail also affords partial answer to the question men have so frequently asked: did Jonathan Edwards ever unbend from his rigidities? Certainly, although the proofs are implied in the general picture, instead of stated directly. One must read the story between the lines; for example, in the hour spent with his family each evening, before the children went to bed and he returned to the study. This was not an hour of devotion but of conversation, in which the whole group took part. One may read this story also in family letters; for example, in his letter to Sarah Edwards, his wife, reporting his care of one of the children taken seriously ill in her absence. It is perhaps most charmingly suggested in the children's accounts kept in his hand in the *Interleaved Bible:* extra pennies for little Jerusha for her diligence in reading; pistareens borrowed from Timothy and paid back again; silver spoons thought of and purchased for the daughters before they were old enough to use them properly. It is in the letters of the daughters after they had grown up and had homes of their own, and in the spirited nonsense of Esther and Lucy and Susannah. Any household which could claim such a trio would have been a household in which there was laughter, much laughter. Perhaps Jonathan Edwards did not join in it, but at least he would not have frowned it down (except on Sunday). It is not likely, however, that a complete transcript of his daily life in its relations with those who knew him best would change the traditional picture very greatly. He was a man consecrated to a religious life before he was husband, father, neighbor, or townsman; and he made few compromises. An entry in his *Personal Narrative* to the effect that if he were in "a good frame for divine contemplation" when dinner was announced, he would forego dinner rather than interrupt himself, suggests a jog in the household schedule such as Sarah Edwards might have expected at almost any time. But, being also consecrated, she probably did not mind.

In the more intimate story of Northampton's weekday life there is record of many friendly favors exchanged between pastor and people. Anyone going to Boston would carry letters or bring parcels for "Mr. Edwards", and he would do likewise for his parishioners and neighbors. The town had been riven by "parties" ever since it was founded; active hostility might break out in either camp at any time, and yet remoteness had emphasized mutual dependence. In the many emergencies of village life, all responded to the need of one, regardless of petty alignments. Perhaps the most picturesque example on the record concerns the burning of Ebenezer Hunt's hat shop in 1733. Immediately other shops were closed while his fellow townsmen lent a hand to set him up in business again. His own account of this nine-day triumph is an unintentional masterpiece, a kind of folk tale of early American enterprise. It appears in his *Journal*, under date of January 19, 1733/4, as follows:

"God was pleased to incline the hearts of my Christian friends & neighbors to help me in that difficult hour. They freely contributed many ways to restore me into business. In nine days time I got to work at my trade in my new shop. the fire happened on a Saturday morning; some timber was got that day for another shop, & the remainder on Monday, and all hewed & some framing done; Wednesday it was raised; Thursday it was shingled, boarded, & my bowroom filled in with brick; Saturday I did something at my trade, & on Monday I was settled to business".[18]

Village life was as friendly, architecture and early American business as simple as that.

As to the personal life Jonathan Edwards lived outside of his pulpit and study, little is known. Tradition denies to him, and probably rightly, any considerable share in the labors connected with his small Northampton acreage. Later generations have not liked the picture of Jonathan Edwards raking hay, picking up stones in the meadow, fanning peas, setting out two hundred cabbage plants in a morning, or going to mill with a hand sled, as other country ministers and intellectuals, including the president of Harvard College, shamelessly admitted in their diaries.[19] The frailty of his health throughout his life and his preoccupation with study made his relation to all such tasks largely supervisory, but he would not have considered them inappropriate to his calling, and with a farm boyhood behind him would have possessed a deftness of hand for any one of them. Samuel Hopkins remembered that he liked to chop wood, and did so daily for exercise; he also set out various trees, and once measured Mt. Tom, finding it sixty-three rods high.[20] He probably also spread ashes in the orchard, put the ink powder to soak, and did many other such chores. He owned sheep and at shearing time was probably out watching the process along with those of his neighbors who had reason to be interested in the price of wool. If a serpent had reared its head at one of the meetings of the Hampshire Association, as had happened in Cambridge during the Synod of 1648,[21] he and every other country minister present would have been equal to the situation, and the slaughter would have made very little interruption in the progress of debate on the question before the meeting. One may be fairly sure, however, that he never pulled a tooth or bled a patient on his pastoral visitations, as ministers in more remote parishes were still expected to do in his generation. Northampton had had the services of Dr. Mather since 1736, and as pastor, Jonathan Edwards kept strictly to spiritual ministrations.

Within the village, he had intellectual companionship with only a few men, notably John Stoddard, Colonel Timothy Dwight, and Major Ebenezer Pomeroy. Otherwise, he found it with ministers and dignitaries who passed by on horseback, *en route* for Hartford or Boston. No week passed without guests. They came in all seasons and at all hours, although to judge from ministerial diaries, they seemed to come chiefly at midnight. Hospitality was simple, but there was a good deal of it, and the parsonage often resembled a wayside inn: a dozen or eighteen for dinner after meeting, the family awakened at all hours, horses to be cared for as well as men, guests sometimes remaining for weeks or taken with sudden illness and obliged to stay until they recovered. "So much Company fatigues me at one time", wrote James MacSparran, a brother minister, who protested thus secretly in his diary. (He should not have minded, however, having been the fortunate host of George Berkeley.)

Jonathan Edwards kept no diary which memorialized his favors in this sort, but some of his guests did, to the praise of his gracious hospitality.

"Very curteously treated here. The most agreeable Family I was ever acquainted with. Much of the Presence of God here", wrote Joseph Emerson. Others gave like testimony.

When his guests left, it was Jonathan Edwards' custom to "ride out" with them for a few miles, by way of extending the hospitality. This custom is often remarked by those who had spent a night under his roof.

"Mr. Edwards was so kind as to accompany us over Connecticutt River and bring us on our way",[22] wrote Joseph Emerson, continuing the story.

Only a very well ordered household or a very careless one could have stood the strain of these continual unexpected demands. Fortunately Sarah Edwards had known beforehand what a parsonage was like. She willingly put herself within the frame, accepted the " how much more" argument applied to everything ministerial, managed her household with scriptural efficiency, cared for her little children, and unfailingly gave that better measure of hospitality than would have been expected of her as the wife of a colony magistrate. As reward she was written down in the travelogues of her guests, not for her hospitality alone, but for the beauty of spirit which distinguished the Edwards home, even to a transient guest.

Of the amenities of American social life outside of the parsonage pattern, neither she nor her husband had any great knowledge or experience. Even the decorous gaieties of Boston in the mid-century would have seemed wasteful to them both, where they were not darkly wicked. Rural America and urban America, even for those inclined to piety, lived in different worlds. In Boston the constables still went forth on the Sabbath day compelling church attendance, and on all days fining those they might catch swearing (one crown per oath) or otherwise breaking the law; but well-bred men were not conscious of these restrictions. Benjamin Lynde of Salem, one of the Representatives to the General Court, and an exact contemporary of Jonathan Edwards, lived what might be regarded as the normal social life of a young man of affairs who was also a prominent church member. His forenoons were spent with the law, his afternoons and evenings in playing keels, drinking spango, attending "great frolicks" or in dancing, usually at private homes. On the day he took his second degree at Harvard College, he celebrated by a "merry evening" which progressed from point to point until daylight. On other festive occasions he attended "great suppers", hog barbecues, huskings, puppet shows (at private houses), and in the company of other young people, spent evening after evening in what he set down as "merriment".[23]

Benjamin Lynde was a devout man, but he gave religion and the church only a share of his thought. By virtue of something in his temperament and something more in his training, he had learned that life was pleasant, the mere living, and within the framework of that concept he had grown up to observe the Sabbath, read his Bible, and save his soul.

Jonathan and Sarah Edwards thought otherwise. Their concept of life left no place for any pleasure to which prayer would not have been a fitting prologue. Approved music consisted of hymns alone; dancing was contrived by Satan himself; feasting was indulgence of the body without profit to the soul. Life was too short and time too precious for the Christian to give thought to anything which did not in some way look ahead to the eternities beyond. Jonathan Edwards traveled considerably, but his journeys did not bring him exposure to a less straitened way of life. On visits to Boston or New Haven he looked out from the sanctity of another parsonage, his thought fixed on the sermon he would preach to a strange congregation on the morrow. If only occasionally he might have sat down with men who were not ministers, a feast before him such as Boston hosts delighted to spread before their guests, and politics or any other undoctrinal subject for a conversational theme, his own conviction that the end of this our life is God, might possibly have seemed more authoritative.

But it would have been useless to invite him. Not only would he have been an anachronism at a "turtle feast", a Boston concert or a week end at some country seat, but he would not have accepted the invitation. His six-day week was lived on the level of the seventh day, and only ministerial functions were in the line of duty. A study of his whole life confirms one in the view that geography and training had little to do with his view of life. Had he not grown up in East Windsor or been educated at Yale College, or accepted a call to Northampton, it might have made little difference. To find God, as he would have put it, was of all deep needs of his nature the most insistent, and he would have gone straight to that goal, no matter in what path his feet had been set. He had pleasures, satisfactions, and deep human joys, but even these had chiefly to do with one area of life; namely, religion. Single-mindedness is costly in any age or society, and it was costly in provincial Northampton. As Jonathan Edwards walked the streets of the village, he earned the respect of his people and to some extent their love. His interpretation of the pastoral obligation was in line with their wish in so far as this meant sympathy, gentleness, and unsparing service. But in a very real sense he walked among them as the most solitary of men. The time would come when they would forget the kindness and remember only that he had never really been one of themselves. But no Northampton prophet would have dared such a prediction in the good years of the 1730's.

Chapter 7

The Doctrine Laid Down

THROUGHOUT these same good years of his ministry, the making of sermons was to Jonathan Edwards one of the chief ends of his reading, his study, his thought. What shall I preach, he asked of himself a thousand times and then wrote down the answer in many notebooks. Also, in his relation to his flock he was more preacher than pastor, for all the week-day disciplining and catechizing. It was on Sunday morning at the ringing of the meetinghouse bell that Northampton had its best chance to know "Mr. Edwards", as he mounted his high pulpit and in a quiet voice, without movement or gesture, laid down his doctrine. His tall, spare figure and his deliberate manner gave him a commanding presence. The piercing eyes went everywhere; the thin tones reached the dim corner of the gallery. Every word was distinctly spoken. One does not fidget under such preaching. The young people, a little surprised at themselves at first, felt his authority and mended their ways. "Indecent carriage at meeting" became a thing of the past. This delicate-looking young man had something to say, and strangely enough his fragility seemed to increase his power.

As a speaker, his chief asset was the quality of his voice—a little languid, with a note of pathos, Samuel Hopkins said; too low for a large assembly, but very distinct and strangely arresting. He particularly commended the well-placed pauses and great distinctness in pronunciation.[1] Thomas Prince spoke of his naturalness of delivery, his low, moderate voice, his freedom from mannerisms, his "habitual and great solemnity, looking and speaking as in the presence of God".[2] Like Emerson, Jonathan Edwards gave the impression of speaking from the immediate inspiration of the moment, in spite of the manuscript before him.

As a preacher in the open fields, he would not have been a success. Whitefield could thunder God's judgments across the meadow, hurling his body about with great agility and by the magic of his oratory causing hundreds to go down before him. The quiet intensity of Jonathan Edwards required walls. Such power as his is rare, and difficult of analysis. John

129

Hooker, a brother minister, called him the most eloquent man he ever knew, defining "eloquence" as the power of "making strong impressions of the subject of a discourse on the minds of an audience".[3] Others made essentially the same comment. People went away from Whitefield's preaching talking about "the great Mr. Whitefield". They went away from the Enfield sermon crying, "What must I do to be saved?" Not even the sermon as a sermon, but only the truth it proclaimed, was the final impression. The Enfield sermon is not a piece of oratory in the usual sense. It is a notable example of almost elementary logic, and the exposition of a very simple idea by means of everyday imagery. It would have gained nothing by such volume as would have awakened echoes. Spoken quietly, and in a manner to suggest that the speaker was a mouthpiece, not one who relied on his own authority, such words had an irresistible finality.

Until George Whitefield began the fashion of extemporaneous speaking, Jonathan Edwards had his complete sermon manuscript before him in the pulpit. Each sermon was carefully written out in a tiny booklet stitched together by hand. The size, $3\frac{7}{8}$ by $4\frac{1}{8}$ inches, corresponded exactly to the sermon booklets made by other ministers, trained similarly to cut their foolscap to the purpose. Jonathan Edwards, who had been brought up in the thrifty East Windsor parsonage, also made use of scraps of paper of all sorts: letter folds, first drafts of letters sent, blank sides of letters received, Yale theses, governors' proclamations, broadsides, bills from Mr. Potwine's general store in Hartford, requests for prayers, marriage banns, children's copybook exercises, ends of Mrs. Edwards' fan papers—whatever came to hand. To assume that poverty was back of this practice is absurd. Writing paper, like other luxuries, had to be carried on horseback from Boston, and weeks might pass before a depleted supply could be replenished. Besides, wastefulness of any sort was not countenanced in the King Street home. Jonathan Edwards saved scraps of paper just as he saved scraps of time. Both could be made to serve a useful purpose. Biographers are glad enough he saved the paper, for these vagrant scraps bring the Edwards home to life in many ways, some of them all but priceless. An order for the latest style in clergymen's buttons, three pounds paid for a hat, eleven pounds for a gold locket and chain, sixteen shillings for "a Pare of gold wiers", bills for spelling books, cables of thread, thimbles, three yards of lute string, a silk handkerchief, a ribbon for Sarah, a broom, a mousetrap, a primer, "one child's plaything", one dozen long pipes, grocery lists showing infinite chocolate for the Edwards consumption, the fragment of a letter expressing parental concern over measles, Dr. Mather's bill for two bloodlettings, a reminder to bring Lucy's shoes—such are the trivia which enable one to sketch in the background for the personal story. The turning of any sermon page is likely to bring to light some intimate detail of family life, not elsewhere recorded.

Tradition says that Jonathan Edwards placed the tiny sermon booklet in the open pulpit Bible, keeping his finger on his place. The writing is so fine and the sermon page so crowded that he must have followed his own script with some difficulty, particularly on a dark day, for the Northampton church was unlighted except by the sun. In using notes at all, he was inviting criticism; for ever since John Warham had dared "carry a quiver full of them" into the pulpit, sermon notes had been an issue. Solomon Stoddard had always preached from memory, and had felt so strongly that this was the only way to preach that he had once inveighed in print against "The Defects of Ministers" [4] who did otherwise. Timothy Edwards, father of Jonathan, prided himself on a memory equal to a two-hour discourse, unaided by a scrap, and was not humiliated by "thumb papers" until well after his seventieth birthday. His son, in the very presence of Solomon Stoddard, read his entire sermon, although his dependence upon the manuscript was probably not such as to render impossible that "Holy Inspection of the Congregation", which Solomon Stoddard thought the *sine qua non* of acceptable preaching. After Whitefield came, Jonathan Edwards, like most other American preachers who had been in sympathy with the new evangelism, spoke extemporaneously, aided only by a brief outline. He continued this practice until the end of his life.

The familiar pulpit legend concerning his extraordinary powers has reference chiefly to his revival preaching, which caused men to cry out in terror as he compelled them to face their eternal doom. The legend, however, is far from the truth except in a few applications. Characteristically, he was not an evangelistic preacher at all, in the usual understanding of the term. It is true that the great and terrible wrath of God and the urgency of personal salvation were his lifelong convictions, and that in times of revival he preached repeatedly on these themes. They were short cuts to the repentant prostration of the multitudes, and he took them as evangelists have always done; but by the month and year, his sermons had more reference to the practical virtues of everyday piety than to anything spectacular either in theme or in treatment. When he was most himself, he was a quiet-spoken teacher, and a kindly though unsparing critic of men's conduct in the light of their religious obligations. Salvation was a recompense in itself as well as an escape from future torment. "It would be worth the while to be Religious if only for the Pleasantness of it", is quite as typical a sermon theme as that of the familiar *Eternity of Hell Torments,* upon which his preaching reputation so securely rests. Even in revival times he did not always preach damnation.

"There is a sweet Harmony between [Christ] & the Soul of a true [Chris]tian",

and

"there never was any man that once came to und[er]stand what manner of man [Christ] was but his Heart was infallibly drawn to him",

are sermon themes from the midst of a revival season.

He owed his reputation as a hell and brimstone preacher to two pieces of printed matter which appeared at extraordinarily propitious times for making a reputation. One of them was his letter to Benjamin Colman, detailing the 1735 revival in his own parish; and the other was the Enfield sermon, preached at the height of the Great Awakening excitement and printed immediately. No preacher ever spoke at a more favorable moment for an immortal broadcast than on this latter occasion. It was a case *par excellence,* of the man, the idea, and the moment. Men would have believed anything in the nature of revival hysteria, and they preferred exaggeration to the truth. When they heard that there were those in the congregation who had fled in terror from the vision of judgment painted by this spokesman, it was enough. In the popular mind, Jonathan Edwards became another Whitefield.

The later chapters are even easier to understand. The tradition was too picturesque to be allowed to die; besides, the sermon was in print. Today not ten in many thousands have read it, but all know the story. Both town and preacher are inseparably connected with the picture of terrorized sinners dangled over the pit by a thread. Jonathan Edwards, the fiery Puritan, has passed into American legend. As a matter of fact, he was neither Puritan nor fiery, but any attempt to contradict the legend in the lay mind is as futile as it is unimportant. For anyone who cares to know the truth, this contradiction is written in very fine handwriting, often difficult to read, on the small pages of some five hundred extant sermon booklets which occupied the crack of the Northampton Bible on successive Sunday mornings.

These extant sermons cover the whole period of his ministry down to within one month of his death. All except those preached before 1733 are dated; if a sermon was preached more than once, subsequent dates and places are added; if a page was omitted, or if only half the sermon was preached, the fact is noted. There are enough extant sermons, marked "Preached at Northampton", to take care of more than half the Sundays in his twenty-three-year pastorate, making the whole panorama of his sermon thought, together with the manner of it, an open record. It appears from these memorials that he reached his preaching maturity early, and that except for changes of emphasis and timely response to events, his preaching changed little during the whole of his pastorate, or, in fact, during his entire life.

As a young preacher he chose more texts from *Revelation, Psalms, Proverbs, Solomon's Song* than in later years, and he also developed his thought more poetically. He liked to dwell on the "Infinitely glorious Perfection of God", the rapture of the saints in heaven, and the mysteries of deep religious ecstasy. These early sermons suggest many correspondences to his own personal experiences, his sweet sense of the divine presence, and his own absorption in religious contemplation. He made much of the beauty of nature as an earnest of celestial glory: as in the following eloquent peroration:

"The beauty of trees, Plants, and flowers with which God has bespangled the face of the Earth is Delightsome, the beautiful frame of the body of Man, especially in its Perfection is Astonishing, the beauty of the moon and the stars, is wonderfull, the beauty of highest heavens, is transcendent, the Excellency of angels and the saints in light, is very Glorious, but it is all Deformity, and Darkness in Comparison of the higher Glories and beauties of the Creator of all . . ." [5]

These are distinctly youthful sermons, written out with the care and precision of college exercises, even to careful punctuation. There are no shorthand abbreviations, no half-written words, no first-draft corrections. He even followed the current rule for printed matter, inserting the first word of the new page in the lower corner of his manuscript. As he grew older, there was less of the mystic's rapture, more interest in doctrine, a more realistic view of human nature, and more emphasis on the practical virtues of Christian living. The manuscript page became less neat; the handwriting more hurried. The booklet became a record of his own thought for his own use, not a specimen exercise. Thought was more important than punctuation.

Naturally, he accepted the preaching formula of his day. This was in accordance with his father's example, his Yale training, and the practice of "learned divines" for more than a hundred years. There was only one way to build a sermon, and thus was it built: first, the Text and the Doctrine to be deduced from it; then the Exposition of the Scripture context, followed by the Defence of the Doctrine; last, its Application or Uses of Instruction, Self-examination, Consolation, Reproof, Warning, or some other purpose appropriate to the sermon emphasis. Unvaryingly he kept to this pattern throughout his life. Individuality came by way of the sermon development, never by any change in the essential design. It remained for another, unfamiliar with the expectation of the American pew, to speak according to a new pattern and in a new idiom. One of New England's own sons, trained at Harvard or Yale, could not have done it, even though he had dared to try. America would not have accepted a home-grown innovation. But after George Whitefield had broken the familiar pattern, anyone could break it; and everyone must, if he would survive.

In following the model set before him, Jonathan Edwards early developed a characteristic pattern of his own. After he had stood before them for a year, his Northampton people knew what to expect. The Text would not be obvious. This young man had a genius for finding Scripture to his purpose, and finding it in unexplored scriptural corners. Characteristically also, he phrased the Doctrine to correspond as closely as possible to the Text.

"I will not change the words of the text for a Doctrine", he once wrote, and when he did change them he added little.

Text: Jam. 1:13, For God cannot be tempted with evil.

Doctrine: Tis Impossible that G[od] should be under any Temptation to do anything that is Evil.

Text: II Cor. 4:18,—but the things which are not seen are eternal.

Doctrine: The Things of the unseen [World] are Eternal things.

Text: Psa. 78:25, Man did eat angels' food.

Doctrine:—those that partake of Christ eat angels food.

Habitually, he gave large space to the Exposition of the Scripture context, repeating the familiar story as though it were being told for the first time. He had skill in narrative, and his simple handling of biblical events is often, as a piece of writing, the best part of his sermon. His clarification of the Doctrine was usually by the method of particularization. To him a sermon idea was not the end of a golden string, to be followed wheresoe'er it led, but an area of space to be cut up into smaller areas, until the whole had been divided and subdivided, and each part numbered and labelled, the categories usually becoming more concrete as he proceeded. His orderly mind found pleasure in these lists of propositions, reasons, examples, carefully arranged in a climactic scheme. It is the easiest of all methods of thought development, and puts little strain on a great mind. Almost any one of his sermons provides illustration. When preaching on the text "Remember Lot's wife" he proceeded as follows:

Doctrine: We ought not to Look Back when we are Flying out of Sodom & that for the following Reasons.
1. Because Sodom is a City full of Filthiness & abominations.
2. Because Sodom is a City appointed to Destruction.
3. Because it is exceeding Dreadful D[estruction].
4. —Swift and Sudden Destruction.
5. There is nothing in Sodom worth Looking back upon because all the Enjoym.[ent] of Sodom will soon Perish in the Common Destruction and will all be burnt up. Tis not worth the trouble to Look back on things that are Perishing.

The sermon was remarked as memorable. Reading it on the manuscript page, one wonders why. The sermon on Christ weeping over Jerusalem, repreached six times and marked "Very good" in his own handwriting, presents a series of reasons why Jesus wept. In other sermons, eternal life is a life of humility, of love, of obedience. The temptations of the world are of three kinds: by circumstances, by worldly objects, by business. He clarifies the spirit of prayer by enumerating the objects to be prayed for; taking Christ's yoke upon us, by a series of biblical illustrations, beginning with Abraham and proceeding through Moses, David, Daniel, down to the Apostle John. What the spirit of prayer, or the taking of Christ's yoke upon him, might mean to the individual Christian, he makes no effort to explain. The text, "Pour out the Holy Spirit", was not translated into life, but developed by the easier path suggested by the headings, "On us, on others, here, in other towns, on the whole land, on the nation, on the world of Mankind". Again and again he directed his appeal to special groups, such as "To natural men, To the godly, Particularly to Heads of Families, To young people, To Children, To all that belong in this little village". These categorical counsels made the sermon organization.

In a series of sermons on the parable of the ten virgins he was content to define wherein the true and the false agree and wherein they disagree; what is symbolized by the oil and by other details—all oblique to the main teaching, as it would seem. His Application consisted of further enumerations, no nearer to life on a weekday level.[6]

Always there was symmetry, orderliness, design. Such sermons lent themselves admirably to the catechizing of the children who heard, for the outline was always clear, the points carefully numbered. Relentlessly he held to the course of these numbered steps, erecting a signpost at every turning and keeping the whence and the whither of his argument clearly before his hearers. The wayfaring man who listened may not have understood the Doctrine or the Application, but he would have been a dull clod indeed if he could not at any moment have told the exact point in the two-hour journey at which pulpit and pew had jointly arrived.

These persistent categorizings, for all their appearance of logic, often leave the questing modern very much in the dark as to the essential inwardness of the doctrine the preacher labored so symmetrically to clarify. What after all was Jonathan Edwards' notion of prayer, as prayer, apart from the objects prayed for, the times and seasons when prayer should be offered? Exactly what did he mean by "eternal life" here and now, or by such a dark phrase as "the cure of our spiritual wound"? His own thought was far too precise for the content of his terms to be foggy in his own mind; why so little effort to translate them into life? Instead, he merely divided them into pieces, met objections, gave reasons. One would think his own intense perception of spiritual truth would sometimes have broken through the stiff sermon formula. Perhaps it did, in his extemporaneous remarks; but if so the sermon booklets give no sign.

His peculiar power as a preacher lay in his ability to paint pictures. He had to an unusual degree the faculty of objectifying his concepts, but his imagination needed something tangible with which to start. This the biblical poet had already supplied. Jonathan Edwards took the biblical figure and pursued it relentlessly, until heaven, hell, God's wrath, eternal glory, as he preached them, lost their vague outlines and became visible, imminent realities. Beginning with the known, he enlarged and intensified familiar details until the boundaries between known and unknown were obliterated and his hearers transported. Analyzed, the method is simple enough; it can almost be reduced to the *how much more* formula. If a real thunderstorm in this town can be as terrifying as last night's storm was, think what it will be when God lets loose his thunders over the whole earth at one and the same minute. With memories fresh in their minds as to how it was when

"thunder fell in Smith's pasture",

superlatives needed no firmer foundation. If God can shake New England as he did in 1727, think what it will be when he shakes the whole earth. If the preacher had stopped there, his idea might not have gripped anyone; but he went on to particularize, until the accumulated horror was all but unbearable:

"What a mighty strength would it Require only to move one mountain how Great a strength then must that be that will shake the whole Globe to which the greatest Mountains are Less than molehills. Less than Clods of Dirt. If we Could stand at a Distance and see the Earth shaking and shivering under the hand of God not only Towns and Cities shaken down but Mountains overturned, and the Islands of the Sea shaken out of their Places and shattered to Pieces what a great Idea would it give of the Power of God. . . . If a small Earthquake is so terrible and it puts you into a Consternation to feel a trembling of the Earth for about a minute, how will it amaze you if you are in a sinfull state when the whole Globe shall be as it were Rocked to pieces and you shall hear the foundations of the Earth Crack and shall see the mountains Overturned and the whole heaven at the same time filled with flashes of lightening and the air tortured with perpetual and Innumerable Claps of Thunder far more Awfull than the most horrible that we hear in thunder storms, and all this at the visible Presence of the Almighty and an angry God".[7]

Such specifications of God's power might have fallen on unterrified ears before 1727, but hardly afterward, earthquake terror being in a class by itself among human fears. To those who in the current language of the newspapers, had "heard a large earthquake", the preacher's words recalled the unforgettable sensation, putting their very souls in a palsy.

Fire as a symbol of God's wrath, he treated in exactly the same fashion. Beginning by thrusting the little fingers of his congregation into the flame, then their hands, their arms, their whole bodies, he presently pushed them headlong into a quivering lake of fire. Even then he did not stop, but forced them to imagine the excruciating pain of fire

> "Running into our Mouths & filling our Lungs,—
> Running into our Ears and Nostrils",[8]

to be endured world without end, while tortured sensibilities remained undeadened to the agony.

His own conscious aim in all this was to make scriptural preachment a reality.

> "The Reason why men No more Regard warnings of Future punishment is because it Don't seem real to them",

he wrote as Doctrine for one of his sermons. He proceeded to make it real by the method most natural to him, particularization of the horror in tangible, visible form. The coming of God in the clouds, the saints in white singing around the throne, the dead coming forth from their graves, were to him literal sights. He would have missed entirely the grim irony and bold unbelief of Stanley Spencer's concept of the Last Judgment (at the Tate Gallery) [9] which has to some extent offended the orthodoxy of modern times. He would have seen only the gravestones tilted back, and the sleepers emerging, but this would have been only the prelude to the real drama. His imagination would have been dilated far more by the vision of the Son of God coming in his glory "in the clouds of heaven with millions of angels, and with thunders and lightning breaking forth from his Presence".[10] How terrible will be the appearance of Almighty God to those who are unprepared to meet him, and how glorious also the bliss of the redeemed!

Yet strangely enough, having asserted that heaven was a very different place from earth, he proceeded to make it out of the same elements. The angels would carry the souls of the saved to the very throne of God. God and Christ would meet them and treat them like brethren; they would eat and drink together; Christ would lead the assembly in their praises. Heaven was a place; he saw it; he heard it. It was something like Northampton on a Sunday morning, only in some vague way purified and glorified. Except for the Catholic imagery, he would have understood and accepted the sculptured vision of judgment on various cathedral west fronts, with the saved gathered to Abraham's bosom (literally) and the damned pouring, like a current, into a lake of fire. He admitted that there was a figurative as well as a literal significance to biblical symbol, yet for sermon purposes he dwelt on the literal. As a result, his treatment of the unseen is two-dimensional. There is all too little to tease the mind beyond today and tomorrow, except the text itself, which he turned from poetry to prose. He even knew what the saints talked about in their heavenly converse—the death of Jesus, of course.

To a day that interprets vision and poetry as symbol, not fact, such literalness is too easily dismissed as naïveté. But to the Northampton hearers, who like their preacher read their Bible for what it said, word for word, these prose details which he added made the Scripture take shape in color and movement until his pictures of heaven and hell and God on his throne were as real as though they had been murals painted with a brush on the gray meetinghouse walls. But with an arbitrariness of which he was probably unconscious, he refused to consider *Solomon's Song* except as symbol. Human love, beautiful as he had found it, belonged in another category. Flat-footedly he wrote down as Doctrine for a sermon, "The Book called Sol[omon's] Song is a divine Song concerning Things of a spr. & divine nature & no human Love Song".[11]

His sermon style was seldom heightened. At its best it was as unadorned as Bunyan's, although lacking Bunyan's distinction. His figures of speech were almost strictly scriptural. When he needed briars and brambles, pastures and water brooks, a cloud the size of a man's hand, the high places of the forest, he took them from David and the Prophets and the Evangelists, as though he had never had a farm boyhood of his own, and had not every year of his life spent weeks in lonely horseback journeys through woods, breathtaking in their spring and autumn beauty. As a part of his own daily devotions, he was accustomed to going to the woods which bordered Northampton, tethering his horse and walking alone in meditation; yet so far as the thoughts he brought back had need to cloak themselves in images, he took them from the Bible, seldom from his own observations. Whatever hunger he had for poetic expression was satisfied by chapter and line and verse from the familiar store:

"Man is like grass, says the Scripture. Yes, man is like grass. I will show you wherein this is a true saying".

"The King in his beauty. Yes, the King in his beauty." And there he stopped. What more was there to say?

His most frequently quoted metaphor, written years before the prison house of theology had closed around him, remains a somewhat lonely example of apparently original poetic phrase:

"To think of nothing is to think of the same that the sleeping rocks do dream of".[12]

One must look closely for the poet in him to speak on Sunday morning with so authentic a voice, although the proofs may sometimes be found. He saw the soul of man craving happiness. It is like an empty vessel which only God can fill. The fire of hell will be something like the lightning flash which drinks up man's spirits and his life. But usually his figures are more conventional.

Like many of his parishioners, he raised sheep, bought sheep, visited his pastures, mended his fences, superintended the shearing, and through the years acquired much precise information about sheep and their ways. An illustration drawn from the familiar scene on Mt. Tom would have been intently heard, yet one never finds it. When he had need of sheep for sermon purposes, he shelved all his own observations, and kept strictly to biblical varieties: sheep dumb before their shearers, sheep for the slaughter, gone astray like lost sheep. Not a word suggesting his own knowledge of lambing time, of the peril of broken hurdles, of the occasional wolf, or of the dog over twelve inches high, unlawfully ("for the sheep's sake") roaming at large in Northampton. Preaching did not deal in such obvious realities.

Nor did American poetry, for that matter. These were still the years in which poets were blind to the world around them. They still rang the changes on the melancholy yew, heather and gorse and skylarks, no one of which they had ever seen. Whippoorwills, goldenrod, and gentians had hardly as yet appeared in their verses; even the maple must wait to be "planted on poetic ground". For a minister to have used his eyes in the interest of sermon illustration would have been quite as unlikely. Wild blackberry vines had nothing to do with sermons; the lilies of the field alone were sufficient. Even a hundred years later, a Harvard audience was to be shocked by Emerson's breach of scholarly proprieties in his "meal in the firkin, milk in the pan".

By his own statement, Jonathan Edwards had "a very plain unfashionable way of preaching".[13] He meant, of course, unadorned, and without the polished phrase proper to printed matter. His verdict was right: he was no stylist. "The Death of Christ is a great Subject of contemplation." "The Misery of the Damned in Hell is one of those Great Things that the Saints in their blessed and joyful state in Heaven shall behold and take great notice of throughout Eternity." "Bridling the Tongue is a Great and Essential Part of Religion." Examples of similarly undistinguished vocabulary occur on every page, to deserve the eulogium spoken by one of his later critics: "His talents were of a superior kind. He regarded thoughts, rather than words".[14] It was a judgment calculated to praise, stylistic excellence being low in the list of criteria for sermon excellence. Was the doctrine "solid, rational and instructive"? Did the preacher avoid the "extreams of the enticing words of men's wisdom"? Did he show a "noble negligence" of mere language? If so, he was well approved.

"Iron can do some things that gold cannot", wrote a brother minister, by way of preface to his humble offering from the press. Was the book useful? Would souls be saved thereby? These were the real tests.

Jonathan Edwards' power to present ideas in pictures might lead one to expect lurid exposure of community sins; but except on a very few occasions the exact reverse was true. His reference to the local scene is seldom specific enough to be recognized. One may read a literal hundred of his sermons, and except for the headings, which name the occasions, know very little more about what was happening in Northampton than might be learned from reading *Leviticus* and *II Chronicles*. What went on at the local tavern did not concern him. He dealt with the springs of action, and the name and address of the offender seldom concerned him. In a sermon entitled,

"Preached On the Occasion of the Excommunication of John Bridgman's Wife, which was July 22, 1739",

neither the culprit nor the offence is mentioned. Text and doctrine alone re-created a town scandal of which all knew the details.

In the *Temptation of Joseph* sermon,[15] one of the most specific against Northampton evils, he called the offences by their family names and went on at once to what was beneath and behind them. After laying down several general principles by which conduct is to be recognized as either good or bad, he warned the young against specific evils, calling the familiar roll, but without going into details. To Whitefield these lost chances would have been inexcusable. He would have pictured the offender, dramatized the offence, called names, and set every tongue in town to wagging. At the end of this particular sermon Jonathan Edwards invited the young people who did not agree with his arguments and were unwilling to give up the amusements he had denounced to bring satisfying answers to the arguments he had presented. "I don't desire", he said, "that young People should be abridg'd of any lawful & proper Liberties." This is completely typical of his governance in his own family. The liberties permitted to his daughters are startling in the light of eighteenth century proprieties: the long journeys, the unchaperoned comings and goings while they were still in their teens. His admonitions in letters to them have no reference to behavior whatever, only to the principles which underlie it.

There are no parallels anywhere in Jonathan Edwards' sermons to the strictures of his predecessor against hooped petticoats, the sinfulness of wearing periwigs, compotations in private houses, and many similar follies. Periwigs had particularly aroused Solomon Stoddard's ire, men's "own Hair [being] sufficient for all those Ends that God has given Hair for".[16] Whether Jonathan Edwards' hair was inadequate or not, no one knows, but he wore a wig and said nothing of it. When country towns were still wearing shoestrings, he followed Boston and put on buckles; such matters, in his view, lying outside the precincts of sin. Foppishness in dress he would have been the first to deprecate, but he had too much dignity and too much sense to lose his balance over such matters. He showed a similar discrimination in wasting no arguments on Sunday morning as to the exact hour of the sixth day at which woman was created, or the exact number of feet from the meetinghouse a private dwelling could stand without affront to God. To a later day many of his two-hour arguments may seem futile, but they were never trivial.

Like any other preacher he read the times to his purpose, and made fitting Sunday response to weekday happenings. When the Lyman house was destroyed by fire and two of the children burned to death, the sermon on the following Sunday was shaped to this tragedy. To do so was a tribute to the members of his flock whom it concerned, as well as a fresh reminder to all, of the swift ways of death. Similarly when the courthouse burned, when the "throat distemper" came, or drought burned up the crops, he used the sermon material God himself had provided. He shared the simple trust of the least intellectual of his flock that God spoke through these accidents and the devastations of nature. His files are full of sermons preached at fasts held for rain, and his remarks on such occasions indicate that he expected a literal answer. He would have rebuked the unfaith of the brother who attended the fast but wrote in his journal:

"Before Mr. Noyes had done prayer, ye rain came down at once on ye Meeting-House to ye great Surprise of ye assembly".[17]

Jonathan Edwards would have been surprised if Jehovah had not "unstopped the bottles of Heaven," and immediately.

What these hundreds of sermons with their carefully selected texts, their closely reasoned analogies and precise divisions within divisions meant to "Sticher Pomroy" the town tailor, to Ebenezer Hunt, Noah Clark, Preserved Bartlett, and all the others, only these men themselves could have said. Pages of careful reasoning to prove the devil a liar were not to them wasted logic. They straightway went home and marked the new evidence in their own Bibles. A sermon's prosperity in any age lies in the ears that hear it, not in the criticism of those who come after. The Northampton pews had paid their annual rate for two hours of Exposition and Application of doctrine fifty-two Sundays in the year. They expected doctrine to be heavily freighted with learning greater than their own, and well annotated by Scripture. They were not theologians, any of them, but they were all detectives.

They knew what they had heard all their lives, and if the Sunday doctrine had swerved an inch toward anything Antinomian or un-Stoddardean, they would all have been on the scent at once. "Sound doctrine" and religion were one and identical; "Mr. Edwards" kept within the white lines of traditional orthodoxy. Hence, when they opened the doors of their pews at the end of the two hours and filed out into the air again, they were well content. Children stayed to catechizing, repeated the sermon outline correctly, straightway forgot it, but remembered all their lives that God and religion were more important than anything else, and that Sunday was a holy day.

Read in print or on their tiny manuscript pages, not one in fifty of these sermons would be likely to suggest that America was to honor Jonathan Edwards as one of the great minds of his century. There is much repetition. Long before his Northampton pastorate was over, his thought had begun to run in grooves. Posterity, interested in the originality of his thought, must find it elsewhere than in the sermon booklets. Read under properly diffused light, two hundred years away from the atmosphere of the meetinghouse and the presence of a believing congregation, lacking the quiet voice and the deep solemnity of the preacher, these two-hour discourses leave one wondering somewhat as to the preacher and his power. In the 1730's and '40's, however, it was quite otherwise. These same closely reasoned, heavily doctrinal sermons made the name of Jonathan Edwards known on two continents.

Chapter 8

Souls Gathered In

THE FIRST signal honor of his career outside of his own parish was a tribute to a sermon he had preached. This was in 1731, when he was twenty-seven years old and had been settled in Northampton for more than four years. He had been invited by the Boston clergy to preach at the Public Lecture on July 8th, and his sermon had so greatly pleased the older brethren that they had urged him to print it at once. This was his first publication.[1]

In the light of his career as a revival preacher, the sermon is of considerable importance, for it laid the foundation of his whole evangelical structure. He called it *God Glorified in Man's Dependence*. It is a carefully reasoned discourse in which he made bold to announce that he could justify the ways of God to men by the basic tenet of traditional Calvinism, divine sovereignty. One cannot of course assign single causes to the complicated process of social change; and yet, fitted into its chronological place, this sermon appears to mark the beginning of both the new emphasis in doctrine and the new fervor in preaching which ten years later were to bring about the Great Awakening.

In 1731, New England was full of very disturbing signs of interest in the more modern plan of salvation loosely called Arminianism. In place of the familiar doctrines of God's sovereignty, His inexorable justice in the damnation of sinners, and the complete helplessness of men to do anything about it all, this new way of thinking held out hope by way of more respectable living, benevolence, and those measurable virtues generally known as "good works". These newer notions had the great advantage of being more concrete, easier to understand, and far more comfortable than the traditional sound doctrines. The conservative clergy were alarmed in proportion as the laity were interested, but in their great concern to speak against the new they had forgotten to preach the old. Here was a young man who, without calling the offensive new doctrine by name, preached the old with such fervor as to make it appear the more desirable. The Boston clergy were delighted, and no wonder.

In Jonathan Edwards' personal story, this sermon made clear what was to be his lifelong theological loyalty. As between the "ancients" and the "moderns", he declared for the "ancients". The "fashionable new divinity", as he saw it, robbed God of his due glory and thwarted the whole scheme of human redemption as God had designed it. In this sermon he was not concerned to argue against these newer doctrines, or even to chart the true scheme of salvation as a consistent whole. He said nothing about eternal punishment, contrition for sin, or even conversion but, logician that he was, went back to the beginnings. The sovereignty of God in the world he had created was the foundation of all right doctrine. Until man had acknowledged this sovereignty unequivocably and had admitted his own helplessness, the gift of free grace could have no meaning for him. Having reasserted this absolute supremacy, Jonathan Edwards went on to define it in terms of personal redemption:

> Man is nothing; God is all.
> Man's very desire for God is God-given.
> Whatever degree of holiness man may attain is not his own, but God's dwelling in him.
> God communicates his own beauty to the souls of his saints.

In doctrine, this is pure Calvinism, purer in fact than New England was accustomed to hearing. In emphasis, it was a timely rebuke to those who were taking credit to themselves for any good works they practiced. In approach, it was frankly speculative; there was hardly a concrete detail in the whole sermon.

Stripped of the young eloquence with which they were proclaimed, these ideas were thoroughly familiar to the Boston divines who listened so approvingly. No phrase had been on the lips of the New England clergy more frequently since Jonathan Edwards was born than "sovereignty of God"; and yet, as he now interpreted this venerable doctrine, he seemed to be preaching a fresh, new truth. The sermon, as the record reads, was "uncommonly impressive". It is easy to see why. Back of the familiar structure of Calvinistic thought, in this basic first *Point*, "sovereignty", the fervent young preacher was putting the authority of his own personal religious experience. When he spoke of a satisfying spiritual joy, "a kind of effusion of God in the soul", he was not speaking the language of catechetical divinity as he had learned it in Ames'

Medulla during his Yale College days; he was speaking out of his own knowledge of spiritual things. Divine sovereignty, by this interpretation, was the doctrine which, hitherto "abhorrent", had immediately after his conversion appeared "exceeding pleasant, bright and sweet". It would be years yet before he would clarify to his own complete intellectual satisfaction the complex psychology implicit in this inner change which he now proclaimed; but throughout his life the communication of God's own beauty to his redeemed creatures, not by virtue of any worthiness in them but by his own sovereign pleasure alone, would be to him the essence of religion, as man might begin to know it on earth. This Boston sermon of 1731 supplies the doctrinal basis for this first step in Jonathan Edwards' own pilgrim's progress.

In the long history of New England preaching, this sermon is not more important as a check to the fashionable new doctrine of salvation than to the much older process of rationalization by which the unfathomable, unpredictable God of Calvin had been gradually changed into a reasonable being. In fact, Calvin's God had not crossed to the American continent at all, but by 1620 had already suffered comfortable modification at the hands of various Cambridge divines: John Preston, William Perkins, Richard Sibbes, and notably William Ames, whose *Medulla Sacrae Theologiae* became the *vade mecum* of Harvard and Yale divinity students for another hundred years. During this same first century, New England Dissent through its own spokesmen, John Cotton, Thomas Hooker, John Davenport, and Peter Bulkeley, had modified Calvinistic doctrine still further in the direction of a reasonable rather than an arbitrary God, until by 1731 a theological system with a strongly legalistic bias had been developed. The "covenant of grace" amounted in effect to a contract, almost as binding on God as on man.[2] Salvation was on terms. God bestowed it. Man did not deserve it, but he might know the terms, and if he chose to fulfil them, God was virtually in his power. God would keep His word. As a reasonable Being, he had to, except perhaps in the hundredth instance. Rationality left a small unplotted area for the inexplicable freakishness of Providence; but, generally speaking, the arbitrariness of an inscrutable Deity had been brought within predictable bounds. Neither the sovereignty of God nor the depravity of man had been denied, but both had been decidedly breached.

Even the great and awesome doctrine of election had come

to mean, in practical pulpit treatment, that the slightest desire after salvation might be God's way of announcing to individual man that he was elected. If he would act on this suggestion, repent, submit himself to God, he might possibly be admitted. God spoke through His ordinances, of which preaching was one. Hence, if a man would only go to church, put himself under sermons (and also the watchful eye of the minister, God's appointed agent), his chance of salvation was greater than if he had not been exposed. Solomon Stoddard had made it still easier by suggesting that the sacred seal of the Lord's Supper might also, under special conditions, be a "converting ordinance". From such arguments it had been only one more step, and a short one, to say that "good works" also might put one in the way of faith. Calvin would have been incapable of such notions. His scorn of them and their proponents would have been sublime. With all his inexorable partiality, or rather because of it, the God of Calvin's *Institutes* dilates the imagination, whereas, by comparison, the God of Ames' *Medulla* merely commands respect. A man might almost deal with such a Being if he knew the answers, and they were all in Ames' *Medulla*. To borrow Calvin's own words, used by him to excoriate those who had imagined God to be corporeal, "the immensity and spirituality of the essence of God" had been accommodated to the narrow capacity of those who could not grasp his true majesty.[8]

Without meaning to be a better Calvinist than his brethren, or even faintly imagining that he was, Jonathan Edwards in this 1731 sermon was predicating a Deity more fit for adoration than for finite comprehension. God was once again inscrutable, immutable, unpredictable. Man's place was in the dust, and when he had once caught a glimpse of the divine glory, he would willingly be there. Later, with other preachers of the Great Awakening, he put the dynamic of fear behind this same doctrine, emphasizing the glory of God in man's damnation; but on this earlier occasion he was content to dwell on the transcendent glory of a Being upon whom men were utterly dependent. In his young fervor for this cardinal doctrine of a lost golden age, the older men were heartened, for they did spy a kind of hope.

The intense conviction of the young preacher, the approbation of the older men, and the far-reaching consequences of this check to newer theological ideas suggest another occasion in American religious history, arresting in its correspondence and also in its direct antithesis. On another July day, a little more than a century later, another young man, similarly quiet-voiced and without gestures, leaned on one elbow and read from a closely written manuscript to another ministerial company, met in Cambridge, three miles away. His words also were uncommonly impressive as he proclaimed man's dependence on God and the satisfying joy of that inner certainty which he also had learned through a personal experience of religion:

"If a man is at heart just, then in so far is he God; the safety of God, the immortality of God, the majesty of God do enter into that man with justice.

"One man was true to what is in you and me. He saw that God incarnates himself in man and evermore goes forth anew to take possession of his World. . . ." [4]

When this later address was finished, no one urged publication or offered to write a flattering preface. The settled ministry went out in rage and consternation, feeling that the temple had been polluted and the cause dishonored. But the souls of the young men were "roused"; they thronged around the speaker as though they had heard a prophet. A generation had been liberated by his words.

What Emerson did was to reassert in quite untheological language the life principle of all religion. To him creeds and theological systems crushed it to death. On the authority of his own vision, he swept them all aside, and said: The Kingdom of God is within you. Forget the creeds and find God for yourself today and tomorrow. Those who identified religion with current theological explanations of it were horrified. What Jonathan Edwards had done a hundred years earlier was to take the life principle of all religion, as he had found it out by his own search, vital and joy-giving, and shut it up in the husk of a dead idiom. He translated a personal experience into a theological system, and a system of which forward-looking men, even among the clergy, had begun to be disrespectful. No wonder those zealous for the old system were heartened. They felt the glow behind the words of this new herald, and thought (wrongly) that the life was in the system he justified. Perhaps this new champion might yet save a dying cause.

The comparison is doubtless unfair. In the history of men's thought a century can be a long time, nor does one read the record backward. Before Emerson began to think for himself, three more generations of courage in thought and action had been built into his heritage. On many paths men had dared to clear away the underbrush of tradition and to look on the bare contours of truth according to life. Emerson was the product of a far mellower culture and had had a few glimpses of the world beyond his own door. Besides, he was a man of intuition, and something of a poet. He could take a leap into the unknown, with no logician's sense to retard his progress. It would have been asking a great deal in 1731, although the like has sometimes happened in the history of thought, for Jonathan Edwards, hedged in as he was by sound doctrine and shackled by too great reverence for authority, to dare to look into his own heart and speak what he knew, independently of all learned divines, past and present. If instead of justifying "vital piety" by the doctrines of Calvinism, he could only have looked past Calvin, past Luther, and past St. Augustine, back to the Sermon on the Mount, putting religion of the spirit in language that the rank and file could understand, there is no telling how the religious history of America and the cultural pattern of America might have been altered. He had the courage. He had the personal experience of religion. It merely never occurred to him that all theological systems are but man-made rationalizations of order in the universe, and therefore worthy of only qualified veneration. Neither did it occur to him that he had in his own hand the key which would have let himself and all his brother ministers out of prison.

The publication of this 1731 sermon one month after its delivery was a distinct compliment. In addition, it introduced Jonathan Edwards to the New England clergy and to the larger audience of divines outside America as a preacher of what were labelled in the preface "evangelical doctrines". This was to be his lifelong reputation. The Boston approval also increased his prestige in his own pulpit and immediate neighborhood. His people took pride in this printed proof that the succession of learned divines in the Northampton pulpit was not to be broken. The Hampshire Association, at the meeting following this Boston occasion, and probably because of it, requested that, with two brother ministers, Jonathan Edwards draw up an address to the County Court, protesting against the growing vice and immorality, and proposing a reform in manners. His championship of evangelical doctrine and his zeal for reform in manners are the two discernible causes for the revival in his own parish in 1735. With this precise end in view, he went to work at once with increased enthusiasm in both directions.

Northampton was favorable soil for revival hopes. Under Solomon Stoddard's vigorous preaching of eternal punishment there had been periodic revivals. The congregation knew the signs and had tasted the excitements. But there had been scarce a sprinkling since 1718, and now a new generation was ready to be stirred. According to Jonathan Edwards' own recital of events,[5] the first indications were visible in the fall of 1733, when the young people began to show an unusual flexibleness and yielding to advice. He had been urging them to examine their own lives lest they be living in some way of sin, and when on one occasion he became more specific and preached a sermon setting forth the evils of mirth-making and company-keeping on Sunday evening, they were so deeply impressed that they straightway gave up these practices. This was the first step toward concern for their souls. While they were in this yielding mood, he pressed his advantage and began to preach on more "awakening" themes: the despair of those who wait too long, the steps to be taken by sinners under conviction, the shortness and uncertainty of life. In April, 1734, two young persons in the town, a man and a woman, died suddenly. While their young companions were still greatly sobered by these deaths, the preacher quickly seized his opportunity, organized the young people into small groups for private meetings, appointed fasts, and in various other ways kept religion in the foreground during the week as well as on Sunday.

During most of the preceding months of the year 1733 he had been preaching on positive themes: the joy of the saints, the beauty of holiness, the rest the true believer enjoys in Christ, the practical Christian virtues, especially benevolence and honesty. In August, 1733, he had preached one of the most notable sermons of his life and also one of the most individual, *The Reality of Spiritual Light*.[6] By the favorite figure of his younger preaching, light, and by his most characteristic method, appeal to the rational understanding rather than the emotions, he sought to prove that for which no concrete proofs avail: the reality of a divine emanation of God's beauty in the souls of those appointed to receive it. He spoke more poetically than was his wont and with a fervency of conviction concerning this "dawning of the light of glory in the heart", changing man's nature and disposing him to service and obedience. Spiritual light not only reveals, it animates that which it shines upon. It is a principle of light within. Supernatural as it is, it is not a divine gift externally bestowed and externally received; it is a participation of God by His redeemed creatures. The soul so animated gives out a light of its own. In attempting to clarify such ideas, Jonathan Edwards was once again on his lifelong track and, had there been no Arminian errors to confute, he might have gone far in a direction of his own.

But the battle was already at hand. By 1734 heresy had filtered into his own parish. Men were beginning to take sides. He set himself to resist the oncoming tide. The result was a series of sermons designed to combat point by point what he believed to be the false doctrines of his theological opponents. His refutation was in Calvinistic idiom: the sovereignty of God, his inexorable justice, particularly justification by faith alone. Some of the more influential members of his congregation, particularly Israel Williams,[7] the "monarch of Hampshire", opposed the bringing of so controversial a theme into the pulpit. Their opposition was strongly put, but Jonathan Edwards chose to disregard their protests. His decision was the beginning of disharmony in the parish. It was also the beginning of the revival. According to his scale of values he had suffered "open abuse" in a good cause.

Opposition had of course created tension. Tension had supplied a favorable background for emotional excitements of the revival sort. In addition, there was deep unrest over the doctrinal issue itself. Even though there had been no opposition and no tension, the pastor would have been sure of an alert hearing for his views. From their childhood up, his people had been taught there was one way to be saved. Now as rumors of this new and easier way began to be insistent on every side, they felt that the very foundations of belief were being cut away. Could the Bible be wrong? Could Solomon Stoddard have been wrong? No wonder their minds were "put into an unusual ruffle" over the whole affair. As Jonathan Edwards saw his pastoral obligation, he must assure them that the scriptural basis on which the old doctrines stood was impregnable. He did so with such compelling vigor that he put his congregation in the way of an eager pursuit of salvation according to the provisions for which he pleaded. The result was the greatest revival in New England history up to this time.

Read on the printed page, these sermons seem too heavily doctrinal and too argumentative to make revival history. One must make allowance for the frame of mind in which the parish assembled to hear them, and also for the current respect paid to the authority of Scripture, which was their particular strength. Years of young zeal in the study of the Bible lay back of the preacher's earnest conviction that old doctrine was also right doctrine. At every point he buttressed his own thought with such weight of proof as seemed incontrovertible to those trained to accept line and verse as authoritative and final. Even so, the revival might never have followed hard on these sermons if the preacher had kept to scriptural proofs alone. In the fourth sermon, *The Justice of God in the Damnation of Sinners,*[8] he added the time-honored revival methods: appeal to fear and denunciation of specific sins. As a result, this sermon proved the climax of the series and the beginning of the shower.

He took for his Text *Rom.* 3:19: "That every mouth may be stopped". Doctrinally, his theme was again the sovereignty of God, this time in relation to sinful man's helplessness. God is just, he argued; never more so than in casting away sinful men forever. Men deserve nothing. They are incapable of any goodness in themselves. God is the Creator of all things, and it is meet that He should act as the sole possessor of earth and heaven. To admit God's justice is the first step in the only path to an undeserved salvation. To Jonathan Edwards such majesty was sublime. The transcendent beauty of a being who ruled the world according to his own sovereign pleasure gripped his imagination and uplifted his soul. Perhaps not many in his congregation felt the sublimity, but the wrath of such a transcendent being sent them to their knees.

Harshness of doctrine begot harshness of manner, and when the preacher came to the Application of his Doctrine, he became more denunciatory than his people had ever known him to be in all the eight years he had lived among them. Relentlessly he called the roll of the town sins which shut men out from God's mercy and kindled the divine wrath to their destruction. "How many kinds of wickedness are there?" he asked, and then proceeded to answer his own question: irreverence in God's house, disregard of the Sabbath, neglect of family prayer, disobedience to parents, quarreling, greediness, sensuality, hatred of one's neighbor. The list was no other than a roll call of the Seven Deadlies in village dress, and would have fitted any congregation in any age; but to Northampton, with nerves on edge after a month of stern preachments, the minister's words seemed applicable to one town and one only. Up and down the village streets he went, pointing his finger accusingly at one house after another, unearthing secret sins and holding them up for all to see.

Now that they no longer matter, those words still seem strangely harsh words for a man to speak to his own friends and neighbors. A minister from Boston, who did not know which neighbors had quarreled, or which merchants had been envious of which, might have named the same sins and gone blameless in the ears of the accused. But not their pastor who had baptized their children and buried their dead. This was the most effective sermon Jonathan Edwards had ever preached from his high pulpit in the fortlike meetinghouse, but he would pay dear for his success. Weeks later, when fear had passed, the sharp edges of these stern accusations would still lacerate. "Mr. Edwards" had lost something he could never quite regain in Northampton. But in 1734 he did not know that. Besides, from every corner men were beginning to cry out, "What must I do to be saved?" and on Monday morning the King Street parsonage was being besieged by those who had not been able to sleep the night before.

The first professional conversions came in December, 1734. The fact that one of these was the conversion of a young woman, by reputation one of the greatest "company-keepers" in the whole town, provided the spectacular element needed to give the "great work" its initial impetus, and accordingly put the parish on tiptoe for marvels at the very outset. The news that she had been saved was like "a flash of lightning, upon the hearts of the young people", Jonathan Edwards wrote. She became the center of attention, and apparently bore herself so well through the ordeal as to cast no suspicions upon the genuineness of her profession of faith. The pastor himself was incredulous at first, so notorious had she been in directions opposite to all things religious; but soon he too became convinced, and with him the whole town. After that the revival moved forward by its own momentum.

First the young people and presently their elders were put under deep concern for their sins. As light broke upon one after another, the despairs of those under conviction increased. The whole town found itself in two camps: the saved who rejoiced, and the unsaved who agonized to join them but could not. Regular business became perfunctory where it was not actually suspended. Religion was the one topic of conversation, and briefly the meetinghouse resumed its central place in the life of the town. The parsonage was the object of pilgrimage night and day, as the saved brought news of their acceptance and the condemned besought the pastor's help. It was apparently a situation which called for unqualified superlatives. "Scarcely a single Person in the whole Town was Left unconcerned about the Great things of the Eternal World" [9] was the pastor's attempt to give faithful report weeks after the rushing mighty wind had passed.

During the early stages, Jonathan Edwards seems to have handled the situation with good sense and practical wisdom. He appointed singing meetings at which overcharged emotions could spend themselves in an orderly manner. He met his flock in small groups—children, young people, old people, sinners, saved—adapting the same counsels to their several needs. He encouraged groups to meet by themselves in private houses. He invited those under deep concern to come to him privately. As a result, there seems to have been little boisterousness. There was also almost universal harmony, great rejoicing as the number of the saved daily increased, and "a glorious alteration in the town". The "Party Strife" which had always divided Northampton was laid aside; neighbor confessed fault to neighbor; differences of long standing were wiped out (supposedly).

"I never saw the Christian Spirit in Love to Enemies so Exemplified, in all my Life as I have seen it within this Half-year",[10]

the pastor wrote. He had seen revivals in his father's parish as a boy, but nothing like this. To him, it seemed almost the millennium, and was the happiest time in all his ministry. Temporarily, he had the sympathy of the whole town in his own single-hearted pursuit of things unseen, and the joy of it was almost unbearable. To hundreds in the parish likewise, "the world was a thing only by the bye". The meetinghouse could not hold those who thronged to service, and when on a certain Sunday morning the pastor received a hundred new members *en masse,* his oldest daughter, Sarah, aged seven, among them, pulpit and pew alike were "deeply affected". No wonder. This was the outpouring for which three generations of ministers had agonized in vain. Now that it had come, it seemed more like a story out of the Bible than like everyday village history.

That by its very nature such a state of emotional strain could not last, seems to have occurred to no one, not even to the pastor. All made the mistake of assuming that continuance of marvel was the sole proof God was still with them, and when all at once they found themselves back on the C major of this life there could be only one possible cause—some one had sinned. God had withdrawn his presence. If only Jonathan Edwards could have taken his harvest, called it a harvest, and been content, he might have been spared much bitterness; but he was too young, too inexperienced, and too much fired by apostolic zeal to attain to so wise a conclusion. Of this same error the most grievous mistakes of the Great Awakening were born.

The revival reached its peak in the early spring of 1735, after about three months of intense excitement. So far nothing had happened to check its progress or dim its glory. About this time similar manifestations began to be reported from other towns, most of which in the beginning had been frankly skeptical. Visitors had come to see for themselves and, as they carried back favorable report, their story bore fruit in their own parishes. As Jonathan Edwards himself observed:

"There is no one thing that I know of which God has made such a means of promoting his work amongst us, as the news of others' conversion".[11]

Northampton also profited as the news of neighborhood successes filtered back.

Late in the spring of 1735 the first sinister note was struck in the attempted suicide of Thomas Stebbins, a man of weak mentality. Several weeks later Joseph Hawley, one of the chief men of the town and uncle to Jonathan Edwards, "cut his throat on Lord's Day morning" and died immediately. The community was aghast. "An awful Providence",[12] wrote Ebenezer Hunt in his *Journal*. A fast was appointed, and the congregation prostrated itself before God. But the turning point had come: the spell was broken, the emotional climate changed at once, and the long delayed reaction set in. For the first time sobered men and women began to question the wholesomeness of the excitement under which they had been living. As a matter of fact, the limit of endurable ecstasies had been reached; but before equilibrium could be established and life could proceed normally once more there were to be many blots on the record. Hawley's death proved to be only the beginning, even in suicides. "Multitudes", to quote the pastor's own word, were impelled to do likewise, feeling it "urged upon them as if somebody had spoke to them *'Cut your own throat. Now is a good opportunity'* ".[13]

Fortunately not all succeeded. Others suffered from equally strange delusions, until at length it was clear to all that God had withdrawn his spirit. The heavenly shower was over.

Incredulous at first, Northampton presently accepted the situation, and settled back unwillingly into a more prosaic way of life. By the end of the year 1735, pulpit and pew together were lamenting the "dead time in religion", and calling the difference between the concerns of six days and the seventh "a decline". Some of the new converts had climbed into the fold by mistake and now had to be disciplined. Dissension had come back into the parish and had become so pronounced that the pastor referred publicly to "our late quarrels". Northampton was again a town with "parties". Early in 1736 a few of the more zealous of his congregation, unwilling to accept the changed situation, persuaded him to print some of his more "awakening" sermons, in the hope that jaded emotions might be whipped into yet one more response, and the glorious work return once more. He printed the sermons, the congregation paid the bill, but nothing happened.

Reviewed as a whole and at long range, this 1735 revival, for all of its extravagance and sensationalism, seems to show more of concern with religion as an inner experience, and more connection between professed conversion and subsequent reform of conduct than one ordinarily finds in later American revivals. No doubt this result owed much to the fact that until the end when rumors began to come in from other towns, this had been strictly a village affair, proceeding step by step under the supervision and counsel of one man, the settled pastor. There had been no models of revival behavior to live up to. Northampton had made its own models. By comparison with later revivals in this and other parishes, this had been a distinct advantage.

The most complete contemporary record is that of Jonathan Edwards himself, written down almost a year later in the form of a letter to Benjamin Colman of Boston under the title, *A Faithful Narrative of the Surprizing Work of God.* In its influence upon American religious history, particularly during the revivals of the 1740's, this was the most potent piece of writing Jonathan Edwards ever planned, and in many ways the most unfortunate. He spoke too soon. Time had not yet winnowed false from true. Neither pulpit nor pew had yet been able to set the supposed marvels in due perspective. Had he delayed report for another year, he would probably have written the story with quite different emphasis, and established thereby a different pattern for later revival behavior.

Inexperienced as he was in such matters, he had been caught, like his people, by the more unusual manifestations; so much so that when he set himself to prove the signal presence and power of God in conversion he chose out of the several hundred conversions to which he might have borne witness, two of the most spectacular: the experience of a young woman in a morbid state of mind immediately preceding her own death, and the precocities of Phoebe Bartlett, aged four, who feared herself in danger of hell and shut herself up in the closet until she received assurances to the contrary. When his readers assumed that such behaviors did greater honor to God than less spectacular deliverances their conclusion was fair enough, and when in the next decade extravagance went out of bounds, and revival marvels were induced by a score of bizarre methods, Jonathan Edwards was himself in part to blame. His own very earnest later rebuke to the emphasis on "bodily manifestation" and other sensational forms of hysteria was less effective than the models he had himself set up in this earlier treatise. Phoebe Bartlett was immediately adopted by all New England as a worthy addition to Cotton Mather's galaxy of unnatural, pious children,[14] from whom she differed only in that she progressed to a healthy though still pious maturity, remaining meanwhile the favorite pattern for extreme minors under conviction for sin. Thanks to Cotton Mather, almost any New England parent would have been glad to observe similar symptoms in his own unredeemed four-year-old, since in familiar pulpit tutelage, the younger the child, the greater glory to God in its rescue from the wrath to come.

To Jonathan Edwards, accustomed to the phrases of sixty on the tongue of his youngest, such a view needed no defence. He would not have exploited one of his own children for any cause, but he considered them fit subjects for God's wrath until they could give evidence of their conversion. God was no respecter of ages. When preaching to little children, he did not greatly simplify his doctrine, or tone down its severity.

"God is very angry with the sins of little children",

he wrote as the Doctrine for one of his revival sermons, designed for a children's meeting, and then went on to amplify his thought under the headings:

> "Live in neglect of Christ"
> "Abundance of Sin on the Sabbath Day"
> "Wicked thoughts"
> "Wicked desires"
> "Hating one another"
> "Multitudinous kinds of wickedness"
> "Serve the devil" [15]

Possibly one should not press his words too far; but, as the father of a small flock, exactly what did he mean by such a catalogue of infant sins? What, in concrete application, could he find in his own nursery to match such ascription of evil? The answer is of course that to him and to the rest of the ministerial brotherhood doctrine was in one category and fatherly affection in another. Doctrinally, children were in a natural state; therefore hell yawned for them. But when he wrote in a family letter, "Tell Esther to be a good Girl",[16] he meant exactly what any father would have meant. Religion as it was preached in colonial times and, in fact, throughout the eighteenth century, did not bring harmony into living. It puts man spiritual at war with man natural, just as doctrine required. Nowhere is this more apparent than in the conflict between parental love and proper respect for a jealous Deity. When a company of ministers, all of them fathers, could spread on the minutes of their association meeting that the wasting sickness among the children of the county was "A Testimony against our Immoderate love of and doating upon them",[17] the brethren were seeing double. The day afterward, when they dismounted from their horses at their own back doors and greeted the little children who ran out to meet them, did they attempt to curb this "immoderate love"? The question answers itself. When Jonathan Edwards preached to a group of little children about neglecting Christ and serving the devil, he was preaching theologically, and his words had little relation to the frailties of his own fatherhood or the sweetness of the Edwards family life. The time was quickly coming when such doctrine could not survive a more realistic and unified view of life. When Phoebe Bartlett's own children had grown to parenthood they might dote on their offspring less guiltily and also desire for them a somewhat different distinction from her quite scriptural infant agonies. But in 1737 hers was still a glorious tale.

As Jonathan Edwards lived over the story in the writing of it, the foreground was full of activity. Three hundred converts filled the meetinghouse to overflowing. A new one must be built and at once. After long debate, the formal vote to build was taken on November 5, 1735. The new structure was to stand as close as possible to the old, on top of Meetinghouse Hill. It was to be almost twice as large, measuring fifty-six by seventy feet. There was to be a gallery at one end and a steeple. Otherwise, the Town left all details to the committee, who henceforth met night and day. Work began in the summer of 1736, while the whole town watched. The oldest inhabitants told the children how it had been in 1661, and the children in their turn stored up another generation's memories. The story as recorded in Ebenezer Hunt's characteristic staccato style is again memorable.

[1736] Summer of 1736 framed it. Mr. Joseph Wright, master.
        Sept. 16. laid the sills (Thurs) were to begin to raise on Mon next, but it rained.
        town met & agreed to hire 60 men at 5/ per day they keeping themselves except drink.
        Tues A.M. they began to raise. Sept 21st. raised all parts except 2.
        Wed. finished body of house & put up 2 beams,
        Thurss. all beams & prepared to raise upper part of belfry.
        Friday finished scaffolding & raised half of belfry.
        Sat—rained till noon:
        in afternoon finished body of belfry.
        Monday 27th finished raising.
        no one having been hurt in the whole process.
1737   July 21. The Spire was raised with good success.
1738   May 5. We pulled down the old house without hurt to any man or the new house.[18]

On the Sunday after the raising Jonathan Edwards, with his superb feeling for texts, preached from *Amos* 9:6:

"It is he that buildeth his stories in the heaven".

No doubt what he had to say on this occasion was heard with a shade more anticipation that usual. Outside, the new structure had within the week, for the first time, assumed the reality of a building; now, although the preacher said less about the actual raising than Ebenezer Hunt had supplied, through the scriptural analogy he linked the work of the raisers with God's own creation. Considered apart from its occasion, this sermon is little different in matter or method from dozens of others shut up in the small booklets. Read with a sense of the village history which it documents, it becomes strangely moving. It may even have been a great sermon. The preacher was not speaking to those interested in the rise and fall of doctrine; he was speaking to men with splinters in their hands, and he knew what he was about.

On March 13, 1737, nearly a year later, an accident gave fresh incentive to haste and temporarily put the congregation under deep concern for their souls. During a crowded Sunday morning service, the gallery of the old meetinghouse fell. Strangely enough, no one was killed, although more than seventy persons were seated directly underneath. They were protected by the tops of the high pews, but to Northampton God had carefully planned it so. Just as any other minister of his generation would have done, Jonathan Edwards interpreted this accident as a "Rebuke of God and a Loud Call to Repent".[19] Why should God not speak through the decaying beams of an insubstantial building? As to that, he had no more doubt than his little Jerusha might have had.

But, bruises healed, the warning of God was promptly forgotten in the new excitement of "dignifying the seats". On November 18, 1737, a committee of five was appointed by the Town with instruction to seat the males at the south end and the females at the north, and to have respect in so doing to men's estate, their age, and in a lesser degree to their usefulness. The current importance of this appraisal cannot well be exaggerated. "Seating the meetinghouse" in any parish was equivalent to issuing a new edition of the *Social Register;* and if any mistakes were made they would probably not be rectified for another generation, possibly not while the meetinghouse stood. Children would in time come down out of the gallery to sit in the family pew, but there would be few other changes. The decisions of the committee were final. The five men set to work. The village waited, and the fruits of the spirit languished until the suspense was over.

The seating of magistrates gave no trouble. It was the assignment of the rank and file which necessitated prolonged debate. They had paid their rates; they felt they had rights in the matter, but they were not likely to be pleased, no matter how the committee disposed of them.

Who should be elevated?
Who should be degraded?

Over this question the committee labored for five weeks. They came back to the Town with one question only:

Should wives and husbands sit together?

No, said the Town, adding as an amendment that if husbands and wives should "incline to sit together", they need not be forbidden. On December 22nd the seaters made report, and after some debate their report was accepted. This drama, strange blend of aristocratic tradition and democratic protest, had been enacted at least twice in every American parish before the 1770's put an end to such a system.

The dimly penciled diagram surviving in the Judd MSS. is the most complete picture of the Northampton parish extant. Here are the town widows in a row to the left of the pulpit. In the pew next to the great ones of the village, Colonel Stoddard and "Mr. Hawley", sits Mrs. Edwards in solitary, elevated state. The oldest Edwards daughter, Sarah, is in the second row, along with several of the "bad book" children, deacons interspersed among them to keep order. Mercy, one of the Edwards servants, so frequently mentioned in family correspondence, is in the first seat of the Lower Tier. In serried ranks, here are also the Lymans, Pomeroys, Clarks, Wrights, Burts, Allens, Clapps, and all the others whose wedding banns, requests for prayers, and thanksgivings for deliverance are bound with the sermon booklets. Here sits Hannah Strong, later to be admonished for contempt of church authority, and also the wife of John Bridgman, who was to be excommunicated. "Timo: Dwight, His mother, wife and Child", sit together, contrary to the usual custom. In the places assigned on this blurred piece of paper, the congregation assembled on Christmas Day, 1737, when Jonathan Edwards formally dedicated the new meetinghouse. His text was inevitable: "In my Father's house are many mansions".[20] This was a memorable day in Jonathan Edwards' life and in the history of Northampton.

The new meetinghouse remained the outward symbol of the great ingathering. It was also a monument to eleven years of successful preaching. No young man in all New England had such a record of souls gathered in. Years later Jonathan Edwards recognized he had been overcredulous as to the number. There had not been so many genuine converts as he had at first assumed. Dross had been mingled with the gold. He had lacked judgment and discretion. He had not been alert to the "False Appearances", the "Corrupt mixtures", the counterfeits and extravagances until it was too late. He lived long enough to know that he had made bitter mistakes, but not long enough even to imagine the far consequences of this truly surprising story in the religious life of America. As all of New England and presently all of America read his account, revivals seemed more possible to those who had previously prayed in vain for just such a spectacle as he described. His story also established a technique of revival behavior for pulpit and pew which endures to the present day, on the edge of America's almost vanished frontier. More immediately came the Great Awakening, as a direct, perhaps an inevitable, sequel. As this spiritual hurricane swept over New England in the 1740's, neither Jonathan Edwards nor those who first learned his name on the title page of his thin volume, *A Faithful Narrative,* had any idea that upon his shoulders more than those of any other American rested the responsibilty for what was happening.

Up to the time he dedicated his new meetinghouse, there had been only one check to the favorable recognition which came to him during his first decade of ministerial labors. This had to do, not with the revival in his own parish, but with the notorious Breck case of 1735 and 1736. In fact, this sensational affair was one contributing cause to the ending of the revival, not only in Northampton but throughout Hampshire County, as pulpit and pew concerned themselves with one of the first major scandals in the church life of their immediate neighborhood. Robert Breck, a young liberal, had been called as minister by the Springfield congregation. The Hampshire Association, having reason as they thought to doubt his orthodoxy, had opposed his ordination, whereupon the Springfield congregation, resenting neighborhood interference in their affairs, had called a council of Boston ministers to hear the charges and, if they could be overthrown, to proceed with the ordination. This council convened October 7, 1735. At the very moment Robert Breck arose to answer the charges as stated, he was arrested by the civil authorities and carried off to jail, presumably at the instigation of Thomas Clap, minister at Windham, who had been spokesman for the Hampshire Association in preferring the charges. In 1735 such an indignity to the cloth as civil arrest and imprisonment was sufficiently unaccustomed to let loose an avalanche of protest, and before the affair was concluded the Massachusetts General Assembly had taken a hand and passed a vote of censure against the Hampshire Association for their interference in parish concerns. Meanwhile, Robert Breck had also been duly ordained and had come to take his seat among the country ministers who had raised the furor against him.

Jonathan Edwards' part in this unhappy series of confusions had been the drawing up of the defence of the Hampshire Association, after the vote of censure against its procedure had been passed by the Massachusetts General Assembly. He had not been present at the October Council at which Robert Breck had been arrested, and unkindly enough, in view of the sequel, was made a member of the Association committee to deal with the case only, in the words of the Minutes,

"to Remove the Difficulty of the Com^{tee} consisting of an Even Number".[21]

Nevertheless, he wrote the defence and was sharply criticized for it. As the years went on, the names of the instigators were forgotten, but because the defence was in print his part was remembered against him by Robert Breck and by all those who had been on his side in this brief though violent battle. Really, it was the Brattle Street Church fight over again, for although in the beginning Robert Breck had been suspected of an Arminian taint, the affair of doctrine had speedily been subordinated to debate over authority. Who has it? The individual church or an association of ministers? Long before this issue was clearly defined in the popular mind, Jonathan Edwards had put himself publicly on the side destined to lose. He had also made personal enemies, who would later have him in their power. The Breck affair was a sad scandal; but unfortunately it cannot be left buried in the attacks and defences it provoked, if the most bitter church battle of the next decade and some of the more virulent personal animosities which helped to ruin the career of Jonathan Edwards are to be understood.

Coincident with his first fame as one highly favored of God in the salvation of many had come the beginnings of that hostility which was to disrupt his peace for the remainder of his life. But for him the poisons worked slowly. Still greater triumphs than the 1735 revival were to come first.

Chapter 9

The Great Awakening

IN THE religious life of America, the year 1740 marks an end and a beginning. Current notions of religious experience underwent swift, determining change. The relation of the church to the community, the minister to his flock, one congregation to another—in fact, the whole structure of community life—was sharply and permanently altered. The Great Awakening was an upheaval. It destroyed much that was good, encouraged lamentable excesses, and ushered in an era of bitterness and calumny unparalleled in American religious history.

But that was by no means all. This revival, or rather series of revivals, vitalized afresh the religious experiences of the average man, and gave to the doctrines and forms of the church an intensely new personal meaning. It poured new life and energy into that which had grown stale and shrivelled. Its very destructiveness testified to the exuberance of the new life principle. According to men's capacities, their minds were stirred and their old thought patterns broken up so that they were forced to reshape the loyalties by which they lived. Somewhat too suddenly also, it gave them a startling new sense of their own power in group action. For these and many other reasons, the Great Awakening, in spite of all its extravagances and tragic mistakes, was the most potent, constructive force in American life during the mid-century.

At first glance, it seemed to come suddenly, and to be traceable to a single cause. A young stranger, George Whitefield, took ship from London,[1] preached in a hundred American towns and villages, and left a millennium behind him. Looked at more closely, however, the amazing chapter of which he was the leading figure appears only as the climax in a long process of change. Without George Whitefield or his like, the sudden phenomenon of 1740-41 might never have come to pass. The change might not have been cataclysmic at all; but, in some form or other, change was imminent. Whitefield's contribution was to make it spectacular. The wave of hysteria which swept over America from 1740 to 1745 was largely his doing, but the inner movements of change which came to open expression during those years owed little to his evangelism. Long before he came the currents had been shifting, as men had grown restive under the old system and wavered in their loyalty. Momentarily, Whitefield sent them by scores back into the fold, unaware that in their frantic desire for personal salvation they were not returning to the old loyalty at all, but responding to a new spirit in a new day. Under fire, he called himself a Calvinist, but his preaching emphasis was essentially democratic. Salvation was for all who would have it. In preaching a "whosoever will" doctrine at this particular moment, he gave a religious application to certain vague impulses toward democracy and turned an individualism as yet inarticulate into a gospel of personal safety. As the older ministry saw it, this was a return to the fabled piety of colonial days. In reality, it was a step toward 1776.

His personal triumph was unparalleled in American pulpit history. Briefly, he held the center of all stages and was crowned with more laurels than any alien who had yet set foot on American soil. As he made triumphant progress from village to village, he was received as no less than an "angel of God". Men of essential greatness are not required for such rôles, and Whitefield was not a great man. Unquestionably he had great powers, but he was not a great man. Colossally egotistical, intellectually shallow and lazy, he was unimpeachably sincere. He believed what he preached. Therein lay his power. In addition, he possessed enormous physical energy, extraordinary ability to play on the emotions of men, and oratorical talents nothing short of amazing. As he proceeded from meetinghouse to meetinghouse, his glory mounted higher and higher, until those who followed him lost all sense of rational discrimination. The story of his amazing pilgrimage through New England in 1740 reads like fictionized biography of the age of the Crusades, not solid history of eighteenth century America.

Unrolled as a panorama of the past, this prostration of whole communities before one man presents no enigma. It might easily have been predicted. At the moment of his coming America, and especially New England, was the likeliest soil in the whole world for his particular gospel. Religion was still very important to the average man, and community life organized to keep it so. Moreover, he came with a gospel sufficiently old to be easily understood and sufficiently new to provide the savor of novelty. The pew was well grounded in doctrine; the plan of salvation was as familiar as the alphabet. Without disturbing the structure of belief as his hearers understood it, he made it seem new by merely changing the emphasis. New England was also conscious of her long apostasy. It was the most threadbare of stories. Men intended to lay aside their "worldliness" and all the other sins of which they were accused; they intended to make sure of heaven, but the time had not yet come. As the clergy said, they were "too comfortable in their sins." Whitefield provided the necessity for immediacy. Under his impassioned preaching each hearer felt himself alone in the whole universe pursued of God. If he were to escape damnation and obtain the key to heaven, he must do it today. After the sun set, it would be too late. Thus are revivals of religion born in all ages.

No American preacher would have been equal to the task. It required an outside stimulus and the dynamic of an unfamiliar personality to bring about a stampede of such proportions. Not if the meetinghouse gallery had fallen a second time could Jonathan Edwards have put such compulsion on his hearers. A new voice must speak, but the audience was waiting. For more than three years all churchgoing New England had yearned for a revival to match Northampton's, and they knew the signs. Seldom has it fallen to the lot of an evangelist to find his way so excellently prepared. George Whitefield burst upon the American scene with almost everything in his favor; the spadework had all been done, and more. He did not even plant; he merely put in his sickle and claimed the harvest.

Advance notices of his coming were almost wholly favorable. For over a year the Boston papers had been printing accounts of his phenomenal success in England, always with much emphasis on the behavior of his audiences. His work among the British colliers was almost as well known in New England church circles as the Northampton revival. In 1740 his immediate arrival in Boston was preceded by the publication of letters from London ministers testifying to his powers, by announcement of the American publication of his sermons, and by a statement of his own large plans for the evangelization of America. Adverse accounts from London were omitted, either because they were not known to exist or because Boston papers of that date would not have dared to print such scurrility concerning an emissary of God. London had no such scruples. Whitefield's departure in 1739 had been labelled a good riddance, his audiences characterized as infatuated lunatics, and his motives in collecting funds for the

Georgia orphanage impugned. The *Daily Post* of May 12, 1739, had reported that his preaching had given such disgust to the civil magistrates that the Lord Mayor had forbidden him to erect his stage in London, adding that pickpockets did a thriving business in his auditory, their gleanings exceeding the donations left on the collection plate.[2] The issue for June 22, 1739, printed a rumor that he had fallen down dead.

He was not even accorded the dignity of serious criticism, but constantly made ridiculous as the target of abusive rhymes and unseemly jests. His replies to such attacks only made him more ridiculous, as he did not have the wisdom to perceive. His collecting of money was criticized more than his preaching. When a hospital fund was languishing in 1740 *Hooker's Weekly Miscellany* suggested that Mr. Whitefield might be sent for in order that he might "lye, prevaricate with Infants, Drunken Folks, Ideots and Madmen". He might "even go so far as to rave, stare, foam, beat his Breast", by way of adding to the entertainment. There is much in the same vein.[3] The contrast between the London farewell of 1740 and the Boston welcome is almost ludicrous.

To what extent his "publicity" on this first tour was supervised is not clear; but that some favorable control was exercised is apparent from the *Journal* of William Seward, his "companion in travel", who speaks of "writing my dear friend Whitefield's letter over for the press", and of dealing with the irate Philadelphia printers who objected to his statement that Whitefield's preaching had hurt the dancing-school business in that city.[4] In the light of such admissions, one rates Seward a good press agent and goes elsewhere for the whole truth. The publication in Boston, shortly before he arrived, of the *Directions How to Hear Sermons Preach'd by the Rev. Mr. George Whitefield* and also of the first instalment of his *Journal* (from England to Philadelphia) was well planned. For an age not surfeited with serial excitements, the phrase "To be continued", at the end of the instalment, was an adroit stroke.

After he arrived press notices were admirably calculated to keep public curiosity at its zenith, and to guarantee a continuance of the hysteria which attended his every appearance. Always the same details were emphasized: the size of the audience, the distance many had travelled to hear him, the fact that they had stood in the rain, or assembled at five A.M., that many had fainted, that the outcries of the repentant had drowned the voice of the speaker, and that the collection plate had not been large enough for the offerings poured into it. As a result, from the hour Whitefield set foot in a town, those who came to hear him felt obliged to outdo all previous records of faintings, shriekings, and souls added to the kingdom with great clamor. The cumulative effect of such advance preparation became almost insupportable as days passed and the list of towns visited lengthened. Had he remained longer in the same town, men's sense of discrimination would have been awakened—they would have passed judgment on him and on themselves alike; but before they had been allowed two consecutive nights' sleep he was away to the next village to better expectation once more. Otherwise, his fame could not have lasted a fortnight. He needed a new flock and a fresh pasture every forty-eight hours. While the holiday was on, nothing mattered but to make sure of heaven; but with shops reopened and life going on as usual, men wondered at their own fears and postponed repentance. The nature of Whitefield's extraordinary talents made this inevitable. His power was of the moment, and the moment only.

His triumphal tour of New England in 1740 lasted a little over a month. He arrived in Boston September 18th, spent ten days there and in the immediate neighborhood, went to Northampton, where he remained four days, and then turned southward through Connecticut and back to Philadelphia. On the day of his arrival in Boston, he was met on the road by a committee of ministers, who conducted him into the city with great acclaim. Those who had doubts (and there were such) kept silent. The city was his.

Then began a veritable "week of Sabbaths". He preached first to a "vast Congregation" at Dr. Colman's, then to five thousand on the Common, and to eight thousand in the fields. For ten days he went to church after church in rapid succession, thousands at his heels, "admired and followed beyond any man that ever was in America".[5] Dr. Colman's aptly chosen text, "Who are these that fly as a Cloud, and as doves to their windows?" [6] was true day after day, as the excitement grew more and more tense. On the fifth day a tragic accident increased the sensationalism. In Dr. Checkley's meetinghouse, someone broke a board to improvise a seat for himself. Instantly, remembering Northampton, someone cried out that the gallery was falling, and in the panic that ensued, three were killed, two more died almost immediately, and many were injured. Whitefield wrote:

"But God was pleased to give me Presence of Mind; so that I gave Notice I would immediately preach upon the Common".[7]

In Boston he had the support of the majority of the leaders among the clergy: Thomas Prince, Robert Abercrombie, William Hobby, Thomas Foxcroft, Benjamin Colman, and many others. Charles Chauncy was almost solitary in his opposition. Those who favored him opened their pulpits and were generous in their sympathy and coöperation, in spite of minor qualms, confessed later. Harvard College received him hospitably, in spite of deeper qualms. Men of affairs gave him audience, showed him the courtesies of their station and, if report be true, more than once unbent from their magisterial dignities to kiss him farewell or be "bathed in tears" at his departure. As to the citizenry, they not only heard him gladly but, while he was in range, would hear no other, nor listen to one word in his dispraise. So charmed were they "with his Manner of Address, that they shut up their Shops, forgot their secular Business, laid aside their Schemes for the world; and the oftener he preached, the keener edge he seem'd to put upon their Desires of Hearing him again".[8] He was indeed and in truth the "Wonder of the age".

The innovations of his method were half the source of his magic. In a week he had changed the whole definition of preaching and pulpit behavior. Instead of doctrine logically stated, proved, applied, according to a carefully prepared plan of argument, he dramatized both the biblical narrative and the application, spoke entirely without notes, made violent gestures, laughed, sang, shed public tears, and literally took New England by storm. Nothing like this had ever happened in the name of religion. American meetinghouses had often enough been the scene of drama, but it had never before come by way of the sermon. Preaching had been a solemn exercise. Sermons had been made according to the pattern. Here was a preacher who substituted human interest stories for sober logic, turned his pulpit into a stage and gave churchgoing America its first taste of theatre under the flag of salvation. Boston's whole routine of life was distorted by the strangeness of going to meeting at three A.M. in order not to be shut out at six, of closing shops at midday in order to hear another sermon, and, perhaps strangest of all for men and women accustomed to decorum in all things churchly, of hearing the gospel preached in the open fields. These novelties alone were sufficient to turn him into the Pied Piper he became in 1740.

New England had always had ears for sermons well spoken, and had approved preachers powerful in tones as well as in truth, but Whitefield's powers of voice were in a new category. David Garrick's alleged remark that he would give a hundred guineas if only he might say "Oh", as Whitefield uttered it, Lord Chesterfield's famous jest of tears wrung from men's eyes at the manipulation of Whitefield's tongue over the syllables *Mes-o-po-ta-mi-a*, Lord Bolingbroke's verdict, "the most commanding eloquence I ever heard in any person," and Hume's remark that it was worth going twenty miles to hear him, suggest, among many others, that only hyperbole could do justice to his powers of oratory and emotional compulsion. Of all his endowments for evangelism, his superb voice was the gift of God, *par excellence*. It had music, flexibility, volume.

"How awfully, with what Thunder and Sound did he discharge the Artillery of Heaven upon us?" [9] wrote Dr. Colman, thinking to praise.

His imagination was as agile as his body, his sensitiveness to the mood of an audience unerring. Had he chosen the footlights instead of the pulpit, he might have shared honors with Garrick and Cibber. He conquered not by force of intellect (for he was not a thinker) nor by spirituality (for he was not a spiritual man), but by the tones, the oratorical wizardry, the personal magnetism he could exert over an audience, particularly if it numbered thousands. It requires only to read his sermons in print to be convinced that his powers were chiefly of the platform. Lacking the golden tones, the sprightly imagination which drew pictures to the life, his pages are as dull as the portfolios of ministerial dispute which they incited. His theology is scaled down to the comprehension of twelve-year-olds (perhaps rightly). He repeated himself endlessly. Everything he had to say in a lifetime he said in any one sermon. Yet he was content to say it over three times daily, if only he had opportunity. The remark in Ezra Stiles' *Journal*,

"Mr. Whitefield preached about Seventeen Thousand Discourses",

would have pleased him, for impressive totals were music in his ears, and round number sufficient.

His appeal for the Bethesda Orphanage provided another element of novelty. He was at his best when picturing the woes of the downtrodden; here was a concrete need, and a need on the American side of the ocean. Moreover, the collection plate gave opportunity for overwrought emotions to express themselves in tangible form, and thus became both a climax and a relief to the revival tension. One remembers also that this same collection plate had much to do with the wave of humanitarianism which swept over America a decade later.

The suddenness of his triumph disarmed even the skeptical and caused them to hold their doubts in abeyance. They had prayed for a revival, and here it was. Not until it was all over did the more discerning quite realize what had been lost along with these unparalleled gains.

"From the days of righteous Abel to the days of pious Whitefield",[11]

as spoken in awe and admiration by the unthinking, had a grain of truth. He had indeed begun a new era and what had been was no more.

The whole story is as understandable for Whitefield as for the crowds which paid him such extravagant honor. No wonder he expanded under such adulation. Accustomed to being heralded as a nuisance, his preaching branded as acceptable only to brainless fools, he was now the "great Mr. Whitefield," to whom even magistrates were respectful. The homage of deck hands, colliers, and apprentices, he knew; but to be invited to sit down in conference with such men as Thomas Prince and Benjamin Colman was a new experience. Momentarily, the favor of such men liberated and dignified him; but he was not able to maintain himself long on this higher level. He lacked the inner resources, and he had already willingly accustomed himself to the easy acclaim of the unthinking. To him their homage was proof of the favor of God. "The mention of my Departure was a Grief to many," he could write,[12] and believe it. Denouncement by his enemies was but another proof which added also the glory of martyrdom. When he was arrested in Charlestown, he wrote in his *Journal*:

"Blessed be God for this further Honour: My Soul rejoices in it. I think *this* may be called PERSECUTION. I think it is for *Righteousness* Sake. . . . Father, forgive my Persecutors. They know not what they do".[13]

He could also write this, believe it, and in his own spirit be blameless for so doing.

The tenacity with which throughout his life he held to an ambition crystallized in his early twenties is one of the most amazing things about him. It is also disappointing, for he allowed this ambition to prevent his own growth. Year after year, despite the varied and crowded experiences which were his, he remained singularly undeveloped. His sermons, letters, published pamphlets at the end of his life show no enlargement of view, no deepening and maturing of wisdom, no reshaping of his own purposes in line with the rich experiences of his life. Success had come too early. Continuation of the same kind of success was too easy.

Preaching was his one thought, his one desire. To feel himself "filled with the Spirit", words coming from his lips unpremeditated, and to see hundreds before him moved to tears by his power—this was his one delight. In his zeal to preach he seemed completely oblivious to the needs of his body. His *Journals* are full of references to exhaustion, illness, inability to eat, to sleep; and yet the preaching program went on, unabated, the totals mounting. On his way to Springfield after his Northampton visit, he was stunned by a fall from his horse; but, having recovered consciousness and strength enough to proceed, he turned the experience into emotional exaltation which registered itself in eloquence, while he preached on schedule. If he preached while suffering intense pain, the greater the glory; hence he continued to neglect his body. That he had rare courage, there is no denying. When sea voyages meant uncertainty and prolonged hardship, he spent two full years of his life *en route* to and from America.

The genuineness of his own religious experience and the integrity of his zeal for other men's salvation are also not to be questioned. Even his extravagant humility may have been sincere: when he said, "It is all God", he probably thought it was. At the time of his 1740 triumph, he was only twenty-five years old—a fact that has too often been forgotten in making up his account. Still in the first fervor of his own religious awakening, newly aware of his power over men, and unfortified with a capacity for cool judgment, he was the easy and defenceless victim of a popularity seldom paralleled in the history of preaching and seldom so well deserved. Would a man twice his age have been equal to the temptations?

In contemporary records his story is usually set down in superlatives, either by his most ardent supporters or by his most virulent enemies. There were just a few men, however, who were able in the midst of the excitement to speak in a quite natural tone of voice, and to appraise him judicially. The verdict of Tutor Flynt of Harvard, a man of solid sense and an academic conscience for fact, needs no revision after two hundred years. While Whitefield was still in the precincts, Tutor Flynt wrote that he was old-fashioned in his logic, neither rational nor argumentative in his discourses,

"not much acquainted with books—wch makes me wonder at his positive & dogmatical way of expressing himself in some things. . . .
"I think he is a composition of a great deal of good & some bad and I pray God to grant Success to what is well designed & asked by him".[14]

There were others who expressed doubts or even dared to speak of his failings; but out of deference to the ministers who opened their pulpits to him, and to the cause he represented, these men kept their adverse opinions to themselves or wrote them down in diaries to see the light lifetimes later. Jonathan Mayhew's entry "I heard him once, and it was as low, confused, puerile, conceited, ill-natured, enthusiastic a performance as I ever heard",[15] was not what New England cared to hear in 1740. Benjamin Colman's account of Harvard students "full of God", not seven out of a hundred unaffected, "the voice of prayer and praise filling their chambers, and their fervency, joy and seriousness sitting visibly on their faces",[16] told the story as men wished to hear it. Had men like Jonathan Mayhew, Benjamin Lynde, or President Holyoke of Harvard spoken out openly in 1740, as they did later, few would have listened. It is the majority approval which directs social change, and in 1740 majority approval was with George Whitefield, in whose presence the multitudes were as plastic as the fabled clay.

Final truth concerning this amazing man and the movement he inspired goes considerably beyond the facts. He was the most spectacular and also the most paradoxical element in the whole cataclysm he induced, but that is not the whole story. One might not hope to find a better example of his own preachment that men may be used of God to do greater than they know. The statue in his honor in the dormitory quadrangle of the University of Pennsylvania, with its inscription,

"Zealous advocate and patron of higher education in the American colonies", is as richly deserved as the tributes to his preaching power and to his pioneer part in American philanthropic enterprise. He would have been as incapable of directing wisely the churches and colleges he helped to bring into being as he proved to be in the sad affair of the Bethesda Orphanage, which he sponsored. He was a beginner, and other men must work out the details; but in an imposing list of American institutions, except for him, they might not have had the chance.

The visit to Northampton came immediately after the ten-day triumph in Boston. He arrived on Friday, October 17th, and remained as a guest in the Edwards home until Monday evening. His own *Journal* preserves the only record of this four-day visit, significant as the first and, so far as is recorded, only meeting of the two men. On Jonathan Edwards' side, it had been eagerly anticipated. Only a week before, he had written to Eleazar Wheelock of the "sorrowfully dull & dead time" [17] in his own parish and of his hope that the coming of Whitefield might be blessed to the good of his own soul and the souls of his people. His own "low state of health" was probably the reason he had not gone to Boston to see the great ingathering for himself.

One might hope for fuller details of this week-end visit. Did Jonathan Edwards' previously expressed fears lest "Satan get any advantage of him", gain any support? Did he observe the flaws in argument, the dogmatical assertions, the sketchy knowledge, the obvious response to the moment in lieu of careful preparation? Was he, like Benjamin Colman, offended by the "harsher epithets and Expressions which dropt from his lips"? [18] If so, did the emotional effect which Whitefield induced counterbalance these flaws? There is no record. Perhaps the answer is that Whitefield used no "harsher epithets" in Northampton. Extraordinarily sensitive to atmosphere as he was, he may have felt himself in no mood for harshness while in the company of Jonathan Edwards. From his own record it is clear that something in the quality of this man affected him. "Dear Mr. Edwards", he called him after one day's acquaintance, characterizing him as

"a solid, excellent Christian, but at present weak in Body. I think, I may say I have not seen his Fellow in all New England. When I came into his Pulpit, I found my Heart drawn out to talk of scarce any Thing besides the Consolations and Privileges of Saints, and the plentiful Effusion of the Spirit upon the Hearts of Believers. And, when I came to remind them of their former Experiences, and how zealous and lively they were at that Time, both Minister and People wept much; and the Holy Ghost enabled me to speak with a great deal of Power".[19]

He preached four times from the Northampton pulpit and once at the parsonage; accompanied by his host, he made the journey to Hatfield, where he also preached. On Saturday morning, at Jonathan Edwards' request, he talked and prayed with "his little Children, who were much affected". All this gave many opportunities for conversation and for taking the measure of this much-talked-of guest. It would have been strange if Jonathan Edwards had not made unfavorable observations in several particulars; but if so he kept his verdict to himself, except to reveal later that he had remonstrated with Whitefield concerning his "Enthusiastic views".[20] Essentially, however, the two were in accord.

To Whitefield, Northampton was marked for special remembrance for Jonathan Edwards' sake. He wrote:

"Our Lord seem'd to keep the good Wine till the last. I have not seen four such gracious Meetings together since my Arrival".[21]

Souls had been savingly wrought upon; there had been much weeping. "Dear Mr. Edwards" himself had wept "during the whole time of exercise" on Sunday morning. Whitefield's own emotions had been powerfully stirred. This was the usual formula for success. The fact that in his own record he accented the Northampton visit not only for these revival manifestations but also for the felicity of the Edwards home is perhaps significant. On tour he spent his days and nights in ministers' homes, and yet something in the King Street parsonage seemed to call for special remark. For one to whom the normal relationships of life were unimportant, and to whom praise of others did not come easily, his tribute is tribute indeed. One may forgive the application to his own wifeless state for the sake of the few sentences which do not follow his usual pattern for *Journal* entries:

"Oct. 19, 1740.
"Felt wonderful Satisfaction in being at the House of Mr. *Edwards*. He is a Son himself, and hath also a Daughter of *Abraham* for his wife. A sweeter Couple I have not yet seen. Their Children were dressed not in Silks and Satins, but plain, as becomes the Children of those who, in all Things, ought to be Examples of Christian Simplicity. She is a Woman adorn'd with

a meek and quiet Spirit, talked feelingly and solidly of the Things of God, and seemed to be such a Help meet for her Husband, that she caused me to renew those Prayers, which, for many Months, I have put up to God, that he would be pleased to send me a Daughter of *Abraham* to be my Wife. I find, upon many accounts, it is my Duty to marry. Lord I desire to have no Choice of my own Thou knowest my Circumstances; thou knowest I only desire to marry in and for thee".[22]

When he departed on Monday, Jonathan Edwards rode with him as far as East Windsor, where Whitefield said good-bye with "some inward Regret". This was the journey on which Whitefield confided his concern over an unconverted American ministry and his hope to send over a few country-men of his own to fill some places more worthily, a sugges-tion which in its later misquotation was to spoil Jonathan Edwards' memory of this week-end visit and embroil him in an ugly personal controversy. But that chapter was still some months distant. Whitefield proceeded southward through Con-necticut, to write a different revival story in each colony he passed through, and Jonathan Edwards turned toward home. The first chapter of the Great Awakening was over. Hence-forth, it would not be such "comfortable travelling toward heaven", but everyone was on march, and sound guidance was needed in New England as never before.

In the second stage, popular response increased beyond ministerial dream. Scores of parishes became centers of re-vival frenzy. Sermons were preached every night in the week, and there were private gatherings at all hours of the day. Meetinghouses were packed; conversion was the theme of the hour. Before one group dispersed, another assembled. Children forgot their night fears and walked miles through the woods to psalm singings. Young people left off their "frolicking" and met together for prayer. Increase and Cotton Mather had died too soon.

Boston set the example for outside leadership by inviting, soon after Whitefield's departure, his friend, Gilbert Tennent of New Jersey [23] to carry on the "great work". Tennent ar-rived on December 13th and found not only Boston but all of New England in a favorable mood for his quite different tactics. Lacking Whitefield's range of oratorical talents, and also the personal qualities which had endeared him to his audiences and all but deified him in their eyes, Tennent chose literally to frighten men into salvation. His pulpit manners were violent instead of persuasive. As Esther Burr remarked in her *Journal,* he "would fain preach 'em to death if he could". His one theme was hell-fire and damnation. He raged, shouted, stamped, roared, and set nerves on edge beyond endurance. Henceforth, this was to be the revival emphasis. Conversion was not to be the beginning of a new life; it was a scramble to safety, and the way led through bedlam.

Accounts of what followed are full of contradiction. Benjamin Colman, who believed this to be a genuine work of God, wrote, speaking for the spring and summer of 1741, "the very face of the town seems to be altered". According to a pamphlet "Christ riding in his chariot of salvation", New England had indeed become God's holy city. Taverns were empty; dancing schools languished; profanity ceased. Ministers who deplored the sensationalism and the unseemly practices of Gilbert Tennent and his brother William, wrote the exact opposite. It was all a show of religion instead of the substance. Not one convert in a hundred led a changed life. The whole story was stuffed with abominable lies. From objective fact, as recorded in many contemporary accounts, the truth seems to be that for the greater part of a year after Whitefield's coming, New England's concern for religion was very intense, reaching a peak during the spring and summer of 1741. There is no question also that this intensity gave rise to many extravagances, and that these were in turn increased by the notice they received. Samuel Finley's sermon, *Christ Triumphing and Satan Raging,* would have made fitting headline for a truthful news report.

Jonathan Edwards' Enfield sermon belongs to this highest pitch of revival enthusiasm. It was preached July 8, 1741. All conditions were favorable for a very "awakening" response. The audience was a rural congregation, the preacher a stranger, except that his name was associated with revival power. Tradition says that Jonathan Edwards was not the guest-speaker whom the congregation had assembled to hear on this occasion, but a last-minute substitute. For the sake of a better story, one hopes this is true, as it very well may be. The ministry was all on horseback during the summer of 1741, with sermons in their pockets for any emergency invitation. The theme was in line with the newest revival emphasis, the wrath of God and the imminence of everlasting punishment. Preparation for effective response to such a theme was excellent, for there had been much talk that the end of the world was nigh. The flocking into the kingdom on every side was one of the signs. The text, "Their foot shall slide in due time", was as good as an oracle.

He had already preached three times from this same text. The first two sermons are undated; the third had been preached in Northampton immediately before the Enfield occasion. All three are distinctly different treatments of the same theme.[24] In the first sermon, obviously early, he had presented the magnificence of God's wrath. It would be a glorious sight to see the world burn up in demonstration of such majestic power. The sermon ends with the contrasting picture of how it will be with those who are safe.

In the second sermon, he developed the same theme from the point of view of man. Taking as his Doctrine, "The punishment of wicked men generally comes upon them when they don't expect it", he pictured men in their false assurance of safety. They flatter themselves that they will never be punished; they think getting out of the path of destruction is in their own power; they trust in their self-righteousness, and in the fact of their baptism. But God is swift and terrible. In the midst of their security comes punishment. The third sermon, marked preached at Northampton, June, 1741, is essentially the same as the Enfield sermon, although slightly less expanded than the printed version. It exists in two drafts, one less fully developed than the other.

The wrath of God was one of the best possible themes for an exhibition of Jonathan Edwards' peculiar power as a preacher, as many previous successes had shown. In this particular sermon he chose to develop the theme not by arguing the justice of God's wrath or presenting its history through biblical instances. He took no time to describe the sensations of the doomed. Taking the eternal consequences of God's wrath for granted, he made it seem personal and immediate for each member of the congregation seated before him. Obliterating the world outside the meetinghouse walls, and foreshortening time until the final judgment was not eons hence but tomorrow and possibly today, he sent each unconverted Enfield citizen to his well-deserved doom. Nothing but God's own hand held him back. God was very angry. At any minute he might loose his hold. Then the feet would slide. In all parts of the land he was gathering in his elect. Possibly all those ever to be saved in this generation would soon be brought in, and thereafter all hope of fleeing the divine wrath would forever be past. Some of those sitting in the pews would remember this very discourse in hell. If we knew who they were . . . But at that point, he might as well have called the names. His hearers knew who they were, as they caught hold of the pillars of the building and cried out in helpless panic.

"A most Terrible sermon, wch should have had a word of Gospell at ye end it, tho I think tis all true",[25] wrote Isaac Watts in his copy of the printed sermon. Jonathan Edwards had added such a word many times, but today he allowed divine wrath to stand unrelieved.

Time has undoubtedly added to the magnitude of the effect this sermon produced, to the greater glory of Jonathan Edwards, although contemporary accounts also are written in superlatives. Stephen Williams tells the story in some detail, under date of July 8th, the day on which the sermon was preached.

"We went over to Enfl— where we met dear M^r E— of N— H— who preach^d a most awakening sermon from these words— Deut. 32-35 and before sermon was done—there was a great moaning & crying out through ye whole House— What Shall I do to be Sav^d—oh I am going to Hell— Oh what shall I do for Christ &c. &c. So y^t ye minister was obliged to desist—ye shrieks & cry^s were piercing & Amazing—after Some time of waiting the Congregation were Still so y^t a prayer was made by Mr W. & after that we descend^d from the pulpitt and discours^d with the people—Some in one place and Some in another—and Amazing and Astonishing ye power God was seen—& Several Souls were hopefully wrought upon yt night. & oh ye cheerfulness and pleasantness of their countenances yt receiv^d comfort—oh yt God wd strengthen and confirm—we sung an hymn & pray^d & dismiss^d ye Assembly".[26]

The best tribute to the power of Jonathan Edwards as a preacher of the last judgment does not concern the Enfield occasion. It is the testimony of Nehemiah Strong of Northampton on the series of sermons preached in the home pulpit in 1739 on the *History of Redemption*. When the preacher came to that part of the sermon which had to do with God's final judgment, the mind of Nehemiah Strong was wrought up to such a pitch that he expected

"without one thought to the contrary, the awful scene to be unfolded on that day, and in that place. . . . Accordingly, he waited with the deepest and most solemn solicitude to hear the trumpet sound and the archangel call; to see the graves open, the dead arise, and the Judge descend in the glory of his Father, with all his holy angels; and was deeply disappointed, when the day terminated, and left the world in its usual state of tranquillity".[27]

Could Dante do more? In fact, one contemplates Dante's hell with pleasurable sensations, knowing it is Dante's, a safely remote place of the imagination. Jonathan Edwards not only made it real enough to be found in the atlas, but made those consigned to it personally responsible for being there. It would have been difficult for those who believed the doctrine, ancestrally as it were, to walk away from the finality of their doom, as he pronounced it, into the sunlight of a normal day.

Perhaps one such success is more important than a thousand ordinary Sunday mornings in one's own pulpit. Perhaps not. The Enfield picture does not show the whole man, but as an abridgment of the Great Awakening in its more worthy chapter, this sermon deserves to be the landmark it has become in American religious history.

Chapter 10

Aftermath

SHORTLY after midsummer in 1741 the "Great Work" was suddenly ringed around with monstrous evils. The outpouring was not coming according to specifications. Ministers found themselves all at once faced by so many problems at every turning that they could take little joy in the abundant harvest which lay all around them.

Novelty had taken the place of inspiration. The pews having no demigod before whom to prostrate themselves, attempted to provide drama of their own making. When revival signs languished, they induced excitement by acting the form of it. Giving free rein to their emotions, they wept, shouted, fainted, went into convulsions, and rolled on the floor. Bodily manifestations became more important than a changed heart. A child screamed, and the revival was on in one parish; other parishes waited, alert for screams. Ministers who believed such behaviors to be counterfeit, were beside themselves, for to brand them counterfeit was to invite the cry, "Unconverted". In Boston, where it pleased God "to speak in a more soft and calm wind", fewer excesses were reported, but even Boston did not escape. Had Jonathan Edwards printed his *Faithful Narrative of the Surprizing Work of God* in 1741, it would not have seemed surprising at all. Excess had gone out of bounds, and only the spectacular seemed genuine.

Although Whitefield was temporarily out of the picture, he was to blame for much of this confusion. He had begun the vogue of breast-beatings and pulpit antics and had measured his own success by the number of outcries and repentant groans from the audience. Before his New England tour, ministers had gone sedately into their pulpits, their little sermon booklets in their pockets. Now they left their notes at home and endeavored to "spread their hands" as Whitefield had done. If no one cried out, the sermon was a failure. One minister who professed to deplore extravagance nevertheless reported, "The first screamings in these Parts on the Sabbath were under my preaching".[1] Charles Chauncy, who was of the opposition, probably felt quite safe in quoting the remark that on a certain occasion "the noise could be heard for a mile".[2]

It was all very disappointing. The ministers who had invited this clamor were men of dignity, most of them, but they had been unable to resist the popular tide. A little of the thumping literalism of Charles Wesley would have been the best dose that could have been administered. Always the first reasons he assigned for "fits in the congregation" were "humbug or gin". Having eliminated these, he was willing to consider a possible nobler cause; but he had sense enough to begin at the lower end. Unfortunately, the ministers who respected "bodily signs" did not, nor had they observed Whitefield's own methods very carefully. He had known how to invite a noisy demonstration from the audience, and then to make the clamor which drowned his voice contribute to his unique mastery of the situation. By a change of tone he could command a silence which impressed the groaners more than their own noise. Not so Messrs. Tennent and Tennent and their New England imitators. They could invite bedlam, but they could not stop it. As a result, the Great Awakening perished in its own noise.

Whitefield was also responsible for connecting in the popular mind the idea of a revival with the coming of a strange preacher. Previous to his visit, parishes had been content to listen to the village minister for life. If revivals came, he reaped his own harvest. The five revivals in Northampton prior to 1735 had been Solomon Stoddard's revivals, and had been so labelled in the popular memory. Whitefield had set a new fashion. The coming of Gilbert Tennent and his brother William had fixed it more firmly. After Tennent, came Davenport, Buel, and others. Jonathan Edwards went on preaching tours for weeks at a time. So did his brother ministers. By the summer of 1741, a ministerial migration was in progress, and pulpit as well as pew was enjoying the novelty of new faces, new responses, new methods. Sermons that had been fruitless at home became "very awakening" when preached under different conditions. It was all a little intoxicating. Only when the clergy returned home did they discover that their extramural successes had been a little too costly. In their absence their congregations had had ample opportunity to make comparisons; they had also heard some startling criticisms of their own pastor by visiting ministers who assumed Whitefield's prerogatives in denunciation and abuse. Soon talk began to turn upon the right of one minister to invade the parish of another. In the pews, there began to be rumors of separation. Ministers became alarmed and cancelled their engagements afield in order to protect their characters at home. It was high time.

Too late, in fact, for no sooner had the shepherds come home than the flocks began to wander. For this too Whitefield was partly responsible. Like John Wesley, he had advocated lay exhorting, urging new converts to tell their experiences publicly, and thereby bring others to repentance. He also encouraged women no longer to keep silent in the churches. At first there had been very little response to these counsels. So long as the pulpit provided novelty the pews were content to be audience; but as soon as the pulpit drama lagged they bethought themselves of these new rights and privileges. Confusion past the telling resulted. Of all the evils of the aftermath, "lay exhorting" was the most persistently disrupting to good order in the churches. Whitefield's willingness to honor humble means had let loose a monster.

Exhorters were for the most part young men of good voice and poor education. They soon discovered that their own parish was a poor theatre of action and sought new pastures, usually travelling in bands. Uninvited and unannounced, they entered a meetinghouse while a preaching service was in progress, stationed themselves at the four corners of the building and began to harangue the congregation. Naturally, they directed their efforts toward the sensationally minded and disaffected members in the congregation, their main object being to stir up those capable of being stirred. If the minister remonstrated, they denounced him as a hindrance to the "great work" and raised their voices higher. Usually there was enough sympathy with the intruders to render the minister helpless in quieting the tumult. The orderliness of mere preaching had grown too dull for the palate of 1742.

Ministerial correspondence, diaries, and other personal records supply abundant detail concerning this strange mélange of ignorance, "overbalancing Zeal for Religion" and dissatisfaction with things as they were. Men of sober judgment and temperate speech could content themselves only with superlatives, as they recounted this sudden reversal of what more than a hundred years of experience had established as decorum in the American meetinghouse.

"This behavior is not to be expressed by words," wrote one dignified layman, who could not believe the sight of his eyes or the din in his ears, as the exhorters took possession of the

meetinghouse on a Sunday morning. Dignity and sobriety
were helpless to quiet the uproar. While this New World
version of a one-time "Feast of Fools" was on, silence in the
meetinghouse was not to be invoked either from the desk or
from the deacon's pew. The floor belonged to anyone, and he
might keep it as long as his voice would last. A single phrase
was sufficient. An Ipswich diary describes a meeting in which
a man cried out, "Come to Christ", without intermission for
a half-hour; an old woman on the back seat denounced
lawyers for an equal space, in boisterous rivalry, while over
her head "a mean fellow preached".[3] What next? said those
who remembered Salem in the 1690's. Had they lived, they
would have found their answer in the patriotic excesses of
this same territory during the 1760's and '70's.

The ministers were almost solidly against these disorders,
but they had to walk carefully in their opposition, remembering that Whitefield had not invented lay preaching. John
Robinson himself had recognized the "gift of prophecy" as a
lay privilege, and so had John Cotton, although these men
would have found another name for the Babel of 1741-42.
There had been lay preachers in America prior to this time;
but as they had been chiefly Quakers, to whom New England
was unlawful territory, ministers were caught off their guard
and for the moment were sorely puzzled. Many of them
made the mistake of attempting to deal with the situation
authoritatively, whereas what was called for was tactful
leadership. The obstreperous element, in so far as it was
sincere, merely desired some participation in the work of the
church. Sitting in straight rows on Sunday was no longer
enough. John Wesley, who in the beginning took no more
kindly to lay preaching than the New England clergy, anticipated this desire and was wise enough to make a place for
lay preaching in his scheme of church organization. He set up
qualifications and assigned duties to his lay preachers, appoint-
ing honors and dignities commensurate. In the New England
church such changes would have meant a more fundamental
reorganization than could have been very quickly accomplished, even though it had been approved. Hence, the exhorters took things into their own hands and brought tumult
and confusion into the sanctuary.

It was not long before indecorum outdid itself under the
notion that the greater the clamor the more the spirit of God
was at work. Zeal was more important than knowledge. An
exhorter who could boast of no education was thought better

qualified to arouse sinners than the minister. A premium was likewise placed on youth and inexperience. A blind boy memorized Whitefield's sermons, spoke them with violent gestures, and was thought a great preacher. Little children declaimed in public concerning repentance and free grace. How could they do it, said their elders, except by the spirit of the Almighty?

The way out was of course to let the frenzy exhaust itself, as it very quickly did, first in Boston and then gradually in the smaller towns to the north and west. In more remote parishes, where the revival had come late, the tumult lingered on a little longer; but by the autumn of 1742 it was well past. If while the frenzy was at its height, the clergy had been wise enough not to antagonize their flocks, they might have emerged with their dignities less sullied; but, having made the mistake of answering hostility by reproof, they found themselves in a bad situation. Congregations were in no mood to be pastorally advised. They had begun to feel the power in their own hands, and whether ministers read the far-off signs or not, the days of pulpit authority were numbered. The worst mistake the clergy could possibly have made was to attempt to tighten the pastoral grip. They can hardly be blamed for trying to restore order, but their methods were poorly timed.

Temporarily the tussle of authority between pulpit and pew was kept from being a clear-cut issue by the controversy among ministers themselves as to the genuineness of the "Great Work". This controversy became more intense as a result of the excesses of James Davenport in the summer of 1742 and the publication of Whitefield's criticism of the American clergy in *Some Remarks on a Late Pamphlet,* published at about the same time. Those who had kept silent during the Tennent extravagances no longer felt need for restraint when James Davenport publicly burned religious books at New London in March, 1743. As the verdict of the Cambridge court stated at his trial, he was of unbalanced mind and to be pitied; [4] but he had done great mischief and injured a good cause irreparably. Something irremediable happened to evangelism when the police were obliged to step in and make arrests. As Charles Chauncy said, Davenport had brought the very word "conversion" into contempt. By writing pamphlets detailing his extravagances and demanding his retraction, point by point, the clergy also hurt the cause. They were to hurt it still more by their vitriolic internal warfare, for in the rapidly shifting meetinghouse drama, the year 1743 was to be the year of "sad divisions among ministers". The outpouring itself was over; the exhorters had exhausted their repertoire and lost their audience. Now the ministers had the stage. In the word of a diarist, who saw it coming months before, "The great awakening &c. seems to be degenerating into Strife and faction".[5]

Whitefield was very naturally the peg on which to hang grievances, since there was now no blinking the fact that he was responsible for much of the confusion. The appearance of the fourth instalment of his *Journal,* with its outspoken criticism of the American ministry, and the American publication of a pamphlet hostile to him, *The Trial of Mr. Whitefield's Spirit,*[6] forced men to take sides openly. The conservative element, quickly dubbed "Old Lights", arrayed themselves against his supporters, called New Lights, and something resembling civil war ensued. Old Lights battled with New Lights, both sides forgetting why churches exist. This is the work of God; support it, said the New Lights. This is not the work of God; suppress it, said the Old Lights. Whitefield's opponents, who out of respect for the cause had kept silent in 1740, now spoke out. His adherents made him even more of a hero *in absentia.* Unfortunately for any healing of the breach, both sides put their accusations in print. Pamphlets poured forth from Boston printing houses in a weekly flood. Merely to read the week's grist was a chore of proportions, let alone to answer it.

This paper warfare continued for months, minister answering minister in a sequel of bitterness discrediting in the extreme to those who so shortly before had joined prayers for the salvation of America. Apparently the dignity and effectiveness of nonresistance occurred to no one. Ministerial diaries, newspaper files, and other contemporary records are full of testimony to the sad quarrel. "The opposition is exceedingly virulent and mad", wrote one Thomas Smith in his *Journal* on May 26, 1743.[7] His adjectives fit the case exactly.

The ramifications of the dispute quickly went beyond the practices of Whitefield and the peace of the individual churches. There seemed no way to end the strife. The entire clergy found themselves in a hopeless tangle, for which the only real solution would have been to cut the knot and begin over again; but, that privilege being denied in an ongoing world, they merely wrote more pamphlets. A "sit-down" strike in the Boston printing houses from 1742 to 1745 would have done more for the cause of religion in America than any other imaginable blessing.

Even the civil authorities recognized the peril to religion. On February 9, 1742/3, Jonathan Law, Governor of Connecticut, and one of the few magistrates who had been on the side of Whitefield and the revival, issued a Proclamation calling for a day of fasting and prayer because of

"the unhappy Divisions and Contentions which still prevail, both among Ministers and People, in the Doctrines and Practice of Religion; and the bitter Spirit of Uncharitableness & Disorder which too much prevails among all Orders in the Land: All which calls for our deep Humiliation before the LORD. . . ."[8]

Similar action was taken by civil authorities in other colonies.

Jonathan Edwards' part in this unhappy warfare consisted in two treatises, *The Distinguishing Marks of a Work of the Spirit of God*, in 1741, and *Some Thoughts concerning the Present Revival of Religion in New England*, in 1742; the series of sermons preached in the same year, later to be made the basis of the *Treatise Concerning Religious Affections*, and his pamphlet controversy with Thomas Clap concerning Whitefield's alleged intention of sending over British clergymen to take the places of the unconverted American incumbents. Although classified among the New Lights, he consistently maintained a middle position, viewing with deep concern the increased emphasis on bodily manifestations—the shriekings, contortions, trances, prophesyings, and ecstatic deliriums—but insisting there might well be a connection between such manifestations and the unusual presence of divine power. It was not man's prerogative to judge in such matters. Ministers were watchmen of men's souls, not their bodies. If Christ had intended that they should count pulses, diagnose the tremblings, faintings, weepings, and convulsions of their flocks, he would have put some book in their hands which would have made them skilled anatomists and physicians. He did not do so; therefore let them concern themselves with souls, not with bodily symptoms.

He admitted that excesses had smeared the "great work", but to him they had not discredited it. Human nature itself was sufficient explanation for the lamentable extremes which were visible on every side. Nothing was happening that was not to be expected. There would be still more excess. If those who were disturbed overmuch

"wait to see a work of God without difficulties and stumbling blocks, it will be like the fool's waiting at the river side to have the water all run by".[9]

Men of balanced judgment should look not at these follies alone, but at the work considered "in the Lump". As for himself, on the basis of his own observation he was ready to declare that if this great stirring throughout the land were not in general the work of God, then

"We must throw away our Bibles, and give up revealed religion".[10]

In his belief, this was a "work much greater than any that has ever been in New England", and only the "beginning or forerunner of something vastly great". God had chosen the Old World as the honored place in which Christ was to be born in the flesh. Through the years it had also been honored with the blood of the martyrs. It would now appear that He had chosen the New World as the scene of that latter glory by which mankind was to be "renewed". The Great Awakening was the sign. America, and especially New England, was about to be turned into a paradise of God. Contrary to the way of nature, the Sun of righteousness was about to arise in the west. Earnestly he set forth the dangers and griefs of missing such an opportunity by failing to read aright the signs of the times. Those who refused to acknowledge the revival as the work of God were making this mistake. Let criticism cease and let the still greater glory of God be ushered in by promoting what was good in the work already accomplished. Through these arguments his own deep interest in current history as the fulfilment of Scripture prophecy, one of the major interests of his later years, begins to be apparent for the first time.

If the section entitled "The Nature of the Work in a particular Instance" is rightly assumed to be a description of the religious transports of Sarah Edwards, wife of Jonathan, his conviction that many of the so-called "excesses" may be wrongly interpreted is more easily understood. For the same reason, this piece becomes also an important chapter in his own more intimate story. "The person", as he calls the subject of these experiences, carefully and somewhat awkwardly avoiding all pronominal reference,

"has more than once continued for five or six hours together, without interruption, in a clear and lively view or sense of the infinite beauty and amiableness of Christ's person, and the heavenly sweetness of his transcendent love. So that, (to use the person's own expressions) the soul remained in a kind of heavenly elysium, and did as it were swim in the rays of Christ's love, like a little mote swimming in the beams of the sun that come in at a window. The heart was swallowed up in a kind of glow of Christ's love coming down as a constant stream of sweet light, at the same time the soul all flowing out in love to him; so that there seemed to be a constant flowing and reflowing from heart to heart. The soul dwelt on high, was lost in God, and seemed almost to leave the body. The mind dwelt in a pure delight that fed and satisfied it; enjoying pleasure without the least sting, or any interruption. And so far as the judgement and word of a person of discretion may be taken, what was enjoyed in each single minute of the whole space, which was many hours, was worth more than all the outward comfort and pleasure of the whole life put together; and this without being in any trance, or at all deprived of the exercise of the bodily senses. And this heavenly delight has been enjoyed for years together; though not frequently so long together, to such a height. Extraordinary views of divine things, and the religious affections, were frequently attended with very great effects on the body. Nature often sank under the weight of divine discoveries, and the strength of the body was taken away. The person was deprived of all ability to stand or speak. Sometimes the hands were clinched, and the flesh cold, but the senses remaining. Animal nature was often in a great emotion and agitation, and the soul so overcome with admiration, and a kind of omnipotent joy, as to cause the person, unavoidably, to leap with all the might, with joy and mighty exultation. The soul at the same time was so strongly drawn towards God and Christ in heaven, that it seemed to the person as though soul and body would, as it were of themselves, of necessity mount up, leave the earth, and ascend thither".[11]

Indications of date in the phrase "about seven years ago", place the beginning of these experiences in the 1735 revival, and the "near three years ago", prior to the coming of Whitefield, as is specifically stated. Since then they have been more frequent, particularly "about a year and a half ago, upon another new resignation of all to God", and again in the immediately preceding winter. Guarded hints toward the identity of the "person" appear in the details,

"not in the giddy age of youth, nor in a new convert, or unexperienced Christian, but in one that was converted about twentyseven years ago; and neither converted nor educated in that enthusiastic town of *Northampton*, (as some may be ready to call it) but in a town and family which none, that I know of, suspected of enthusiasm".[12]

There are also correspondences with his own earlier sketch of Sarah Edwards, particularly in the words,

"a wonderful access to God by prayer, as it were seeing him, and immediately conversing with him, as much oftentimes (to use the person's own expressions) as if Christ were here on earth, sitting on a visible throne, to be approached to and conversed with".[13]

This identification would seem to be confirmed by the many parallels between this account and the known recital of Sarah Edwards concerning her experiences during a revival season earlier in the same year, 1742. Jonathan Edwards was away from home at the time, and Samuel Buel, a brother minister, was in charge. It appears from her own record that she was the central figure in the meetinghouse drama, and that her bodily state under stress of her ecstasies was such as to cause alarm to some of her neighbors, who feared that the "effect might be fatal before Mr. Edwards' return".[14] Many of the excesses so much condemned by the conservative clergy—the faintings, cryings out, unavoidable leapings for joy, and the irresistible desire to tell others—were part of her story.

Nothing in Jonathan Edwards' own religious experiences matched these violent emotional disturbances, at least so far as the record goes. He confessed several times to being overcome by "floods of tears", which continued for an hour or so, but nothing more uncommon. The fact that his wife was given to these more extreme manifestations no doubt inclined him to a more hospitable attitude toward them, although his conviction that such demonstrations might be evidence of divine power went far deeper than loyalty to his own household. Even when religious emotion took forms impossible to one of Sarah Edwards' refinement, he still refused to judge. Human bodies were frail, and spiritual ecstasies might easily be insupportable.

"Such a bubble is too weak to bear a weight so vast", he wrote. For one of his dignity and restraint, such an attitude was something of a triumph.

In 1742 it also put him on the wrong side of the ministerial argument. In the excitement of debate, there was no middle ground. A man was either for or against. By leaving any room at all for emotional expression, he was unqualifiedly a New Light, who had said "Yes" when he should have said "No", with the result that his two carefully reasoned treatises were mere wasted words so far as any effective rebuke to extravagance was concerned. Neither those who were bringing the cause into disrepute by unseemly excesses nor their impassioned critics were in any frame of mind to consider the true signs and the false signs as he had so carefully listed them. He was on the wrong side. He spoke too late and too temperately. Besides, all New England remembered Phoebe Bartlett.

He also spoke too abstractly. It was highly colored incident, rich in objective detail, which was attracting the attention of 1742. What were the most bizarre excesses yet reported? Which "marvel" might most debatably be the devil's work instead of God's? Instead of satisfying popular appetite in these directions, Jonathan Edwards applied himself to a distinctly minority interest—the laws of human nature which lie behind these behaviors. Exactly what is the relation between "soul" and body? Exactly what do these supposed marvels mean in terms of the workings of man's mind? The "root and course of things" must be inquired into. By such speculations, which quickly lost him his contemporary audience, he gained the respect of another generation. By the time his son was able to think abstractly, these two treatises were of interest to religionists for the same reason they were neglected in 1742. Looked back upon today, they are important chapters in Jonathan Edwards' contribution to religious psychology.

In a word, he was concerned to distinguish between what is "imaginary" and what is "spiritual". To him there was no possible confusion. Imagination was one of the operations of that faculty of the mind currently known as "understanding". By it one perceived objects of the senses when those objects were not actually present. Rightly used, it was most helpful; but, allowed free rein, it would overbalance the other workings of this same faculty of the mind—understanding. The devil liked nothing better than to lead men on to such extravagances. Not that imagination was the devil's instrument only. God himself made use of it, sometimes causing "strong impressions" to be made on the imaginations of His saints. They saw visions; heard voices. These impressions were indirectly divine gifts, and often very extraordinary. To the Old Testament prophets, for example, God was as immediately and visibly "there" as

"we perceive one another's presence when we are talking face to face".

But this faculty, by which objects of sense seem present when they are not, is wholly natural. It is part of man's mental equipment as man. Things "spiritual" are quite otherwise. Conversion is a "sense of God in the heart"—a God-given faculty which has no counterpart in unredeemed man. It is supernatural. As between the two, Jonathan Edwards did not hesitate to declare:

"I had rather enjoy the sweet influences of the spirit, showing Christ's spiritual divine beauty, infinite grace, and dying love, drawing forth the sweet exercises of faith, divine love, sweet complacence, and humble joy in God, one quarter of an hour, than to have prophetical visions and revelations the whole year".[15]

This distinction, so fundamental to any understanding of his whole concept of religious experience, was not new to him in 1742. It had been both implied and directly expressed in the *Faithful Narrative* five years before; but, obscured by the emphasis on individual case-histories, it had been missed by his readers. By 1742, it was far clearer in his own mind. Meanwhile, he had been observing conversions as he had once observed spiders. How many kinds are there? What do these differences mean as to the basic laws of human nature and the divine plan? He would have still more to say of this in the *Religious Affections*.

In his pamphlet controversy with Thomas Clap he seems out of character. For the first and only time in his life he was airing a private grievance through the press. In the light of the circumstances, however, his procedure was not strange. Whitefield had been maligned over his signature and must be exonerated, no matter how distasteful the process:

"I had no other Way left for me to take [he wrote], tho' it was very contrary to my Inclination, but to go into the Press too, and from thence declare the Matter as it was, and publish those very Letters of mine, and endeavour to convince the World that you had greatly abused Mr. *Whitefield* and me".[16]

The circumstances back of this skirmish were embarrassing enough. Thomas Clap, Rector of Yale College, published a statement that upon Whitefield's visit to Northampton in 1740 he had confided to Jonathan Edwards a plan by which certain of the American clergy were to be replaced by British incumbents. Thomas Clap, for reasons of his own, had kept this inflammable item until the tide against Whitefield was well turned, although he claimed to have heard it at the time from a third person who also was present at the Whitefield-Edwards conference. The publication of Clap's statement naturally let loose a torrent. Civil as well as religious authorities were in a rage. Disgruntled laymen, forgetting their grievance against the minister, leaped to his defence. It was a case of American countrymen against a British invasion, and particularly against Whitefield for having suggested it. No previous charge had raised such a furor against him.

At the distance of two centuries, it would seem that an hour's conference between the disputants would have been a good way to get at the truth of the matter, but such was not the way of the 1740's. Both disputants took to the press, Clap leading off. Anyone who will take the trouble to reconstruct this utterly dead issue from the pamphlet remains, will be partially rewarded, on Jonathan Edwards' side, for the illustrations it holds of his clear-cut logic, his legal precision of phrase, his knifelike discriminations, and his tenacity in argument. One must honor his motive to exonerate Whitefield from a false charge; and yet, by any interpretation, the whole affair comes dangerously near to gossip in high place, and it is difficult to feel that any of it mattered so much as either of the disputants imagined. In practical sequel it meant that Thomas Clap never forgave Jonathan Edwards for putting him in a corner on page after page, and that in consequence Jonathan Edwards was thereafter *persona non grata* at his own alma mater. Henceforth, he attended the Princeton instead of the Yale commencement.

In the fall of 1744, before any measure of peace had settled upon the meetinghouse, Whitefield again landed in America. Nothing more unfortunate could possibly have happened. Should he or should he not be admitted to the pulpits of the settled ministry? Accusers and defenders again took their positions on the battle line, and again schism followed.

For six more months the fray assumed formidable proportions. Forced to take sides, some ministers tried to conciliate their congregations by opening their pulpits to Whitefield and taking the consequences. Others forbade him to darken the doors of their meetinghouses. Resolutions for and against him again poured forth from the presses in a weekly flood.

The most dignified statements of opposition in this new crisis were those issued by the colleges. The Harvard declaration, which appeared December 28, 1744, was entitled

"The Testimony of the President, Professors, Tutors and Hebrew Instructor of Harvard College in Cambridge, Against the Reverend Mr. George Whitefield and his Conduct".

A corresponding statement was issued by Yale College three months later.[17]

The plain-spoken accusations of the Harvard manifesto outlined the course of attack followed by ministers individually and in groups throughout the ensuing months. Whitefield's extemporaneous preaching was lazy; his criticism of the college teaching and his offer of a substitute list of books which might properly be taught were flagrant arrogance; his account of moneys spent for the Bethesda Orphanage (in answer to previous charges of misappropriation of funds), was very summary. To dispose of one thousand pounds in a single item was to render no account at all. It was time for the ministry to take a united stand. The New Haven clergy followed a similar line of attack, labelling his treatment of the college, "Our Beauty and our Glory", uncharitable censoriousness. The framers of their statement were astonished at his impudence. On the whole, they declared, "Religion is now in a far worse state than it was in 1740".[18]

Whitefield's answers to these charges were lamentably weak. To the charge of "Enthusiasm", he replied that he professed himself a Calvinist, and

"preached no other Doctrines than those which your pious Ancestors and Founders of Harvard College preached long before I was born".

To the charge of misappropriated funds, he merely said,

"How can it be proved that it was not used for the Support and Education of the Dear Lambs at the Orphan-House?"

As to the remaining accusations, he disposed of them one and all by saying they were not answered,

"On account of the Variety of Business in which I am necessarily engaged, and my Daily calls to preach the everlasting Gospel. . . . But why should I say more, it would be endless as well as take up too much of my precious Time".[19]

This was the precise truth. Whitefield had less than no interest in yesterday's quarrels. He bore no grudges and was apparently serenely untroubled by the estrangement from those who had shown him such gracious hospitality on his previous visit. To a degree, in this indifference to criticism he was an example of his own Christian preachments, and just so far he put the settled brethren to shame for their much speaking. There was, however, another side. His absorption in the one business of his life, preaching, was in many respects admirable, but in so far as it was an absorption which involved complete unconcern for the consequences of his words and actions it can scarcely be called the single-mindedness of a great man.

To a later day, the whole quarrel between Whitefield and the New England ministry seems pitifully provincial, although that greater issues were at stake than most of the pamphlets revealed, is apparent to the naked eye, and was at the time. The small fry, naturally, went no further than personal recrimination, which merely added to the mutual hatred. Others dodged the issue, lamented the dissensions, and once more painted a lost golden age in which there had been unbroken harmony between church and church, minister and people. Others, but only a few, made bold to approach the question of authority, congregational and pastoral, which was fundamental to the dispute; but they approached it timidly. This issue was finally brought bluntly to the fore, and in a measure clarified as a fundamental issue, through a trivial circumstance. On November 19, 1744, two Yale students, John and Ebenezer Cleaveland, were expelled from Yale College for attending a New Light meeting. Immediately there was a great stir throughout the colony. The much-argued pros and cons of New Lightism were completely obscured as the laity rose up in anger against the "stretch of the College Power" which this action represented. To deny degrees to two students who had done their work acceptably, and whose only offence was that in vacation they had gone with their parents to a meeting in a private house, was denounced as a piece of ecclesiastical arrogance. The punishment was unwarrantably "cruel", but the fact that the college authorities had inflicted it for a "crime not committed within their Jurisdiction" [20] was the real point of attack. Quite clearly the issue concerned outside authority as against personal privilege.

The immediate action of the Yale College seniors is significant to those who would read the 1740's for their shadows of the 1770's. Seemingly as a rebuke to the college authorities, the students arranged for the printing of Locke's *Essay on Toleration,* a book on every student's private reading list in those days. When the Rector heard of the plan, he ordered the guilty instigators to make public confession, with their diplomas at stake. One senior refused. When Commencement day came, his name was not on the list. He made inquiry and was given opportunity for tardy confession. He refused, protested that he was of age, had property, and would appeal to the King. The further record may have suffered deletion, for it merely indicates that he was sent for, treated with "complaisance" and given his degree with his class. For the main issue involved, this episode is an exact parallel with the Northampton "bad book" case except that in the conclusion Yale College made concessions and Jonathan Edwards did not. His victory, if victory it may be called, was hardly worth what it was to cost him.

Except for a few belated skirmishes, the Harvard manifesto put an end to front-page interest in the Whitefield quarrel. The clergy still had to deal with the problems he had brought them, but as a person he could no longer command the center of the stage. On his later visits he had brief mention, both for praise and for blame, but the praise had a warmed-over flavor, and the criticism was a querulous rehashing of old bitterness. His day was over; America had other and sterner battles ahead. The taking of Cape Breton definitely reduced him to secondary importance. An entry in the *Journal* of Thomas Smith documents this shift in interest almost to a day. Under date of February 2, 1745, he wrote,

"Great talk about Whitefield's preaching, and the fleet to Cape Breton".[21]

Henceforth the meetinghouse was to have a more insistent rival than ever before in America. Revivals also were thoroughly out of favor. New England had had enough of such excitements to last for a generation. The term "New Light" was an insult. As a committee of ministers expressed it, to leave off one's wicked ways and show a concern for religion was to invite laughter from one's companions. They spoke it sadly, not realizing perhaps that the reaction would be proportionate to the frenzy. Observers from the laity disposed of the whole affair as a "superstitious panic" which had run high for the moment, but had required only cool consideration to be seen in its true character. They too were wrong.

After two hundred years, the truth of the matter is more easily arrived at than such facts and figures as are available. At the time both sides spoke so immoderately that statistics are wholly unreliable. To Whitefield and Tennent every outcry was a new convert. One may read that as many as 50,000 or as few as 5,000 were "added to the kingdom" during 1740-41. To study church membership rolls against such totals is to be greatly puzzled. Sixty-nine added to the membership of Old South Church, Boston, during the peak year, 1741, does not look like the great ingathering the Boston clergy wrote about. Neither is the number of new churches during the middle forties larger than would seem natural with a growing population and the settling of new towns. Correct totals at this distance are perhaps impossible, but in any case, they are not very important.

The significance of the Great Awakening has little more to do with statistics than with dull pamphlets—objections to objections and replies to replies. What mattered socially, politically, as well as religiously, to Americans of the next generation was the readjustment of their thinking which this upheaval had imposed on them. The language of the meetinghouse had been translated into the vernacular, somewhat too suddenly. Man's notion of his own individual dignity and importance had been greatly increased, also too suddenly. The form of worship had become less important. Whitefield had honestly not cared what ritual a man used so long as his heart was changed. By his deference to men and women as individual human beings he had added a timely potency to his words of entreaty; he had also planted seeds that would bear fruit in later independence of action which had nothing to do with life in the meetinghouse. That religion was to emerge from this, its greatest hour of triumph in American life, to take henceforth a secondary place, is of all results of the Great Awakening the most ironic. Prior to 1740, there was already a cleavage between religion and the broader stream of American thought. The Great Awakening made the rift wider.

More permanently, this upheaval in American life had to do with the spread of an idea, an idea as old as Christianity; namely, that religion is an individual, inner experience or it is nothing. Decent living is not enough. Without a changed heart, "good works", no matter how good, are shell without substance. Scarcely less important to American social as well as religious history, was the new type of religious leader which this brief hysteria produced. An illiterate exhorter disturbing the Sunday morning peace in 1742 was a nuisance, if he were not worse; he might also be a counterfeit. At his sincere best, he did not belong in the New England meetinghouse, but there would be a place for him on the frontier during the next century. Undoubtedly something valuable was lost from the traditions of the American pulpit when to the average man "learning" no longer seemed of first-rank importance among ministerial qualifications; but the new concept would be translated into life, for good to many, during the covered wagon era. The Great Awakening was hardly over in 1742.

Jonathan Edwards' personal participation in the evangelism of 1740-42 had been considerable, but at the time it was hardly more important than that of other ministers whose names have been forgotten. However, his share in clarifying the idea of conversion and giving it sound doctrinal standing was greatly more significant than the share of any other American. His notion of religious experience as expressed in the *Treatise Concerning Religious Affections* was basic to the new theology, both as it would be debated by intellectuals of the cloth during the next generation and stoutly professed by a half-educated ministry and itinerant evangelists who would hold "protracted meetings" on the prairies in the next century. By applying himself to the "root" of the matter, as his mind demanded, he had made revivals theologically possible.

Chapter 11

Trouble in the Parish

DURING the restless years 1742-45, almost any parish disagreement would have served as a model on which to build mischief. Northampton had escaped the more indecorous manifestations of congregational defiance, but mischief, grim and long continued, came by way of the salary dispute of 1742 and the notorious "bad book" case of 1744.

The salary dispute had roots stretching back into the peaceful thirties, when it had amounted to no more than pastoral impatience over delay in collection of "rates". A letter fragment as early as 1734 expresses more than an edge of annoyance on this score.

"Sir
"By this I would Signify to you that I never have been at so much Difficulty to get in my Salary as I have been this year. Never any Constables were in any measure so Backward. There is Considerable of my Salary that is yet behind which I very much need & have been Put to Considerable Inconveniences already for want . . ." [1]

The "Backward Constables" may with some warrant have been nettled in return.

Such complaints were very common. Ministerial diaries are full of them. When family needs were insistent and the salary was overdue, ministers met their bills by orders on the town for unpaid rates. It was a clumsy procedure, distinctly irritating to one with a feeling for meticulous regularity in all things and a conscience for paying his bills promptly. Payment by parish donation was an even more sorry substitute, and undignified in the bargain. The itemized lists of such favors credited to parishioners in ministerial rate books read like burlesques. Jonathan Edwards kept no such lists, but he probably did not escape, any more than his brother ministers in rural parishes, the indignity of a firkin of butter, half a tub of onions, a pair of gloves and a load of hay, a red petticoat and one hog, deposited now and then at the back door. Such business dealings did not sort well with the idea of a minister as the emissary of God, bearing upon his shoulders burdens too great for angels.

By 1740, even though his salary had been paid promptly and in cash, there was not enough of it for his growing needs. He had a house full of children; there was much illness; more servants were necessary; he was buying books, pastures, sheep; the budget would not balance. He took his case before the town and asked for more money. It was promptly granted. Action was also taken about his wood supply, which he had reported to be insufficient. Parishioners who had not yet brought in their loads were given until Tuesday night to do so; if by that time, there was still an insufficiency, the remaining amount would be paid for out of the town rate. This was on January 20, 1741, while the revival was still in its brighter stage.

In the following spring there was a second increase—this time of fifty pounds—apparently without request, and shortly thereafter a "great uneasiness in the town" over pastoral expenditures. The standard of living on King Street was sharply criticized, even the clothes the family wore becoming a subject for reproof. Mr. Edwards was of "a craving disposition", abusing the generosity of the town by "lavish" expenditure. So much was said that he was obliged to make public the family budget, in itemized array, and then to suffer still greater humiliation as the parish critics fell upon the list and made it prove their own thesis—just as many children could be maintained for exactly half the sum. Portions of a letter written on sermon notes dated March, 1743, detail this humiliation.[2] The text, "Be ye kindly affectioned one to another", was probably received coldly by those who looked closely to see whether Sarah Edwards were wearing her new "locket and chane", costing £11.

A year later one item on the town book reflects the continued spirit of censoriousness in the parish:

> "The question was put whether the Town will pay the charge of bringing Mr Edwards' his Daughter from Brookfield & it passed in the negative".[3]

Certainly an ungracious gesture in response to what would seem a strange pastoral assumption. Why should he have allowed such a question to be put at a time when feeling was so inflamed against him? In the following spring he made request for a fixed salary instead of an amount to be determined annually, but the town refused to comply. No reasons were given, but the fluctuation of bills of credit at the time may have been one reason for the denial, as it was for the request. Three more times he made the same request and was twice denied, both times with evidence of bad feeling on the part of the town and a deep sense of injury in the parsonage. One of the few surviving scraps from Sarah Edwards' pen is a note presumably addressed to one of the town constables, immediately following the 1744 request for a fixed amount.

> "Northampton March ye 26
> "1744

"Sir

"Mr Sheldon jest now informs me that you cannot Send all the money at the time Mr Edwards is Rid out and therefore I write to Desire you to Send Some as much as you Possibbly can for Mr Edwards is under Such obligations that he cant Possibbly do without it and therefore mustr up all possible Pains to procure it.

> "This from your friend and Servt
> SARAH EDWARDS" 4

The town did not grant his request for a fixed salary until 1747, and then "provided he and the people Can Agree on a Sum & a proper Rule to Compute the Sum from Year to Year." A committee was appointed, which reported in the following March, and

"the matter being long debated," it was finally "passed by a great majority".5

Jonathan Edwards signed his acceptance of the new arrangement in the town book, May 16, 1748; and thereafter pastor and committee met at stated times to compute the amount on the basis of existing prices, price of beef to be determined in the fall, pork in the spring, and so on through the list of necessities. It would seem to have been a problem for trained economists, but the village deacons went at it as though they were rebuilding Ebenezer Hunt's hat shop, from foundation to shingles in nine days. Had the parsonage burned at any time while salary adjustments were still on the town agenda, the parish would have done the same for Jonathan Edwards and his family; and the week after, they would have gone right on quibbling. Neighborly assistance in disaster was one thing; the rights of the pew versus the pastor might be quite another. As the dispute dragged on through the years, it became shot through with personal elements; but in the beginning it had not been primarily personal. In the end it meant victory for the pastor, but victory without peace. The affair had smeared his relations with his flock and made a distinct rift in the parish. A letter of his daughter Sarah's, written in the spring of 1748, indicates that the situation had grown so unpleasant that he had considered removal, "if a Convenient Opportunity Present".[6] An entry in the *Itineraries* of Ezra Stiles supplies the further hint that the presidency of the College of New Jersey had been suggested to him at this time by Governor Belcher.[7]

Back of this unpleasant interlude, on the parish side, was a feeling for democratic principles under other terminology. Why should King Street have its clothes tailored in Boston and wear a hat costing three pounds? For that matter, Ebenezer Hunt valued his village-made beavers (best variety) at sixty-five shillings each and he had cheaper varieties. The minister could be hatted locally at exactly the Boston price, and why not? The Edwards ménage already included several servants. Why the purchase in 1747 of the "negro girl named Venus"[8] for eighty pounds? Perhaps the village deacons did not mean to be unkind. Questions of privilege were already touchy questions in the 1740's, and in objecting to anything which savored of aristocratic privilege the pews forgot the offices of kindness and friendly consideration. So did many a village patriot of honorable memory thirty years later, and today a monument marks his resting place.

At the very height of these money troubles, even to the exact month of the town's first denial of his first request for a fixed salary, came the "bad book" episode, which, aside from his dismissal in 1750, was the most sensational news item in all Jonathan Edwards' twenty-three-year pastorate. In normal times, he might have had the coöperation of his people in such a case of discipline, but not after more than three years of petty criticism and back-door gossip directed at the private affairs of the parsonage. Jonathan Edwards was not insensitive; nor, for all his alleged absent-mindedness, was he unaware of what was going on around him. He knew that he was standing on a volcano in March, 1744, and yet to be tactful and not speak out in public on this occasion was to him unthinkable. If the children of his parishioners had been disorderly, the moment of discovery should be the moment of reproof, even though reproof might set off another explosion.

With his eyes wide open, he walked into the danger zone and lighted the fuse himself. Twenty years in the pulpit had taught him nothing about the delicacy of human relations.

In the fact of misbehavior of members brought before the whole church body, there was nothing in the least unusual. Hardly a parish got through a given year without its "case"; and the sharing of details by pastor and people was merely routine procedure. Offences generally considered were two— adultery (by far the most common) and drunkenness—although occasionally variety was introduced through stealing watermelons, "borrowing a horse", mixing a superstitious brew, or merely talking back. The Hampshire Association on one occasion had to consider the complaint of a brother who demanded satisfaction of his fellow worshipper for "Defamation", particularly for calling him a "Swine"; but usually such cases merely interrupted a morning's study at the parsonage. For the more frequent offences, adultery and drunkenness, the procedure was brief and stereotyped. For the numerous cases of women called before the church at the birth of a child born seven months after marriage, the process involved: first, the formal inquiry; second, the confession; third, the baptism of the baseborn child, all three actions usually being recorded as of the same date. Drunkenness involved public confession and public admonishment, also at one appearance. Only when the culprit failed to confess, or was possibly "somewhat mincing in his replies", was the inquiry prolonged. Otherwise the congregation held up their hands in token of satisfaction with the confession, the pastor dropped a word of caution upon the offender in particular and the church in general, and the case was declared closed. Church records are occasionally enlivened by accounts of the behavior of recalcitrants, but usually the process of rebuke and reinstatement was swift, sober, and unvarying.

The Northampton "bad book" case is important in Jonathan Edwards' story because, like the salary dispute, it contributed directly to the parish resentment which culminated in the dismissal of 1750. It also makes concrete in a single instance the drama of village life in its relation to the parsonage, and in the larger drama of church life outside the village illustrates the increasing rebelliousness of the pew under any assertion of pastoral authority. The Northampton case was more spectacular than most parish discipline cases because the offenders were younger. They were boys and girls in their teens. To assume as some have done that in this instance

Jonathan Edwards was meddling in that which did not properly concern him, is to forget the control which the colonial church permissibly exercised over men's private affairs. What a church member did in the privacy of his own home, whether he "gave thanks at his eating", read the bedtime chapter with his family, or did not, was by no means his own business. Every church member had an obligation not only to walk acceptably himself, but also to look out for the sins of his fellow members. So it had been from the beginning of the colonial church. When a new congregation was to be gathered, the would-be gatherers were instructed as a first step to meet together, "and seriously examine the spirituall conditions one of another, even untill they be actually satisfied . . . of each other".⁹ In most parishes, as late as 1740, such espionage was no longer very troublesome. Men had other things to do, and besides they had grown lax themselves. But the ministry still held tenaciously to their earlier prerogatives. The Northampton affair went out of bounds because the large number of culprits involved necessarily prolonged the investigation, and because the parish lost zeal for the inquiry when the wrong children were found to be implicated. The pastor also made the initial mistake of reversing traditional practice, and instead of first dealing with offenders in private, bringing the whole affair before the congregation at the outset. Thereby hangs the tale.

Reduced to its lowest terms, the story is as follows: five or six boys from families of lesser standing in the town obtained possession of a book of instructions to midwives, aroused the curiosity of other young people in its content, and passed the book around. Before long a large circle, including sons and daughters of the élite, shared the secret of the book, and had either read it themselves or heard some of the comment concerning it. How long this suppressed excitement continued before word of the affair was brought to the minister's ear is not recorded; but, once apprised of it, he immediately and publicly set in motion the regular machinery of investigation. At the close of a preaching service, he told the congregation what had happened, took a vote authorizing the investigation, and appointed an hour for the committee to meet. So far, all was well, and thoroughly regular. Before dismissing the congregation, however, he read out a list of names of young people who were to appear at the investigation, making no distinction between supposed culprits and sustaining witnesses. Immediately the sentiment changed, and "the town was all in a blaze". No wonder, for children of committeemen and first families had been summoned along with sons and daughters of the less eligible. If a strip of paper preserved among the Edwards manuscripts be the memorandum in question, as it probably is, the names are separated into groups and differentiated by various signs, possibly to indicate degrees of guilt and to distinguish offenders from witnesses. Explanation of these shorthand notes at the time of the announcement might possibly have saved the whole situation.

From this ill-fated Sunday in March until June 3rd, more than two months later, the village seethed. The record of official action in the case may be pieced together from testimony given before the committee of investigation and written down by the pastor. Testimony is recorded from twenty-two witnesses,[10] of whom only six were named in the original list. These witnesses implicate eleven culprits, of whom only five were included in the original list. From the fact that no testimony is recorded for half the persons in the original list or from any of the culprits, it appears that history of the case is not complete; but this recorded testimony, connecting as it does a grand total of fifty-six persons with the village tempest, leaves very little doubt as to the chronology or nature of events.

The book which caused the uproar was entitled, according to report, either *The Midwife Rightly Represented*, or *The Midwife Rightly Instructed*, probably the latter. Whether the book had been taken from Dr. Mather's library or had been imported into the village by one of the children, does not appear. It does not seem to have been produced before the committee at any time. In fact, less than half the testimony given concerns the book at all. Very early in the procedure, the nature of its content, its various hiding places, the names of those who read it or listened to the discussions—all this was subordinated to the more important issue: how the culprits behaved in response to the summons of the church. The public confession of two of the ringleaders, Timothy and Simeon Root, officially closing the affair, makes no mention whatever of the original offence, merely of their "scandalously Contemptuous Behaviour towards the Authority of this Church", and their promises in the direction of conduct more humble, meek, and decent, "treating those that are ouer me in the Lord with due honour & Respect as becomes a Christian". Oliver Warner's confession concerns the "unclean and lascivious expressions" of which he had been accused, and his promise to behave in future "with that Sobriety & Purity that becomes the Gospel".

Doubtless the minister's tactlessness in giving premature publicity to an unsorted list of names was in part responsible for the shift in emphasis; but, whatever the cause, the "bad book" was forgotten in the battle between pulpit and pew which it precipitated. The main issue was soon clarified in the village mind. Was this a private affair and therefore none of the minister's business? Was there a limit to church interference in matters of conduct? Hitherto, when Northampton parishioners had been dissatisfied with the ruling of the pastor, they had taken their grievances to the Hampshire Association, and had accepted the ruling of the higher body. Now they began to talk boldly of individual rights as against ecclesiastical authority of any sort. The fact that in this case pastoral authority took precedence somewhat over parental authority, just as in the expulsion of the Cleaveland boys, made the resentment of the pew more intense than might have been the case had the offenders been adults; but the main issue was none the less clear. A principle was at stake and the village knew it. It is this fact which gives importance to an episode which in the pettiness and shabbiness of its details would not warrant reconstruction. As parish history, the whole affair would be mere routine, had its implications not become so serious and so far-reaching.

From beginning to end the tale strains one's credulity, as a procedure directed by a master mind. The three ringleaders in the affair, Simeon and Timothy Root and Oliver Warner, appear to have been the town hoodlums, but the committee treated them as though they had been Pomeroys, giving their insolence far more attention and importance than it deserved. The spectacle of the best born sons and daughters of the village drawn into a network of talebearing against three boys, whose offence could have surprised no one, is amazing. How ministerial discretion, built up and tested aforetime during a pastorate of almost twenty years, could have permitted the parsonage to be turned into a court of inquiry, the minister's children to testify against the children of parishioners, and the minister's wife to quote the insolence of Timothy Root, who said over and over again, "I won't worship a wig", passes belief, even assuming an ethical background which made talebearing an obligation. The fact that the whole investigation was conducted without harshness is beside the point.

The method of investigation invited to restlessness, as every parent should have known. Culprits were summoned to the parsonage in groups, and while they waited their turn to be questioned, they fell into "scandalous mischief". One boy, growing tired of waiting, climbed a ladder which stood against the parsonage, and looked in on a bevy of girls waiting their turn in an upstairs room. Two others, without permission, left the parsonage yard, went to the tavern and called for a mug of flip. Those who were left behind, goaded by Timothy Root's "Go away, and if you were not such devilish cowards, you would have gone away long ago", dared a bravado they probably did not feel, and played leapfrog, thereby touching the marginal area of insubordination before God's messenger. Under such conditions, a game of leapfrog becomes something other than leapfrog. Jerusha Edwards, watching at the window, came forward helpfully at the proper moment to supply the names of the participants.

The lowest depths had been reached, however, in the laughing and whispering "in the open face of the church", when the offence was first detailed at the close of the church service, and again in the contempt implicit in Simeon Root's insolent remark, "What do we here? We won't stay here all day long", spoken in the very hearing of the committee, or, worse still, in his brother Timothy's perversion of scriptural teaching in the insolent remark that the committee themselves were "nothing but men molded up of a little Dirt". That Colonel Stoddard, Northampton's leading citizen and a man of distinction in Massachusetts colony, should take such remarks from boys under durance seriously enough to report them to a committee of five other men, met in solemn session, and that not one of these men, or even Dr. Mather, the town physician, had the wisdom to see the whole affair in relation to community peace or the prestige of the pulpit, probably mitigates somewhat the impression of the pastor's blindness in this affair, but not enough to save him. They were all blind.

On June 3rd the confessions of the three ringleaders, composed by the pastor and read out in meeting, officially closed the affair. The congregation had listened to many such confessions through the years, but these confessions would have had a more alert hearing than usual. This episode had clarified and crystallized several important issues in the parish mind. And the end was not yet.

The pity of the sequel is increased by the suggestion that the pastor himself had qualms as to the rightness of his procedure, even while the affair was in progress. On a small scrap of paper, one side of which had been used for a child's A B C copy, are these two queries in Jonathan Edwards' handwriting:

"Whether the chh. did any thing contrary to the Rules of the Word of G. in determining to search into the matter as they did".
"Whether thereof since they did so determine to make thorough search, the committee should not go on till they think they have made a thorough search".[11]

The other seems more like a post-reflection. It is written on the back of a "Down Country" memorandum of letters, books, papers to be taken to East Windsor, and books, sermons, and the usual chocolate to be brought back. He may well have made the jottings *en route*, preparatory to a talk with his father:

"Whether if it be I say that these things were the things that were reported whether these things were of a scandalous nature".
"Whether it was to be Looked upon as a private offence".
"Whether I ought to have done any thing about it as the pastor of the chh".
"Whether I ought to have gone and talked privately with them".

These doubts strike at the root of the whole controversy. Moreover, they indicate a realization that something had gone wrong. There is also, on a piece of fan paper, an outline for what would seem to be a public presentation of the grounds for action in the case. The course of argument is directed toward the main issue, that of authority.

"To deny Power in a Church to meddle without a Complaint is to deny a Power of self preservation common to all societies".
"Shall the master of a ship not Enquire when he knows the ship is running on Rocks."

Objections to this line of argument are listed with arguments in reply. There is also a heading, "Give Reasons why I think it was not a private offense". Whether or not these memoranda have reference to the 1744 case, they indicate that the pastoral prerogative had been challenged.

In a similar battle concerning the limits of pastoral authority in a private matter, Timothy Edwards, father of Jonathan, had remained obdurate even after a church council, called to hear the case, had acquitted the culprit, and after he had subsequently withdrawn his charge of pastoral maladministration. The offender had been Joseph Diggens, a former pupil. The offence had been marrying without securing the consent of the bride's parents, in Timothy Edwards' eyes an unpardonable affront to parental dignity. He had refused to baptize the child of this marriage, or to permit Joseph Diggens to apply for admission to another parish until he had confessed his fault publicly. This the culprit refused to do, and had the church vote to support him. But Timothy Edwards stood fast, claiming ministerial right to veto the decision of the congregation. For three years the sacrament of the Lord's Supper could not be celebrated in the East Windsor parish because of the state of disharmony which existed between pastor and people, and at the end of this time Timothy Edwards yielded only upon signed entreaty from the leading men of his parish that peace be restored. This was four years before the Northampton "bad book" affair. Jonathan Edwards would have agreed with his father. As emissaries of God, they fought His battles, not their own. The jottings in Jonathan Edwards' handwriting show no hint of belligerency in his support of the traditional view. Put in the form of queries, they suggest rather that too late he had entertained doubts which might have saved him one of the most unfortunate episodes of his ministry.

Quite naturally, posterity has not forgotten the affair. The facts have usually been sadly garbled, but the impression of Jonathan Edwards, the harsh disciplinarian, has survived the generations. In a sense, he has deserved to be the victim of his own lamentably bad judgment, but it was bad judgment and not harshness which caused the mischief. He merely pushed a familiar assumption of pastoral prerogative further than a restless time could bear, and discovered to his own surprise that it was no longer the current view. Something had happened during the ten years since the Hampshire Association had considered the question:

"What is the Duty of ministers, when any Under their Jurisdiction and Government refuse to come to them when sent for upon account of Misbehaviors?

"Ans. They ought to look upon them as Guilty of contemning Christ's authority, and to deal with them accordingly.

"Voted in the Affirmative".[12]

To the end of his ministry, Jonathan Edwards clung too literally and too tenaciously to this interpretation of ministerial duty for his own good; but in his attitude toward the individual wrongdoer he was not harsh. Quite the contrary. Characteristically, he was concerned to justify the law which had been transgressed and to set up safeguards against a repetition of the offence, not to dwell on the circumstances in the case, or to denounce the culprit. His own report of such cases is often quite as abstract and generalized as one of his sermons might have been. But in troublous times, reputations are quickly changed.

During the decade following the Northampton uproar, the issue of pastoral authority was forced into the open in almost every New England parish. In 1752, eight years later, the Hampshire Association took account of this unrest in a debate on the question,

"Whether in general an offence can be so circumstanced as to render it improper to bring it to the chh. in the first instance superceeding private Steps?" [13]

Such debates were futile; the pew would settle this question, not an association of ministers. But it would be a long fight. The ministry would continue to argue that pastoral authority was delegated authority, straight from Christ itself; the pew would continue to feel it to be an invasion of personal rights. The ministry would prove their case by Scripture, giving line and verse; the pew would listen, and perhaps wonder at their own lack of conviction. In the mid-century, the American laity could not have called by name the oracles to which they were unconsciously responding.

In Northampton's test case of 1744, the pulpit had won. But more had happened through this affair than appeared on the church records, and thereafter, for a reason no one could have stated, "Mr. Edwards'" reproofs would fall on ears more dull for the hearing. In the fall of 1744, he took for his text at the Quarterly Lecture, Psalm 144:12,

"That our sons may be as plants grown up in their youth; that our daughters may be as corner stones, polished after the similitude of a palace",

and announced as his *Doctrine*,

"Tis a peculiarly lovely & pleasant sight to behold young People walking in the ways of vertue and piety".

Addressing his remarks to the gallery, he said:

"I dare appeal to those young People that have in a great measure neglected Relig. & given the Reins to their inclination & spent a great Deal of their time over wine mirth & those Diversions that are inconsistent with a serious Religion. . . ."

Ten years before, such an appeal might have been a landmark of changed behavior. In fact, it had been so. But those days were past. During the following year and periodically thereafter, such items as the following occur on the Town Book.

"The Town being Sensible of the Irreverent & disorderly behaviour of many of the young people & children in the house of God in the time of publick worship, and at the Same meeting made choice of Ensign John Clapp, Gideon Henderson, Caleb Strong, Ellisha Pomeroy, to inspect the behaviour of the young people & children in time of publick Worship & to prosecute them for their irreverent & disorderly behaviour, & Voted at the Same time the Inspector have power to order Such disorderly persons to Sit in Such places in the Meeting-house in the time of publick Worship as they think proper." [14]

In some ways it had been smoother going when the word of the minister was law.

The years 1744-1748 were barren years. Not one new candidate applied for membership. The salary dispute dragged on; the "bad book" children grew up. Opposition and resentment were no longer veiled. The house on King Street was the target for attack on the slightest provocation. The town "parties" realigned themselves on this new issue, while the whole parish waited for an occasion which would force removal.

Extra-village events were also conspiring to loosen the tie with the meetinghouse. The French and Indian War claimed village attention in a very direct and personal way. The town was again fortified. Watch houses were constructed on the outskirts.[15] Northampton men and boys enlisted, and subsequently the progress of events became a matter of intense community interest. Week by week Jonathan Edwards' sermons reflect the contemporary excitement and deep anxiety. The general course of events can be followed in the sermon headings for special days:

"Fast on Occasion of the War with France, June 28, 1744."
"Fast on Success in the Expedition against Cape Breton, April 4, 1745."

"On Occasion of the Return of our Soldiers from Cape Breton, August, 1745."

"On a Fast on Occasion of the Proclamation of War with the Indians, Septem. 19, 1745."

"Fast Occasioned by the Rebellion, Mar. 13, 1745/6."

"Preceding the Expedition to Canada, June, 1746."

"Thanksgiving for victory over the Rebels, Aug. 1746."

"Fast, Oct. 16, 1746, on Occasion of the Arrival of the French Fleet, &c."

"Thanksgiving, Novem. 27, 1746, after the Confusion of the French Fleet."

These sermons supply little detail as to the successive campaigns of the war, but in accordance with Jonathan Edwards' habitual practice, keep closely to the scriptural analogy. For the "Fast preceding the Expedition to Cape Breton", he took as his text:

"If thy people go out to battle against their enemy, . . . then hear thou in heaven their prayer, and maintain their cause".

For the sermon commemorating the return of the soldiers from this same expedition:

"Then they returned, every man of Judah and Jerusalem, and Jehoshaphat in the forefront of them, to go again to Jerusalem with joy; for the Lord had made them to rejoice over their enemies".

The presence of the returned soldiers in the congregation would have caused eyes to turn in their direction as this text was announced. So also would the reading of their personal thanks by the pastor, probably at the close of the sermon. One such page bound in with a sermon for this same month contains the awkwardly phrased, badly spelled "Thanks of Seth Pomroy" (later to be Major Pomeroy), preserved sound of life and limb. It would seem strange if on such an occasion the pastor did not add a few words on his own account. Doubtless he did.

Occasionally he commented directly on the progress of the war. In the sermon marked, "Preceding the Expedition to Canada, June, 1746", he became almost impassioned:

"The call to us in this Part of the Land especially seems to be very loud. The Land never had such a Call".

Such a sermon would have made recruits.

"When a People of God are molested & endangered by injurious and Bloody Enemies For them Cheerfully to ex— — &
expose Thems[elves] in a war tending to their Defence and
Safety or good . . . is a Duty they owe to G[od] their Country
and Thems[elves]",[16]

he declared, making a plea for defensive warfare which is
almost vehement. Such sermons—and there are a considerable number of them—suggest that, had he lived on into the
1770's, he might have been a powerful force behind the
Minutemen. He would also have been obliged to make one of
the most difficult decisions of his life.

In the study these were fruitful years, despite all the distractions within and without the parish. By 1746 he had
finished his *Treatise Concerning Religious Affections*, significant as his most deliberate answer to his own insistent question, "What is the nature of true religion?" In attempting to
make this answer he was within the area most congenial to
his own thought. As he acknowledged in his Preface,

"It is a subject on which my mind has been peculiarly intent,
ever since I first entered on the study of divinity".[17]

It was also a subject on which he was peculiarly qualified to
speak.

His treatment bears the marks of long study, matured
thinking, and the ability to detach himself from what he calls
the "dust and smoke of present controversy". Five years
before, his *Distinguishing Marks* had been a specific attempt
to check current evils. He had been the practical pastor, bent
on discharging his responsibility as spiritual guide after his
Sunday morning manner, and therefore keeping the weakest
member of the flock in his eye as well as his brother intellectuals. In this later treatise he frankly addressed himself to his
peers; and, although always aware of the counterfeits and
gaudy shows which must be distinguished from true religion,
he was now more concerned with abstract distinctions than
with the timely correctives. He dealt with the subject in its
essence, not with the externals of the current panorama. His
clean-cut discriminations, his coolness in argument, his recognition that although the devil "had foiled them" in the late
revival, the history of religion in America was not thereby
ended, reveals much as to the quality of his thinking and the
nature of his faith. While Satan, as he said, seemed to be
leading both parties, one on the extreme right and the other

on the left, he strove to find the deeply obscured but, as he believed, the "right" path in the middle. In doing so he made one of his most determining contributions to the religious thought of his time, for this is not merely a polemic. It is a philosophical argument as to the nature of religious experience.

With respect to the current debate, this treatise is an argument for the central place of the emotions in all religious experience. Not the intellectual faculties (perception, judgment, speculation) but the "affections" are the springs of action in all things religious, as in all things worldly. The deists declared otherwise, reducing religion to that which may be rationally apprehended and rationally demonstrated. Six years after the excesses of the great revival, they had gained many American supporters. The sober-thoughted majority in both pulpit and pew had long since declared for the enlightened mind rather than the "raised" emotions. Let religion be a rational exercise; let men be guided by reason in their search to apprehend the divine. Then might the counterfeits and extravagances of 1741 be at an end indeed. "Heart religion" had been fatal to good order in the churches; let the ministry preach common sense instead. So spoke the Old Lights, who still had heart for the conflict.

In his unqualified opposition to this rationalistic trend, Jonathan Edwards was not advocating a return to emotionalism; he was attempting to prove by the laws of human nature, as he understood them, that religion is not primarily an affair of the intellect, but an affair of the heart, or, as he put it on page after page of this treatise,

"True religion consists very much in affections".

For modern readers, his thought is somewhat obscured by his terms, particularly by his seeming identification of "soul" and "mind", "heart" and "will", "emotions" and "affections". He recognized the inadequacy of language in such matters. It was "imperfect" and "unfixed". The things of religion lay beyond the purpose for which language was contrived; yet he attempted to bring his distinction within the current idiom. The Soul had two faculties: the discerning faculty, known as Understanding; and the choosing and governing faculty, known as Will or Inclination (in the contemporary view, Will being not yet differentiated from Emotion). With a slightly stronger push to his own thought at this point, he might have separated them; but this was not the distinction which engaged him. He was concerned to prove that exercise of the discerning or passive faculty alone could never bring a man to a sense of the divine. The devil can discern true from false; the devil knows the doctrine, but he is still the devil. Religion must take hold of a man's heart, and powerfully affect his emotions, which are the living springs of all human action. "In nothing is lukewarmness so odious" as in religion, he declared. Vigor is requisite. Religion, being powerful, manifests itself in the "exercises of the heart, its principal and original seat". The enlightened understanding without an "affected fervent heart" is light without heat. Light one must have, but light alone is not sufficient:

"If the great things of religion are rightly understood, they will affect the heart".[18]

Taken out of its eighteenth century idiom, his idea is simply that feeling lies nearer than thought to the source of religious consciousness, and is the gateway to "religious experience" as distingushed from religious knowledge. The "sense of God" is an emotional, not an intellectual experience. This was in line with his own religious experience of more than twenty-five years, and he had not the shadow of a doubt. As he now attempted to clarify his own certainty to the conviction of others as well, he wrote the most cogent piece of reasoning which had yet issued from his pen, and the first in direct fulfilment of his early intent to make

"a Particular Enquiry into the Nature of the Human Mind, with respect to both its Faculties—the Understanding and the Will—and its various Instincts, and Active and Passive Powers".[19]

By so doing he also gained a learned audience on both sides of the Atlantic, and wrote a pioneer chapter in religious psychology.

He did even more. This treatise put the experience of conversion on a sound scriptural basis, and thus cut the standing from beneath those who branded all emotion in religion as "enthusiasm", and found Scripture to prove it anathema before God. Jonathan Edwards outdid them by finding scriptural proof for that which lay behind these manifestations: the visions, voices, and joyous outcries. If a man's emotional nature be indeed the "principal and original seat" of his religious consciousness, then emotion had been made not only respectable but important. The emphasis accordingly shifted from the outward manifestation to the inner certainty, and in that shift the cornerstone of the new theological structure was laid. Jonathan Edwards and John Wesley stood together in their insistence on the inner witness, not of the mind, but of the emotions, although otherwise their concepts of the experience of conversion differed widely.

"You cannot reason concerning spiritual things", John Wesley declared over and over. Eventually, he was the more successful of the two in safeguarding emotional expression from extravagance by elaborate churchly supervision; but this is a different matter entirely. Basically, the two men were in agreement on that point of the new theology which was to take strongest hold of the popular imagination in a new generation—individual certainty in the experience of conversion.

In Jonathan Edwards' own personal story, this treatise is important as defining clearly the issue on which he was soon to make the fight of his life, and lose. The church to which he ministered was full of those who admittedly had never received the "inner witness". They were trusting to the "means of grace" and to their own endeavors; and, as he saw it, they were wrong, pitifully wrong. Those who had guided them had been mistaken. As their pastor, responsible for their souls, he must change all this. Those of his congregation who read this treatise knew there was trouble ahead, and so did he.

More permanently, the *Treatise* is also important as a piece of religious literature. Jonathan Edwards was not writing logical exposition alone, with abundant biblical footnotes. He was giving personal interpretation to the "beauty and amiableness of true religion", this communication of God to his creatures, this revelation which is such that the natural man can discern

"nothing of it, any more than a man without the sense of tasting can conceive of the sweet taste of honey; or a man without the sense of hearing can conceive of the melody of a tune; or a man born blind can have a notion of the beauty of the rainbow".[20]

As he wrote thus out of his own deepest experience of living, elevation of style often matched elevation of theme.

Everywhere there is self-revelation. In dwelling on the transforming power of the "gracious affections", he set down his own religious aspirations. Nothing but the religion of heaven was worthy enough, as a standard of measurement.

"All who are truly religious are not of this world",

he wrote. Heaven is their country. They are strangers here on earth. God is fitting them for that other world by this communication of himself. Absorbed in his own vision, he was doubtless unaware that he was painting a picture of the perfectibility of man which his Dissenting forbears would neither have recognized nor have approved, and that at the same time he was greatly diminishing the number of the visible saints. This was his own vision, and these were his standards of Christian attainment. Nothing Jonathan Edwards ever wrote, aside from his *Personal Narrative*, reveals so clearly as this *Treatise* the plane on which his own inner life was lived. Neither could anything suggest more clearly why he walked alone.

While his thought was thus engaged through many months, he continued to go to and fro in response to the appeals of distressed ministers in parishes where trouble was brewing. He wrote numerous letters to aggrieved parties; he attended fasts and sessions of prayer, looking toward the averting of an open breach; he was a member of councils called when quarrels could not be settled out of court. Fragments of surviving letters concerning such affairs suggest that his name and advice carried weight, and that his calm, judicial temper fitted him for the rôle of peacemaker. Time after time he urged moderation in thought and action, complete frankness between disputants, and, above all, that the cause of religion be not dishonored. Unfortunately, his appeals to reason instead of emotion, and his unwillingness to treat with personal detraction, were methods too quiet for the aggrieved parties in most parish disputes of the middle forties; but they were the only methods Jonathan Edwards knew. This same calmness of temper was to inflame his own detractors the more in the crisis so soon to come in his own parish.

Late in the year 1747 David Brainerd, missionary to the Indians, died of tuberculosis at the King Street parsonage. He was betrothed to Jerusha Edwards. Months earlier, Dr. Mather, the town physician, had given him up; but the Edwards family had still hoped. Jerusha, in pitiful ignorance of the risk she incurred, nursed him through many weeks. In June, 1747, when he was too ill to travel alone, she went with him to Boston, and brought him back a fortnight later. He died October 9th. Four months later, on February 14, 1748, Jerusha died. She was seventeen years old and, in her father's word, "generally esteemed the Flower of the Family".[21] This was the first break in the family circle.

Reticent as Jonathan Edwards was about all that concerned him most nearly, one might have expected him to retire further into himself and never speak her name again. Instead, five days after her funeral, he stood before his congregation and spoke an intimate eulogy. A week later this might not have been possible, but in the first shock of bereavement, his habitual restraint was broken, and he opened his heart, speaking more freely and more intimately of that which concerned his own affections than on any other recorded occasion in his whole ministry. The sermon he used `had been preached before. In the MS. booklet it is headed,

"To a private Meeting of Young People after Billy Sheldons Death Feb. 1740/41.
"Job. 14. 2 He Cometh forth like a flower & is cut down.
"Afterwards preached the Doctrinal Part with the new application at the End on occasion of the Death of my Daughter Jerusha, Feb. 21, 1747/8".[22]

The application is distinctly personal. He speaks of Jerusha's presence at meeting "Sabbath before last—without any signs of approaching Death", of her five-day illness, the speedy calling of physicians (more than one), the consultations.

"But notwithstanding all means there could be used, she soon departed. Gods apparent Time was come."

No love or tenderness could hold death back.

"Her Place here in the House of G. you now see empty."

He refers to her as "My own dear Child", describes her virtues, takes comfort in her abhorrence of wicked ways, adding:

"I can now be sensible what a bitter cup it would be to me if it had been contrarywise".

More touching even than his tributes to her is his appreciation of the sympathy he has received from his people. They must have known how deep was the affliction,

"at least many of you were so Pleasant and Comfortable while G[od] continued it. . . .

"Some of you have shown affection on occasion of her death."

His closing exhortation, as was usual with him on such occasions, was directed to the young people. He hoped that this might be the beginning of a general awakening and reformation. If so,

"I shall think I had much more Cause to admire Gods mercy in such a happy Consequence than to mourn for my own Loss tho it is so great".

This was not mere pulpit language. It was the precise and lifelong truth. No wonder the village could not understand this man who stood before them.

For Jerusha's sake, Jonathan Edwards may have taken a measure of comfort in the editing of the Brainerd memorials, which immediately engaged his attention. The task of disposing of these voluminous private papers "for God's glory and the interest of religion" had been laid upon him by David Brainerd himself as a dying request. It could scarcely have been refused. As he set himself to the sorting and arranging of these intimately personal materials, he must often have been sorely puzzled. Such morbid reflections and melancholy self-torturings concerning an inward state of grace were strangely out of key with his own recent thought upon the nature of the Christian's experience. Yet they were also strangely similar to his own agonizing after assurance of salvation in his younger days. Possibly with these similar experiences in mind, he made generous allowance for the "imperfections" which belong to all saints "while on this side heaven". David Brainerd's "imperfections" had been many, but these were far less important than the truly eminent state of piety to which he had attained.

Jonathan Edwards would scarcely have been "on this side heaven" himself, had he not used Brainerd's case as occasion for a little special pleading in the "enthusiasm" controversy. During the hysteria of 1741, Brainerd had been an undergraduate at Yale College, had been a victim of the campus excitements, and in the end had paid dear for his indiscretions. In a luckless moment he had made bold to remark that one of his tutors was devoid of grace, and as a result, he had been expelled from the college. Jonathan Edwards had been unsuccessful in his subsequent, repeated attempts to win Brainerd's reinstatement, in order that he might receive his degree, but he had taken great satisfaction in seeing the younger man's mistaken zeal turned into nobler channels. New Light extravagance had given place to a truly vital piety. A man should be judged, not by an early mistake, but by his ability to learn from it. This David Brainerd had done.

Quite apart from its relation to current discussions of New Lightism, this *Life and Diary* deserves more notice than it has received, as a piece of biographical interpretation, written by one whose pen had been trained to other matters, and apparently without a model at hand. In spite of the ever present temptation to sermonize, Jonathan Edwards seldom loses sight of his obligation to the subject of his story, and in the editorial remarks from page to page succeeds amazingly in bringing Brainerd to life, clad in all his depressing humilities, pieties, and unspeakable sufferings. If it is impossible to share his admiration for such a man, it is at least possible to honor him for the portraiture, which, one may suspect, is a picture to the life.

Coming so soon after his *Treatise Concerning Religious Affections,* this volume naturally furnishes occasional addenda in the same line of thought. The concluding section, entitled "Reflections and Observations on the Preceding Memoirs",[23] for example, contains one of the clearest as well as one of the most eloquent delineations of the Christian's experience to be found in all his writings. As he speaks of eternal safety forgotten in the abounding joy of the new experience, of the divine beauty which powerfully draws his heart and causes his whole soul to flow toward God, the supreme excellence, there is more than a suggestion that biography has become autobiography. Momentarily, as he went on to describe the deepening joys of the Christian's experience, Jonathan Edwards seemed to have forgotten also the nagging specifications of current controversy. But only momentarily. Time after time he forced his definition back to the confutation of error. This is the weak point in all his writings. If only he might have felt free to tell! But no: to tell was important, but to confute was more important.

One might think the publication of this book, so late as 1749, after emotional religion had been widely discredited in the popular mind, would have been distinctly unsuccessful, but the very reverse was true. David Brainerd's New Lightism was far less important to those who read his story than the account of his labors among the Indians, which in addition to being a new chapter of American adventure, was also new proof of God's power. The conversion of "savages" did special honor to divine grace. Jonathan Edwards' name on the title page of course carried weight, giving the book its initial hearing; but on its own merits it was distinctly successful. In fact, the influence of this *Life and Diary* toward a new era of missionary labor would be hard to measure. Suprisingly enough, it also made the name of David Brainerd better known to the average churchgoer of the next generation than the name of Jonathan Edwards.

Before this long labor of friendship had issued from the press, he was again deep in his studies, looking toward the attack on Arminianism. It is apparent from his purchase of books and from direct statements in his correspondence, that the subject of the freedom of the will was already taking shape in his mind as the first offensive in this attack. But it would have to wait. The foreground was too much disturbed. He would have to give his whole thought to parish affairs. It must have seemed an ominous foreboding when, on June 19, 1748, Colonel John Stoddard,[24] Northampton's leading citizen and the pastor's unfailing friend in every preceding crisis, died. His staunch loyalty and wise counsels would be sorely missed in the bitter days ahead.

Chapter 12

Defeat and Dismissal

DISMISSAL from his Northampton pulpit gave Jonathan Edwards his best chance to belong to the ages. In the wilderness of Stockbridge he could preach old sermons to a handful of Indians and a smaller handful of whites, close the door of his four-by-eight-foot study, and make up his mind about the freedom of the will. Distance would bring its immunities. Not so many ministers would come by on horseback; the routine of parish life would be greatly simplified; in this lonely place he would be almost as close to England and Scotland as to Boston. He would be a free citizen of a larger world; not a small-town minister.

But had he known all this on June 22, 1750, the knowledge would have brought him scant consolation. Dismissal not only blotted his personal record and wrote failure over twenty-three years of earnest endeavor; it also brought the whole ministerial calling into reproach and injured the cause which meant more to him than his own happiness. Northampton would no longer be known as a peculiar center of God's power; it now became a symbol for strife and bitterness. Under his ministry the church had prospered. He had built the new meetinghouse. He had seen a generation grow up and take their places in church life. Many of those who accused him had professed conversion under his preaching. Now, ten to one, they had voted for him to go.

In part, he had brought the disaster upon himself, as he quite clearly recognized. To some degree, also, he was the victim of a community feud which had nothing to do with the question at issue, and, still more, a victim of the widespread unrest between clergy and laity over the matter of authority. The pews knew their power, and after more than ten years of opposition to ministerial autocracy, they were swift and ruthless in the exercise of it. Ministerial tenure was no longer for life, but quite openly at the will of the congregation. The Northampton dismissal had dozens of parallels in the mid-century, and for that reason made very little stir except in ministerial circles. To the laity at large it was just one more church quarrel. Jonathan Edwards himself had expected it for years and was making his arrangements. Only six months before it happened he wrote:

"I expect to leave my Pastoral office here when this year is out, which Ends in the last of April, as the People have reckoned from the Beginning for the Payment of my salary".[1]

He was dismissed in June.

On the surface, the dispute concerned the basis of admission to the sacrement of the Lord's Supper. Did the privilege belong only to those who had given public testimony of their own inner regeneration, or might it belong also to those who, failing such assurances, were not living "scandalous lives"? In other words, who is a Christian? He who has the evidence as an inner possession, or he who observes the ritual? Stripped down to its essentials, this is seen to be no petty dispute. "Experimental Piety" was the very rock on which New England Dissent had built its whole structure. Long before battle was joined, Jonathan Edwards had made his position clear; and now that the test had come he would pay dear for his championship, too late, of a cause already lost. But he was returning to the central principle from which the American church had taken its life. No wonder this quarrel could not die.

There was a peculiar irony in the fact that once again it reared its head in Northampton, where fifty years earlier Solomon Stoddard had dared to abandon "Experimental Piety" as the basis for admission to the Lord's table. Not the ghost of the old dispute, but the very body and bone of it now returned to ruin the career of his grandson and former colleague. The issue itself was unchanged, but the intellectual climate was so hostile to any such reversal that Jonathan Edwards was beaten before he renewed the battle. One does not with success, or even with safety, attempt to turn the clock back fifty years on any issue in any age, and Jonathan Edwards was not so naïve as to think he was an exception to the rule. Why then? The answer is implicit in every chapter of the story.

His grandfather, Solomon Stoddard, had been a very practical man. He knew people, and he knew what would work in church polity. He also knew that he was not living in John Cotton's day, and that in attempting to do so his own contemporary, Increase Mather, was something of an anachronism. Accordingly in 1700, when he put his ear low to the ground and heard ominous whispers of discontent from the Halfway members who were shut out from the Lord and he recognized that the Halfway Covenant, which in 1661 had seemed a vast concession to second generation Christians, was not good enough for their grandchildren. Accordingly also, when he decided to take his courage in hand, go one step further than 1661, and throw the door wide open to Covenant and non-Covenant members alike, he was not obeying a reckless impulse. He was initiating a plan which he thought would work. He had considered the hazards carefully and had decided the risk was worth taking. Besides, it might turn Halfway members into better Christians. His faith was justified. The plan did work.

It worked because, even as early as 1700, the old restriction had begun to look slightly too aristocratic. Men had already become more interested in working together than in being a peculiar people. By 1750, with Whitefield's preaching immediately behind them and the first rumblings of the Revolution dimly audible, their minds were fast becoming closed to any arguments for special privilege, as any one who read the Boston newspapers might have known. Whitefield's greatest mistake, in terms of his own popularity, had been his attempt to purify the ministry. To attempt to purify the membership was to invite mutiny. Solomon Stoddard's innovation had worked also because, in 1700, he had had the incalculable advantage (for such a rôle) of being a young man and the champion of a liberal cause. He was opening doors, not shutting them. This had also been the strength of Whitefield's preaching. To attempt to restrict any privileges whatever in 1750, let alone to withdraw privileges already enjoyed, was to go against the whole spirit of the mid-century. Jonathan Edwards' talk of restoring the sanctity of the Lord's Supper meant little to a generation for which church rites were not symbols of inner reality so much as personal prerogatives, to be protected at all cost. On its merits, the Halfway Covenant was a dead issue; revived, it acquired a significance which had far more to do with fair governance than with the communion of saints. The church member of 1750 was a democrat, although as yet he did not know it; and a good many of the "Boys of '76" were already born.

Still another weakness of Jonathan Edwards' position was the fact that he was reversing his own practice of twenty-three years. To revoke a privilege he had apparently sanctioned after it had been enjoyed beyond the memory of any but the oldest in the congregation, was madness. Any minister with a sense of fact and even an elementary understanding of human nature should have known he was courting his own destruction. In fact, Jonathan Edwards knew it; but, being an Edwards, he did not draw back from a losing fight. How could he do otherwise, he reasoned, once convinced that he had been wrong for twenty-three years? As to the expediency of such a move, he did not even consider it. "Expediency", in a matter of principle, was not a word in his vocabulary.

One must respect his honesty, at least, and his independence in announcing such a change of front. As for the change itself, the reasons are clear. As a young pastor he had naturally approached "Stoddard's Way" with a favorable bias. Grandfather Stoddard had been a kind of demigod to the Edwards children, and acceptance of his ideas was only natural. As a college student Jonathan Edwards had entered *The Safety of Appearing* and *The Appeal to the Learned* in his *Catalogue*, and had no doubt read them with pride in his relationship to so great a man. As a colleague pastor he had accepted the existing order, and then through the years had made his own observations. Theory and practice did not agree.

He had come to this decision unwillingly and had held his peace for years, having, as he said later, "no strength to oppose received notions and established customs—till it was too late".[2] By the early forties many of his brother ministers and many in his own congregation knew of his changed view, and by 1745 it was an open secret. In his *Religious Affections*, he had declared himself still more plainly; but no public statement was made to his people until 1748, when an application for membership brought the whole question before the parish in accordance with regular procedure. He made a formal statement before the Committee of the Church, announcing a state of controversy to exist between pastor and people, and as a first move requested the privilege of expressing his views in print. His request was granted. The result was his treatise, *A Humble Inquiry into the Rules of the Word of God, concerning the Qualifications Requisite to a Complete Standing and Full Communion with the Visible Christian Church*, published in the early autumn of 1749. In his own word, he had undertaken his part in this controversy (which proved to be "a contention between me and a great part of New England") "with the greatest reluctance that ever I undertook any public service in my life".[3] His phrase "public service" expresses exactly his own sense of the importance of this battle. It was so important that he put everything he had into the balance.

In the beginning the doctrinal issue had real validity for the congregation also. "Mr. Stoddard's Way" mattered for itself. Before long, however, the interpretations of pastoral motive in wishing to change it became more important than the scriptural or unscriptural basis on which it rested. Of all the interpretations expressed, the most damaging to the credit of the pastor was that in demanding evidence of "Experimental Piety" he himself wished to be judge of the "degree" of piety. This he stoutly denied in his treatise, in his statements before the committee, the church, and the council. He did not even insist that the applicant be able to state the time or the manner of his conversion. All that he asked was that church members be able to profess sincere belief in their own "renovation of heart" instead of mere knowledge of the doctrine and decent living. Once again, it was "heart" religion as distinguished from "head" religion. The "visibility of saints" to all but the eye of God was at best relative, he declared, but in his own inner consciousness a man might have assurance of his regeneration. As the outward symbol of this assurance, the sacrament of the Lord's Supper belonged only to those who could profess it as a reality. The rest, no matter how decently they lived, were mere spectators.

In the attempt to clarify his position, he submitted to the committee four forms of public profession, any one of which he was willing to accept, or to modify in any reasonable fashion. All four were rejected. Of these the two shortest were the following:

"I hope, I do truly find a heart to give up myself wholly to God, according to the tenor of that covenant of grace which was sealed in my baptism, and to walk in a way of that obedience to all the commandments of God, as long as I live".

"I hope I truly find in my heart a willingness to comply with all the commandments of God, which require me to give up myself wholly to him, and to serve him with my body and my spirit, and do accordingly now promise to walk in a way of obedience to all the commandments of God, as long as I live." [4]

When such seemingly noninflammable pledges could sound a battle cry, the nonsectarian of the present may well wonder what the great quarrel was about.

Painstakingly Jonathan Edwards set forth the scriptural basis for his position in the *Humble Inquiry*, a labor of several months. Temporarily, as he reported, "the Fermentation was much quell'd" by its publication, but only temporarily. In the summer of 1749, while he had been absorbed in writing it, rumors had continued to spread and community feeling had grown so greatly inflamed that the majority did not wish peace. They wished to be rid of "Mr. Edwards",

"root and branch, name and remnant".

Only twenty copies of the treatise were distributed in the town, and these were read by very few. To a modern judgment, it might seem that he flattered his people by expecting them to read it; but, if so, he had flattered them on every Sunday morning of his ministry, for neither in method nor in matter was it greatly different from the weekly sermons. Heavily freighted with Scripture, cogent in argument, it was addressed to those who knew their Bibles and cared for the doctrine. In the heat of controversy, it might have made good reading by candlelight, even in a parish which numbered few intellectuals. It was not read in Northampton in 1749, because the parish mind—at least the mind of the opposed faction—was already closed to any and all pastoral arguments, however cogent they might be. Jonathan Edwards might have known this from the rejection in April, 1749, of his offer to resign if, after the parish had had an opportunity to read his book, they still wished him to go. The majority wished it, without reading the book. Feeling ran so high by the time of its publication, that some of his parishioners would not even permit it to be brought into their houses.

To his adherents, some of whom were ready to defend it unread, he had proved his case, and had done so without casting dishonor on Solomon Stoddard's memory. Briefly stated, the point of this more than eighty-thousand-word treatise is that the Scriptures recognize not two kinds of saints, but one —those who can profess godliness. Those who can profess only the "common virtues" have no sanction in Holy Writ for their "promiscuous admission" to Christ's church. In support of his position Jonathan Edwards called to witness the history of the Israelites, the sayings of the prophets, and the parables of Jesus. Warrant there was none for admitting those whose only qualification was that they had not been guilty of scandalous living. Solomon Stoddard had been wrong. As for himself, the biblical authority was final; and, standing firmly on *Leviticus* 10:10, *Jeremiah* 15:19, *Ezekiel* 22:26 and 44:6-8, he rested his case, leaving the issue with God.

In terms of logic alone, victory was his. Solomon Stoddard also had been an encyclopedic student of the Bible—in his day, powerful in argument; but on the printed page he was no match for his grandson and former colleague. One by one Jonathan Edwards undermined his structure of proofs, keeping unswervingly to the doctrinal points at issue and treating his dead opponent with the respect and reverence which were his due. He had merely been mistaken.

Placed side by side, the arguments of the two men are seen to rest on entirely different foundations. To Solomon Stoddard the practical test was the final test. In order that God's work should prosper, public worship must be maintained and the Gospel ordinances celebrated. If godly men only might carry on such matters, there would soon be no one left to officiate in a church, not even a minister. In apostolic days it had been different: then indeed many might be called and few chosen. But now "Religion runs very low among the people of God; and . . . there is a great scarcity of Godly men". In some countries especially,

"Godly men are very thin sown" [5]

indeed. There may be only two or three in a parish. If all but this pitiful remnant be excluded from the celebration of God's ordinances, how will His work prosper? Therefore let the ungodly have a share; besides, participation may help them to be more godly. To Jonathan Edwards such service was lip service only, and exceedingly displeasing to God. Numbers were of no account. The hope of the church was that it should be one company, purged of the unregenerate and united in heart religion.

After his months of careful labor to assemble proofs of his position, the village indifference to his treatise was most disappointing. He must use other means. He therefore requested permission to preach his principles before the congregation. This was in October, 1749. The town at first flatly refused. After weeks of parley, however, and much persistence on both sides and much increase in the tenseness of community feeling, a grudging permission was granted. Five public lectures, delivered in March, 1750, were the result. On these occasions the aggrieved portion of the membership defeated the purpose of the request by staying away. It helped matters not at all that their places in the meetinghouse were taken by strangers from neighboring parishes who, having heard of the boycott, hastened to Northampton and thereby added to the ferment. Obviously the case of the pastor versus the congregation was deadlocked, and a crisis imminent. The time had come to call a council.

Even that was not so easy. In the fifty years since the Brattle Street Church was founded, both ministers and congregations had learned that the decisions of councils are determined beforehand, if the right delegates are picked. Mindful of this, the Northampton congregation wished to choose delegates opposed to the pastor. They also wished to restrict him to delegates chosen from Hampshire County, which almost to a man favored Solomon Stoddard's view of sacramental privileges. Jonathan Edwards objected. In so doing, he was adhering to the provisions of the Cambridge Platform, on which the practice of Massachusetts churches was based. The committee appointed by the town to treat with him concerning the make-up of the council based their arguments on the ruling of the Saybrook Platform, which was less liberal in this respect. In session after session the committee endeavored to wear down the pastor's resistance on this point, but in vain. After weeks of harassing argument, the town agreed to permit him the choice of two delegates outside the county, but reserved for themselves the right to make final choice from the nominations he submitted. He had really been defeated—in his own word, made a "Cipher".

Conduct of the whole affair was in the hands of a standing committee composed of nineteen men from the town and fifteen from the church. From these two groups smaller committees were chosen to wait upon the pastor from time to time and report back to the town. This detail of the procedure was one of Jonathan Edwards' main points of grievance from the beginning. He wished to call a church meeting and to speak to his people directly; not to plead his case with five men in his own parlor and have his words interpreted by them. One can hardly blame him. There is no indication that the final verdict would have been different had he spoken directly, or that he thought it would have been. He was merely contending once again for a ministerial privilege. As the leader of the flock a pastor should meet his people face to face on any matter which concerned them all, and not deal through interpreters. He also protested strongly the control of the affair by the precinct. This was not a precinct affair at all; it was an affair of the church membership. He had no controversy with the town, only with those who were of the communion. Why should the precinct be in control, and the congregation taking orders from them?

But his objections and protests were unheeded. As he wrote to his friend Joseph Bellamy:

"The People have a Resolution to get me out of Town speedily that disdains all Controul or Check. To make the matter strong, there is a Precinct meeting kept alive by adjournment".[6]

As a result the town was kept in ferment. After the March lectures opponents and adherents lined up openly and the battle was on.

The leader of the opposition was Joseph Hawley, a young cousin of Jonathan Edwards. At the time only twenty-six years old, he was gifted and spoiled. Massachusetts was later to know him as one of her leading public men, a vigorous "Son of Liberty", member of the Stamp Act Congress, and author of various inflammable slogans, notably,

"The Parliament of Great Britain has no right to legislate for us";
"Fight we must finally, unless Britain retreats."

He was the son of Joseph Hawley, who had committed suicide during the revival of 1735, and like his father, was given to fits of excessive melancholy. Eventually he became insane. In 1750, his college training behind him, he had returned to Northampton to begin his career as an attorney, and was naturally greatly flattered by being asked to become spokesman for the "aggrieved brethren". He also had private reasons for animosity toward the pastor. During the preceding two years his brother, Lieutenant Elisha Hawley, had been the target of town talk because of a shabby affair which pastoral censure had made public property. In such a case Jonathan Edwards was no respecter of cousins. Had he lived long enough, he would probably have rebuked his own son Pierrepont through the customary channels of church discipline, as well as privately, if Pierrepont's delinquencies had come under his pastoral jurisdiction.

Joseph Hawley's right-hand man was Major Seth Pomeroy, village blacksmith, already known to his fellow townsmen as "very high in liberty". Untutored, natural-born leader of men, he was everything Jonathan Edwards was not. If only the two could have joined forces, they would have made an invincible team. In the 1770's Seth Pomeroy also was to be a member of provincial congresses and a soldier whose fearlessness became a legend. Getting wind of the trouble at Bunker Hill, he raced to the scene, walking the last lap of the way because, according to his standards of Yankee integrity, a man had no right to risk a borrowed horse in the danger zone. He was then an old man, but he gave what he had left to the cause which men in that day called patriotism. In 1750 he was twenty-five years younger and twenty-five years more energetic. The blacksmith shop could not use all of him. Naturally combative, he needed a cause in which to fight; and, although doctrinal quarrels were hardly his theatre of action, here was a ready-made situation into which surplus energy and a vague resentment against personal privilege might be poured. Protest against the excise laws as yet lacked a concrete channel of expression. Besides, this grievance was still too far away. He took the cause at his own door.

Jonathan Edwards' strongest supporter was Colonel Timothy Dwight, Northampton's leading citizen since the death of John Stoddard. Wealthy lawyer and man of considerable importance in Hampshire County, he could not cope successfully with a man of Major Pomeroy's brusque effectiveness. He was not a good fighter; he had made the wrong alignments so far as the town "parties" were concerned and, like John Stoddard, he lived with a shade too much elegance to suit the villagers who gathered at the tavern to speak their minds. Deep down, too deep to come to open expression in 1750, the essential cause of this village rupture was neither doctrinal nor personal. It was a protest against an aristocratic minority. Jonathan Edwards had always had the wrong friends. For twenty years he had allied himself with a dictator, a man of Tory principles and a dignity too imposing for a one-street village. Now he had done it again. Besides, he lived with too much elegance himself, as his family budget had already proved. In this affair he was attempting to dictate to the town; one man to a whole population. His insistence upon presenting his case to the entire membership, instead of being willing to deal with the committees appointed by the town and the church to wait upon him, was high-handed Tory procedure. But the committees outnumbered him thirty-four to one, and they had the town and the membership behind them.

Dismissal was of course written in the stars from the beginning. It was only a matter of procedure. Town councils and church councils had learned to step warily in such matters, and above all, to move in the direction of the congregational wish, if this were at all consistent with a fair judgment. They remembered the decision of the Massachusetts General Court in the notorious Breck case of 1735, which, although ostensibly a question of doctrinal soundness or unsoundness, had speedily resolved itself into a tussle over final authority. No one had ever accused Jonathan Edwards of so crude a maneuver as the arrest of Robert Breck at the moment he was to appear in his own defence, but neither had anyone who disliked him ever forgotten that it was he who had drawn up the defence of the Hampshire Association when it came under the censure of the General Court. Certainly the opponents of Jonathan Edwards in Northampton did not forget, and when it came time to call the council they saw to it that Robert Breck was appointed. As for Robert Breck himself, he would have been a saint on earth if his vote against Jonathan Edwards had not been in part a vote of remembrance.

While the committees argued their way to a decision as to how to call a council, and also cast about for someone to answer the *Humble Inquiry,* the weeks passed. Peter Clark of Salem Village had been invited in January, 1750, to write the answer, and had been supplied with the notes Solomon Williams had prepared for this purpose. He kept the committee waiting until April, and then declined; whereupon the task devolved upon Solomon Williams himself. His reply took still more time while the village situation became still more tense. During all these months the communion, over which pulpit and pew were battling, could not be administered, for want of brotherly love between believers.

Extant sermons for the same period, however, show very little change from the customary Sunday preaching. Jonathan Edwards kept the controversy out of his pulpit, although with the town feeling so greatly inflamed almost any text he might have chosen would have seemed a veiled allusion to the subject uppermost in all their minds. Sometimes it was not even veiled. When, for example, in the month before the dismissal he preached from *Nehemiah* 1:3-4,

"And they said unto me, the remnant that are left of the captivity there in the province are in great affliction and reproach", he meant that his people make application to their own state. From the second of the two verses,

"And it came to pass, when I heard these words, that I sat down and wept, . . . and prayed before the God of heaven",

he framed his Doctrine, as follows:

"It becomes Saints in case of special Dis—?— & Calamity of Gods Children to betake thems.[elves] to G[od]".

He meant this also as specific counsel in the local dilemma.

One sermon particularly, preached in June, 1750, the month of the dismissal, must have been poignant in its effect, no matter what the mood of the congregation. He took as his text *Isaiah 32:17-18*,

"And the work of righteousness shall be peace; and the effect of righteousness quietness and assurance for ever.
"And my people shall dwell in a peaceable habitation, and in sure dwellings, and in quiet resting places".

The sermons themselves bear out the implications of the texts, suggesting that he was not using his pulpit as his personal stage during these trying months. Various letters written to other ministers indicate that he deliberately curtailed his journeys so as not to be absent from his people on Sundays, being as he said,

"especially loth to leave 'em destitute at this critical & difficult time with me & Them".[7]

Some of his enemies would not have credited him with such a motive.

The Council convened on June 19, 1750. It was not full, the church of Cold Spring having refused to join. This meant that there would be only nine lay delegates, and that Jonathan Edwards would lack one supporting vote. Edward Billings, pastor at Cold Spring, acted in his ministerial capacity only; he had no power to represent the church. The ten ministerial delegates were equally divided, as follows:

For Jonathan Edwards:	*Against him:*
Peter Reynolds (Enfield)	Robert Breck (Springfield)
Robert Abercrombie (Pelham)	Joseph Ashley (Sunderland)

For Jonathan Edwards:	Against him:
Edward Billings (Cold Spring)	Timothy Woodbridge (Hatfield)
David Hall (Sutton)	Chester Williams (Hadley)
William Hobby (Reading)	Jonathan Hubbard (Sheffield), Moderator.

That the ostensible issues were not the real issues, and that the spirit of the deliberations was anything but judicial, is clear enough from various subsequent statements, chiefly from the "confession" of Joseph Hawley, leader of the opposition. This "confession" was made twice over: once in a letter to Jonathan Edwards four years later, and again still later, in a letter to David Hall,[8] one of the supporting minority. This second letter, at Joseph Hawley's request, was printed in a Boston newspaper in 1760, after Jonathan Edwards was dead and the whole affair forgotten, except by a few who had occasion to remember. In the letter to Jonathan Edwards, Joseph Hawley's assumption of full blame for inciting the church to take action against the pastor, for presenting the written complaint of the church before the council, and for opposing the suggested adjournment of the council for a two-month period in the interest of a fairer verdict suggests the course of procedure and also its motivation. Joseph Hawley made unqualified admission of his own wrong spirit and disrespectful attitude, and recognized the "uncharitable conjecture" and the "unchristian heat", which had been back of the whole proceeding. He recalled his own sense of shock at the behavior of the opponents when the church vote was taken, saying that until that time he had not himself realized the "undue engagedness of the people", which even then had excited in him a sense of horror and filled him with great "concern and sorrow and melancholy".

The decision was of course a foregone conclusion. It was announced on June 22nd, after three days of deliberation. The questions put to the council were:

1. Whether it be the opinion of this council, that the reverend Mr. Edwards, persisting in his principles, and the church in theirs in opposition to his, and insisting on a separation, it is necessary that the relation between pastor and people be dissolved?

Resolved in the Affirmative.

2. Whether it be expedient that this relation be immediately dissolved?

Passed in the Affirmative.

A vote of the church body had previously been taken. Two

hundred and thirty male members had voted against him; twenty-three had voted for him; the remainder had refused to declare themselves. By his own statement most of his adherents were women.

A minority report, drawn up by William Hobby and signed by seven of the delegates, was presented under the same date. It was labelled *A Protest*. The grounds were: (1) Jonathan Edwards' sentiments on the subject of the dispute were thoroughly Christian, and his practice in harmony with that of the apostles; (2) his dismissal was out of proportion to the importance of the controversy; (3) there had been no attempt to convince either party of the truth or falseness of the conflicting principles; (4) the grounds for dismissal had not been set forth.[9] But protest was futile, as those who made it knew.

According to the *Diary* of David Hall, a close friend, Jonathan Edwards received the verdict calmly. The entry reads:

"that faithfull Witness received ye Shock, unshaken: I never saw ye lest Symptoms of displeasure in his Countenance. the whole week. but he appeared like a man of God, whose Hapiness was out of ye reach of his Enemies. and whose treasure was not only a future but a present good: overballencing all Imaginable Ills of Life, even to the Astonishment of many. who could not be at rest without his Dismission: it manifestly appeared to me".[10]

Jonathan Edwards' own journal of the whole affair, which runs to ninety printed pages, has the impersonality of an official record.[11]

He preached his farewell sermon on July 2, ten days after his formal dismissal. No church member able to walk would have missed it. With what inner quakings some must have taken their seats, or with what boldness others dared look straight at the Edwards pew, one may only imagine. In the long progress of the quarrel the whole village had become enmeshed. There had been no such thing as keeping aloof. Far too much had been said on both sides. This morning "Mr. Edwards" would have the last word. He was noted for his plain speaking. Had either his friends or his enemies ventured a guess as to what he would say, they were probably wrong. But few who heard would ever forget.

On such an occasion a man reveals himself, and on July 2, 1750, Jonathan Edwards revealed himself. Judged as a sermon, this farewell sermon is no masterpiece. It is not even a great sermon, but it is a biographical document of importance. He had had only ten days in which to make up his mind what to say. The immediate past was confusion; the future was a blank. His own emotions had been deeply stirred. Now that he had nothing more to lose, he might say what he wished. This last chapter was also his best chance for drama. He could cast opprobrium on his accusers, and berate his flock for disloyalty. He could make himself a martyr for righteousness' sake, or he could indulge in sentimental reminiscence. He chose to do none of these things. He had a genius for unforgettable texts; but this morning he chose one which would not have caused the slightest ripple of sensational anticipation. On first pronouncement its import would have been dark to the majority; and when the sermon was over not three persons in the congregation would have remembered what it was. Looked back upon, it appears to have been a superb choice:

"As also ye have acknowledged us in part, that we are your rejoicing, even as ye also are ours in the day of the Lord Jesus".*

With the statement of the *Doctrine*, "Ministers, and the people that have been under their care, must meet one another before Christ's tribunal at the day of judgment," it was clear that this sermon was to be definitely personal. Even so, it would not have made headlines. The preacher did not ignore the late unhappy events or make subtle allusions to them. His own sense of wrong was deeply and plainly apparent, particularly in such a phrase as "unhappy debate and controversy managed with much prejudice and want of candor". His triumph was rather that he dwarfed the importance of the whole affair by accepting it, and treating it as though it were already of the remote past. The time would come when mistakes would be known as mistakes, and the motives of men, worthy or otherwise, would be known and judged in their true light. He would wait. Discussion and debate were over. He was saying goodbye, and in saying it he chose to direct the thought of his people to that far future when minister and people would answer before God.

He addressed himself to group after group: the professors of godliness; those in a Christless condition; those under awakening; the young people, whose souls had ever been his

* II *Cor.* 1:14.

"peculiar concern"; the "lambs of the flock"—reminding each group in turn of that far-off day of reckoning. To each group it was the same message. The simplicity and clear sincerity of these repeated farewells must have been profoundly moving in spite of the unsympathetic attitude of the majority. There were no theatricals, no innuendoes. There was nothing to be angry about. The record was now finished.

"How often have we met together in the house of God in this relation? how often have I spoke to you, instructed, counselled, warned, directed, and fed you, and administered ordinances among you, as the people which were committed to my care, and of whose precious souls I had the charge? but in all probability, this never will be again. . . .

"It was three and twenty years, the 15th day of last February, since I have laboured in the work of the ministry, in the relation of a pastor to this church and congregation. . . .

"I have spent the prime of my life and strength in labours for your eternal welfare. . . .

"I have found the work of the ministry among you to be a great work indeed, a work of exceeding care, labour, and difficulty. . . .

"But now I have reason to think my work is finished which I had to do as your minister. You have publicly rejected me and my opportunities cease. . . .

"I desire that I may never forget this people, who have been so long my special charge, and that I may never cease to pray fervently for your prosperity. . . .

"And let me be remembered in the prayers of all God's people that are of a calm spirit, and are peaceable and faithful in Israel, of whatever opinion they may be with respect to terms of church communion. And let us all remember, and never forget our future solemn meeting on that great day of the Lord; the day of infallible decision, and of the everlasting and unalterable sentence.

"Amen." [12]

These are disarming last words. Except for Jonathan Edwards' own record that "many seemed to be much affected and some . . . exceedingly grieved", there is no news report of this occasion; but certainly many who heard must have found their mood changed by this quiet, poignant farewell. There was not much to say about a sermon like that, coming immediately in the wake of loud hatred and recrimination. He had pushed the whole quarrel years away, making it only an incident in the long panorama of a mutual relationship. His dismissal was now past history. He was content to let it stand

as a fact, as bare of comment as the statement on the Northampton Church Record:

"June 22, 1750. Revd Jonathan Edwards was dismissed".

What might be called his own private comment on his dismissal consists in a single word, and that word deleted. In
the manuscript rough draft of his farewell letter to his congregation, preserved among his papers, the final sentence
reads as follows,

"I am dear Brethren He who was your once affectionate and I
hope through grace faithful pastor & devoted servant for Jesus'
sake. J. E."[13]

The word *affectionate* is carefully crossed out. There is no
more eloquent personal detail in the whole sad story.

As a news item, his dismissal attracted very little attention
outside of Northampton. A letter of protest appeared in the
Boston News-Letter of July 23rd, one month later; but this
provoked no comment in the press. The "great noise" Jonathan Edwards spoke of concerned the doctrinal dispute only
and was confined to ministerial circles. The requisite sensationalism for a news broadcast was lacking. Jonathan Edwards did not march to the meetinghouse with his adherents,
as "Mr. Fisk" of Salem was moved to do; he was not arrested
by the civil authorities, or pushed down the stairs. The meetinghouse was not locked against him. Qualifications for admission to the Lord's Supper had no chance of making headlines in 1750; and the personal quarrel, lacking any central
incident, had become so generalized that almost any one of
the "aggrieved brethren", if quizzed by a reporter, might have
fumbled in his reply. The council hearings had been decorous
and thoroughly regular. There had been no public exhibitions
of temper, no personal defiance. In spite of numerous precedents for sensationalism in the current meetinghouse drama,
Northampton had at least regarded the external proprieties.

What action the Hampshire Association took relative to his
dismissal is not known, as the pages for the years 1748 to
1751 have been cut from the record. Why, only those who
mutilated the book could say. He had been a charter member,
and had performed valuable service. Did someone wish to
protect him from unfavorable comment? or possibly to protect the Association from criticism for action later recognized

as unworthy? When the record resumes in 1752, the brethren were dealing with the issues his dismissal had raised. Ironically enough, the 1752 meeting was held at Northampton, and one subject for discussion was

"Whether Ministers have an exclusive sole right to determine the proper Subjects of Baptism".

It is encouraging to read that in the following year they bent to the prevailing winds sufficiently to recognize a new problem,

"Mr. Bascom moved
Whether he can hold Communion with those Chhs * who tolerate members in the evil of Rebellion against Government? And also what is the duty of a chh. respecting its own members who have thus offended?" [14]

Before such a question could be admitted to discussion in such a body, much water had flowed under several bridges.

In 1750, the village tension having been relaxed by finality, both pulpit and pew looked ahead: Jonathan Edwards to find a new post, and the church to find a new pastor. Neither search yielded immediate results. Jonathan Edwards' personal problem was peculiarly acute. He was forty-six years old and, as he thought, well past his prime. He had a "numerous and chargeable" family to support, and no prospect of a suitable position, being as he himself admitted

"fitted for no other Business but study".

Had he known that he had less than eight more years to live, he might have felt vanquished indeed. Personal fame was no part of his thought. Even to lay down his burden was no relief. His chief concern, in the midst of his anxiety for the future and his very real sorrow at leaving his home and the people he had served for exactly half of his life, was that in spite of this "awful frown of Heaven" God would still "improve him for the good of souls". His letter written to his friend Thomas Gillespie in Scotland, the day after the Farewell Sermon, [15] is the word of neither a defeated nor an embittered man. He faced the difficult situation ahead of him with clear-eyed directness and unclouded vision, and although

* Churches.

the chance of another appointment as desirable as Northampton was scanty, he hoped for some door of usefulness to be opened speedily. Having so said, he went immediately to work to find it.

Unfortunately, it took him a long time. He remained in Northampton during the greater part of the following year, occupying the pulpit numerous times at the request of the supply committee and preaching at the homes of his adherents. So far as sermons and outlines bearing 1750-51 dates tell the story,[16] he avoided the controversial issue entirely; but his presence in the town naturally aroused the hopes of his friends and the fears of his enemies that he would consent to be pastor of a second church. Such was the usual sequel to parish schism. By his own statement, he did not consider such a project favorably at any time, although he was strongly urged to remain, particularly by Colonel Timothy Dwight, who offered to divide his own salary in order to make this possible. The project went as far as the addressing of a formal statement to five friends of Jonathan Edwards—Thomas Prince, Thomas Foxcroft, Peter Clark, William Hobby, and David Hall—presenting reasons for the proposal, and requesting ministerial advice as to procedure. According to this document [17] some preliminary canvass had already been made, for the proponents of the scheme state that "a Considerable Number in the Neighboring Towns" have declared their agreement with the principles of "Mr. Edwards" and will join such a church; also many in Northampton who either are in doubt as to his principles, or have been intimidated by his opponents and are "Cautious of Appearing for him", will undoubtedly be convinced and reconciled.

The conclusion of this appeal suggests that the whole project proceeded more from friendliness toward one in search of a station than from any large degree of confidence in the wisdom of the venture. The conclusion reads:

"If all above fails, Enquire of the Afores'd Gentlemen Messrs Rogers's & others about an Accadamy & put them all in mind for Encouragement that Mr Edwards dwell in a part of the Country where provisions are plenty & cheap & avocations & diversions rare & unusual".

All that was needed to set the town in another blaze was the rumor that a rival meetinghouse was in prospect. This was exactly what the opposition had expected, but exactly what they did not intend to permit. Excitement ran far higher over this alarm than over the dismissal itself. Besides, some scores had not yet been paid off, and here was a fresh opportunity. Doctrinal issues were again forgotten in a campaign of personal bitterness and recrimination which touched depths not reached in the earlier crisis. Jonathan Edwards' opponents laid aside their remaining reserve and badgered him openly. For some unexplained reason, the core of this second attack was an accusation made by Major Pomeroy in a church meeting prior to the dismissal, but carried no further at the time. He had asserted that it was plain to see the pastor was regarding his own "temporal Interest" rather than the good of the church, and thus laying a snare to catch them all. Rumors of the rival meetinghouse now confirmed this suspicion. The opposition speedily organized their campaign on this platform, assembling data to prove their case.

The adherents promptly drew up a formal protest [18] expressing their sense of shock at this procedure, and declaring that they would not take communion beside those who had thus reviled their former pastor. The surviving fragment of this protest contains quoted excerpts from the "traitors" which add touches of local color to grave dispute, as the great quarrel descended to lower and lower levels. One John Miller —labelled "another traitor"—allowed personal rancor to clothe itself in a barnyard figure, "uttered openly and in the hearing of several". Said he of "our late Pastor", according to the quoted summary:

"It would be well if his head was seven feet underground but he thot Six would do his turn and Mr Edwards was Just like his old Cow Lowing after a good mess".

The more unseemly abuse of Colonel Dwight, the pastor's staunch supporter, has been clipped from the manuscript, taking with it the signatures of the protesters. The "traitors" of course replied to this attack, and were again challenged. Even after Jonathan Edwards had accepted the Stockbridge post, the "accused brethren" went on replying to the "aggrieved brethren" until it would seem the whole dish must have been unsavory stale to all palates. Jonathan Edwards' word, "edged on by some at great distance, persons of note, —great men in civil authority," suggests a possible spur to continuance.

The Town Book tells the same story. There was no precedent for action in the case of a dismissed pastor who was still supplying the pulpit for ten pounds per Sabbath, and complications accordingly arose over nonessentials. On July 20th, a month after the dismissal, he asked a continuance of his rights for the current year in the meadow land formerly used by him. The town objected. The phrasing of their action is revealing. A committee was appointed

"to Confer with Mr Edwards on that affair, and to Convince him (If they Can) that he hath no right to that land, and if they Cannot convince him—
Then the Com.^{tee}, if they see Cause, may, if they will leave that matter to men, and that to be a final issue of the Case".[19]

Apparently they could not convince him, for at the meeting two weeks later the use of the land was denied to him by town vote. Jonathan Edwards' tenacity on this point was no doubt annoying, but the refusal of the town to make so slight a gesture of hospitality, while he still lived in their midst, is shocking enough as revealing the degree of bitterness which had been engendered. The Covenant of 1742, by which the congregation had pledged themselves anew not to "allow ourselves in backbiting," to "avoid all unchristian inveighings" and "reproachings", had been buried under too many grudges to be subject to recall.

Meanwhile several offers had come—one from Canaan, Connecticut, one from Lunenburg, Virginia, and one from Scotland;[20] but he appeared more interested in Stockbridge, having gone there to preach and to look the situation over six months before the first council had convened. Immediately after the dismissal he went again. It is easy to see why he was interested. His physical strength was hardly equal to another large pastorate. For ten years he had considered that he was living, as he said, "on the brink of the grave". Stockbridge seemed also to promise leisure for writing, and twenty-five years of study and thought were awaiting harvest. Moreover, in the long task of editing the Brainerd memorials, he had seen afresh the urgency of missionary work among the Indians. John Sergeant's place was vacant, and only a day's journey from his former life. In the midst of the Northampton clamors, Stockbridge seemed a haven. But first he would ask the advice of a council. Unfortunately there was still further delay.

The second council convened on May 15, 1751, six months

after the formal call had come from Stockbridge. Joseph Hawley was again spokesman for the disaffected members, who now saw their opportunity to dismiss "Mr. Edwards" from the proposed second church, which existed only as a friendly wish. In preparation for any move in the direction of turning the wish into a reality, the opponents drew up a "Remonstrance", which Joseph Hawley himself later characterized as "vile". The council asked for a conference with the church on the charges as stated. The church, prompted by Joseph Hawley, refused, nor would they appear before the council to sustain the charges they had preferred. Some members of the church protested such action, even in the intense partisanship of the moment; but Joseph Hawley was successful both in preventing the council from going before the church and in preventing representatives of the church from going before the council. The council of course advised Jonathan Edwards to accept Stockbridge, thus confirming his own private decision. This was on May 19, 1751.

In permitting this second council to be called at all, he had made a sad mistake. His own personal refusal of the proposal made by his adherents should have been enough. Yet such was his feeling for the customary proprieties that he wished to write finality on the whole affair through the channels recognized as official in such a case. Seven years later he followed the same course upon his removal from Stockbridge, and for the same reasons. Personal decisions were best made impersonal through the support of a council. Not to act thus was not to do things decently and in order. His reasons are understandable, but his judgment was poor. In fact, he had made a crucial mistake ever to enter his pulpit after July 2, 1750, thereby preventing the farewell sermon from really meaning farewell. Every sermon he had preached thereafter had merely been a fresh invitation to abuse, and though the vote of the town four months later had not expressly denied him the further privilege of his former pulpit, the implication was unmistakable. On November 19, 1750, the town settled his account to date, and henceforth made other arrangements.[21]

He entered on his Stockbridge labors in the summer of 1751, immediately after the adjournment of the advisory council. The warring brethren may have entertained sudden doubts as to their various procedures, when, coincident with his departure, the church was struck by lightning and the steeple damaged.

"The thunder of his power, who can understand",[22] wrote Ebenezer Hunt in his *Journal*.

With the church divided in two unequal parties, agreement on a new minister was well-nigh impossible. After two more years of dissension they decided to make no further attempt until the difficulties with the "aggrieved brethren" could be adjusted, and not until September of 1753 was it possible to settle on John Hooker, "no one contradicting". He accepted the call, and was ordained December 5, 1753, three years and a half after Jonathan Edwards had been dismissed. The Rev. Robert Breck gave the right hand of fellowship, a theatrical gesture indeed.

After his removal to Stockbridge, Jonathan Edwards put the whole affair behind him; and when, three years later, he was obliged to answer the "confession" of Joseph Hawley he did it with extreme reluctance, since it obliged him, as he said,

"renewedly to revolve in my mind, and particularly to look over that most disagreeable and dreadful scene, the Particulars of which I have long since very much dismiss'd from my mind, as having no Pleasure in the Thoughts of them".[23]

Joseph Hawley did all that a man could do: admitted his error, humbled himself, and asked forgiveness; but to Jonathan Edwards even this fell somewhat short of "proper Christian satisfaction—made as public as the offense Committed." He spoke quietly and without rancor, but it is plain to see the years had not dulled his deep sense of wrong nor obscured the details of the whole painful story. There was no resentment, only an inexorable insistence on the truth.

"I looked on my self, in the Time of the affair, as very greatly injured by the People in general, in the general Conduct, Managem[en]t, & Progress of it, from the Beginning to the End."

Even to ease a repentant man's conscience he would not soften the blow.

"Thus sir, I have done the Thing which you requested of me. I wish you may accept it in as Christian a manner as you asked it. . . . One thing I must desire of you, & that is, that if you dislike what I have written, you would not expect that I should carry on any Paper or Letter controversy with you on the subject. I have had enough of this Controversy, and desire to have done with it. I have spent enough of the precious Time of my Life in it heretofore. I desire and pray that God may enable you to view things truly, & as he views them, and so to act in the affair, as shall be best for you, & most for your Peace, living & dying." [24]

Three years later, Jonathan Edwards was dead. Fortunately for Joseph Hawley's peace, he had spoken in time.

The phrase "so contrary to the treatment due to me from that People" suggests exactly the aristocratic view of ministerial prerogative to which Jonathan Edwards was born and from which he never receded. If the Northampton people had been actuated by Christian principles, considering how long and how faithfully he had been their pastor, they would have treated him with "Tenderness, Calmness, and moderation, not to say Honour & Reverence".[25] Their successors have endeavored to make what restitution was left for them to make. Jonathan Edwards would like the symbolism he would quickly find at the doorway of the present church, as modern footprints still wear down the stone which was once the doorstep to the meetinghouse he built. The simple inscription on the upright to the third step would please him better than any eulogy.

> "The semi-circular stone below was the step of
> The Third Meeting-House
> 1737-1812
> Here Jonathan Edwards preached
> 1727-1750."

His defeat and dismissal were after all mere incidents; the "great work" went on.

BOOK THREE:
A New Beginning

Chapter 13

Missionary to the Indians

In the Judd MSS. there is the following entry:

"Mr. Edwards preached here Oct. 13, 1751 in P.M. from Heb. 11.16. (J. Judd preached A.M.)
"Oct. 16, Mr. Edwards & family removed. J.J. met them at Bartletts".

The *Diary* of Jonathan Judd adds,

"Oct. 16. Met Mr. Edwards and family at Lonard Bartletts. rd. some miles".[1]

With his formal installation as missionary over and some three months of active service already behind him, Jonathan Edwards had returned for his family and household goods. This was the real break with Northampton. Had removal followed hard upon dismissal, more than a year earlier, finality might have been a poignantly bitter experience; but after all the months of anxiety, abuse, and suspicion this farewell on October 16th must have been mainly a relief. At last the long uncertainty was over, and he knew where he was going.

That he already had deep qualms is a matter of record, despite his faith in the leadings of Providence. In leaving Northampton he was breaking every familiar association and changing the well-ordered pattern of his whole adult life. Less than a fortnight before, the passing of his forty-eighth milestone had reminded him that readjustment to a new scheme of life would not be easy. He admitted willingly that for the teaching of "savages" he had neither aptitude nor training. Furthermore, during the three months already spent at the mission, he had learned there was to be no peace from strife. He had walked into a veritable net, spread by the same enemies he was leaving behind. But the die was now cast. He turned his horses out of the King Street yard, taking with him his wife, his infant son Pierrepont, and seven other children, and headed toward the wilderness. His eldest daughter, Sarah, had already preceded him to Stockbrodge as the wife of Elihu Parsons. His daughter Mary had married Timothy Dwight, Jr. of Northampton, and was left behind in a new home next door to the Edwards parsonage on King Street. Stockbridge, by the road he followed, was slightly less than sixty miles away. It might just as well have been six hundred.

Henceforth, those who came would come on specific errands; no one would merely pass by, for Stockbridge was beyond the line of the frontier and a mere dot in the wilderness. Twelve white families, and two hundred and fifty Indian families, made up the population. The Mission stood in the center of the town. Around it were huddled the wigwams of the Indians who accepted its bounty, received blankets and food as they had need, but otherwise lived their tribal life with slight modification. They neither spoke nor understood English. The white settlement was entirely separate, a village within a village, and entirely dependent on itself for whatever had justified migration to this lonely spot. Beyond lay the larger wilderness, uncharted and full of manifold dangers. This was the farthermost edge of civilized America.

Temperamentally, Jonathan Edwards was fitted for isolation and solitude, even danger. Fear he did not know. Given some reasonable assurance of safety for his wife and children, and freedom to think his own thoughts, he would have welcomed the immunities of the wilderness. He had been born in "the Lord's Waste" and, surrounded by forests, felt completely at home. But unhappily, Stockbridge was to bring him peace neither without nor within. He might so easily have known this that he is hardly to be forgiven for not recognizing it months earlier and acting upon his knowledge. This new battle would not be one in which the outside world would take much interest. Stockbridge and the salvation of Indian souls were far remote from the daily thought of New England in the 1750's. She was already girding herself for a new struggle in which man's freedom on earth would become more important than his heavenly crown, and village disputes over doctrine and quarrels with the minister would be forgotten in the need for unity in a common cause. Joanthan Edwards might have been of little help in the counsels which laid the first foundations of American independence, but at any rate he was to have no part in them. The frontier was out of the current picture, and so was he, after he returned to it.

The Stockbridge mission had been born in Northampton

in 1734, at the home of Colonel John Stoddard, leading man of both town and church, and was therefore a foster child of the parish. This fact explains in part Jonathan Edwards' hospitality to the offer of the missionary's post. He had been one of the orignal group interested in launching the project, and had followed the fortunes of the mission through the intervening years.[2]

At the time of its founding, Colonel Stoddard had been more conversant with Indian affairs than any other man in Masachusetts. When he had been consulted as to the best location for a mission, he had advised the territory of the Housatunnocks, because they were not under French control, and therefore not Catholics. The Williams family, through Israel Williams of Hatfield and Stephen Williams of Longmeadow, had been prime movers in the affair. Stephen Williams had gone to secure the consent of the Housatunnocks, and when an agreement had finally been reached it was he who had sealed the bargain by presenting the Indians with a wampum belt. He had also been asked by Governor Belcher to find a suitable missionary and schoolmaster, and had named John Sergeant and Timothy Woodbridge. Both men had immediately been appointed. The Williams hold on the situation had been further strengthened at the outset by the settlement of Ephraim Williams and his family in Stockbridge, as one of the four families originally secured by the Commissioners to set an example of civilized living before the Indians. Shortly after the family had taken up their residence, Abigail Williams, daughter of Ephraim, had married John Sergeant, the first missionary. As a result, for thirteen years, Ephraim Williams had enjoyed a paternal relation to both the town and the mission. Naturally, at John Sergeant's death, neither he nor his family wished to relinquish this hold.

The Williams nominee for John Sergeant's post had been Ezra Stiles, a young friend of the family, then a tutor at Yale College. He was twenty-four years younger than Jonathan Edwards. It was only when Ezra Stiles refused to accept the post,[3] to the great disappointment of Abigail Sergeant, that Jonathan Edwards had his chance to become a candidate. When he went to Stockbridge in September, 1750, three months after his dismissal, to look the situation over with a view to settlement, he could hardly have failed to know that he was second choice. His sponsor was Samuel Hopkins, his close personal friend, then minister at Great Barrington, an hour's ride from Stockbridge. Samuel Hopkins should have known better than he spoke, when he told the Commissioners that Jonathan Edwards was "the most proper person for that mission" and also recommended him to both the Indian and white congregations as "the most suitable man for their minister".[4] Obviously this recommendation was dictated by affection rather than by critical discernment, for Jonathan Edwards was in almost all ways unfitted for the appointment. Besides, he was walking into a Williams stronghold, and therefore a veritable cave of the winds so far as currents of personal opposition were concerned.

There are vague suggestions that the roots of the Williams-Edwards disaffection went back to a remote feud between the Stoddard sisters, but remote causes are not necessary. Enough had happened in the preceding seven years to explain the concerted hostilities of the seven more still to come. Ephraim Williams was the uncle to Solomon Williams of Lebanon, who had replied to the *Humble Inquiry,* and was still to be replied to in devastating fashion. He was also uncle to Israel Williams of Hatfield, formidable opponent during the Whitefield era, and to Elisha Williams, long estranged tutor of the Weathersfield days. Within this frame, a network of minor hostilities crossed and recrossed the family alliances, until it would seem that nothing but polite tolerance would have been possible on either side. To make matters worse, coincidently with Jonathan Edwards' appointment, Elisha Williams, while on a visit to England, had been made a member of the governing board of the mission on behalf of the London Society for the Propagation of the Gospel, which paid the bulk of the missionary's salary. Shortly after this appointment, Madam Sergeant became the wife of Major Joseph Dwight,[5] appointed with Jonathan Edwards' approval Stockbridge resident in deputy charge of Indian affairs for the Boston Commissioners. By these two initial shifts in the situation, Jonathan Edwards was officially delivered into the hands of his enemies.

Hospitality and friendliness would have made the Stockbridge years pleasanter to live, but they could hardly have turned an ill-advised project into a successful venture. The Stockbridge mission had been conceived in error and was doomed to fail from the outset. Even the founding of the town was artificial. Stockbridge had not originally been an Indian trading post at all. It was merely a point on the map, equidistant from two small Housatunnock villages. Funds being lacking to build a church in each village, this halfway point was chosen as a seat of operations. By the original plan, the Indians left their own lands in the fall, came to Stockbridge and set up their wigwams around the meetinghouse. During the week they went to school, and on Sunday they went to church. When spring came, they returned to their farm lands, planted their crops, and cheerfully forgot all they had learned. In the fall, they traded their harvest to the Dutch for rum, and those who survived the consequent orgy came to Stockbridge for more alphabet and more sermons. No wonder they thought preaching and prayer and Sabbath keeping were for the winter; freedom to go their own wilderness ways, and chiefly to get drunk, was for the summer.

In 1736, the Commissioners for Indian affairs had sought to rectify the original mistake by offering the Housatunnocks land nearer to Stockbridge in return for their own holdings. After long parley and much persuasion, the Indians consented; but they were suspicious and, some of them, openly resentful. The suspicion and resentment resulting from this land transaction persisted as long as the mission endured, returning in various forms to plague the missionaries, Jonathan Edwards among them.

An equally serious handicap to success had been the coming of the Mohawks as co-settlers with the Housatunnocks. The motives behind this invitation were practical, even financial. By it the Boston Commissioners thought to foster their trade interests by preventing the steady migration of the Mohawks into Canada, and the Mission authorities thought to secure the annual gift of Isaac Hollis, conditional upon the finding of twelve Indian boys to live in the boarding school he had founded. There were not twelve Housatunnocks willing to come. Hence the invitation to the Mohawks. Once again it was a compromise, and a poor one, for the Mohawks were the terror of every other Indian tribe in the north country and also, because of the labors of the Catholic missionaries among them, they inclined strongly to the French interest as against the English. With rumors of war in the air, the presence of the Mohawks jeopardized the peace of the Indian settlement, already riven with jealousy and suspicion, and greatly increased the peril of the small English minority.

But the chief barrier to the success of missionary work among the Indians was the concept the missionaries themselves had of their task. Indians had long since ceased to be curiosities or, except in war time, even a terror. King Philip had been long dead. They were now souls, "lost heathen souls", "among whom Satan's Kingdom has remain'd so long undisturb'd".[6] Missionaries were God-appointed agents of their salvation, and were to be especially rewarded for the heroism and sacrifice their labors entailed. David Brainerd, thanks to Jonathan Edwards, had become the saintly example of the ideal missionary. To a modern reader, he is an example of the exact opposite. His story can hardly be read with composure, much less with admiration. Instead of attempting to endure rigors which would have been challenging enough to a hardy woodsman born to them, David Brainerd should have been in a sanitarium from his college days forward. To force himself between hemorrhages to take long horseback journeys in all weathers, to live alone in rude huts, or to be carried to the mission when he was too ill to go on foot—these are the specifications of heroism set down to his heavenly glory. Before his death he admitted that he had mistreated his frail body; but, like other missionaries of his day, he failed to see that he had been pursuing sainthood, and to that end glorying in the very hardships and sufferings which hastened his death.

Gideon Hawley, another young missionary, a protégé of Jonathan Edwards, by his own statement, would have given up his labors among the Indians a hundred times, except for the glory of the sacrifice he knew himself to be making, and the "sanctity" of the missionary's character as he aspired toward it. In one of his saddlebags he carried the *Life of David Brainerd,* and when it seemed he could not endure loneliness and hardship another day, he read a chapter and was spurred to emulation. When even this failed, he turned his horse toward Stockbridge, and spent a few days with "Mr. Edwards".

These men had little interest in Indians except as souls to be saved. They believed them as a race to be of a low order of creation, "a base, ungrateful People, insensible of Kindnesses done them".[7] In current sermon epithet they were "the miserable Natives". Their customs were foolish and wicked, their traditions ridiculous, their language a "barbarous and imperfect Dialect", their worship of the "Great Spirit" blasphemous. Samuel Hopkins narrates a teasing scrap of folk-tale of the heavenly visitant who descended to earth with snowshoes on his feet, cleared the land of monsters, taught the people charitable customs, and was annually remembered in a ceremony of gratitude to the Great Spirit; but he tells it only to "excite compassion toward such ignorant creatures".[8] There is among Jonathan Edwards' Stockbridge papers a single sheet on which two lines of copy are set for Ebenezer Manumaseet on a school day. One of these, for the sake of ironic rebuke, might stand beside Samuel Hopkins' compassionate motive. In a large, inexperienced hand, Ebenezer (his thoughts no doubt far away), crookedly traced his copy in the legend,

"He that pities another thinks on himself",[9]

and then signed his hybrid name twice over.

Missionary work proceeded on the hypothesis that only as the Indians laid aside their own customs and lived according to the English fashion could Satan's kingdom be overthrown. Above all, they must be baptized and keep a New England Sabbath. Among his evidences for the prosperity of the Gospel, John Sergeant, the first Stockbridge missionary, listed the fact that the marriage banns of Ebenezer and his chosen squaw, Sarah, had been duly published at the Sunday service, and that the Indians taken to Yale College to see their sons, had behaved "with much decency", particularly when they were being shown the "Library, and the Rarities of the College". Apparently the humor of this "conducted tour" dawned on no one.

The intense zeal of these men who counted baptisms so eagerly, and seized upon any evidence that Indian ways were being eradicated, pays tribute to the human capacity for endurance, self-sacrifice, and tenacity of purpose; but it is a tale which belongs in the annals of grim asceticism rather than in the annals of man's labors for his fellow man. For heroism and the ability to endure hardness, the tales of the forty-niners of the next century, in their admittedly selfish quest, are greatly more thrilling. By comparision, the tales of David Brainerd, and those who followed the pattern he had set, are merely pathetic, although that was least of all their fault. In their concept of Christian service toward a saintly end, the more difficult the more saintly, they were the children of their own day, as all men must be.

Jonathan Edwards had written David Brainerd's *Life* and edited his *Journals*. He had paid him tributes without number and thought him a very eminent Christian, but in the whole record of his own missionary labors there is not a suggestion at any point that he regarded the missionary's life as peculiarly saintly, or the slightest hint of an ascetic attitude toward his own labors. He had more than his share of illness and pain, but within the limits of his rigorous program of study and pastoral ministration he guarded carefully what health was permitted him, took sensible precautions, and in his own allusions to his physical state was almost apologetic for his frailties. Naturally he shared the current view that the Indian was a soul to be saved, but he took this for granted. It was no more true for Indians than for his own children and his Northampton parishioners. Baptism might be the beginning, middle, or end of the missionary's labor, but it was not the goal. His understanding of the Stockbridge problem and his administration of Mission affairs, for one of his day, were surprisingly realistic.

When he arrived in Stockbridge in 1751, the Mission had been in existence for seventeen years. For two years, since the death of John Sergeant, no one had been in direct charge. Mission affairs had been loosely handled through long-distance control from Boston. Mohawks and Housatunnocks were now living side by side, filled with mutual hatred and jealousy. The original nucleus of four families in the English settlement had been increased to twelve, most of them closely related to each other. Jonathan Edwards faced the problem of ministering to an Indian population fatally divided against itself, and to a small clique of whites, half of whom were his personal enemies and that half in control of the town. Nominally the head of the Mission, he was actually helpless to direct its affairs.

How much or how little he knew about all this before he took charge is not clear; but three weeks after his formal installation as missionary [10] he wrote a letter to the Boston Commissioners for Indian affairs, setting forth the whole situation in plain language and proposing a plan which he thought would end the Williams domination at one stroke, and put him as missionary in actual as well as nominal control of the situation. His proposal called for the appointment of resident Trustees to coördinate the activities of the Mission, exercise disinterested supervision, make inspections, and be held accountable for all moneys. Thus, he concluded, would the confusions which had hitherto prevailed be ended and impartiality take the place of profitable control. His clear-cut analysis stripped the situation down to fundamentals, his arguments for centralized authority and the disinterested handling of public funds were based on principles which commend themselves as sound to anyone acquainted with administrative problems. That his own personal peace would be greatly increased under such an arrangement, he doubtless also foresaw. What neither he nor anyone else could have foreseen was that Major Joseph Dwight, an erstwhile friend, and a man thoroughly competent for the post of resident agent for the Commissioners, would straightway marry Madam Sergeant, thereby allying himself to the Williams family and becoming an enemy to the missionary, with power to act. By this turn of events, Jonathan Edwards' position became almost untenable.

In this same letter he made suggestions for internal improvement in the administration of mission affairs, which show that he had a grasp of the problem in its larger aspects, and a concept of missionary work which looked toward the far future. The first necessity, as he saw it, was the appointment of a young and likely scholar to learn the Mohawk language and to introduce English among the Mohawk children. He should be offered a good salary and have two English boys under his direction. The previous fifteen years of instruction in the school had been wasted; Indian children had merely made sounds for signs, having no notion whatever of what they were reading. In addition, he advocated either bringing the English children into the Indian school or else farming out the Indian children for a year or two in the English families and then returning them to the school. The latter plan he regarded as the more practical; it would also be more agreeable to the Indians.

He wrote this letter in August, two months before he returned to Northampton for his family. Meanwhile he had gone ahead with temporary arrangements for a house and had petitioned the General Court for permission to purchase land from the Indians. There was no parsonage, no land purchasable from the whites on which to build one, and no land sequestered for the ministry. The winter was coming on; his numerous family would require a large and immediate wood supply as well as a commodious shelter. His petition called for two tracts: one as near as possible to the center of the town for a homestead, and the other, a plot of woodland. He was making plans for permanent residence. In the following year, when the house was finished, he allowed a petition to be presented to the Court that it be purchased as a parsonage, but this petition was denied. Colonel Ephraim had been present at the session and was

"constantly busy with the Representatives, with his Lime-juice

Punch & Wine. Objections were made against the Petition which could come from none but He",[11]

Jonathan Edwards wrote, in explanation of this defeat. At every juncture he was to be reminded that his presence in the town was not agreeable to its leaders.

Even apart from personal hostility, the situation presented problems enough. His duties, while not arduous, called for readjustment in his whole thought of the pastoral relationship. Instead of one congregation he had two, with distinctly different needs. In Northampton he had been directly responsible to the people he had served, and had received his salary from them. He was now responsible to the Society for the Propagation of the Gospel in London,[12] to two congregations, and to the Boston Commissioners, who had general supervision of all matters pertinent to Indian settlements, and power to disburse all moneys. Communication with remote centers of authority meant long delays; often before the reply came the situation had changd completely. The Boston Commissioners were in sympathy with the missionary's labors; but naturally they were more interested in Indian trade and Indian loyalty in time of war, regarding the mission as a valuable means of promoting friendship toward these ends. To Jonathan Edwards this was a result of his work, not a motive for doing it. For this reason, even though the local agencies of coöperation had been friendly, he would have found it difficult enough to share his pastoral responsibilities with those to whom "God's work" was a profitable investment, to be promoted for selfish ends.

Moreover, he was responsible for the Hollis boarding school for Indian boys, white elephant of the Stockbridge missionary. From the beginning Housatunnock boys had been most unwilling to be enrolled; they would not stay after they had agreed to come, and yet the missionary must see to it that the number of pupils did not fall below twelve, else the annual gift would be withdrawn. To complicate matters still more, the Hollis schoolmaster was responsible only to Isaac Hollis, who paid his salary, but the missionary was responsible for the school and, by the terms of his appointment, obliged to deal with complaints from the pupils. It was a clumsy arrangement and made for endless friction. At the time of Jonathan Edwards' appointment, Captain Martin Kellogg, a friend and relative by marriage of Elisha Williams, held the post of schoolmaster. He was clearly incompetent.

The boys poured their complaints into the missionary's ears, but he could do little to help them. Isaac Hollis would not answer his letters. Captain Kellogg would have no dealings with him. The Boston Commissioners were not interested in such petty details. The situation was deadlocked. Meanwhile, Elisha Williams had persuaded the London Society to open a similar boarding school for Indian girls, thus doubling the problem and more, for the society had agreed to support this new school,

"provid⁴ Mrs. Sergeant [undertake] ye management & education of such girls".[13]

They had sealed the bargain by paying her a year's salary in advance "for her trouble", while the project was still a project, and had also made generous grants looking toward the necessary preparations. From the missionary's point of view, the prospect of a second school was anything but hopeful, as the dissatisfied boys from the school already in existence continued to interrupt parsonage mornings with their complaints and appeals.

If the Stockbridge story were to be told in pictures, one of these would be the picture of Jonathan Edwards listening with difficulty to the broken English and sign language of Solomon, Hendrick, Jacob, and the others, asking questions himself in broken Indian, and making careful jottings under each name as the conference went on. Not enough blankets, said the boys; not enough to eat; salt meat and porridge only; lumps of bran in the meal; boys going ragged to meeting; some boys have no breeches; all boys hired out to work six days in the week; catechism on Saturday nights only, and the Bible read but once. Such was their story, and such was one item of everyday reality in the missionary's life, as the surviving jottings reveal it.[14]

Minutiae of this sort did not irk Jonathan Edwards. He was well accustomed to stories of distress which would have seemed petty to those of another calling, and he made friends for life of those who sought his help. But he could not, in his full maturity, content himself with such a foreground of pastoral duties when he saw so clearly the mistakes and handicaps of the situation in which he found himself. Disqualified as he was by temperament and maturity for the post of a hireling, and miscast as a preacher to "savages", his analysis of the mission problem, past, present, future, political and educational as well as religious, suggests that the trustees of New Jersey College were probably not making any mistake when, too late, they invited him to take charge as president. He had the detachment of the administrator, and saw the problem which lay underneath the details of a given situation. In fact, the entire sheaf of his voluminous correspondence with the Boston Commissioners and the London Society contradicts the oft-repeated notion that he was incapable of handling practical affairs. He may have preferred to split metaphysical hairs, given a morning free from the complaints of Solomon, Hendrick, and Jacob, and he may have been as absent-minded as some have been pleased to assume; but he could also balance a budget, plan a vocational course of study for those whose I.Q.'s were on the minus side, and direct mission activities with reference to the daily lives of those for whom it existed, as well as preach toward their eventual Christianization.

He also had a grasp of the larger aspects of the missionary problem surprising for the mid-eighteenth century. A letter written to Joseph Paine,[15] official of the London Society, six months after his appointment, sets forth the conflict between commercial and religious interest, the waste of public moneys, the duplication of effort by rival missionaries, and outlines a plan of centralized effort, with education the main objective, which sounds more like missionary planning a century later than that of pre-Revolution days. There is nothing whatever of the evangelist's point of view in this letter; he might be speaking of a program for a business enterprise. His suggestions are those of a practical man, who faces conditions as they are and acts accordingly.

A fundamental disqualification is apparent, however, in this same letter, for one who would be a leader of men. Jonathan Edwards lacked tactfulness, and he lacked it pitifully. Although writing on this occasion to a British clergyman, he summarily disposed of the Church of England missionaries by saying they were

"almost universally High Churchmen, & great Bigots, using all manner of methods to promote their own party, & to Encroach upon & root out the N— England Churches, & engross Everything to themselves".

He adds that he had found them no less active in their own interest than the Papists. His point as to the waste of money would have been entirely clear without this derogatory judgment, but it would never have occurred to him to delete it out of consideration for his British correspondent. Moreover, to say unpleasant things other than unpleasantly was not among his talents. He reaped much unhappiness thereby.

No doubt during his two-year struggle to free himself, at least officially, from the tangle in which he was enmeshed, this propensity to speak bluntly at inopportune times added materially to his distresses; but it would have taken more than tact to iron out the difficulties in the Stockbridge situation. This was a case for plain speaking, and he spoke out. The essence of his complaint was that Ephraim Williams and Joseph Dwight had turned their legitimate prerogatives into a despotic control of both the town and the mission, and that this control was highly profitable to themselves but fatal to the peace of the town and the success of the mission. Control was paying dividends and creating posts for one member of the family after another. Public money was being shamelessly wasted, to the great advantage of the Dwights. As the headmistress of the new girls' school, Madam Sergeant (now Madam Dwight) expected her children to be educated at the public charge. Joseph Dwight's son would be a teacher in the boys' school. Joseph Dwight himself would be steward of both schools. The government bounty was being distributed through his shop, with great profit to himself. In fact, Jonathan Edwards concluded, events were fast shaping

"to establish a Dominion of the Family of Williams's over Stockbridge affairs".

This letter was written to Speaker Hubbard in August, 1752. There was no invective, no expression of personal resentment. He was merely stating facts, adding:

"You may use this letter as you wish:—I have used freedom in this case of extremity".[16]

Had he merely been making criticism of the Williams family, the Commissioners would have turned a deaf ear. Men of Ephraim Williams' ability who were willing to spend their lives in the wilderness had been hard to find. If he and his family connection had profited financially, why not? They had earned their reward. As to Joseph Dwight, he was a man of force. Indian affairs were in a precarious state; at any minute the colonial government might have a war on their hands, and in that event, the fact that their representative was reaping private gain from his official position was of less importance than that he would be a good man to keep the peace. At least, so they thought. It was only when Jonathan Edwards pointed out the deep distrust with which the Indians had come to regard both Ephraim Williams and Joseph Dwight that they began to give ear to his charges. His argument was deeply strengthened by the burning, in the spring of 1753, of the boys' boarding school, and the loud whispers that this had reference to party faction.[17] When the Commissioners realized that violence was already at hand, they took a new view of the situation and looked afresh into the array of facts before them. As a result, their eyes were opened, and the subsequent fight of the united Williams cohorts was powerless. Their domination was swiftly ended.

In the spring of 1754 Jonathan Edwards wrote to Colonel Timothy Dwight of Northampton:

"Brigr D. is doubtless about to remove; and I hear that Elijah Williams is in a Disposition to sell. our Difficulties with the Indians I think are all over".[18]

He was wrong. They were just beginning.

Fortunately for the part he was to play during the coming months of anxiety and danger, his three years of residence had won for him the confidence and to some degree the esteem of both congregations. His pastoral labors had been more successful than his preaching. The Indians liked him. His patience and disinterested service on their behalf had convinced them of his friendliness, in spite of his fine distinctions as to sacramental privileges, particularly baptism, a ceremony by which they set great store. There were occasional explosions over his unwillingness to baptize all who presented themselves or their children for the honor, but these were after all relatively infrequent and of minor importance. Within the strict limits of the meetinghouse and its blessings, the pastoral scene was pleasant.

His success as preacher to the Indian congregation was seriously qualified by his inability to handle either the Housatunnock or Mohawk languages in public. For practical weekday purposes he could negotiate in the Housatunnock, but in the pulpit he kept to English. It was a serious handicap and, as he himself recognized, legitimate basis for some of the criticism that he was unsuited to his office. Before he came, the Indians had heard Sunday sermons in their own language; now they were obliged to piece them together sentence by sentence through an interpreter. He made repeated efforts to overcome his infirmity, as he called it, but was unable to do so. His children, who heard more Indian than English, all spoke it fluently, but his own proficiency in the tongues was reserved for ancient Hebrew.

His sermons to the Indians were mostly New Testament sermons, explaining very simply the joys of heaven to which drunken Indians do not go, the anger of God against sinners, particularly drunkards, and the practical virtues of Christian living, of which temperance is mentioned twice as often as any of the others. For "their darling vice", drunkenness, according to Housatunnock imagery,

"is a great logg across ye path which ye traveller cant climb nor go round".[19]

On a page headed "A Talk to St. Indians about Drink", Jonathan Edwards set down ten points for counsel and reproof. This skeleton preachment is representative of the spirit and method of his missionary labors. He wrote:

"1. I am sorry to hear of such things among you as are the occasion of this meeting. It will [be] sorrowful to all good People to hear such things of the Indians at Stockbridge with whom so much Pains have been taken & so many means used to bring em to God.

"2. But none have so much Reason to be concerned about it as you for if this Trade of getting too much Drink goes on among [you] it will Tend more to Hurt than any Bodies else.

"3. You pretend to be Christians & some of the People of J[esus] X but how unworthy & unbecoming Xtians is it to follow such a practice as this. By this Practice, men instead of being Xtians make Fools of thems. & make thems. like Beasts. It is beneath man.

"You hope to be the Child[ren] of G. and go to Heaven when you die but who can think that the great & holy G. will take such as make Beasts of thems. to Heaven. Who can believe He will take such to live with glorious saints and angels forevermore.

"If you go on with this Practice all the Instructions you have had & your Baptism & your coming to meeting will never do you any good.

"You have greater Light than other Indians but if you go on in sin your Light will do you no good but Hurt. God will be much more angry with you than with the Indians that never heard of the Gospel.

"You know your Duty more than others, & G. has done more for you than others & therefore if you dont do your duty you will have a hotter Place in Hell than the Heathen that never heard of J.X." [20]

He went on to remind them of the pains Mr. Sergeant had taken to make them into good Indians, of the interest "Gentlemen abroad" had shown, in laying out their money on the mission. Housatunnocks will be a "stumbling block before the Mohawks" if they persist in this wickedness. It is time to make a great resolution. If they do they will be very happy, both in this world and in the world to come. But if they do not they will be very miserable, both now and forevermore.

Whether metaphysics and theology gained or lost by such tasks in the foreground, who shall say? Certainly to Jonathan Edwards there was nothing inconsistent about the picture of himself in the rôle these memoranda suggest. For a later day, like so many other pictures which might recall his story, this one is made of strangely incongruous elements: the log meetinghouse, a handful of grave-faced Indians sitting in straight rows, their blankets drawn close around them; behind the desk one of the great intellects of his time, and a quiet voice saying, It is not good to get drunk.

His sermons both to Indians and to whites were all old sermons, for with the removal to Stockbridge his preaching days were definitely over. He merely went back into his files, marking sermon parts to be omitted, making slight additions here and there, but rarely working out a new sermon from an old text. His preparation was still meticulous. He would not have stood up before a dozen illiterate Indians without a carefully prepared outline before him. It would seem that almost anyone who had twenty-five years of public speaking behind him would have welcomed the Mohawks extemporaneously, but not Jonathan Edwards. Carefully he wrote out his speech:

"Your Coming here will rejoyce the Hearts of all Good men as They will hope it will be a means of your coming into greater Light & Knowledge in the Xtian Religion and so be a means of your Et[ernal] salvation and Happiness.

"We dont desire to keep you from the Kn[owledge] of the Bible the Word of G. as the French Priests do their Indians. We are willing that you could read the word of G. as well as we & know as much as we.

"While I continue here I shall be willing to come from time to time & to do my utmost to instruct you in the true Xtian Relig[ion]." [21]

With the outbreak of war in 1754, the whole mission situation changed abruptly. Many of the Christian Indians enlisted, leaving only a remnant to hear sermons and write in their copybooks. Most of the mission work was at a standstill. For the next three years there was scarcely a month in which those who remained in the settlement were not in actual danger. Hostile Indians without and treacherous Indians within kept the community on continual tension. A climax of terror came in the early fall of 1754 when several whites were murdered in the near vicinity. Immediately the town residents, together with settlers from the outlying territory, flocked to the Edwards home. A fort was hastily built around the house, and within this enclosure what Jonathan Edwards referred to as "great numbers" were fed, sheltered, and warmed until the peak of danger had passed. In his report to the General Court of moneys spent, he estimated that no less than eight hundred meals had been served, the equivalent of twenty-four hours' pasturage for a hundred and fifty horses provided, and seven gallons, one quart, of the Edwards supply of good West India rum consumed. While the fort was being built, he had also made provision for the laborers, who had consumed a hundred and eighty more meals; and when their building materials ran short he had supplied fifteen rods of new log fence which had cost him ten shillings per rod. To these items must also be added the fact that during the whole of this autumn and winter of fear, Jonathan Edwards was severely ill with what numerous family letters refer to as "Feaver and Ague, having a severe fit almost every day". In the following spring, when he wrote for increased military protection and protested that he could not much longer house the four soldiers then quartered at his house, he gave as one of his reasons his own "low state of health", which still incapacitated him from going after the necessary provisions with which to feed them. To read between the lines of such a record is to find a truer picture of the missionary's place in a frontier society than the number of baptisms could possibly suggest.

The Edwards parsonage was also a haven of hospitality to visitors on horseback, just as it had been in Northampton. If guests from afar came less frequently they stayed longer, and if they belonged to the wilderness they counted Stockbridge a second home. The *Journal* of Gideon Hawley [22] includes entry after entry telling of spending "several days very agreeably" at "Mr. Edwards' House", of dropping in unexpectedly, of being cared for through illness, and of meeting others there who had done likewise. On one such occasion, he found *Pamela* on the family table, and wrote that he was "exceedingly delighted with it". The suggested picture is pleasant. Life was not all discord and fear. The wilderness had even its conveniences, as one of the Edwards daughters put it. Not a week passed, she wrote, without some chance to send or receive letters. If danger added four soldiers to the household for weeks together, the circle was merely enlarged and the family altar surrounded as usual.

During another troubled period in 1756 Esther Burr, the second daughter, returned to pay her parents a visit, bringing with her Aaron Burr, her infant son, later to be the center of so many storms. Esther had married during the first summer after the family left Northampton, and this was her first home-coming. It was also to be her last. She hardly enjoyed her visit, for, not having lived with the Indian danger as her sisters had done, she was beside herself with terror during the whole of her stay, and would have gone home immediately except for her father's disapproval. His word was still law to her, as it had been when she was a child.

"So I must tarry the propos'd time, & if the Indians get me, they get me",[23]

she wrote in her *Journal*. Beautiful, fragile Esther Burr was made for the adventures of the spirit, not for the rigors of the wilderness, and for all her expressed willingness to die, if it were her time, she could scarcely have taken horse and ridden away to Northampton, as her mother did during this perilous time.

In this *Journal,* written in the form of letters to Sally Prince of Boston, she left almost a day-to-day record of her Stockbridge visit, as also of many other adult experiences. Her self-revelation in these entries is more important than her news. Her sparkling gaiety and gift for witty repartee, the "peculiar smartness in her make and temper", which had troubled the peace of more than one young minister during her eligible years, are on nearly every page. "Form'd to please", Samuel Hopkins had called her; and, in different epithets, so had various other young admirers, who aspired but did not attain. She had the Pierrepont gaiety and charm, the Edwards sharpness of tongue. Even her sisters were careful not to push her too far.

"You know she never could bear pestering very well, but I think She grows worse about it [Lucy wrote]. So we must take care what we say." [24]

Her quite typical comment on the Stockridge troubles had been:

"I think Mr Dwight deserves to be Licked".[25]

Her training is reflected in every view she expressed. She was so loyal to it that she did not know she was loyal. It had become her own standard of measurement. When General Braddock was killed and his army defeated, her remark might have been spoken from a pulpit:

"Our Sins, Our Sins, they are grown up to the very heavens".[26]

When her husband put tickets in a Philadelphia lottery, including one for little Sally, she wrote:

"But none for me, because I am against it".[27]

"Mr. Burr" might make deletions of her gay nonsense from an occasional letter, but not even he was guardian of her conscience. When she discovered that her little Sally, like Timothy's Mary, had a "crooked neck", the deformity feared in each of the Edwards generations, she wrote:

"Perhaps God foresaw yt we Should be too Proud of her, & so has Sent this calamity to mortify us & her".[28]

It was a characteristic Edwards answer, spoken without a shadow of self-righteousness.

On the long journey to Stockbridge, in a wagon with her baby and a servant, she was obliged to spend Sunday in a one-room house already overflowing with its occupants, and yet she had no word of complaint for the inconvenience of the experience, only regret that a Sunday had passed without religion. She made up for the lack as best she could by taking a Bible and walking to the woods to be "retired". When on the same journey she passed through New York, she disposed of urban life in one sentence:

"I would not live here a fortnight for any money".

She preferred to "dine eight Ministers" on Wednesday, ten on Thursday, or on a special occasion possibly thirty-one, for social gaiety look forward to the annual "wood-frolic", and for her soul's good, anticipate a visit from "Mr. Whitefield". She had heard her father's sermons all her life and yet on his frequent visits they were still news, to be recorded with appreciative comment.

"Mr. Edwards preached all day two charming Sermons from those words, 'When a wicked man dieth his expectations perish, & the hope of unjust men perisheth'." [29]

The beauty of holiness was to her the all of beauty, and when she read such quatrains as the much lauded Mrs. Rowe was capable of penning, she was transported. Yet by no means was her life meager. She lived within the pattern to which she was born, and lived happily, even richly. Her brief story is by all odds so much the brightest patch in the Edwards annals that its loss would have been loss indeed. As for Esther Burr herself, she was so joyous, so high-spirited, so thoroughly alive, that one cannot but be grateful she did not survive her own griefs.

Whether she was closer to her father than her sisters, there is no knowing; but her intimate talks with him about her own religious experience bespeak an unusual bond of sympathy. Perhaps it is only that her *Journal* has given this intimacy the emphasis of record. She seems also to have been like him in the intensity of her religious transports. Father and daughter spoke the same language, and they were able to speak it to each other. On the Stockbridge visit, she took occasion during her mother's absence to talk over her experiences with him, as she had done when she was a little girl in Northampton.

"[Sept. 11, 1756]
"last eve I had some free discourse with my Father on the great things yt concern my best interest— I opened my difficulties & he as freely advised & directed the conversation has removed some distressing doubts yt discouraged me much in my Christian Warfare— He gave me some excellent directions to be observed

in Secret yt tend to keep the Soul near to God, as well as others
to be observed in a more publick way— O what a mercy yt I
have Such a Father— Such a Guide." [30]

The letter which she wrote to him after the death of her
husband is further testimony to the closeness of the relationship, and also of the similarity between her experiences and
his own at her age. As she contemplated the "glorious State"
to which her husand had been released, her

"Soul was carried out in Such longing desires after this glorious
State yt I was forced to retire from the Famaly to conceal my
Joy, when alone I was so transported & my Soul carried out in
Such Eager desires after Perfection & the full injoymnet of GOD
& to Serve him uninterrupedly yt I think my Nature could not
have borne much more— I think dear Sir I had yt Night a fore-
taste of Heaven".[31]

She was soon to know the reality.

Many other informal glimpses into the Stockbridge home
come by way of letters exchanged between the sisters after
marriage separated them. In these intimate pieces, with their
scraps of family news, Sarah and Lucy, Mary and "Sukey",
"Timmie" and Betty, become fairly definite personalities.
Lucy's letters are the most individual. Like Esther, she indulged in gay quips, wrote nonsensical postscripts, and told
the news in more picturesque style than the others. She was
warm-hearted, tempestuous, swift to anger, and sometimes
reckless. She later made a marriage which displeased her
sisters, and then withdrew proudly from their displeasure. It
is easy to understand from her sprightly letters that to her the
making of a quilt, even for Betty, would be, as she said, "very
dull happiness to undertake alone". Betty was the delicate
one, for whom they all made sacrifices and expressed affectionate concern. "My tenderest love to Betty and tell her to
accept the inclosed ribbon as a token of My Love": such a
message closes more than one letter. They kept in close touch,
responding to one another's need, regardless of weathers or
Indian wars. "Who shall come, Mother or I?" wrote Lucy,
when Mary was expecting another child. Lucy could stay
longer, but Mother could come; that is, if she did not stay too
long. Only Lucy, on this occasion, expressed this possibility
in the negative: "for my father will not be willing if she stays
a great while".[32] This sentence recalls another from a fragment of one of Jonathan Edwards' own letters to Sarah, his

wife, written years before, when she had overstayed his
expectation at a family bedside which needed her:

"We have been without you almost as long as we know how to
be; but yet we are willing you should obey the Calls of Providence
with regard to Col. Stoddard".[33]

This was the spirit of the home Jonathan and Sarah Edwards
had founded.

The sheaf of family correspondence during the Stockbridge
years is also all the tribute they could have wished as to the
kind of religion of which their lives had been an example
before their children. The naturalness with which the daughters speak of their own faith and trust, report the state of
their souls or ask for one another's prayers, suggests that
religion as they knew it by precept and example was no
Sunday exercise alone. It was a way of life. One of the most
revealing suggestions in all the Edwards memorials as to the
values for which they lived comes in a letter which it would
be a breach of faith to reprint. It was written by Sarah
Parsons, the eldest daughter, to her sister Susannah in 1760,
after both parents were dead. After detailing a few personal
circumstances which had made the preceding winter particularly hard to bear, she closed with this postscript:

"If you let any Creature See this Letter I shall never forgive
you, burn it as soon as yo've read it, yours, S. P".

Record of this brief lapse from her accustomed grace somehow escaped the burning, to give eloquent testimony to the
view of life in which she had been reared and to which she
was committed in loyalty. This world was not a happy place
at best; but one filled the place appointed, gave grateful service, and made no complaint, no matter how hard the winter.

Even during these seven years of exile, Jonathan Edwards
would have admitted no cause for complaint. He believed
himself to be where the leading of God had placed him, and
that was enough. No more fitting text could have been chosen
to suggest the spirit in which he lived his life than the words:

"My times are in thy hand",

inscribed on the sundial which now marks the site of the
Edwards homestead in Stockbridge.

But quiet acceptance was not the whole story. The seven years of exile were also years of intense labor, and labor toward an abundant harvest. In the small room known as the "study"—a tiny nook at the west end of the house, large enough only for a desk, a chair, and many books—Jonathan Edwards found the most effective rostrum he had ever known.

Chapter 14

"Life Passed Through the Fire of Thought"

IF STOCKBRIDGE from a distance had looked to him like a philosopher's paradise, he wasted no time bemoaning his mistake. Favorable or not, he would make it serve his turn. The books would be written. He began immediately, first applying himself to the unfinished business of replying to Solomon Williams. This was during the first winter and spring, when he was building a house, making a first effort to learn the Housatunnock language, writing voluminous letters to the Boston Commissioners for Indian affairs, and attempting to adjust himself to a completely new routine of life. It was just as well, for the peace and leisure which had made Stockbridge seem a desirable choice were never to come. The first fruit of his mornings spent in the new study was *Misrepresentations Corrected and Truth Vindicated,* published in 1752.

Defeated as he was, and driven from the field on the issues involved in this controversy, one might reasonably ask why he bothered to reply. The answer is simply that in the highly charged atmosphere of the mid-century no one who had convictions on the inflammable subject of church authority or church sacraments, was beaten so long as there was an opponent left to answer. Had Solomon Williams deigned to answer a second time, Jonathan Edwards would probably have written a third treatise. He could not desist from strife, while what he considered false arguments on this subject so vitally important to the purity of the church remained in print, unchallenged.

As the title suggests, this is a polemic. In his *Humble Inquiry,* he had given relatively untrammelled expression to his own views of the sacrament as a Christian institution. In this second treatise he was concerned solely to confute and confound the arguments of Solomon Williams. He dealt in negations almost entirely. For that reason, *Misrepresentations Corrected* has little interest for another day. Furthermore, it is the only cause one need ever seek for the continuing hostility of the Williams family. Without descending to personal abuse, Jonathan Edwards neatly decapitated his opponent by showing that he had failed to inform himself correctly as to the facts in the case, and had therefore spent all his arguments in vain:

"It would have been no great condescension in Mr. W. if he had allowed that *I* knew what the question was, which was disputed between me and my people, as well as *he*, in a distant part of the country".[1]

"I will not say, that Mr. W. knew it to be a false representation which he here makes: but I will say, that he ought to have been better informed, before he had thus publicly ridiculed this as a fiction of *mine*." [2]

Instead of answering Solomon Williams' arguments, he shows them not to be arguments. They are "peremptory and confident assertions", "great *exclamation*, in the room of arguing". He has begged the question, been inconsistent with himself, and, without recognizing it, has argued against his own scheme as much as against the one he is attacking. Such ridicule of his opponent was in the current controversial manner, but it did not make for even tolerable relations between members of families already estranged.

Laboriously Jonathan Edwards went on, giving attention to the minutiae of error: words and phrases inaccurately used, unfair interpretations, insinuations, paucity of proof. The spirit of this one-hundred-and-fifty-page confutation is epitomized in the sentence:

"Perhaps instances enough of this have already been taken notice of; yet I would now mention some others".[3]

By the time the last page is reached, one has the impression that nothing which might possibly have discredited Solomon Williams has been omitted. The caution which Jonathan Edwards expressed in a brief note to Colonel Dwight as to the safe delivery of the manuscript is entirely understandable, once the treatise has been read. He wrote,

"Sir,

"I have just sent the Copy of my Answer to Mr. Williams by my son Parsons, to be conveyed by you to Mr. Foxcroft. I need not tell you that extraordinary Care had need be taken in the Conveyance. There are many Enemies who would be glad to destroy it. I know not how in the world it can be well got to Mr.

Foxcroft's Hand, especially by Reason of the small Pox, but I
desire you would do the best you can.   "J. E." [4]

Timothy Dwight was successful. The manuscript arrived
safely, and the book was straightway printed by subscription.
Its publication raised a brief tempest in Northampton, which
still further delayed agreement on a new minister, and also
brought the Stockbridge situation to a climax of hostility
almost insupportable. Nevertheless, Jonathan Edwards had
delivered his soul, and he had also the last word. That he
would pay dearly for whatever satisfaction finality brought,
did not concern him.

This treatise adds nothing to his lasting fame, but it illustrates better than his more important works his detective
quality of mind, his sureness of argumentative aim, and his
ruthlessness as a controversialist. He not only felled his
enemy, but bludgeoned him after he was down. Considered
as a polemic, the *Reply* is not great. It is an answer to an
answer, negative in its purpose and dull in its method. The
point-by-point exposure and ridicule of fallacious argument
and textual error, instead of being incidental to a larger purpose, determine the course of his thought. Even as a warfare
of words, the piece lacks brilliance. Jonathan Edwards was
expert in using a rapier, but this time he took a cudgel, and
as a result the attack is not pleasant to watch.

There is ample reason for recording his complete share in
the controversy, however, since it was a share toward an
eventual victory, and a victory of great importance in the
church life of America. His "qualifications" prevailed, although he did not live long enough to know it. In New England church practice of the next thirty years, not only Solomon Stoddard's amendment to the Halfway Covenant, but the
Halfway Covenant itself fell into disuse. It was a bloodless
surrender and had more reference to what happened on the
battlefields of the Revolution than to any synodic decree.
With the reorganization of American life after the Revolution, parish and village were no longer one. The church still
stood on the green, and in many towns continued to be the
unofficial center of community life; but constables no longer
collected rates or enforced church attendance. Ministers were
no longer obliged to devise a basis of church membership
which might include the whole citizenry of the town. The
people of God accordingly became a peculiar people in a new
sense, which was really an older sense. They might henceforth

guard the doorway to the sanctuary, as they had demanded the right to do when they became Dissenters. As the church body split up into sects toward the beginning of the new century, all groups, and especially the evangelical wing, made a change of heart the basis of admission rather than any of the previous substitutes. In the end, "heart religion" had won. To Jonathan Edwards this would have been reward enough, and more.

The importance of these two controversial treatises, the *Humble Inquiry* and the *Reply to Solomon Williams*, in Jonathan Edwards' long championship of "heart religion" is that they gave it a concrete and timely application in relation to church polity. In his *Religious Affections* he had spoken more permanently, because he spoke more abstractly, but in both books, he spoke to his own day, and while he lived, he seemed to have spoken in vain. Twice he had taken the unpopular side of a current argument in an inauspicious hour, and twice he had been defeated, but by leaving his views in print for another generation of ministers to ponder, he did more for the cause of "heart religion" than any other minister of the mid-century. Twenty years later, some one he had never known was saying:

"So I think sir, if I was to engage with you in this controversy, I would say, *Read Edwards.* And if you wrote again, I would tell you, *Read Edwards,* and if you wrote again, I would say *Read Edwards.* For I think it needless for any man to write after him, and fruitless for any man to write against him upon this subject. Nor do I think any man need blush to say that Mr. Edwards has sufficiently answered all that ever has been, and ever will be, wrote on the opposite side".[5]

When Solomon Williams did not essay to reply a second time, Jonathan Edwards was at last free to complete his studies looking toward *The Freedom of the Will*, a project he had had in mind for years.[6] To undertake such a task in 1753 took courage, as well as an uncommon degree of concentration and detachment from his surroundings. This was the year in which his Stockbridge enemies were showing their hostility most openly. Half of the town was engaged in a whispering campaign against him; the other half, against Colonel Joseph Dwight. The burning of the boarding school made new administrative problems. His own health was more precarious than ever. Yet in this atmosphere of outer turmoil his thought took final shape with regard to this problem, more difficult and currently more important than any other to that wing of the clergy which had arrayed itself against the moderns and their "new divinity". Late in the fall he began to write, and with feverish rapidity brought to completion the work on which his fame rested securely for more than a hundred years. The book was published by subscription October 17, 1754.

The subject of the Will had presented more than one dilemma in American theology. An assembly of churches met at New Town as early as 1637, when attempting to catalogue the erroneous opinions which had been brought to America, put first on the list the notion that in conversion the "faculties of the soul" (understanding and will) are destroyed. According to the confutation of their spokesman, they were able to prove that these faculties exist after conversion. With naïve but, as they thought, scholarly dependence on the exact phraseology before them, they reasoned:

"Peter is said to be led whither he would not; therefore he had a will".[7]

As this dilemma took other forms in other generations, synods and councils of ministers continued to deal with it to the best of their ability; but in some form or other it was always with them. As they well knew, denial of free will in man was basic to the whole Calvinistic structure. If man's will were free, and he might accept divine grace or reject it, then his eternal salvation could no longer be foreordained by a power outside himself: he would be saved by his own choice, not by an immutable decree. And if this were true, then God's sovereignty was limited, not absolute. There would be reins on His omnipotence, and man would hold them. It was unthinkable. If man's will were free, the Calvinistic system was ruined.

The intellectuals among the American clergy had followed the pros and cons of this ticklish subject for three generations, but few had been so bold as to touch it with their own logic. In their sermons they had merely reiterated the traditional Calvinistic position within the safe frame of recognized authority. Now, as another generation of English "Arminians" began to challenge the traditional position more insistently, it became increasingly apparent that a champion must arise who could do more than reiterate; else the cause was lost.

Meanwhile, the pew also had begun to have suspicions. One

indirect result of the revivals of the early forties had been to weaken the authority of traditional doctrine in the popular mind, particularly the doctrines of sovereignty and election. It is easy to see why. Congregations had listened to too many pulpit attempts to batter down man's stubborn opposition to God, and had witnessed too many swift changes in their own eternal prospects, not to become a little skeptical over the finality of predestination. One day a man was "lost" because he would not; the next day he was "saved" because he would. How could he be merely a puppet? After he repented, God did the rest, of course; but the permissive power seemed to be within his own control. At least so the mid-century American preferred to think. What else did the urgency of revival preaching mean? What else did "whosoever will" mean?

The pulpit of course had an answer to this apparent paradox, but that was easily forgotten, as the leaven worked. By the mid-century both "Elect and Reprobates" were responding to whatever flattered their new sense of dignity as human beings, an impulse to which they could not possibly have assigned a cause. It was getting too late in the drama of human thought for God to be made in the likeness of an inexorable sovereign, or for man to accept a fate assigned him before he had so much as come into existence. The Arminian assertion that man's will was not bound but free was both a cause and a result of these timely stirrings. The time spirit was on the anti-Calvinistic side, and the anti-Calvinists knew it. The rebuttal of their new boldness would task stronger powers than had yet been consecrated to the support of Calvinistic doctrine for several lifetimes.

Jonathan Edwards was well aware of the gravity of this crisis, and when he entered the lists on the side of "sound doctrine" he was both well prepared and well disposed to be a defender. He had informed himself thoroughly as to current argument on both sides. He was fresh from another doctrinal battle which had sharpened his wits and his tools for just such a warfare.

His refutation of the Arminian position amounts, in essence, to a new definition of human liberty by which he thought at one stroke to save both the dignity of man and the omnipotence of God. He grants man freedom of action to carry out his own choices, but insists that these choices are determined by motives which lie outside of man's control. Reduced to aphorisms, his reasoning proceeds in the following sequence:

An act of will is an act of choice.
Choice is not only a deliberate act, but an inclination in one direction or another.
Man is free to act upon his choices and inclinations.
These choices and inclinations are, however, directed by motives.
These motives lie outside of man's control.
The will is therefore not active, but passive.

In other words, the area of human liberty is definitely restricted to the area of action upon human choices. It has nothing whatever to do with the causes which lie back of these choices. As Jonathan Edwards himself puts it,

"Let the person come by his choice any how, yet, if he is able, and there is nothing in the way to hinder his pursuing and executing his will, the man is perfectly free, according to the primary and common notion of freedom".[8]

This is not pure Calvinism or Calvinism as modified by New England Dissent. Jonathan Edwards' contribution was to make man's freedom an intermediate step. He had qualified freedom rather than denied it; or, in more modern phrase, he had represented human liberty as "conditioned". He had further modified the traditional view in his insistence upon the passivity of the will, an idea which was consistent with his own experience of intuitive awareness of divine truth. The mind does not create impressions; it receives them. This is not impotence. It is not even inactivity. Like the professed passiveness of the mystic, it is a state of receptivity in which the self is denied, in order that it may be merged in God. Such an idea was to him not ungrateful doctrine. He could assume the will to be passive, because he had felt his own to be passive under impressions he believed to be divine. He had agonized to have his own motives God-directed. Beyond these limits he did not wish to be free. It would by no means be the whole story, but it is worthy of remark that the clue to this notion of the passive will leads one back to Jonathan Edwards' own religious experiences, and that his qualification of man's freedom in favor of God's sovereignty had an emotional basis before it buttressed an argument. This conclusion would seem to be inescapable in the light of the whole panorama of his thought.

In its application to man's salvation, this qualification of his freedom meant that those whom God had chosen might repent if they would, but the desire to do so came from God. Man's responsibility lay in acting on the choice, no matter whence the inclination toward that choice might come. To this extent only was man's salvation in his own hands. This was very useful ammunition for the practical pastor who had had difficulty reconciling man's helplessness with man's responsibility. Even though a man were one of the elect, he must seek with his whole heart that to which he is foreordained, and admit that, even though God were to deny it to him, He would still be just. To this end, of course, was revival preaching. Ministers, as God's emissaries, helped Him gather in the elect of any generation whenever God signified, particularly through a revival, that He was ready to receive them.

By far the more brilliant portions of this treatise, as well as nine-tenths of the space, concern the point-by-point bombardment of the Arminian position. Jonathan Edwards' dexterity in accomplishing what at times appear to be logical impossibilities is thrilling to watch. He is in thorough command of both materials and weapons. With pitiless accuracy he finds the weak places in the enemy's armor, mows down objections, holds the opposing view up to scorn and defiance, labelling it as "absurd", "impertinent", and sometimes so "nonsensical" as hardly to merit reply. His own assurance is all but unbounded, and quite without respect to the credit of authorities on either side of the argument:

"As to Mr. Hobbes maintaining the same doctrine concerning necessity; I confess, it happens I never read Mr. Hobbes. Let his opinion be what it will, we need not reject all truth which is demonstrated by clear evidence, merely because it was once held by some bad man".[9]

Truth is still truth even though proclaimed in a loud voice by the devil himself, he adds in the next sentence. Such gibes abound, showing him to be thoroughly at home in the controversial manner. Freight of minutiae does not retard his progress. The whole argument moves with a rush and celerity, as though carried from point to point by its own momentum. His resources seem exhaustless; his intellectual energy is astounding. With his readers winded and left far behind, he turns a new corner, as though the race had just begun. Even though the issues of this controversy have been long obsolete, it is impossible to read this treatise dispassionately. It is an amazing performance, not only for its agile dialectic, but for the dynamic behind these missiles, the coherence of these intricate arguments. It is a web: one must take it or leave it, as a whole.

At no point is his writing more spirited than in his defence of the metaphysical method, which he knows will draw fire from his opponents. What of it, he says in effect.

"If the Reasoning be good, it is as frivolous to enquire what science it is properly reduced to, as what language it is delivered in: and for a man to go about to confute the arguments of his opponent, by telling him, his arguments are *metaphysical*, would be as weak as to tell him, his arguments could not be substantial, because they were written in *French* or *Latin*. The question is not, whether what is said be metaphysics, physics, logic, or mathematics, *Latin, French, English*, or *Mohawk*? But whether the Reasoning be good, and the arguments truly conclusive? . . . It is by metaphysical arguments only we are able to prove, that the rational soul is not corporeal, that lead or sand cannot think; that thoughts are not square or round, or do not weigh a pound. . . . It is by metaphysics only that we can demonstrate, that God is not limited to a place, or is not mutable; that he is not ignorant, or forgetful; that it is impossible for him to lie, or be unjust; and that there is one God only, and not hundreds of thousands. And, indeed, we have no strict demonstration of any thing, excepting mathematical truths, but by metaphysics." [10]

At its best, the treatise fulfils the promise of such a passage. As controversialist, he is freer in illustration, more lucid, and far more eloquent than in his usual Sunday sermons, despite the text on the title page and the familiar wares from the preacher's storehouse.

As the argument proceeds, amazement deepens, but for reasons which have nothing to do with the issues involved; rather with the mind which espoused this lost cause with such uncanny deftness in the proofs supplied, such dexterity in the use of weapons unfitted to the hand of an eighteenth century theologian. Having gone so far, why could he not go one step further? How could a mind, capable of fashioning such an architecture of defensive proof, fail to turn its own incisive powers against the premise upon which the argument rested? Yet with apparently not a qualm as to the eternal verity of his assumption, Jonathan Edwards dealt only with that which it based. Those who came after him could find no loopholes in his fabric of proof, but they demolished his premises with the weapons he had taught them how to use.

His method is also inconsistent. He overthrew the arguments of his opponents by metaphysics; at more than one last ditch he established his own position by the argument from authority. One must remember, however, that in using metaphysics at all in a theological argument he was a pioneer on a new track. Had he, as an eighteenth century theologian, left his sermon analogies behind, freed himself from the dependence on line and verse, and launched out into pure philosophy, he would have defied all the laws by which great thinkers both are of their day and are not. When he concludes the whole argument with a panegyric on the Scriptures and the unimpeachable wisdom of God, he is thoroughly within the pattern to which he belonged. He was an eighteenth century divine defending a theological system, a controversialist bent on slashing through the defences of his opponents, a logician winning an argument, not a free explorer in quest of the truth.

Is the *Freedom of the Will* then not a great book? Say rather, it is a great polemic; great enough to have dignified the American battle between conflicting systems at a time when dignity was sadly lacking; great enough to offer substantial check to the new order and to infuse new heart in the old; great enough also to remind theologians of another day, who were not Calvinists, that man's self-importance must not be allowed to go too far. It is not a great book in the sense that its thought begot thought, or that it laid foundations for a better system. It was an ultimatum, an argument to end argument, a "No Admittance" sign over a sacred gateway. It paralyzed debate when debate needed most to be stimulated. From the point of view of another century, it would seem that the inevitable rôle for one of Jonathan Edwards' powers, would have been to cut the theological knot and begin over. Yet for reasons stretching back to his birth he did not know how to cut knots. Laboriously he must untie them, and he untied this one, to the praise of a remote posterity more interested in the spectacle than in the result.

To the uninitiate of his own day, his metaphysical method obscured his thought, exactly as he had predicted. Unfortunately a current sermon which announced itself,

"Heaven shut against all Arminians and Antinomians:
Shewed in a sermon from Revelations 14:12",

was more sure of a sympathetic hearing. His advance intimations of defeat could hardly have prepared him, however, for the fate assigned him by his ministerial critic James Dana, who some sixteen years later, having admitted himself "discouraged with only reading this elaborate and intricate performance", proposed to enshrine "Mr. Edwards and some celerated infidels, ancient and modern" in parallel columns because of "a specimen coincidence" between them in the views expressed,[11] or the verdict of Jeremiah Day that the subsequent influence of this master defence of the Calvinistic position had been on the whole "unfavorable to the cause of truth and piety".[12] Even the honor of having his arguments "recited by the Senior classes" at Yale College for thirteen years (1762-1775) would have been nullified by the crispness of the final record, "this giving offence was dropped".[13] The deference of those who were reluctant to reject the views of one "of Mr. Edwards's merit and Eminence" would have been scant comfort.

"If his Scheme is recd. for true Orthodoxy, some, I fear, will become Deists from ye dislike of what is said to be orthodox Christianity",

wrote James Dana.[14] Even atheism might result. Worst of all, Jonathan Edwards had destroyed the sinfulness of sin. Irony could conceive no more complete paradox. By going beyond the intellectual range of his own generation, he had been cast out by the brethren themselves.

To his own thought he had saved the whole system. By "clearing and establishing" the Calvinistic position with regard to free will, he had also confirmed the other basic doctrines of the modified Calvinism he professed, and thereby scattered his Arminian enemies. But he could not rest until he had built the whole edifice. Largely from materials collected years before, he went on to defend *The Great Christian Doctrine of Original Sin,* and to define *The Nature of True Virtue.* The first was in press at the time of his death, appearing later in the same year, 1758; the second lay in manuscript for seven years, being published in 1765, when the biography by Samuel Hopkins brought the name of Jonathan Edwards to the attention of the clergy afresh.

These two treatises are companion pieces, presenting two views of "that creature called man": one as he is by nature, in all the blackness of his inherited and unredeemed corruption, the other as he is not, a being purged of self and given up to the pursuit of virtue in its perfection of beauty. Obviously, for man as he is commonly known here below, neither view is a recommendation.

In his defence of the doctrine of original sin, Jonathan Edwards was making a timely, though late, contribution to a new outbreak in an old war. The battle had first been sounded twenty years earlier in John Taylor's *The Scripture-Doctrine of Original Sin Proposed to a Free and Candid Examination*,[15] an examination which proved to John Taylor that man was not by nature depraved. The complicated history of economic and social change which found expression in this bold challenge of long accepted doctrine is more interesting to a modern day than the uninspired but courageous and able presentation of the arguments therefor. In the mid-century Taylor's book was regarded both as an emancipation proclamation and as an impious blasphemy. It had been answered and reanswered before Jonathan Edwards spoke out late in the fifties. His defence of the doctrine of innate depravity, though late, really belongs with the defences of Watts and Wesley, and is by far the strongest and most profound of the three. His line of argument is for the most part conventional and thoroughly orthodox. He had dealt with this same doctrine in his *Freedom of the Will,* and in part returns over old paths to the same goal. He is at great pains to amplify his previous point that the corruption of man consists in his very nature, and that it is this corruption which takes him straight to eternal ruin. Carefully he reiterates that he is not blind to human goodness in its multiple manifestations, as his opposers might assume. He is not speaking of crime or villainy before the law, but of "moral corruption", that inner state of evil which shuts man away from God everlastingly. The best of men, as humanly judged, are in this state, and must be.

The touchy point in all "original sin" discussions had long been the relation of Adam's sin to the spiritual state of man since the fall. Why was not each birth a new beginning? By what logic, or more insistently, by what justice, was Adam's sin the sin of all men? Jonathan Edwards accomplished this dubious equation by a theory of the unity of the race, which was his most original contribution to the long standing controversy. The race is one, he argued, by the will of God in its creation. Just as

"a *tree,* grown great, and a hundred years old, is *one* plant with the little *sprout,* that first came out of the ground from whence it grew",[16] so the race, brought into being by the creative act of God, and continuously upheld by that same power, is one through each continuing moment of each man's existence. God's preservation of the race in continued being is equivalent to continued creation. Hence the sin of Adam, who is the scriptural head of the race, becomes the sin of each man, inescapably so. It is no taint or tincture, implanted in individual man by some positive agency, it is a "property of the species". In this sense is sin original, and in no other.

He was also concerned in this treatise once again to exonerate God of all blame for the sin which is in the world. His defence on this point is even more vigorous than in *The Freedom of the Will,* though the argument is essentially the same. Man at his creation was endowed not only with the principles of human nature, but also with the "spiritual image of God". When man sinned, and broke God's law, "these superior principles left his heart".[17] God Himself withdrew them, and corruption followed inevitably upon that withdrawal. God allowed it to be so, and by this permission preserved His omnipotence. Permission, however, does not imply blame. The sin is man's; hence, man's punishment is just.

The reiteration of his position on both of these issues bears no relation whatever, except in theme, to the American skirmish resulting from Samuel Webster's *Winter Evening's Conversation,*[18] a mere paraphrase of Taylor which appeared almost simultaneously with Jonathan Edwards' completion of his treatise. Had he lived to have part in the controversy which Webster's book provoked among the New England clergy, one may be sure he would not have represented himself as a "candid neighbor" engaging in a fireside chat with other more or less candid neighbors. He would have considered the persiflage of Webster's title beneath the dignity of the theme he essayed. His own defence is as direct as his title announces, and his method suited to his purpose, which is essentially a refutation. He is on the defensive. His argument was spirited, but his conclusions were doomed. John Taylor's view would win—not because of John Taylor or any superiority in his argument, but because theology must reshape itself in accordance with a changing world, as it presently did after both John Taylor and Jonathan Edwards were gone. By the logic of events and by the whole slope of American thought, it was foreordained that God should grow less arbitrary and more benevolent and that as soon as benevolence had been emphasized for a generation, the doctrine of election would have ceased to function. Christ would then die for all men, and once again the Scripture would prove it. Man also would change. As he lost his helplessness before God, he would grow in personal responsibility, gradually losing the burden of imputed sin, until presently he could take full blame for his own evil doing and make free choice of the salvation provided. Thanks to the Revolution, which hastened men's thought along many new paths, one generation would be sufficient. It was to be Jonathan Edwards' own son and namesake who would make forceful challenge of his father's thought of both God and man, and be willingly heard. A major prophet might also have known that presently, and inevitably, the divine spark in every man would more than balance any hereditary taint of Adam, and that man would thereby exchange impotence for a far more becoming humility. Jonathan Edwards also was hastening the day. By bringing "the great objections and outcries against Calvinistic divinity to the test of the strictest reasoning", he put the whole traditional system in such sharp focus that it must be dealt with; and to be dealt with in such an intellectual and emotional climate as the sixties and seventies and eighties supplied, meant to be rejected.

Of these two pieces, *Original Sin* and *The Nature of True Virtue,* the second is the more original. It is a kind of sequel to the *Religious Affections,* proceeding from the same basic conviction. Virtue is not of the intellect, or perceiving faculty, but of the emotions, the acting faculty. Its foundations are benevolence, or as Jonathan Edwards insisted, "disinterested benevolence". There is nothing of self in it, nor can be. It is pursued for itself alone, not for any advantages it may confer upon the possessor. It is not a path to a greater good, but an end in itself. The nearest he can come to a definition is to say that it is a kind of beauty, the beauty of God himself. In other words, virtue is holiness, and to perceive it, one must possess it. To be ethical, one must also be religious. Obviously, this is an ideal to which natural man cannot reach, save as the grace of God changes his corrupt nature. It is the ultimate attainment of redeemed man.

Whether Jonathan Edwards realized it or not, from this particular peak of his argument, he was looking more directly over into the new century than from any other point in his whole panorama of thought. In this very abstract reasoning, which would have been well over the heads of any congregation to which he might have attempted to preach it, he was giving a new turn to ethical theory, which in the sequel proved to be determining. By making what he called "benevolence" worthy only in proportion as it was without self-interest, he changed completely the motivation of "good works", hitherto regarded as the Arminian substitute for heart piety and a sure key to heaven. Translated into more practical terms by Samuel Hopkins and his colleagues, this notion of "benevolence", called by other names, was presently laid on Christians as an obligation, and as such became a potent driving force in the humanitarianism of the next century. It was a trust, not a means to personal salvation. In Jonathan Edwards' word, it was "disinterested".[19]

At some time, probably during the Stockbridge years, he brought together his ideas as to the precise nature of the divine power, theologically labelled "free grace", the keystone of his whole system of thought, although the result was not in print for another hundred years. Under the title "Treatise on Grace", it was included in Alexander B. Grosart's *Selections from the Unpublished Writings of Jonathan Edwards* (Edinburgh, 1865). There is no essential change in this piece from his concept as expressed in many previous statements, only a more symmetrical presentation of them. Simply stated, his idea is that saving grace is more than a divine influence surrounding and upholding man; it is a principle implanted within his own nature. It is not gradual, but immediate; not an intensification or quickening of something already present, but a new creation. God is the Author and Giver, and God only. Natural man cannot cultivate it, for not only does grace not exist in him, but he does not possess the sense by which it may be discerned. Since man's eternal salvation hinges upon his possession of that which he is helpless to find for himself, "free grace" therefore becomes the final proof of God's sovereignty in the world he has created.

In Jonathan Edwards' own thought, his *History of the Work of Redemption,* upon which he was engaged before his removal from Stockbridge, was to be the great work of his life and his most significant contribution to theology. In his own word, it was to be a philosophical treatment cast in the form of a history, embracing not only all of Christian theology in its relation to redemption, but also the chief events in church history and those revolutions in secular history which have affected the state of the church, and concluding with a consideration of that perfect state of things which will finally come to pass for all eternity. This vast design was to be still vaster in that it would have regard for all three worlds: heaven, earth, and hell. Against such a background of time and space, he proposed to set forth the "whole body of divinity" so that "every divine doctrine" would appear to its greatest advantage, and the "admirable contexture and harmony of the whole" be apparent. This Gargantuan undertaking was destined to be left as a mere project. Doubtless better so. Who could write such a book? Hardly Jonathan Edwards. Nevertheless on the more peaceful Stockbridge mornings and afternoons, in company with his two ministerial neighbors, Samuel Hopkins and Joseph Bellamy, he pleasured his imagination and no doubt quieted his spirit by laying the plans and working on the foundations of such an edifice.[20]

The last piece of writing from the Stockbridge study appears to have been *God's Last End in Creation*. It is both a fulfilment and a promise. The whole of his intellectual history is epitomized in these hundred pages, for which his first editor apologized lest they prove "too fatiguing to the mind, and wearying to the constitution". Posterity has not shared this dull verdict. If one is looking for what this same editor probably meant when he went on to praise the "natural play of genius" by which the mind of the author would "freely and spontaneously" outstrip his pursuers, then these pages seem more alive than any other hundred which came out of the years of exile.

His subject is speculative. Why did God make the world, this "astonishing fabric of the universe"? Because divinity must, by its very nature, flow outward from itself. God made the world to satisfy himself through an emanation of his own divine glory. To the mind of a poet, this is an idea to be apprehended and clarified in symbol. Jonathan Edwards, however the idea came to him, endeavored to clarify it by a process of reasoning, proceeding to the inescapable conclusion by carefully chiselled steps. There are chief ends and ultimate ends, each of many sorts. There is also, "according to the dictates of reason", one last end and one only, in the highest sense. Reason tells us that in the mind of God, this last end can be none other than a "disposition to communicate His own fulness". Divinity must diffuse itself as the root and stock of a tree must diffuse itself through branch and leaf and bud, not to the end that there may be fruit, but only that fulness must needs diffuse fulness. The process is eternal. Like the punishment of sinners and the felicity of saints, the satisfaction of God is of everlasting duration. God can never reach the moment at which His satisfaction will be realized in its completeness.

The creature also may know something of this, as the

"water in the stream is something of the fountain; and the beams of the sun are something of the sun. . . . The beams of glory come from God, are something of God, and are refunded back again to their original".[21]

But God in creating the world was not thinking first of the good of His creatures; he had rather a "supreme regard to himself and his own infinite, internal glory". As the creature becomes one with God, God's happiness becomes his own.

"The more happiness, the greater union: when the happiness is perfect, the union is perfect." [22]

As he answers his own question in this wise, articulating his progress by Scripture, and relating his answer to the moral order of the world, his thought seems to come full circle, and to connect again with his boyish meditations in the East Windsor meadows. Veteran of many wars as he was, he could not at this writing have retraversed the many battlefields of his thought to find again the God of those early visions. He could not have been satisfied to "view the moon for continuance" and in sweet abstraction of soul to sing forth his meditations. He was on a different track entirely and in a different world. Intellect must probe the mystery, so far as intellect might. Perhaps this was a great pity. It is significant, however, that in this final piece, not theology, but a kind of mystical speculation is being subjected to calm analysis. Was his thought turning back to this early world? And where would it have taken him? On this track, would he have freed himself? He did not live long enough after the writing of this piece for one to know. Nevertheless, two conclusions may perhaps be safely drawn: one, that more than orthodoxy and unorthodoxy would have been involved (thinking such as this does not permit of so neat a classification); and the other, that Jonathan Edwards himself had never been more wrong than when he wrote that he was past his prime. These are not the thoughts of a thinker who is ending his work, but of one who is freshly beginning.

Chapter 15

Honor Too Late

THE PRINCETON chapter is quickly told. The call to the presidency of New Jersey College was wholly unexpected. It was also unwelcome. For seven years Jonathan Edwards had shaped his life to the rigors and limitations of Stockbridge, until, in spite of danger without and disharmony within, the situation was more than bearable. The mission parish was a refuge. According to ministerial standards, he had a dignified living. He owned his homestead and several hundred acres of land, enough to take care of his needs. His wife and three unmarried daughters had accepted the life of the village, had made their place, and were content. His son Timothy, just graduated from college, already had prospects. His three younger children had grown up on the frontier and knew no other background. A little way down the street, his oldest daughter, Sarah Parsons, was bringing up her family of young children. There was no loneliness for his own kin. His ministerial friends had made the long journey northward so often now that they no longer minded the distance. They came frequently, bringing him news and books. His two closest friends, Samuel Hopkins and Joseph Bellamy, were only a few miles away. The wilderness had its compensations. Besides, it was home.

Late in 1757, for the moment all was serene. The Indian uprising of the spring had been quelled. There was preaching and catechizing as usual. Local jealousies were quiescent. Jonathan Edwards was deeply engrossed in his studies. The plan of the great *History of Redemption* was taking clearer shape in his mind, and he knew that if it were ever to be finished he must hurry, for his frail body was frailer with every winter. Then without warning, a messenger brought news of the death of his son-in-law, Aaron Burr, President of New Jersey College. Shortly afterward came the offer of the presidency.

For the trustees to turn to Jonathan Edwards was natural. He had been mentioned for the post in 1748, before Aaron Burr was elected, and ever since had kept in close touch with college affairs, attending the commencement regularly and usually preaching on his visits. The trustees were in sympathy with his theological views and also with his evangelistic emphasis in preaching. Seventeen of the twenty members of the Board present at the meeting, September 29, 1757, had voted to elect him. Had he been personally ambitious, he might have been distinctly pleased by this new opportunity; instead he was deeply troubled. He had no mind to another uprooting, and if his decision had been uncomplicated by the likelihood that he might again be forced out, he would most certainly have chosen to stay with the mission. But he had no choice. For several years all parties to the Stockbridge arrangement had merely been waiting a convenient opportunity. Now it had come.

Accordingly and almost at once, he replied to the trustees, setting forth in detail his disqualifications—"defects", as he called them—and his unwillingness to exchange his present situation for responsibilities likely to be hostile to his studies. As a piece of self-analysis and a statement of plan for the books which were never to be written, this letter of October 19, 1757,[1] has great biographical interest. He was direct in stating what he believed to be his weaknesses: he had a constitutional sluggishness which made him low-spirited and unfitted him for conversation, and particularly for the government of a college; he lacked the alertness which such responsibilities demanded, being as he thought in the decline of life; he was also deficient in knowledge of the higher parts of mathematics and the Greek classics, "my Greek learning having been chiefly in the New Testament".

In his defence of those studies "which have long engaged and swallowed up my mind, and been the chief entertainment & delight of my life", he mentioned three projects: his answer to the prevailing Arminian errors, still to be completed, the *History of the Work of Redemption*, as yet only a project, and the *Harmony* of the Old and New Testaments, toward which many materials had been collected to his great profit and entertainment. Some of these things, he concluded,

"if divine providence favour, I should be willing to attempt a publication of. So far as I myself am able to judge of what talents I have, for benefiting my fellow creatures by word, I think I can write better than I can speak".

But in any case, he was not willing to give them up. In his own words:

"My heart is so much in these studies, that I cannot feel willing to put myself into an incapacity to pursue them any more in the future part of my life, to such a degree as I must, if I undertake to go through the same course of employ, in the office of a president, as Mr. Burr did".[2]

His substitute proposal, or rather statement of the conditions under which he would be willing to accept the offer, shows that he had given thought to educational work. His clearly defined concept of presidential responsibilities as distinguished from purely instructional duties went considerably beyond current practice. Instead of instructing in all of the languages and taking entire charge of one class in all branches of study, he proposed to undertake "general inspection of the whole society", to instruct the senior class in arts and sciences, and "to do the whole work of a professor of divinity." If this definition of the president's duties met with the approval of the trustees, and if the Boston Commissioners would release him from his present post, he would proceed to ask the advice of his friends in the matter.

There was no secrecy concerning these negotiations and apparently no doubt as to the outcome. The same issue of the *Boston News-Letter* (October 20, 1757) which contained the account of Aaron Burr's life, carried also the announcement:

"The rev. Mr. Jonathan Edwards, is chosen to succeed him in the presidentship; a gentleman of whose piety and learning, the public has frequently had the amplest attestations".

His daughter, Esther Burr, in acknowledging a letter of condolence from one "Mr. Hogg" of Scotland, wrote on December 22, 1757, that she had shown the letter to the trustees

"& then I Sent it to my Hon^d Father the Rev. Mr. Edwards who is chosen to Succeed my dear companion which I hope will be gratefull to the friends of this College in Scotland".[3]

The calling of the council was merely a formal gesture in accordance with regularly sanctioned procedure. It met in Stockbridge January 4, 1758. The members, chosen by Jonathan Edwards himself, were all close personal friends: Messrs. Hopkins, Bellamy, Ballantine, Farrand, Brinstead, and Leavenworth. The trustees sent two representatives to present their side, in case the Stockbridge church refused to grant release. According to report, Jonathan Edwards shed tears at the announcement of the decision of the council, but he could scarcely have been surprised. Four days later, January 8, 1758, he preached his farewell sermon to the Indians from the text,

"Remember them which have the rule over you, who have spoken unto you the word of God; whose faith follow, considering the end of their conversation. Jesus Christ, the same yesterday, and today, and forever".

For the sermon to the whites he chose another text:

"For here we have no continuing city, but we seek one to come".

His plans for departure were already completed, and within a few more days he was on his way to Princeton, accompanied by his daughter Lucy. The plan was for the other members of the family to follow in the spring, after the President's house had been made ready for their occupancy.

He arrived on February 16th, and was formally inducted into office on the same day. In the language of the Trustee record for this date,

"The Rev.ʳ Mr. Jonathan Edwards, at the repeated requests and Invitation of this Board and agreeable to a Vote passed at a Meeting of the Trustees in September last, attending, and having been pleased to accept the office of President of this College, so unanimously votd him was qualified as the Charter directs. And the [said] President Edwards was at the same time qualified as a Trustee of the College, and took his Seat accordingly".

This was the only meeting he ever attended. One week later, February 23rd, he was inoculated for smallpox, and after one month, lacking a day, he was dead.

For his very brief term of active service, there is record of a sermon preached in the college hall, a few questions in divinity given out to the senior class, and a cordial welcome and approval by the whole society. Speculations as to what might have followed are of course futile, but difficult to resist. Ezra Stiles may have been right in his remark:

"The Volatility of 100 youth would have disturbed his calm Quiet & made him unhappy".[4]

Possibly; but after the opaque stolidity of Solomon, Hendrick

and Jacob, youthful volatility might not have been unwelcome. Certainly to find himself back in the active world
again and, after years of battle, to be surrounded by an
atmosphere of sympathy and approval, might have been
sufficient reward for whatever it cost. Such an atmosphere
might also have quickened and mellowed his thought in many
ways. But his brief beginning, though hopeful, was too brief
for conjecture as to what the future might have been; possibly
too brief for his own doubts as to the wisdom of removal
from Stockbridge to have been resolved.

Few details are preserved as to the end. There had been a
serious outbreak of smallpox in the vicinity of Princeton
during the preceding months, and many had died. People
were submitting themselves for inoculation more willingly
than a decade earlier, but because of the great risk they still
incurred by so doing, and also because of the notion still
current that this procedure was an affront to the Almighty,
such willingness was still regarded as highly debatable. On
this point, Jonathan Edwards had no doubts; he was firmly
convinced as to the wisdom of inoculation. In a letter written
six years earlier to a friend about to embark for the British
Isles, he had proffered advice thus:

> "One thing I will venture to give you my thoughts on, viz.
> That since you have not had the smallPox, If you find a skilful
> and prudent Physician, under whose care you can put your self,
> you would take the small Pox by inoculation before you go, after
> properly preparing your Body for it, by Physic & Diet".[5]

Such counsel was in line with his own personal practice. He
had always taken precautions when diseases known to be
communicable were epidemic, and he had shown an alert
interest as to the progress of medical science in his day. In
the spring of 1758, his fears for himself may have been increased by the fact that his daughter Lucy had contracted
smallpox in Princeton during the preceding summer, and had
been seriously ill for many weeks. His own health also had
been greatly enfeebled by another illness during the winter of
1757. Whether the suggestion that he take the precaution of
inoculation came from himself or from the trustees is not
clear, but at any rate he consulted them. They gave consent,
and the inoculation was performed. In the medical idiom of
the day, he first had the disease favorably, but after it was
thought all danger was past,

"a secondary fever set in, and by reason of a number of pustules in his throat, the obstruction was such, that the medicines necessary to check the fever, could not be administered".[6]

He died on March 22, 1758. Of his own family only his two daughters, Esther and Lucy, were with him. His wife was on the way, but did not reach him in time. When told there was no hope of his recovery, he was "a little perplexed for a while". If God had led him to these new duties, why should He not permit them to be performed? But his questionings were brief. Characteristically he accepted the verdict as the will of God, sent messages to his wife and other children, gave directions for his funeral, and died in complete peace. An account of these last moments is preserved in the letter of Dr. William Shippen, a Philadelphia physician who attended him, as follows:

"and a very short time before he expired, he spoke to Lucy to ye following purpose dear Lucy it seems to me to be the Will of God that I must shortly leave you, therefore give my kindest Love to my dear Wife & tell her that the uncommon Union that has so long subsisted between us has been of such a Nature as I trust is Spiritual and therefore will continue for ever: and I hope she will be supported under so Great a trial and submit chearfully to the Will of God; And as to my Children you are now like to be left Fatherless which I hope will be an Inducement to you to seek a Father who will never fail you; & as to my Funeral I would have it to be like unto Mr Burrs, and any additional sum of Money that might be expected to be laid out that way, I would have it disposed of to charitable uses".[7]

A letter of Sarah Edwards, written to her daughter Susannah after she knew the end had come, echoes the same spirit of resignation:

"O my very Dear Child
"What Shall I Say. A holy and Good God heas Cover'd us with Dark Cloud. O that we may all kiss the rod and Lay our hands on our mouthes. tho heas Done it. he heas made me adore his Goodness that we had him So Long. but my God Lives, and he heas my heart. O whatt A Legacy my Husband and your Father heas Left us.
"We are all given unto God, and their I am and Love to be—
                                        "SARAH EDWARDS." [8]

A fortnight after her father's death, Esther Burr died. She

had been inoculated at the same time as her father, and was thought to have fully recovered. Her death was so completely unexpected as to be an even greater shock to her sisters than the loss of their father. At first they were incredulous, but their training quickly triumphed and they bowed in submission to what they assumed to be God's will for her and His plan for them all.

"How fast has she been ripening for that world",

Sarah Parsons wrote to her sister, Mary Dwight.

But this was not the end of their sorrows. In the following autumn, Sarah Edwards, widow of Jonathan, also died very suddenly. She had come to Philadelphia for Esther's two children, Sally, aged four, and Aaron, two, with the intention of taking them into her own home. At this time Pierrepont, her own youngest, was eight years old. Although in good health when she began the journey, she became violently ill with dysentery upon her arrival in Philadelphia, and died on October 2nd. Her body was taken to Princeton and buried beside the graves of her husband, her daughter, and her son-in-law.[9] Samuel Hopkins' comment,

"Surely America is greatly emptied by these deaths",

was repeated in various forms by the small circle to whom these losses meant personal bereavement.

In terms of his own family heritage, Jonathan Edwards should have had a longer span. His father died only two months before him, at eighty-nine; his mother lived on to be ninety-eight; Grandfather Stoddard had been eighty-five; Grandmother Warham-Stoddard, ninety-two. Five of his sisters and four of his children lived past their seventies, several of them very long past; yet he was dead at fifty-four.

In the language of his will,[10] made five years earlier, the "Infirmity of his Constitution" had long made him "Sensible of the great Uncertainty of [his] Life", and he had accordingly put his affairs in order. The detailed inventory of his modest personal effects is eloquent of the simplicity of his tastes and the essential unity of his life. For him there was little conflict between outer and inner; "things" had never been in the saddle.

"Best Beever Hat" and "One D[itto] poorer"

"Best Wigg" and "One D[itto] poorer"
"Great Coat" and "Old D[itto]"
"Black Coat" and "Two poorer D[itto]"
"1 pr Specticles" and "pr D[itto]"

Why should one's possessions outstrip one's needs? His did not. He had a pocket compass but no watch; two pairs of knee buckles but no other jewelry. His wealth, in so far as it could be called such, was in his books, listed as 38 folio, 34 quarto, 99 octavo, 130 duodecimo, besides 25 volumes of his own writings, and 536 pamphlets. His manuscripts were listed according to size: 15 folio volumes, 15 quarto, and 1,074 sermon booklets.

Characteristically, he left his sons free to follow their own choice of profession. A legacy was provided for college or for an apprenticeship to law or medicine, and if any one of the three should "take up Learning", the entire library should be his. This share fell to his second son and namesake, who was thirteen years old at the time of his father's death. Through this Jonathan,[11] whose life so strangely paralleled that of his father, even to dismissal after a twenty-six-year pastorate and death soon after election to a college presidency, greater honor came to the Edwards name in the immediately following generation than through any other of his nine children who survived him.

The newspapers took scant notice of his passing. When Solomon Stoddard had died in 1729, the Boston News-Letter had printed a eulogy of more than a column, prefaced by the statement that he was

"too Eminent a Person to be suffer'd to slip into his Grave in silence".

Yet in most American newspapers the death of his more eminent grandson was recorded in a sentence.[12] Had Jonathan Edwards died during the month of the Enfield sermon, or even at the time of his dismissal, he too might have been similarly honored, but not after seven years in Stockbridge had put him and his reasons for honor out of the mind of even church-going America. Besides, popular interest had shifted. Sermons and the death of those who preached them were no longer items of first-rank importance. The newspaper issues carrying news of his death gave much space to the recent excise law on wines and spirits, numerous commissions of bankruptcy incident to the hard times, letters of protest against the details of British governance, usually signed by some "True Friend of Liberty". The *News-Letter* of the following week (March 30, 1758), announced as "This Day Published",

"Father Abraham's Speech to a great Number of People",

credited long afterward, doubtless for the sake of its author, with having turned the tide in a great depression.

Sermons and treatises on religious subjects were still numerous among the volumes advertised for sale. Even

The History of the Martyrs, Alphabetically Epitomized,

wherein was to be had "the Cream of the larger Martyrologic skim'd off, the very spirits of them extracted", still sanctified the leisure of those who had a mind to martyrs; but such titles now shared space with

The Art of Preserving Health. A Poem in Four Books. Book I.
Air. Book II. Diet. Book III. Exercise. Book IV. The Passions,
The Way to Health, Long-Life and Happiness; Or, A Discourse
on Temperance,

and many others suggesting that life in America had acquired a new dimension, and that this earth was no longer the vale of tears it had formerly been.

Even more significant of the changing time spirit was the announcement, on the same newspaper page with Peter Clark's

Defence of the Divine Right of Infant Baptism,

of "Dr. Chauncy's Sermon preached of the Society for Encouraging Industry and employing the Poor", or an announcement that

"The Spinners are expected to appear upon the Common with their Spinning Wheels at Four o'clock in the Afternoon".

The clergy had always wrestled with the practical problems of ignorance and poverty, and it was only natural that they should take a leading part in the organization of relief measures, as a wave of friendly feeling for the unfortunate swept over America during the 1750's. Scores of items appearing week after week in the press attest this new accent in community life. Shut away in the wilderness of Stockbridge, Jonathan Edwards had missed this timely emphasis.

Even ministerial disputes had dropped downward to take a more practical turn. One such battle had concerned "sharp points", or lightning rods, and the doctrinal implications of protecting one's self thereby. There were the "Electricians" who thought "sharp points" no insult to God, and their opponents, the "Anti-Electricians", who esteemed them a presumptuous meddling with the artillery of heaven. The dispute had presently resolved itself into an attempt to define the legitimate use of one's intelligence and to determine the exact limit at which the instinct of self-preservation became a defiance of omnipotence. When in 1755 "electrical points" had been fixed to the steeple of the Old Brick Meetinghouse in Cornhill, and upon Dr. Cutler's church at North-end, the Boston "Electricians" may be said to have triumphed. Rural communities took note, and either capitulated or became still more militant against change.

In 1757 religious controversy had been brought sharply back to traditional issues by the publication of Samuel Webster's anonymous tract, *A Winter Evening's Conversation*, which challenged the doctrine of original sin. By comparison with earlier pamphlet wars, the ensuing battle was hardly more than a skirmish; but at least it brought the champions of sound doctrine to the printing house in militant formation. On the day after Jonathan Edwards' death, a book by his friend Peter Clark of Danvers, having for its purpose the demolishing of Samuel Webster's arguments, was announced for sale under the title, *A Summer Morning's Conversation*.[13] It included a *Recommendatory Preface*, signed by five divines who urgently entreated and solemnly advised all vacant churches to

"beware of settling any Man in the Pastoral Office who does not profess a firm Belief of the Great Doctrine here defended".

The signature of fifty divines would not have seemed authoritative to Americans in 1758. The cause of Original Sin was a lost cause. It was also a cause without a defender who could command a respectful hearing. Peter Clark and his cohorts would not be equal to the fight. The great champion had gone.

Epilogue:

What Is His Greatness?

SINCE his death, the greatness of Jonathan Edwards has changed with the generations; inevitably so. As American life since 1758 has written itself afresh many times, new ideas and new modes of thinking them have reshaped the past as well as the present, postponing the final word. That at the distance of nearly two centuries what survives as his imprint upon the pattern of American culture bears little resemblance to what he put into the religious battles of his own time is also inevitable, and perhaps unimportant. His greatness as a religious leader, although it must have reference to both the timeliness and the permanence of his contribution, is strictly bounded by neither. What is his greatness? In a word, it is the greatness of one who had a determining part in initiating and directing a popular movement of far-reaching consequence, and who in addition, laid the foundations for a new system of religious thought, also of far-reaching consequence. Religious leaders have often directed popular movements. Less often they have founded systems of thought. Less often still has the same leader done both. This was, in part, the distinction of Jonathan Edwards. He was a compelling preacher and also a master logician; an evangelist and also a thinker; a metaphysician on the side of the New Lights.

In both of these directions, his significance had chiefly to do with his emphasis on religion as a transforming individual experience, an emphasis he was privileged to make at one of the most favorable moments a religious leader could possibly have asked. His consequent success in what quickly became a great popular movement owed much to the hospitable time spirit, possibly more to the compulsion of his own personality and the force of his convictions; but it owed most of all to the idea itself, which really amounted to a redefinition of religion in terms of an inner, personal experience. By this new emphasis, which was really a much older emphasis, Jonathan Edwards became the initial, exciting force in a great religious crusade.

His mistake in choosing to speak through an outworn, dogmatic system instead of letting the new truth find more appropriate form of its own, was costly both to himself and to the truth he proclaimed. While he lived to speak directly,

297

his ideas seemed more and the supporting framework less; but later, when he had gone and the traditional system came to be recognized as obsolete, his ideas seemed obsolete also. Actually, he had made substantial changes in the modified Calvinism he professed; but he had made them by way of amendment only, substituting new elements for old, and keeping the traditional phraseology, even when he had changed the meaning behind it. What he did not see was that amendment was not enough. The whole theological system needed to be demolished, most of it thrown away, and the few remaining pieces used in the formulating of a quite new order. He had already gone a long way in this direction himself, possibly further than he knew, but not far enough to put him beyond the arid stretches of theological quibbling. The winning of many arguments became far too important. By his agility in dialectic he threw dust in the eyes of his brother intellectuals and also in his own. What he had to say did not require defence. It required only to be told. His failure to exchange a defensive warfare for leadership in a quite peaceful advance greatly limited his effectiveness in his own day. To a later judgment, it must also seriously qualify his greatness as an original thinker.

Considering the texture of his mind, one may wonder why he could not take the one more step and be free. Sometimes he did take it, but not habitually. He lacked the imagination; he lacked the mellowness and the flexibility which would have enabled him to get outside of the system and view it with enough detachment to judge it. He was on too narrow a track, and the surrounding walls were too high. For one whose thought was capable of telescopic range, and one who exhibited so large a degree of intellectual subtlety, his bondage seems almost a tragic pity. More than most men he was the prisoner of his own ideas. Yet this bondage presents no enigma. Back of it, in addition to the limitations of his personal heritage, lay three generations of Dissenting literalness, and far too many years of his own life spent in the far too industrious and too respectful study of pedestrian theologians, who trusted their hopes to logic and to logic alone. The vigor of Jonathan Edwards' moral earnestness has often enough been traced to the soil and the society from which he came. With equal reason one might say that his intellectual zeal and persistence and, in a measure, his intellectual blindness are traceable to the same sources. Among great Americans, he is perhaps the best example of one whose mind was cast strictly in the New England mold.

As an eighteenth century theologian, he was great in the scope and symmetry of his design. He saw the plan of redemption as a vast drama, stretching back to the fall of the angels and forward to the promise of just men made perfect in infinite ages beyond the last trump. Nothing was single; nothing was final; every end was merely a new beginning. His mind could not rest until he had brought the whole system within his ken, and unified it by a single idea.

Had he lived to complete the proposed "body of divinity", it might have borne little resemblance to the Edwardean scheme of theology as evolved by Messrs. Hopkins, Bellamy, Emmons, and their successors in another generation. These men were scarcely equal to their self-imposed task. Zealously they amassed proofs, filled in gaps, added argument to argument; but when all was finished they could not give the breath of life to what they had assembled. They had brought forth a system eminently useful for confronting point by point the system of their enemies, but one which had little to offer a generation which needed not to be convinced so much as to be won back to a religious way of life. Men were tired of polemics. They needed a new challenge to belief, and it was already at hand. While the "New Divinity Gentlemen" had been busily amplifying, explaining, and neatly fitting part to part, the doctrines which their system was designed to confute had been quietly accepted by the larger portion of worshipping America. The great battle of argument, for which they were so excellently prepared, was never called. A chapter had ended, and there was no going back.

The impetus, however, which Jonathan Edwards had given to theological speculation is not to be judged by the ill success of the Edwardean scheme. Out of his own unfinished thought had come an intellectual movement which determined the main stream of religious debate for over a generation, and in its further sequel opened the way for the sectarian developments of the new century. To say that this same sectarianism is to be laid at his door is to credit one man with too much. For a hundred reasons, all roads led to separation in the church life of the mid-century, and no one man or group of men was responsible. Faint praise though it is, it would seem to be true that the attempt of a little coterie of friends, first to vindicate the master and later to modify his scheme in line with a more timely emphasis, was finally effective in the overthrow of the major tenets he had set himself to defend. The victory of the Arminian way of thought, as opposed to the Calvinistic, was perhaps inevitable in a post-Revolution America. God must be made more kind and man more worthy. But that the Edwardeans hastened the victory by their clarification of the doctrinal issues involved, and that by their intense zeal for a dying cause they forced men to declare their loyalties afresh, there can be little doubt. More ironically still, the triumphing idea as to the relation between this new kind of God and this new kind of man was once again the power of religion in the individual life. Under the very banner of his theological enemies Jonathan Edwards' concept of "heart religion" was still vital. It required only to be caught up by a new time spirit and shaped to answer to a new need. Looked back upon, the essential differences between his modifications of strict Calvinism and John Wesley's were slighter than might be supposed. John Wesley merely chose to make a different emphasis, and he proved to have made it in a fortunate hour. Methodism and the other evangelical sects made the experience of conversion once more a reality in the life of the average man, and thereby gave direction to the religious aspirations of another whole generation.

What has he for a later day? Exactly what he had for his own, once his thought is taken out of the theological idiom. What is the divine sovereignty, as a conviction to live by, but the hope of a world order that can be trusted? What is eternal punishment but the insistence that right must eventually triumph over wrong, if that world order be essentially stable and just? What is "election" but the recognition that there are those who can find God and those whom no amount of teaching and leading and compelling can ever bring to a desire even to search for Him? One cannot confer sight upon the blind. What is human depravity but the reluctant notion that, left to himself, man is no credit to his kind. Certain modern novelists have called it "realism" and have written screeds which make Jonathan Edwards' view of original sin seem mild indeed.

Occasionally in his polemics and very often in his sermons, he laid by his theology and spoke his view of life directly. It is a pity he did not do it more often. If he had lived long enough to justify the ways of God to man in the whole panorama of the divine plan, and had then taken thought as to the essence of it all, he would have found in his hand a very simple thing. In the beginning it had been simple and in the end it would have been simple. Unfortunately he left it at a middle stage when specifications still seemed important. Fundamentally, his beliefs were the beliefs of the great religionists of all ages. He believed that man's life is of eternal consequence. He believed that the imperfect world we see cannot be all. He believed that reality is of the spirit. He believed that there is a pathway to present peace in spite of the frustrations of life, and that man can find it, but not of himself. Had he been able to clothe these ideas in images which would have stirred men's minds as the Enfield sermon stirred them, Emerson in his turn might have found other soil to plough.

As the details drop away, and his significance becomes clearer within the present century, the conclusion persists that as a shaping force in American culture, the man himself has been more important than anything he ever did or said or wrote. Among the great men of America, he is a lonely figure —perhaps the loneliest; and yet in spite of his severance from life as other men lived it, he stamped his personal imprint deep enough to outlast the generations. He was a man of one loyalty, and yet the total impression of his life, lived as it was without wide margins, or open spaces, or hearty human delights, is not an impression of narrowness or incompleteness. As an achievement in human living, the whole seems greater than the sum of its parts. Why, it is difficult to say, unless unity within the areas he knew helped to balance the realms he was content to let alone. By virtue of this same singleness of loyalty, there was and is no mistaking what he stood for. Even while he lived, he became the bright symbol of what he called a thousand times and more, "the things of religion". It has been his peculiar triumph to make that identification permanent.

NOTES

Prologue

1. From the Section on Angels, in "Miscellaneous Observations," *The Works of President Edwards,* edited by E. Williams and E. Parsons, 8 vols., Leeds, 1806–11, together with the two-volume Supplement, edited by R. Ogle (Vols. IX and X), Edinburgh, 1847, X, 368.

2. From the MS. draft of a letter to the widow of Elisha Williams of Weathersfield, dated Sept. 21, 1755 (Andover Collection). Having accused her of circulating false reports which had greatly injured him, he quite characteristically concludes the letter with an expression of sympathy in the loss of her husband.

Chapter I, *The Edwards Family*

1. Samuel Hopkins, *The Life and Character of the Late, Reverend, Learned, and Pious Mr. Jonathan Edwards* (Boston, 1765), p. 2. This selections was seven years after his death. The volume also contains selections from his works.

2. In a letter to Jeremy Belknap, Aug. 4, 1779 (*Massachusetts Historical Society Collections,* 1877, 5th series, II, 8).

3. P. 167, *recto*. This record is duplicated in another volume owned by St. Botolph's Church, a notebook, from which entries were copied into the formal record. The Edwards entry is identical in both volumes, except for the insertion in the notebook of the article *a* before the word *minister*, and for the omission of the letter *e* in the final syllable of *Edwards*. These records are unpublished.

4. From the will of Julian Munter, dated Jan. 8, 1646 (Somerset House, London):

> ". . . Imprimis I give and bequeath unto my grandsonne William Edwards the sonne of Richard Edwards deceased the summe of thirtie poundes of lawfull money of England Item I give and bequeath unto my granddaughter Abigaile Cole the daughter of James Cole the sume of threescore and tenn poundes of lawfull money of England which said sume of threescore and tenn pounds I desire my executors' hereafter named to imploy to the best benefitt, they can for the use of my said granddaughter until shee shall attaine the age of one and twentie years or be married which shall first happen. But if itt shall happen shee shall die or decease before shee shall accomplish the age of one and twentie yeares or bee married. Then I do will and my meaneinge is that ffortie pounds of the said threescore and Tenr. pounds shalbe and remaine to the use of my said grandsonne William Edwards And the other thirtie pounds (residue of the said Threescore is Compounded) I give and bequeath unto my daughter Anne Cole mother of the said Granddaughter Abigaile Cole Item I give unto my said daughter Anne Cole the wife of the said James Cole All my wearinge apparrill . . ."

5. From the will of Henry Munter, dated Sept. 8, 1638 (Somerset House, London):

". . . Item I give and bequeath unto my nowe wives' daughter Anne Cole the wife of James Cole Cooper the some of thirtie shillinges sterlinge And to the said James Cole twentie shillinges sterlinge To bee paid unto them within six monthes next after my decease; Item I give & bequeathe unto Timothie Cole and Abigaill Cole Children of the said Anne Cole ye some of thirty shillings sterling apeece to bee paid unto them when they shall attaine to their severall ages of one and twentie yeares. Item I give & bequeath unto William Edwards sonne of the said Anne Cole by her former husband Richard Edwardes the some of thirty shillinges sterlinge to bee paid unto him within six monthes next after my decease . . ."

6. Under date of Oct. 11, 1647 (*The Aspinwall Notarial Records,* Boston, 1903, pp. 113–14). William Aspinwall was recorder of the Suffolk County Court from Nov. 13, 1644, to Oct. 14/23, 1651.

II (10) 1647, "Agnes the wife of Wm Edwardes of Hartford uppon Connecticot by vertue of a procuration from her said husband dated 4 (9) 1647 signed Wm Edwards & sealed, witnessed John Talcott & John Steele, ordained Timothie Prout of Boston mariner her lawfull Attorney, granting him power in her & her husbands name to aske &c: all such money plate household goods or chattels of & from the Executors of the last will of Jeelian late wife of Henry Mumter of Buttalls Algate parish in London deceased & to acquitt, sue &c: arrest: & power to substitute one Attur. or more. Also to receive six pounds of Mr Wm Hoare due from Thomas Olcott."

7. Records of the Coopers' Company, Coopers' Hall, Basinghall Street, London (by the courtesy of Sir William Foster).
At a Court held May 18, 1620:

"This Day a Petition preferred to this Howse, by Mr Richard Edwards M^r of Arts, uppon the next avoydance the Schoolm^r his place at Ratcliffe, to be admitted to the same place, was here redd, and the said Mr Edwards to be warned before any ellection be made".

Henry Munter
. . . . .
. . . . .

At a Court held July 24, 1620 (Mr. Munter present as warden):

"Mr Edwards admitted Schoolmast^er at Ratcliff According to a promise made unto Richard Edwards M^r of Arts long since to be admitted Schoolemaster of the ffree schoole belonging to this Company at Ratcliff uppon the next avoidance thereof. It is this daye ordered the said Richard Edwards shalbe admitted thereto at or before Michaelmas next for as much as Mr Lownes hath written unto this Company that they should admitt another for that he will leave it".

At a Court held Oct. 27, 1625 (Mr. Munter named among those present):

"Whereas Mr Richard Edwards our late Schoolem^r, is lately deceased and that the Schoolmaster his place is thereby voyd now uppon a petition exhibited to this table by Richard Baker our usher requesting the favour of this Courte for his admission therein It is ordered he shalbe admitted in the place of Schoolmaster in regard of his sufficiency and paynes takinge in the place of an usher & finding two sufficient witnesses to be bound in bond of one hundred pounds . . ."

In accounts book, under "Ordinary Payments" (entries for the other years being identical):

"Paide Mr Edwardes our Schoolemaster for one yeares wages ending at our Lady day 1622 £20.
"Payd more to him as a legasie from Mr Cloker £ III XI s XIII^d".

8. Records of the Consistory Court of London, *Liber Vicarii Generales*, 1623–27, Vol. XIII, p. 155 (Somerset House, London).

9. The record of Faculty Office Licenses for 1625, which might have given her maiden name, is not extant. The marriage records of Stepney parish for this year are in print (*The Marriage Registers of St. Dunstans', Stepney, in the County of Middlesex*, 1568–1639, edited by Thomas Colyer Fergusson, Canterbury, 1898. Vol. I). The Edwards-Cole item is on p. 153.

10. It had been founded in 1538 by Lady Avice, wife of Nicholas Gibson, grocer and Sheriff of London. Originally provision had been made for the instruction of sixty poor children, and the maintenance of fourteen aged persons, seven from the parish of Stepney, and seven from the "mystery" of the coopers. Through later gifts, these numbers were increased. In 1552 the property was surrendered to the Coopers' Company, and subsequently the governance of both school and almshouse was in their charge. Similar charities were maintained by other guilds. In Richard Edwards' day the Schoolhouse probably stood on what was later the site of Free Trade Wharf. For further details, see James F. Firth, *Historical Memoranda, Charters, Documents, and Extracts, from the Records of the Corporation and the Books of the Company, London*, 1848.

11. Such record is to be found on a fugitive leaf dated Sept. 29, 1592, unsigned, and bound with various other items in other hands (British Museum, Sloane MSS. 2177, p. 22, *recto* and *verso*). It is entitled, "Orders to be observed by such poore people as shalbe admitted into the Almeshouse at Radcliffe agreed upon by the Master Wardens and Assistants of the Company of Coopers of London the xxix day of September 1592".

12. It is dated Oct. 27, 1620, three months after his appointment (Records of the Consistory Court of London, *Liber Vicarii Generales*, Vol. XII, p. 181, *verso*). In margin, "Licentia docendi".

In the published list of *Canterbury Marriage Licenses*, First Series, 1568–1618, edited by Joseph Meadows-Cooper (Canterbury, 1892, p. 49), there is mention, under date of Jan. 14, 1612, of "Richard Edwards, Clerk, B.A. schoolmaster of Sutton V".

This was probably the Sutton Valence Free School in Kent, maintained by the Clothworkers' Company of London. Detailed records of the school for the year 1612 have perished, but for the year 1618, when Richard Edwards, father of William, was presumably in London, there is record of another master in Sutton Valence School. Previous experience as a schoolmaster would make application for the Ratcliffe post more natural, although such a suggestion is purely conjectural. There is no evidence for the identification of these two schoolmasters.

13. *Registrum Onniversitatis Oxon* (5 vols., Oxford, 1885–89), 2, III, 261.

Magd. H. Edwards, Richard; dispensed towards B.A. (then of S. Jo.) 16 Mar. 1604/5 suppl. B.A. (Magd. H.) 13 Feb., adm. (Magd. H.) 17 Feb. 1605/6 det. 1605/6 [? I. 399] Richard Edwards, Ch. Ch. (possibly this man) suppl. M.A. 25 June 1617, inc. 1617.

There is mention of Richard Edwards in another entry, quoted from the Book of Matriculation, as follows, 2, II, 268.

9 Dec. 1603, Exeter, Richard Edwardes, Cornw. pleb. f. 18.

Joseph Foster's *Alumni Oxonienses* (Oxford, 1891), II, 449, assumes these two records to refer to the same man.

Cambridge records also show a Richard Edwards whose dates do not preclude identification:

Alumnae Cantabrigienses, Ed. John and J. A. Venn (Cambridge, 1922), II, 89. Edwardes, Richard. Matric, sizar from Christ's Michs. 1607; B.A. 1614-15.

14. Cf. note 5, *supra.* In extant parish records there are several entries showing marriage of one Richard Edwards to one Anne, but no trustworthy evidence has come to light in favor of any one of these. The marriage record of Julian, wife to Henry Munter, which might supply the maiden name, also has not come to light. In the will of Henry Munter, Anne Coles is referred to as "my nowe wives' daughter", indicating that Munter was not her name.

15. British Museum, Sloane MS. 922. The volume is entitled, *Coppies of profitable and Comfortable Letters.* Four letters written by James Coles during 1634–35, and one letter written after he came to America, are included. There are also two letters written to him by Nehemiah Wallington, one by his father John Wallington during 1634–35, and two written by Nehemiah Wallington after James Coles came to America.

16. Undated, but copied into the *Letter-Book* immediately after a letter dated June 30, 1634, p. 179. This letter of June 30, 1634, also mentions, in addition to "my Sonne William Edwards", "my littel dere Dafter Abigall" and "my Lest and derest Littel

one Timothy". The birth of these two children by Anne Cole, and also of a son James is recorded at St. Mary's, Whitechapel, London (Parish Register, Vol. I, published):

P. 128, *verso,* October 29, 1626, "James so. of James Cole & Anne".

P. 134, *verso,* April 6, 1629, "Abigaile d. of James Cole and Anne".

P. 205, *verso,* November 17, 1633, "Timothy so. of James and Anne Cole".

Mention of Abigaile Cole in the will of Henry Munter and in various Hartford records becomes an important clue to the later history of James Cole. The two other children cannot be certainly traced.

17. Dated 1634, *Letter-Book,* p. 185.

18. From a letter written to him on that date by John Wallington, urging him to return to London. *Ibid.,* pp. 191–93.

19. *Hartford Town Votes, 1635–1716* (*Connecticut Historical Society Collections,* 1897, VI), 18, 23. This record was in accordance with a vote of the Town Meeting, Dec. 26, 1639, and had as its intention the listing of all landholders since the founding of the town. Properties listed as of this date may have been owned for three or four years previously. For James Coles' later holdings, see *Original Distribution of the Lands in Hartford* (*Conn. Hist. Soc. Coll.,* 1912, XIV), Index. William S. Porter's *Hartford in 1640* (Hartford, 1842) includes a map showing James Coles' home plot of two acres bordering on the Market Place in Meetinghouse Square. There is also record of his ownership in 1639 of the northern portion of Pennywise Island, later known as Cole's Island. *Weathersfield Land Records,* I, 93, quoted by Henry R. Stiles, *The History of Ancient Weathersfield* (Hartford, 1892), p. 84, note 1. James Coles may even have resided at Weathersfield before coming to Hartford.

20. Cf. note 16, *supra.*

21. Frank T. Cole, *The Early Genealogies of the Cole Families in America* (Columbus, Ohio, 1887), p. 2. In James Coles' letter to his wife, Nov. 29, 1634, referring to the bitter letter of Henry Munter, his father-in-law, he had written, "My Lord's desier is to imploy me for New England". This is the most direct clue to his emigration. Very probably, he obtained license to sail soon afterward. A later letter (1642) of Nehemiah Wallington referring to his flying "to New England as to a City of refuge", together with the urgent entreaties of his family and friends that he return to London, and his own expressed terror at the thought of imprisonment, supply the motivation.

22. Mentioned in his will, Nov., 1652 (Connecticut State Library, Hartford). His estate was valued at £112 3s. 4d. His signature is a mere scrawl. A copy of this will is contained in Charles W. Manwaring's *A Digest of the Early Connecticut Probate Records* (Hartford, 1904), I, 108–9.

23. Actually, she fared somewhat better, for shortly after James Coles' death, their daughter Abigaile and her husband Daniel Sillivant, to whom the house had been willed, also died. The property then reverted to Anne Coles, who at her death willed it to her son William Edwards.

24. Her will had been taken down verbally, Jan. 20, 1679/80 (Connecticut State Library). A digest is included in Manwaring, *A Digest of Early Connecticut Probate Records*, I, 292.

25. For his landholdings, see *Original Distribution of the Lands in Hartford*, pp. 39, 70, 75, 106, 111, 354. Cf. also Index.

For his community services (1667–68), see *Hartford Town Votes*, 152, 154. Earlier entries occur on pp. 77, 88, 336. Cf. also Index.

The rebuke from the court is recorded in *Connecticut Particular Court Records, 1639–63 (Conn. Hist. Soc. Coll., 1928, XXII)*, pp. 196–7: Court of Magistrates, Dec. 14, 1658. Cf. also pp. 67, 89, 136, 174, 204, 236 and Index.

There is unofficial mention of a court record naming him as early as 1639, in *Thomas Lechford's Notebook, 1638–1641* (Cambridge, 1885), p. 184. The action concerns an apprentice.

For other entries, see *The Public Records of the Colony of Connecticut* (Hartford, 1850), Vols. I and II, Index.

26. Mayoralty lists for Exeter and Barnstaple during the mid-century show several possibilities; James Tucker was mayor of Exeter in 1637 and Walter Tucker of Barnstaple in 1639. Extant parish records for neither town furnish evidence of family relationship, but all three names, Walter, James, and Agnes Tucker appear in the Barnstaple records. Other names which occur in both mayoralty lists for these years are John Modyford, mayor of Exeter in 1621, and Richard Medford, mayor of Barnstaple in 1630; John Ackland, mayor of Exeter in 1626 and again in 1665, and Arthur Auckland, Mayor of Barnstaple in 1663. Extant parish records show no Agnes for either name in either town.

27. The last entry for William Spencer in Hartford records is dated Apr. 15, 1640; this entry bears his signature (*Hartford Town Votes*, I, 37). His will is dated May 4, 1640, and was probated Mar. 3, 1640/41 (Connecticut State Library, *Private Controversies*, I, 66, a). On Jan. 11, 1640/41, Agnes Spencer is mentioned as a widow (*Hartford Town Votes*, I, 51). She was still unmarried on May 2, 1642 (*Aspinwall Notarial Records*, p. 141). On Dec. 3, 1645, William Edwards was collecting damages on property listed in 1640 as belonging to the "widow Spencer" (*Hartford Town Votes*, I, 77). The marriage had presumably taken place before the latter date.

28. From a manuscript booklet (*Rev. Timothy Edwards' Notices of his Father Rich. Edwards, Esq.*) numbering 86 closely written pages, in Timothy Edwards' hand: his own lengthy title begins, "Some things written for my Own use and Comfort" (Andover Collection). An abstract of this record is printed by

Dwight, *Life*, pp. 654–61. The inventory of Richard Edwards' estate, taken May 2, 1718, lists several of these books by title as follows: "The old Boston Law Book, The Common Wealth of England, The Young Clarks Guide, Three History Books, and two or three old Books unbound". George F. Tuttle, in his *The Descendants of William and Elizabeth Tuttle* (Rutland, Vermont, 1883), reported having seen in 1877 at the sale of a private library in New York City a manuscript volume, dated 1686, made up of excerpts from Richard Edwards' reading, but this clue to his intellectual interests is unfortunately lost. The Tuttle entry reports (p. 347, note), "It was written in a small, round, very neat and plain hand".

29. From *Rev. Timothy Edwards' Notices of his Father*.

30. From the inventory of his estate, Connecticut State Library.

31. For numerous entries concerning him see *Public Records of the Colony of Connecticut*, Vol. II, 105, Vol. III, Index; *Hartford Town Votes*, 168, 204, 230, 264. Cf. also Index; *A Digest of Early Connecticut Probate Records*, Vols. I and II, Index.

In a record for 1702, *Hartford Town Votes*, p. 339, it is of interest to note that he kept his father's mark "for his Creatures". Cf. p. 336: "Richard Edwards his Mark for his Creatures is a slitt under each Eare".

32. From *Rev. Timothy Edwards' Notices of his Father*.

33. *Ibid.*

34. Record of this case is to be found in the Connecticut State Library under the classification *Crimes, Misdemeanors, Divorces, 1664–1732*, III, 235 ff. The statement of Richard Edwards is dated July 2, 1689. It is written throughout in his hand and signed by him. There are also affidavits from his two eldest children, Timothy and Abigail, corroborating his statement of Elizabeth's failure in wifely conduct, and her "unamicable carriage" toward himself. A summary of this case is included in the Judd MSS. (Forbes Library, Northampton, Mass.), V, 118–20.

35. The marriage took place in New Haven, Nov. 19, 1667. According to Elizabeth Tuttle's baptismal record, dated Nov. 9, 1645, she was two years older than her husband. She was the daughter of William and Elizabeth Tuttle of New Haven. In the Old World, according to the passenger list of the *Planter*, in which he had come to America, William Tuttle had been a "husbandman". In New Haven he was a merchant. English origins of the family are obscure, but are believed to have been Welsh. Cf. George F. Tuttle, *op. cit.*, pp. xviii–xxv.

36. Richard Edwards mentioned this child in the second codicil to his will, dated Apr. 17, 1718 (Connecticut State Library). She is referred to as "Mary the eldest child of my first wife". She was to have "two shillings upon her demand".

37. *Public Records of the Colony of Connecticut*, IV, 37, 52–53, 59.

38. By this second marriage he had five sons and one daughter. By his first marriage he had five daughters and one son. He died Apr. 17, 1718, aged seventy-one years, and is buried in the Ancient Burying Ground, Hartford, Conn.

39. This case is recorded in Hartford Archives under *Crimes*, I, 80–84. There is also reference to Benjamin Tuttle's imprisonment and death under record of action taken by Richard Edwards concerning his property (*Private Controversies*, under date of Oct. 4, 1677). He asks to be reimbursed for moneys spent toward the comfort of "My Broth^r in Law Lying Long in prison last Winter".

40. The oft-repeated assumption that a lower social rating was responsible for the fact that his name stands last in the list of graduates in the class of 1691 is not borne out by the researches Mr. Samuel Eliot Morison, who observes that the order of graduates followed the order of seniority on the "buttery table" through the years of residence (*Three Centuries of Harvard, 1636–1936*, Cambridge, 1936, p. 27). There are two entries in the steward's records for Timothy Edwards, one under date of Oct. 16, 1687, and the other of Jan. 24, 1688. In both entries he is mentioned as of the class of 1691, although he was not charged with the commencement dinner in 1691, nor was his name on the Theses Sheet with the names of the graduates. After the "ominous mark" against his name in the *Punishments* column during the first quarter of 1688, he had disappeared from the record (*Sibley's Harvard Graduates*, edited by Clifford K. Shipton, Cambridge, 1933, IV, 93–94).

41. East-side residents had petitioned annually, since 1680, for a church and a minister of their own, but the parent church of Windsor had been reluctant to grant the separation. General Court action in May, 1694, had granted partial separation, thereby opening the way for the candidacy of a minister. It was in response to this action that Timothy Edwards came. His ordination was delayed until Nov. 3, 1697, following court action permitting the gathering of a church and the calling of a minister. He was formally installed May 28, 1698, after a residence of three and a half years. Final action, granting power to east-side residents to order the affairs of the society and collect rates, did not come until Oct. 12, 1699. For record of this successive action, see *The Public Records of the Colony of Connecticut*, IV, 71, 77–78, 128, 144, 167, 156, 299.

42. On May 11, 1732. From the text, *Heb.* 9:27, "And as it is appointed unto men once to die, but after this the judgment". He used the fact of death as an incentive to righteous living, placing his emphasis on the practical virtues: pay your debts; don't sell corn short in time of great scarcity, or take up large tracts of land in new plantations; do all things "regularly" so as not to "hurt poor men".

43. The inscription reads:

In Memory of
The Revd Mr Timothy Edwards,
Pastor of the 2^d Society in Windsor,
(whose singular Gifts and Piety, rendered
him an excellent, and in the Judgment of
Charity, by the Blessing of Heaven a
Successful Minister of the Gospel)
who died *January* ye 27th A.D. 1758,
In the 89th year of his Age, and 64th
of his Ministry————And his Remains
Bury'd under this Stone.

There is also an *Epitaph* in rhymed verse.

44. Born June 2, 1672; married Timothy Edwards, Nov. 6, 1694; eight days later came to East Windsor, where she spent her life; died, aged ninety-eight, Jan. 19, 1771. She is buried beside Timothy Edwards, in South Windsor churchyard.

45. For whom Downing Street, official resident of the Prime Minister, was named.

46. *Diary*, under date of Sept. 4, 1716 (*Mass. Hist. Soc. Coll.* 1882, 5th Series, VII, 101).

47. The sermon is marked "On occasion of the Death of Mrs. Stoddard who Died Feb. 12, 1736". (Yale College Collection.) It contains nothing personal.

CHAPTER II, *A Frontier Childhood*

1. This was the fourth and last part of this voluminous work. The first part had been published in 1693. No evidence of a connection between the Edwards family of Denbighshire, to which Jonathan Edwards of Oxford belonged, and Richard Edwards of London, father of William Edwards of Hartford, has come to light. The name Jonathan had been bestowed once in the American branch of the family before 1703. Richard Edwards of Hartford had given it to his second son, first child by Mary Talcott. The child had died in infancy.

2. This tragedy took place Mar. 4, 1703/4. According to the Diary of Daniel Fairfield, a mason of Braintree, 57 were slain and 90 carried away captive. Judd MSS., III, 375. A scrap of current philosophizing, added to the statistical report, is more illuminating than the figures: "If these things be done in the green tree what shall be done in the dry. We see all things come alike to all".

3. Two years after the Deerfield tragedy an East Windsor resident was killed by an act of Indian violence. John A. Stoughton (*"Windsor Farmes": A Glimpse of an Old Parish,* Hartford, 1883, p. 67) quotes a letter from William Pitkin to Captain Stoughton, June 30, 1706, concerning this later episode.

4. Numerous quotations from one of these books containing dated accounts with his parishioners (1723–45) are included in Stoughton, *op. cit.,* and also in I. N. Tarbox, "Rev. Timothy Ed-

wards and His Parishioners", *The Congregational Quarterly,* 1871, XIII, 256–74. The present owner of the book has not been located.

5. *Life,* p. 12.

6. *"Windsor Farmes",* p. 46.

7. Henry R. Stiles, *The History and Genealogies of Ancient Windsor, Connecticut* (2 vols., Hartford, 1891–92), includes opposite p. 556 a drawing of the Edwards house, showing most of these details with the exception of the "porch". For many illustrations of similar houses, see J. Frederick Kelly, *The Early Domestic Architecture of Connecticut* (New Haven, 1933).

8. Frontispiece, *"Windsor Farmes".*

9. *Ibid.,* pp. 47–48.

10. Stiles (*op. cit.,* p. 556, note) includes an entry from the diary of the "Rev. Mr. Robbins", mentioning the demolition, under date of Mar. 30, 1812. Cf. also p. 586, note.

11. From the essay "Of Insects", Andover Collection. First printed by Dwight (*Life,* pp. 23–28), but first accurately transcribed from the original MS. by Egbert C. Smyth (*Andover Review,* 1890, XIII, 5–13). The text as transcribed by Smyth has recently been reprinted in a most convenient one-volume edition, *Jonathan Edwards,* edited by Clarence H. Faust and Thomas H. Johnson (New York, 1935, pp. 1–10).

12. "Of the Rainbow", probably written as early as "Of insects", Andover Collection. Accurately transcribed by E. C. Smyth, together with other early pieces ("Some Early Writings of Jonathan Edwards", *Proceedings of the American Antiquarian Society,* n.s., X, 212–47).

13. Smyth argues for his eleventh year, on the evidence of handwriting, spelling, sentence structure, and general attitude. Assignment of a precise date is dangerous, but assumption of precocity beyond what was previously imagined would seem a sound enough conclusion. For a recent treatment of the very interesting questions raised by this early effort, see Clarence H. Faust, "Jonathan Edwards As a Scientist," *American Literature,* 1930, I, 393–404.

14. From the original first draft, Andover Collection.

15. Marked Jan. 1745/6. Yale College Collection. The text is Prov. 30:24–28.

16. From "The Mind", a series of jottings belonging to his college days. Dwight, *Life,* Appendix, p. 668, sec. 12.

17. He had been appointed by the General Assembly of Connecticut to serve as alternate chaplain with Thomas Buckingham of Milford in the 1711 expedition against Canada. He was taken ill at Saratoga and went no farther. Four letters written during his two-month absence have been preserved (Andover Collection). The letters of Aug. 17 and Sept. 10 were printed by Dwight, *Life,* 13–15, but not accurately. There are omissions, transpositions, and what amount to free translations. The sense is not

greatly altered by these changes, but the style is considerably changed, or, as the editor thought, "improved".

18. From a college letter of Jonathan Edwards, dated July 24, 1719 (Andover Collection).

19. This transcript is made from the original (Andover Collection).

20. In a letter written Oct. 11, 1725, during Jonathan's illness at the home of Isaac Stiles of North Haven: "Forget not to thank Mr Stiles & Mistress for any kindness y^y have showed to you & for their Care of him, & put Jonathan in Mind to pay Mr Stiles for y^r Entertainment. You may Let him read this Letter". Another letter dated Nov. 10, 1725, reiterates the same counsel. Both letters are in the Andover Collection.

21. Undated and incomplete (Andover Collection).

22. Of 1754. Interleaved and bearing the name Edmund Williams. American Antiquarian Society.

23. *The Works of Samuel Hopkins, D.D.* (Boston, 1852, 3 vols.), I, Memoir by Edwards A. Park, p. 12.

24. In his *Personal Narrative,* perhaps the best known of all his writings. The manuscript is unfortunately lost. First printed by Samuel Hopkins in 1765, and included in Dwight, *Life,* 58–62, 64–67, it has since been reprinted numerous times. The most recent careful printing is that of Faust and Johnson, *op. cit.,* 57–72. References in the present volume are to the Hopkins text.

25. From "Of insects".

26. From a letter dated Oct. 20, 1725, written during Jonathan's illness in North Haven (Andover Collection).

27. From manuscript tributes to Jerusha (Andover Collection). Two of these, apparently written by her sisters, are undated and unsigned. Of these, one is complete in four pages; the other breaks off before the end. A third, thought by Franklin B. Dexter to be in the hand of Samuel Hopkins of West Springfield, husband of Jerusha's sister, was by the author's statement intended for publication. No printed copy has come to light. There are two more, both in the hand of Timothy Edwards. One of these, headed "My Daughter Anne of her Dear Sister Jerusha", follows the first three very closely; the other, headed "An Acct of ye Last Sickness of my Dear D: Jerusha of the Intermittent, malignant fever", announces as its purpose "in order to move others to emulation". Apparently father and daughters had in mind some project to honour Jerusha in print, and had agreed upon details to be emphasized.

28. Andover Collection. Transcribed from the original. See reproduction, pp. 49–50.

CHAPTER III, *An Embattled Education*

1. Two dates are given for this founding meeting: September, 1700, and September, 1701. Thomas Clap in his MS. Annals, 1747, and his printed pamphlets, 1754, dated it 1701; in his *Annals or History of Yale-College* (New Haven, 1766) he dated it 1700. Franklin B. Dexter accepts the later date, establishing it by a letter known to have been written Aug. 7, 1701, asking for the draft of a charter ("The Founding of Yale-College", a paper originally read before the New Haven Colony Historical Society, and later included in his *A Selection from the Miscellaneous Historical Papers of Fifty Years*, New Haven, 1918, p. 62).

2. In 1699. The "Manifesto" issued Nov. 19, 1699, declaring the intention of the membership to form a new church, and the choosing of a pastor (Benjamin Colman) without asking the advice of neighboring churches, had provoked sharp controversy, Increase Mather leading off in his *Order of the Gospel*, 1700. He had immediately been answered by Benjamin Colman in his *Gospel Order Revised*. Other pamphlets followed in rapid succession.

3. Clap's *Annals or History of Yale-College*, p. 17.

4. In a letter to Gov. Saltonstall, Aug. 25, 1718 (Franklin B. Dexter's *A Documentary History of Yale University, 1701–1745* [New Haven, 1916], pp. 170–71).

5. The son of William Williams of Hatfield, whose second wife was Christian Stoddard, a sister of Esther Edwards. Elisha was the son of the first wife, and therefore no blood relation.

6. Colman Papers (Massachusetts Historical Society). The letter is dated Apr. 10, 1718. The request was based upon the argument that "our Scholars here are wholly an Intirely Separate Company by themselves & their Education is therefore private".

7. Clap's *Annals*, p. 29. The "Papers of Importance" were the minutes of trustee action since the founding of the college.

8. Transcribed from the original (Andover Collection).

9. Jan. 27, 1717/18 (Andover Collection).

10. Dated June 30, 1719 (Andover Collection). Years later, Timothy Cutler did not altogether retain this good impression. Writing from Boston, Aug. 28, 1754, apparently to the Bishop of Oxford, he made the following comment:

> "I have known the man for many Years, and think him superior to Mayhew or Prince, a man of much Sobriety and Gravity, and of more decent Language than they, but odd in his Principles, haughty and stiff and morose".

At this time Jonathan Edwards had less than four more years to live. The letter is preserved in Lambeth Palace Library, London.

11. First published in 1690. Tutors Johnson and Browne, later

to be "excused" for heresy, had apparently introduced the study of Newton and Locke in the college.

12. These pieces were first printed by Dwight, *Life*, Appendix: "The Mind", pp. 664–702; "Notes on Natural Science", pp. 702–61.

13. From the section labelled Existence, No. 27, in "The Mind" (Dwight, *Life*, Appendix, pp. 668–69).

14. The entries are on pp. 3 and 4: p. 3, "Berkley's Principles of human Knowledge & New Theory of Vision"; p. 4, "Alciphron or the Minute Philosopher in 2 vols. in Octavo against the Deists by George Berkley".

15. Thunder, No. 67 (Dwight, *Life*, Appendix, p. 742); Comets, No. 86 (p. 759); Mountains, No. 42 (p. 725); Atom, No. 29 (p. 724). These last two occur in a list of "Things to be Considered or written fully About", 2nd series.

16. Dwight, *Life*, pp. 682–83.

17. Yale Collection.

18. July 24, 1719 (Andover Collection). This is the letter in which he reports his "great Content" in "Mr. Cutler's" management of the college, and the ill news of "Stiles'" failure in the preterit.

19. Andover Collection. The date is missing. Elisha Mix was the son of Stephen Mix and Mary Stoddard, and older sister of Esther Edwards. According to Timothy Edwards' statement of the case, the Rev. Mr. Mix had requested urgently that Elisha be allowed to room with Jonathan, and Jonathan had consented on condition that Elisha "be helpfull to him in yᵉ business he had to do in yᵉ buttery". It was, however, in personal services that cousin Elisha had been found wanting.

20. Transcribed from the original (Andover Collection).

21. This was a Harvard case of discipline, as reported in the *Diary* of Noahdiah Russell, tutor, 1682. The offence had been "the abusing of a Freshman", the punishment, expulsion, and recall of the gifts given him by the college (quoted in the *New England Historical and Genealogical Register*, 1853, VII, 53).

CHAPTER IV, *"A New Sense of Things"*

1. As first printed by Samuel Hopkins, *Life and Character*, p. 23. Cf. note 24, Chap. II.

2. *Ibid.*, p. 26.

3. *Ibid.*, p. 29.

4. He describes such an experience in "The Fire of Love", *Early English Text Society*, Original Series, Vol. 106, Bk. I, Chapters 12, 16, 23.

5. George William Russell, *The Candle of Vision* (London, 1919), pp. 8–9.

6. *Personal Narrative* (Hopkins, *Life and Character*, p. 26).

7. Hopkins, *Life and Character*, p. 27.

8. *Ibid.*, p. 27.

9. Quoted in *The Religious History of New England*, King's Chapel Lectures (Cambridge, 1917), p. 33.

10. A complete list of these books with their respective donors forms one of the *Papers in Honor of Andrew Keogh*, by the Staff of the Library (New Haven, 1938), pp. 423–92. The list is prepared by Louise May Bryant and Mary Patterson.

11. Herbert and Carol Schneider, *Samuel Johnson, President of King's College: His Career and Writings* (4 vols.), New York, 1929, I, 64.

12. Dexter's *Documentary History*, p. 232. This action was taken Oct. 17, 1722. Cutler, Browne, Johnson, and, later, Wetmore, went to England to take orders. On his return, Johnson was the only Episcopal rector in Connecticut, although there had been secessions to Episcopacy in other colonies.

13. The church was built in 1719 although petition for incorporation had not at that time been granted. Opposition had come from the Episcopal Church. For details as to the history of early Presbyterianism in New York, see Jonathan Greenleaf, *A History of the Churches, of All Denominations in the City of New York* (New York, 1846), pp. 126–27; "The Case of the Scotch Presbyterians of the City of New York" (New York Historical Society, *Hazard Pamphlets*, 1773), 46; *Documentary History of the State of New York* (Albany, 1850), III, 460–65. Cf. p. 403 for the "Original Survey of the North side of Wall St. 1685." For details concerning the section of the city in which the church was located see John J. Post, *Old Streets, Roads, Lanes, Piers and Wharves of New York* (New York, 1882), p. 48. The church stood until 1844.

14. There is mention in the *Minutes of the Common Council of New York* (III, 266), under date of Oct. 3, 1721, of the house of "John Smith, the Currier in Queen St." Cf. also p. 204. This was the neighborhood of Gilbert Livingston, petitioner for the charter of incorporation of the First Presbyterian Church (*Ibid.*, III, 172). The name of John Smith also appears in connection with a lot in the same district (*Ibid.*, VII, 12), and years later (Feb. 27, 1766), among the names of Presbyterian trustees who petition for land on which to build the new church.

15. From a letter of Thomas Grant to the Rev. Timothy Woodbridge, Jan. 14, 1723/4 (*The Willys Papers, Conn. Hist. Soc. Coll.*, 1924, XXI, 404–5). Jonathan Edwards had preached from Aug., 1722, to Apr., 1723.

16. *Personal Narrative*, p. 31.

17. Bolton Town Records. For a summary of these negotiations, see Samuel Morgan Alvord, *A Historical Sketch of Bolton, Connecticut, for the Bolton Bicentennial Celebrations, September 4, 1920*, pp. 21–22. For mention of letters exchanged between Jonathan Edwards and his father relative to this offer, see Stoughton, *"Windsor Farmes,"* pp. 83–85. Concerning his likeli-

hood of leaving the New York post, Jonathan Edwards wrote, Jan. 16, 1722/3: "Considering the circumstances of the Society, and my Father's inclination to the contrary, it seems most probable I shall not settle here, but am ready to think I shall leave in the spring".

18. From his famous tribute to her, said by Dwight to have been written on a single sheet, now unfortunately lost. First printed by Dwight, *Life*, pp. 114–15, and reprinted innumerable times since. For complete text, cf. p. 117, *infra*. The fact that John Stoughton (*"Windsor Farmes"*, p. 82) speaks of this sheet as still extant in 1883 leads one to hope it may yet be found.

19. From his *Resolutions*. First printed, though not entire, by Samuel Hopkins, 1765 ed., pp. 6–9. Printed entire, Dwight, I, 68–73, and often thereafter. For a recent careful reprint of Dwight, see Faust and Johnson, pp. 38–45.

20. From *The Correspondence and Diary of Philip Doddridge* (London, 1829–31, 5 vols.), III, 7–9. Of the *Diary and Correspondence*, this is I, 97–99. These resolutions are printed with the correspondence of 1722, but are not otherwise dated.

21. Quoted by Dexter, *Documentary History of Yale University*, p. 260.

22. *Ibid.*, p. 256.

23. Hopkins *Life*, p. 20. The *Diary* extends from Dec., 1722, when he was in New York, through the period of the Yale tutorship, 1724–26, with a few later entries to 1735. The manuscript is lost. First printed, though not entire, by Samuel Hopkins, 1765 ed., pp. 10–21; first printed entire by Dwight, I, 76–94, 99–106, and numerous times since. Included, Faust and Johnson, *op. cit.*, pp. 46–55.

24. The Andover Collection has three letters of Timothy Edwards to his wife, written during this period of anxiety. They are dated Oct. 11, Oct. 20, and Nov. 10, 1725.

CHAPTER V, *Ministerial Legacy, 1727*

1. Parish action prior to this date was as follows: Apr. 14, 1725, a colleague pastor for Solomon Stoddard had been voted; Aug. 29, 1726, Jonathan Edwards had been invited "to assist" Solomon Stoddard; Nov. 21, 1726, he had been invited "to Settle", and his salary, subject to increase, had been determined (Northampton Town Records).

2. In their *Testimony to the Order of the Gospel* (Boston, 1701).

3. In his *Ichabod, Or a Discourse, Shewing what Cause there is to Fear that the Glory of the Lord is Departing from New-England* (delivered in two sermons, printed, Boston, 1702).

4. From Thomas Prince's Election Sermon at Cambridge, May 27, 1730. In his later *Account of the Revival of Religion in Bos-*

ton, In the Years 1740–1–2–3 (Boston, reprinted, 1823), p. 4, he summarized as follows:

"There was scarce a prayer made in public by the elder ministers without some heavy lamentation of this decay: in their sermons also they frequently mourned it: and the younger ministers commonly followed their example therein".

This verdict is borne out in the scores of sermons which found their way into print from 1650 to 1740. In his *Christian History* (Boston, 1743–4), I, 107, he added,

"It wou'd fill a volume, tho' it would be very affecting to repeat their heavy Lamentations published in their Election Sermons".

5. From his *The Heart of New-England Rent, at the Blasphemies of the Present Generation* (Cambridge, 1659).

6. According to tradition, delivered to the "House of Lords & Commons with the Assembly of Divines at Westminster" (*The Christian History*, I, 104).

7. Benjamin Trumbull, *A Complete History of Connecticut, Civil and Ecclesiastical, 1630–1764* (2 vols., New Haven, 1818), II, 19, 20.

8. In his *Diary*, printed in *Mass. Hist. Soc. Proc.*, 1861, V, 115, 117.

9. In his almanac for 1740 (*New England Historical and Genealogical Register*, 1881, XXXV, 29).

10. For a recent discussion of the Halfway Covenant see Perry Miller, "The Halfway Covenant" (*New England Quarterly*, 1933, VI, 676–715).

11. According to the *Judd MSS.*, V, 39–40, the church had originally been organized with eight members. By the end of 1661, eighteen children of six members had been admitted, and by Mar. 24, 1662, there were fifty-six members, counting children. Up to 1672, the year Solomon Stoddard settled, there had been no baptisms of children whose parents were not in full communion, but immediately, on Dec. 11, 1672, Solomon Stoddard had put into effect his system modifying this practice.

12. Particularly his *The Doctrine of Instituted Churches* (London, 1700). Although he argued for the Lord's Supper as a means of regeneration as well as a means of strengthening the saints, he made a careful though not very logical distinction between "Members of the Church walking orderly" and the unconverted.

13. From *"A Dissertation,* wherein the Strange Doctrine Lately Published in a Sermon, The Tendency of which, is to Encourage Unsanctified Persons—to Approach the Holy Table of the Lord, is Examined and Confuted". (Boston, 1708.) This was a direct answer to Solomon Stoddard's widely discussed sermon entitled, "The Inexcusableness of Neglecting The Worship of God, Under

a Pretence of being in an Unconverted Condition, Shewed in a Sermon Preached at Northampton, The 17th Decemb. 1707". Increase Mather's point was that Solomon Stoddard's arguments were contrary to the scriptural teaching in both Old and New Testaments. The ceremonially unclean might not meddle with holy things.

14. In a small MS. notebook of 7½ pages (Yale University Library). His arguments were obviously simplified for popular understanding, his apparent purpose being to put an end to the controversy by showing that the new way was only a reform of the old. The MS. itself is undated, but in the Library catalogue the date 1725 is assigned.

Plymouth colonists had brought Henry Ainsworth's version of the *Psalms,* which continued in use until 1692. This book had tunes. Massachusetts Bay colonists had brought Sternhold and Hopkins' version, which also had tunes. After 1640 this had been replaced gradually by the *Bay Psalm Book,* which did not have tunes. A new school of hymn writers began with Isaac Watts, whose *Hymns and Spiritual Songs* (1707), *Divine and Moral Songs for the Use of Children* (1715), and *Psalms of David Imitated in the Language of the Testament* (1719) enjoyed wide favor. Philip Doddridge and Ralph Erskine made still later contributions. Reform began about 1720.

For a recent discussion bearing on this whole subject, see Percy A. Scholes, *The Puritans and Music in England and New England: A Contribution to the Cultural History of Two Nations* (London, 1934).

15. The "Narrative of Hugh Adams" is owned by the Massachusetts Historical Society. The cow horn episode is on p. 5 of the MS. As might be imagined from this episode, the career of the writer was filled with sensation. Dover was his sixth pastorate. Along with his preaching, he had also practiced surgery and physic.

CHAPTER VI, *The Parish Round*

1. Northampton had first been settled in 1654 as Nonatuck. The original petition presented to the General Court in May, 1653, for liberty to "plant possess and Inhabit the place . . . Called nonotack", had expressed the confidence that it was

"a place desirable to erect a towne in for the furtherance of the public weale by prouiding Corne and raising cattell not only for their owne but Likewise for the good of others the probogating of the gospell the place promising in an ordinary way of gods prouidence a Comfortable Subsistance whereby people may Liue And Attend upon god in his holy ordinances without distraction". Quoted by James Russell Trumbull in *History of Northampton, Mass., from Its Settlement in 1654* (2 vols., Northampton, 1898-1902), p. 6.

2. As was stated in an ordination sermon preached by Thomas

Clap in 1732, under the title, *The Greatness and Difficulty of the Work of the Ministry, and the Insufficiency of humane Abilities for it.* Almost any ordination sermon repeated the same idea. "It is an awful thing to enter into the ministry," wrote Peter Thatcher of Boston to a recruit in 1727, the same year Jonathan Edwards came to Northampton. In his own sermons preached on such occasions, he reiterated these preachments, always with emphasis on the scriptural injunction, "Submit yourself unto your minister", obedience to which was also part of the current view.

3. Under date of Nov. 21, 1726 (Northampton Town Records).

4. Born Jan. 9, 1710. The Pierrepont family was of Norman origin, tracing its beginnings beyond the Conquest. The American line was descended from William Pierrepont, son of Sir George, Knt. of Holme Pierrepont. The Rev. James Pierrepont of New Haven, father of Sarah, was American-born and a graduate of Harvard College. He was minister in New Haven from 1685 until his death in 1714. Mary Hooker was his third wife. For details of the family history, see R. Burnham Moffat, *Pierrepont Genealogies from Norman Times to 1913.* Privately printed, 1913.

5. Cf. Note on Frontispiece, *supra.* The portrait reproduced on p. 21 of Frank William Bayley's *Five Colonial Artists of New England* (Boston, 1929) as the portrait of Sarah Edwards, is incorrectly so assigned. This is the portrait of Mrs. John Edwards (Abigail Fowle), 1679–1760, of Charlestown, Mass. It is now the property of the Boston Museum of Art as the gift of Mr. Charles Wendell Townsend, her descendant.

6. As first printed in Dwight, I, 114 15. Cf. Note 18, Chap. IV, *supra.*

7. This was not the funeral sermon. It had been preached a week earlier by William Williams of Hatfield.

8. From a letter to his daughter Anne, written Sept. 12, 1729 (Andover Collection). On Oct. 6th he wrote again concerning a

"very Comfortable account of y^r Brother, who now hath for a Considerable [time] preach^d both parts of ye day, and Done the whole Work of ye Ministry."

9. Yale Collection. A transcription made by James A. Caskey (1931) is in the library of the Chicago Theological Seminary. Various excerpts from this *Catalogue* are quoted in a valuable recent article by Thomas H. Johnson, "Jonathan Edwards' Background of Reading", *Publications of the Colonial Society of Massachusetts,* 1931, XXVIII, 193–222.

10. John H. MacCracken, "The Sources of Jonathan Edwards' Idealism", *Philosophical Review,* 1902, XI, 26–42. The *Catalogue* entry of the *Clavis Universalis* is on p. 35, between an item copied from the *News-Letter* of May 30, 1754, and mention of a booklist "brought from N.York by my wife June 1754". Although so late an entry halts positive argument as to Edwards' indebtedness to Collier in the college essays, it proves nothing. He may have

been rereading Collier in 1754, or merely intending to read him. The *Clavis Universalis,* published in 1713, would have been a timely discovery during his college days, almost too much so to be likely, although correspondences between the thought of Collier and Edwards make the suggestion worthy of the investigation it received in this article.

11. The *Minutes* of the Association from the meeting of Oct., 1731, to that of Nov. 7, 1756, are deposited in the Forbes Library, Northampton, Massachusetts. Pages from Oct. 13, 1747, to Aug. 5, 1752, have been cut out of the book. This was the period of the trouble in Northampton. Two pages are also missing at the time of the trouble at Springfield over Robert Breck, although no meeting is omitted for this period. The minutes for several meetings are in Jonathan Edwards' hand.

12. A case at Stoughton, Mass., reported in Daniel T. V. Huntoon, *The History of the Town of Canton,* Norfolk County, Mass. (Cambridge, 1893), p. 183.

13. In an entry dated Jan. 1, 1737, *Clapp Memorial* (Boston, 1876), p. 130:

"I find the number of them to be seven hundred and twenty-two. A great number of souls to depend on the care of one weak and sinful creature!"

Thomas Clap had been settled as pastor in Windham in 1726, the same year Jonathan Edwards went to Northampton.

14. From a notebook of 16 pages (Yale Collection). In an undated fragment headed, "Instruction of Children" (Andover Collection), he suggests a plan for parents to follow in religious training of their children. Much more than mere reading of the Bible was expected. Children should know Jewish and ecclesiastical history, chronology of biblical events, correspondences between Old and New Testament well enough to be able to answer such questions as

"How long was it after the Destruction of Jerusalem by Nebucadn [ezzar] till Babilon was destroyed by Cyrus?
"How long after the beginning of the Persian empire before the empire was overthrown by Alexander?"

15. From a notebook of 103 pages (Yale Collection).

16. Dated Northampton, June 3, 1745; a little booklet of 14 pp. (Yale Collection), beginning:

"Dear Child,
"As you desired me to Send to you in writing Some Directions how to conduct your Self in your Christian course: I would now answer your request; . . ."

17. Notebook (Yale Collection). Included in "Miscellaneous Observations", No. 41, *Works,* Leeds Ed., VIII, 168.

18. Judd MSS., I, 28.

19. *Holyoke Diaries,* 1709–1756 (Salem, 1911), entries of Edward Holyoke. Many such items can be found in many other ministerial diaries; for example, *Diaries of the Rev. Timothy Walker,* 1730–1782 (Concord, N.H., 1889); "Diary of the Rev. Justus Forward, 1755–1812", Bethlehem, Mass. (*MS.* owned by the Boston Public Library); "Diary of the Rev. Joseph Green of Salem Village", *Essex Institute Historical Collections,* VIII, 215–24, XXXVI, 325–30. Many such records have been preserved.

20. *The Literary Diary of Ezra Stiles,* ed. Franklin B. Dexter (3 vols., New York, 1901), II, 561.

21. The incident is variously told. It appears that while a sermon was in progress the serpent wriggled into the elder's seat, behind the preacher and was promptly killed by the Rev. William Tompson of Braintree. An allegorical interpretation favorable to the business of the session was straightway written into the record. The serpent was the devil; the Synod was the Church; through its representatives the devil had recently attempted the dissolution of the Church; now the faith of the Church, newly declared by action of his Synod, would overcome the serpent and crush his head.

22. "A Journal of Rev. Joseph Emerson, Aug. 1, 1748, to Apr. 9, 1749," *Mass. Hist. Soc. Proc.,* XLIV, p. 267.

23. *The Diaries of Benjamin Lynde, and of Benjamin Lynde, Jr.* (Boston, 1880). This was Benjamin Lynde, Jr., 1700–1781. Upon the death of his father, he became Chief Justice of the Province of Massachusetts. His diary, pp. 131–208, was apparently summarized by himself from interleaved almanacs.

CHAPTER VII, *The Doctrine Laid Down*

1. In the *Memoir* prefixed to *The Great Christian Doctrine of Original Sin Defended* (Boston, 1758; included in *Works,* Leeds ed., II, 82, 84).

2. *Account of the Revival of Religion in Boston,* 1740-1-2-3, p. 18.

3. Quoted, Timothy Dwight, *Travels in New-England and New-York* (4 vols., London, 1823), IV, 316. The same remark is attributed by Sereno E. Dwight to "Dr. West", *Life,* pp. 607–8.

4. First preached as a sermon, May 19, 1723, three years before Jonathan Edwards came to Northampton. The "Preface to the Reader" in the printed edition is signed by Solomon Treat, Jan. 28, 1723/4. He stoutly reaffirms Solomon Stoddard's preachment: "to carry along the Finger with the Line" is a "despicable way" of preaching, "like Learners in Spelling" (p. iv).

5. From an early sermon (undated) preached from Psa. 89:6, (Yale Collection). There are no dated sermons before 1733.

6. All of these examples are taken from MS. sermons in the Yale Collection.

7. From an undated sermon in his early handwriting. It might very well have followed the 1727 earthquake, which was of unusual violence and caused much terror.

8. From a sermon preached in 1741, shortly after the Enfield sermon; "Vessels of God's wrath" was the theme (Yale Collection).

9. No. 4239 in the current Catalogue.

10. From an undated sermon in his early handwriting (Yale Collection).

11. In a notebook (Yale Collection).

12. From the college essay, "Of Being" (Dwight, *Life*, 706–8).

13. From his Preface to *Five Discourses* (Boston, 1738; *Works*, Leeds ed., VI, 231).

14. Samuel Hopkins, in his Preface to *The Great Christian Doctrine of Original Sin Defended* (*Ibid.*, II, 84).

15. Preached Mar., 1737/8, and again Mar., 1757, a year before his death; printed in 1765 by Samuel Hopkins and in later editions. (*Works*, Leeds ed., V, 517–40.)

16. In his *Answers to Cases of Conscience* (Boston, 1722), pp. 4, 7, 9. Having asked the question, "Is it Lawfull to wear long Hair?" he answers in the negative. "It is a great Burden and Cumber; it is Effeminacy, and a vast Expence". In the same year, 1722, the Rev. Hugh Adams had written "a thesis at ye Commencement" inveighing bitterly against these idolatries and prognosticating judgments upon the land if they were not laid aside.

17. From "The Diary of Rev. Joseph Green, of Salem Village" (*Essex Institute Historical Collection*, 1866, VIII, 224). This was an entry for July 26, 1704. An item in the *News Letter* for Nov. 9, 1749, advertising a printed sermon of Thomas Prince entitled, "The Natural and moral Agency of God in Droughts and Rains", as dedicated to the Royal Society, attests the current dignity of such ideas.

CHAPTER VIII, *Souls Gathered In*

1. The first title page to the first edition reads,

"Mr. Edwards's Sermon to the Publick Lecture in *Boston,* July 8, 1731. God Glorified in the Work of Redemption, By the Greatness of Man's Dependance upon Him in the whole of it. *Judges*, 7,2. 'Lest Israel vaunt themselves'. Boston, 1731".

The preface, signed by T. Prince and W. Cooper, begins:

"It was with no small Difficulty that the Author's Youth and Modesty were prevailed upon to let him appear a Preacher in our publick Lecture, and afterwards to give us a Copy of his Discourse, at the Desire of divers, Ministers and Others, who heard it. But as we quickly found him a Workman that needs not to be ashamed before his Brethren; our Satisfaction was the greater to see him pitching upon so noble a Subject, and treating it with so much strength and clearness as the judicious Reader will perceive in the following Composure".

"We Cannot therefore but Express our Joy and Thankfulness, that the great Head of the Church is pleas'd still to raise up from among the Children of his People, for the Supply of His Churches, those who assert & maintain these Evangelical Principles; . . . And we cannot but wish and pray that the *College* in the neighbouring Colony, (as well as our own,) may be a fruitful Mother of many such Sons as the Author, . . . so we heartily rejoyce in the special Favour of Providence in bestowing such a rich Gift on the Happy Church of Northampton, . . ."

2. For an excellent recent discussion of this subject, see Perry Miller, "The Marrow of Puritan Divinity," *Publications of the Colonial Society of Massachusetts*, 1937, XXXII, 247–300.

3. *Institutes*, Bk. I, Chap. 13, "One Divine Essence".

4. From the Divinity School Address, delivered July 15, 1838, before the Senior Class in Divinity College, Cambridge (*The Complete Works of Ralph Waldo Emerson*, Riverside ed., Boston, 1903, I, 117–51).

5. Entitled, *A Faithful Narrative of the Surprizing Work of God* (in a Letter to the Rev. Dr. Colman, of Boston, 1737; included in *Works*, Leeds ed., III, 5–71). A MS. draft of this piece is in the Andover Collection. It fills 8 folio pages.

6. In the MS. booklet it is dated, "Aug. '33". First printed in 1734; included in *Works*, Leeds ed., VIII, 1–21. Throughout his life, but particularly in his early sermons, he used light, "the most glorious thing in the material world", to suggest the greater glories of heaven. For example, in a sermon of Apr. 1734 (Yale Collection):

" 'Tis sweet to see the Natural Light. A Pleas[ant] Thing it is to behold the Sun but how much more pleasant it is to Enjoy This Light to dwell serene with [Christ] in the brightn[ess] of God's Glo[ry]. The Saints in Heaven are in the full enjoym[ent] hereof; they have their Souls forever wrapt in that Light. They enjoy it in an unspeakable Full and Intimate manner they not only behold the bridegroom but they have it in them. Their souls are filled with it".

There are many such passages.

7. Of Hatfield, the son of William Williams and Christian Stoddard. He was half-brother to Elisha Williams, the Yale tutor, and a cousin (by blood) to Jonathan Edwards. He was a man of considerable wealth and, partly by virtue of it, exercised a domineering control over the affairs of Hampshire County, civil, military, and ecclesiastical.

8. Printed with other sermons of this series under the title, *Discourses on Various Important Subjects*, Boston, 1738; included in *Works*, Leeds ed., VI, 391–430.

9. *Faithful Narrative*, MS. draft. Cf. *Works*, III, 15.

10. *Ibid.*, MS. draft.

11. *Ibid.*, cf. p. 39.

12. Judd MSS., I, 24.

13. *Faithful Narrative,* p. 68.

14. In his edition of Janeway's *Token for the Children of New-England; Or, Some Examples of Children to whom the Fear of God was Remarkably Budding, before they Dyed* (Boston, 1700).

15. Yale Collection.

16. From a letter fragment bound in with a sermon of 1744 (Yale Collection).

17. Minutes of the Hampshire Association, for the meeting held at Longmeadow, Apr. 18, 1738.

18. Judd MSS., I, 27. The "old house" was the second meetinghouse in Northampton. The first, used 1654–61, had been built of logs. It was twenty-six by eighteen feet, and nine feet high, had a chimney, two windows, and a thatched roof.

19. From the MS. booklet headed, "for a day of Prayer appointed on occasion of the front Galleries falling which fell on March 13, 1737" (Yale Collection). This accident is recorded in several diaries and in the Boston newspapers.

20. The MS. booklet (Yale Collection) is headed, "The Sabbath after the seating the New Meeting House Dec. 25, 1737". There is another booklet headed, "After the finishing of the new meeting house" (Yale Collection). The Doctrine for this second sermon is, "The Greatest Glory of an house for Publick Worship is the Pres[ence] of [Christ] in it".

21. Minutes of the Hampshire Association, for the meeting of Apr. 8, 1735. See subheading "[Breck Case]" under "Books and Periodicals" in the Bibliography for titles of Jonathan Edwards' contributions in this affair.

CHAPTER IX, *The Great Awakening*

1. This was his second trip to America. He had first come in the preceding year, 1739. Subsequently he made five more trips.

2. Quoted among various similar excerpts by W. J. Payling Wright, "Whitefield and the Newspapers, 1737–1741", *Congregational Historical Society Transactions* (1927–29), X, 11–21.

3. *Ibid.*

4. William Seward, *Journal of a Voyage from Savannah to Philadelphia, and from Philadelphia to England, 1740* (London, 1740; also reprinted in Boston), pp. 9, 22, 30. The Preface is dated July 24, 1740.

5. From an interleaved almanac of Paul Dudley, under date of Sept. 18, 1740. Cf. note 9, Chapter V.

6. Preached Oct. 21, 1740, immediately after Whitefield's departure for Northampton and printed immediately. The title page announces, "Preached to a very crowded *Audience,* and printed at the Desire of many".

7. *Journal of a Voyage from Gibraltar to Georgia* (Philadelphia, 1740); under date of Sept. 22nd.

8. From Benjamin Colman's preface to his *Letter to the Lon-*

don Ministers (Colman Papers, Massachusetts Historical Society).

9. *Ibid.*, p. 12.

10. *Literary Diary*, I, 70, under entry of Oct. 2, 1770. He had just heard of Whitefield's death.

11. *Some Observations on the Reverend Mr. Whitefield, and his Opposers* (Boston, 1740), probably by Josiah Smith. The word *opposers* is of particular interest so early as this, since criticism was hardly articulate enough as yet to be publicly challenged.

12. *Journal*, p. 152. Such entries were very numerous. His letters duplicate them at many points. For example, on Nov. 6, 1744, he wrote: "All seemed to be melted, and were drowned in tears. The cry after me, when I left the pulpit, was like the cry of sincere mourners when attending the funeral of a dear departed friend". (*Works* [6 vols., London, 1771], II, 71.)

13. *Journal*, p. 81; under date of Jan. 4, 1740/41.

14. *Tutor Flynt's Diary*, 1724–1747 (MS. owned by Harvard College Library).

15. Quoted in the *Diary of Rev. Daniel Wadsworth* (Hartford, 1894), p. 56, note. Daniel Wadsworth himself wrote under date of Apr. 18, 1741 (p. 63), after he had read Whitefield's account of his 1740 New England visit, "Scarcely yet know w^t to think of ye man & pray God to direct me in ye way of my duty".

16. In his letter to the London ministers, Oct. 7, 1740. Later on, May 15, 1742, he wrote, "Mr. Whitefield's friends have been too free with my letters, in printing part of them, and mixing them with Parts of others, without Distinction". Yet he remained a staunch supporter throughout the whole controversy.

17. On Oct. 9, 1740. The letter, framed, hangs in the Kingsley Room, Forbes Library, Northampton.

18. Colman's *Preface*, p. 10.

19. *A Continuation of the Reverend Mr. Whitefield's Journal, . . . to the 11th of March, 1741* (London, 1741), pp. 45–46.

20. One later record of this remonstrance is to be found in the postscript to the second letter in the controversy with Thomas Clap, dated Nov. 3, 1744:

"I may possibly have said that I thought I dealt more plainly with Mr. Whitefield about his errors than any other minister; & that when I talked with him about *impulses,* he apparently did not like to have much conversation on the subject". (From a draft of this letter in the Andover Collection.)

At this time Whitefield's fame was in eclipse. Jonathan Edwards took the side of the ministerial minority in upholding Whitefield, but his sanction was by no means complete.

21. *Continuation of the Journal,* p. 47.

22. *Ibid.*, pp. 46–47. His own marriage would seem to have been a mere incident. He had met his bride two weeks before. Several days after his marriage, he referred to her thus (Nov. 19,

1741): "On Saturday I was married, in the fear, of God, to one who, I hope will be a help to me". *Works*, I, 338–39.

23. He was exactly Jonathan Edwards' age. His father, William Tennent, is remembered as the founder of the "Log College", replaced in 1746 by the College of New Jersey (later Princeton University).

24. Sermon booklets for all three are in the Yale Collection. The third sermon, in its printed form, is somewhat expanded, as is true for all the printed sermons, in comparison with the manuscript version. Such expansion was probably also true for all the sermons as they were preached from the pulpit.

25. Written in his own hand on the title page. The book is owned by Forbes Library, Northampton.

26. From the *Diary*, as printed by Oliver Means, *A Sketch of the Strict Congregational Church of Enfield, Conn.* (Hartford, 1899), p. 19. According to this account, the revival went right on. His entry for the following day is, "Ye word came with mighty power".

27. As related in Timothy Dwight, *Travels in New England and New York*, IV, 316.

CHAPTER X, *Aftermath*

1. *Mr. Turrell's Dialogue Between a Minister and his Neighbor about the Times* (Boston, 1742). p. 8.

2. Charles Chauncy, *Seasonable Thoughts on the State of Religion in New England* (Boston, 1743), p. 239. After supplying detail as to the "Confusion in the house of God"—the screaming, shrieking, talking, praying, laughing, congratulating each other by shaking hands and sometimes kissing—he remarked, "It may seem incredible to relate these Facts; but they are the real truth". Chauncy's statement of opposition is valuable because he spoke temperately.

3. From the Almanacs of Nathan Bowen, quoted in the *Diary of William Bentley, 1784–1819* (4 vols. Salem, 1905), entry for Mar. 31, 1743, III, 477.

4. The Connecticut legislature also pronounced him insane.

5. Wadsworth *Diary*; entry of Sept. 1, 1741, p. 71. This entry is of interest as indicating that the term "Great Awakening" was in contemporary use.

6. Announced in the *Boston News-Letter* of Oct. 27, 1741, as "Published this Day". This was less than four months after the Enfield sermon. Already criticism against the revival had gained considerable momentum.

7. *Journals of the Rev. Thomas Smith, and the Rev. Samuel Deane* (Portland, 1849), p. 107.

8. Printed in the *Boston News-Letter*, Apr. 14, 1743.

9. *Works*, VIII, 632.

10. *Ibid.*, 628.

11. Section V, *Works*, VI, 42–43.

12. *Ibid.*, p. 44.

13. *Ibid.*, p. 50.

14. This account, written down at the desire of Jonathan Edwards, is printed by Dwight, *Life*, pp. 171–186.

15. *The Distinguishing Marks*, VII, 640.

16. "An Expostulatory Letter from the Rev. Mr. Edwards of Northampton, to the Rev. Mr. Clap, Rector of Yale-College in New-Haven, in reply to his late printed letter to him" (Boston, 1745), p. 15. The other publications in this controversy were:
"A Letter from the Rev. Mr. Thomas Clap, Rector of Yale-College at New-Haven, to a Friend in Boston—concerning what Mr. *Edwards* told him that Mr. *Whitefield* said—about turning out the generality of Ministers,—and replacing them by ministers from England" (Boston, 1745).
"Copies of Two Letters Cited by the Rev. Mr. Clap, Rector of the College at New-Haven, in his late printed Letter to a Friend in *Boston,* concerning what he has reported, as from Mr. Edwards of *Northampton,* concerning the Rev. Mr. Whitefield," by Jonathan Edwards (Boston, 1745).
"A Letter from the Rev. Mr. Clap,—to the Rev. Mr. Edwards,—expostulating with him for his injurious reflections in his late letter to a friend; and shewing that Mr. Edwards—plainly contradicts himself" (Boston, 1745).

Clap's accusation, partly because it came first, and more because it was in line with current disapproval of Whitefield, appears to have been more widely believed than Edwards' denial.

17. It was entitled "The Declaration of the rector and tutors of Yale College, in New Haven against the Reverend Mr. George Whitefield, his principles and designs, in a letter to him" (Boston, 1745). Whitefield's criticism had concerned the neglect of tutors to pray with their students, and the use of "Bad Books", meaning books written by men less "evangelical" in their principles than Solomon Stoddard.

18. Declaration of the Association of the County of *New Haven,* . . . Feb. 19, 1744/5. Concerning the Reverend Mr. *George Whitefield,* . . . Boston, 1745, pp. 4–6.

19. Whitefield's *Letter to the Rev. President and Professors, Tutors, and Hebrew Instructor, of Harvard-College, in Cambridge* (Boston, 1745). pp. 7, 21, 22.

This *Letter* was answered by Edward Holyoke, President, in a pamphlet, *The Reverend President's Answer to the Things charg'd upon him by the Reverend Mr. Whitefield, as Inconsistencies.* The reply was dated Feb. 20, 1744/45. Other declarations, replies to declarations, and replies to replies followed in rapid succession.

20. Various papers relative to this affair are included in the Cleaveland Papers owned by Essex Institute, Salem, Mass.: (1) three folio sheets, dated Nov. 19, 1744, signed by both offenders

and by Thomas Clap, detailing the college action in the case; (2) the examination of the culprits, with detailed question and answer, under the title, "A Narrative of the proceedings of the Government of Yale College in the Expulsion of John and Ebenezer Cleaveland". These materials show clearly that the offence of the boys was their disposition to justify their action in the face of the college criticism. John Cleaveland's *Journal* for 1741–42, also owned by Essex Institute, shows that as a freshman he had been greatly concerned over his soul's salvation. The Cleaveland affair is briefly recounted in Trumbull, *History of Connecticut*, II, 178.

21. In Joshua Coffin's *A Sketch of the History of Newbury, Newburyport, and West Newbury* (Boston, 1845), p. 215.

Chapter XI, *Trouble in the Parish*

1. Written across sermon notes dated Dec., 1734 (Yale Collection).

2. A portion of what would seem to be the first draft of his letter in reply to community criticism on this point is preserved in the Yale Collection. The purport of his reply is suggested by the following excerpt: "since there has been so much uneasiness and some —?— with respect to our manner of spending I will yield to give the Town an account of some of these things concerning which I have understood some of the uneasiness has been".

3. Action of Mar. 5, 1743/4.

4. Yale Collection. Sermon notes are written on the back.

5. Action of Mar. 14, 1747/8.

6. Written to Elihu Spencer. The letter was cut apart and the two portions bound with two different sermon booklets. Her reference to her father's insistence "this winter" on a fixed salary, and her allusion to the demand of the town for an itemized statement of family expenditure, might place this letter as early as the spring of 1742/3. If so, her statement of Jonathan Edwards' willingness to leave his people is of particular interest. Sermon notes of 1748 written on one portion of this letter, however, and an allusion to Jerusha's illness, might place it as late as 1748. At this later date, the willingness to leave would not be surprising.

7. *Extracts from the Itineraries and other Miscellanies of Ezra Stiles,* ed. by Franklin B. Dexter (New Haven, 1916), p. 246.

8. A portion of the bill of sale is preserved among his papers (Yale Collection). The girl was purchased of Richard Perkins of Newport.

9. [T. Welde], *A Brief Narration of the Practices of the Churches in New England* (London, 1645), p. 1.

10. The more important MS. items pertinent to this investigation were printed by Thomas H. Johnson in the *New England*

Quarterly, Vol. V, No. 1, 1932, pp. 37–54, under the title, "Jonathan Edwards and the 'Young Folks' Bible' ". The MS. originals are in the Andover Collection.

11. These memoranda are among the papers in the Andover Collection. The issue of church authority as against pastoral authority, with which they are concerned, was not raised for the first time in Northampton, in connection with the "bad book" case. According to entries in the extant records of earlier action, the Northampton congregation was first given a share in such administration in 1740. At that time, by vote of the congregation, fifteen brethren were chosen "to be present at the Hearing & considering causes and matters of Difficulty that should arise in the Church and to be assisting to the Pastor therein for a year." First Church Records, Northampton. It was this committee of fifteen before which the hearings of the accused young people were held. In 1748 the functions of this committee were defined more explicitly, and their authority made final, unless they happened to be in disagreement with the pastor, in which case a council must be called. This progressive curtailment of pastoral authority must be recognized as in part a response to the general movement toward more democratic rule, as well as indication of hostility toward Jonathan Edwards.

12. Minutes of the organization meeting, Oct. 1731.

13. Meeting of Aug. 5, 1752, held at Shelburne.

14. Action of Dec. 20, 1745.

15. In spite of these precautions, several Northampton residents were killed in surprise attacks by the Indians.

16. All of these excerpts are quoted from MS. sermons in the Yale Collection.

17. *Works,* IV, p. iii.

18. *Ibid.,* p. 33.

19. A portion of the heading for his "The Mind", presumably written in his college days.

20. *Religious Affections* (*Works,* IV, 111).

21. In a letter to John Erskine, Aug. 31, 1748 (Andover Collection). The letter is printed in Dwight, *Life,* 251–52. The context (MS. draft) reads:

"It has pleased God, since I wrote my last to you, sorely to afflict this Family, by taking away by Death, the last February, my second Daughter, in the 18 year of her Age, a very pleasant & useful member of this Family, & that was generally esteemed the Flower of the Family. Herein we have a great Loss; But the Remembrance of the remarkable Appearances of Piety in her, from her Childhood, in Life, and also at her Death, are very comfortable to us, & give us great Reason to mingle Thanksgiving with our Mourning. I desire your Prayers, dear sir, that God would make up our great Loss to us in Himself".

22. Yale Collection.

23. *Works,* III, 533–73.

24. The son of Solomon Stoddard, born Feb. 17, 1682; died

June 19, 1748. Jonathan Edwards' sermon at his funeral, preached from the text, "Her strong Rods were broken and withered", was immediately printed. The sermon booklet, marked "On Occasion of the Death of Col. Stoddard", is in the Yale Collection. It was written on pieces of fan paper, some of which are delicately colored, as though by a brush.

Chapter XII, Defeat and Dismissal

1. In a letter to Joseph Bellamy of Bethlehem, Conn., dated Jan. 15, 1749/50 (Library of Congress).

2. In a letter to Thomas Gillespie, July 1, 1751 (Andover Collection; printed by Dwight, *Life*, 462–68).

3. *Works*, VII, p. 5.

4. *Ibid.*, p. 200.

5. Repeated in these same words several times in his printed works: in his *Inexcusableness of Neglecting the Worship of God, Under a Pretence of being in an Unconverted Condition* (Boston, 1708); in his *Defects of Ministers Reproved*, and elsewhere in slightly different form. Such an observation suggests his point of view. He looked at the facts and framed a policy to suit.

6. Dec. 6, 1749 (Yale Collection; printed by Stanley T. Williams, *New England Quarterly*, 1928, I, 237–40).

7. From a letter of Sept. 11, 1749. The name of the addressee is missing (Collections of the American Antiquarian Society). In this same letter he speaks of an awakening among the young people, greater than for the five preceding years, and expresses surprise in its "coming at so unlikely a time".

8. Hawley's letter to Jonathan Edwards is missing, but the reply which it elicited is preserved among the Hawley papers in the New York Public Library. This reply was somewhat inaccurately printed in *Bibliotheca Sacra*, 1844, I, 579–91. It has recently been carefully reprinted in Faust and Johnson, *op. cit.*, pp. 392–401. Hawley's letter to David Hall was printed in Dwight, *Life*, pp. 421–27. It had been previously printed by Samuel Hopkins, 1765, *Life and Character*, pp. 66–72.

9. For the complete text, see *Works*, VII, pp. 386–87.

10. The MS. is owned by the Massachusetts Historical Society. The *Journal* contains various friendly allusions to Jonathan Edwards. David Hall had been a supporter of Whitefield, and like Edwards, had believed the revival to be genuine. He came as a delegate to the second council, May, 1751, but his friendly support was again helpless against the opposition.

11. Included in Dwight, *Life*, pp. 313–403.

12. *Works*, VII, 349–82, particularly pp. 368, 369, 382. The sermon has been reprinted numerous times since 1751, when it was first published. There are two notebook entries entitled "Farewell Sermon". One names as text, *Jer.* 25:3:

"From the thirteenth year of Josiah the son of Amon king of Judah, even unto this day, that is the three and twentieth year, the word of the Lord hath come unto me, and I have spoken unto you, rising early and speaking; but ye have not hearkened".

The other, entered several pages farther on in the same notebook, is the text chosen. In the fact, these two entries merely support what is apparent from various letters and other memorials; namely, that Jonathan Edwards expected the dismissal months before it happened. In his rejection of the more spectacular text, he revealed his own attitude toward the whole affair. An accusing sermon would have been out of line with his conduct throughout the crucial months. The first entry suggests that his earlier thought may have been otherwise. The notebook is in the Yale Collection.

13. Yale Collection. There is a copy in the Andover Collection. The *Letter* is printed as an Appendix to the *Reply to Solomon Williams, Works,* VII, 343–48.

14. Minutes for the meetings of Nov. 5, 1752, and Feb. 5, 1753, respectively.

15. The letter itself is dated Apr. 2; the P.S. is dated July 3. There is still another letter to John Erskine dated July 5. Both letters are in the Andover Collection; both were printed by Dwight, *Life,* pp. 287–97, 405–13.

16. A sermon marked "August, 1750", only one month after the dismissal, is typical. It had as its text *Prov.* 3:16–18: "Length of days is in her right hand; and in her left hand riches and honour". His Doctrine was phrased thus:

"True Religion is no other than the true Method of becoming really & durably rich and honourable and joyful".

17. Yale Collection. This document, which is undated, is very carefully drawn up. The following statements and questions were proposed for consideration:

1. It is difficult to obtain a young candidate with sound principles.

2. If Mr. Edwards goes, the cause he has espoused will suffer.

3. Does the Gospel rule permit the church to remain together under two practices, as at present?

4. If not, what is the lowest number of members over whom Mr. Edwards could suitably be installed?

5. For "Encouragement and Inducement" it may be reported that a number will join from neighboring towns. Many will join from Northampton, once the project is assured.

6. Lastly, if Mr. Edwards leaves, what are those of us who adhere to him to do about Communion? Must we partake with those who believe otherwise?

18. Undated (Andover Collection).

19. Action of July 20, 1750, three weeks after the Farewell Sermon. The granting of what would seem to have been a small favor would have been a great convenience. Jonathan Edwards had sheep and other animals requiring pasturage. He could hardly have been expected to dispose of his possessions within the month.

20. The Canaan prospect is mentioned by Ezra Stiles, *Extracts from the Itineraries*, p. 182. The Lunenburg offer is recorded in a letter from Samuel Davies, printed in *The Memorial Volume of the Edwards Family Meeting at Stockbridge, Mass. Sept. 6–7, A.D., 1870* (Boston, 1871), pp. 110–11. Dwight mentions the offer from Scotland, but gives no details. His statement that Jonathan Edwards received substantial financial aid from Scotland at this time is not corroborated in surviving letters, but the closeness of his relation to John Erskine and Thomas Gillespie, for example, would have made such aid fully natural.

21. The entry on the Town Book (Nov. 19, 1750) reads as follows:

"Voted To give The Revd Mr Edward Ten pounds Old Ten^r p^r Sabbath for ye Time he has preached to this Parish since he was dismissed".

Up to Nov. 15, he had preached twelve times, according to dated sermon booklets which are extant. This amounted to almost every Sunday he had been in town. The settlement of his account on Nov. 19 may very well have been at his own request, and in accordance with his plans for Stockbridge. There is no warrant in the town record for the statement that he was forbidden to preach in Northampton after this date. The arrangement had been "from Sabbath to Sabbath".

22. Judd MSS., I, 24.

23. Letter to Hawley, dated Nov. 18, 1754 (Hawley Papers, New York Public Library; Faust and Johnson, *op. cit.*, p. 392).

24. *Ibid.*, pp. 393, 401.

25. *Ibid.*, p. 393.

CHAPTER XIII, *Missionary to the Indians*

1. Judd MSS., I, 192.

2. The story of this mission, up to the time of John Sergeant's death, is most completely told in Samuel Hopkins' *Historical Memoirs, Relating to the Housatunnuk Indians; or, An Account of the Methods used, and Pains taken, for the Propagation of the Gospel, among that Heathenish Tribe, and the Success thereof, under the Ministry of the late Reverend Mr. John Sergeant* (Boston, 1753).

3. They may not have initiated action in his favor; but they had sanctioned it, and their approval carried weight. A letter from Andrew Oliver, May 26, 1750, written to Stephen Williams

of Springfield (Congregational Library, London), asks for a frank statement as to Ezra Stiles' qualifications, and suggests Ephraim Williams as a source of "such information as would be most likely to satisfy the commissioners about it". Ezra Stiles refused the post Sept. 17, 1750 (*Literary Diary*, I, 209–10). A letter of Abigail Sergeant, Aug. 10, 1750, quoted by Stiles, speaks of malice abroad. A letter of Oct. 6, 1750, expresses her disappointment that Ezra Stiles is not coming (*ibid.*, p. 211).

4. *Memoir* of Samuel Hopkins, I, 44. Cf. note 23, Chapter II, *supra*. (This was Samuel Hopkins later of Newport, not Samuel Hopkins of note 2, this chapter.)

5. A merchant-lawyer of Brookfield, Mass., who had distinguished himself in the 1745 French and Indian troubles, and had been made brigadier general in consequence. Previous to his Stockbridge residence, he had been friendly to Jonathan Edwards. It was his marriage into the Williams family which changed his attitude.

6. From a letter of George Drummond to John Sergeant, Feb. 9, 1740 (quoted in Hopkins' *Historical Memoirs, Relating to the Housatunnuk Indians*, p. 85). From this letter and those written subsequently to Colman, Hollis, and others interested in the project, the professed lack of self-interest on the part of the missionary and his sponsors is unquestionably to be taken at its face value; but the approach to the problem could hardly have been more unfortunate.

7. *Ibid.*, p. 100. Such phrases occur over and over in contemporary discussions of Indian problems.

8. *Ibid.*, p. 13.

9. Yale Collection. The same sheet contains also the grim aphorism, copied eleven times, "HE WHO LIVES UPON HOPE MAY DY OF DISAPPOINTMENT".

10. Dated Aug. 31, 1751 (Andover Collection). Jonathan Edwards had been installed as missionary Aug. 8, three weeks earlier.

11. From a letter dated June 30, 1752, to Col. Timothy Dwight of Northampton (Andover Collection). The letter concerned the selling of land owned by Jonathan Edwards at Winchester, since by refusal of his Stockbridge petition, he was, as he said,

"in greater need of money than I expected".

The petition of Jonathan Edwards, dated Oct. 5, 1751, together with other memoranda relative to the affair is included among the Stockbridge papers, Andover Collection. There is a summary of the transaction in the Judd MSS., V, p. 77.

12. There are also suggestions of help from the Scottish branch of the same society. In surviving records these organizations appear under various names. For example, fragmentary minutes of the London society, relative to the Stockbridge mission, are pre-

served under the heading, "The New England Company". These records are to be found at 26, Bloomsbury Square, London. In the minutes of this organization, the Scottish Society is referred to as "ye Scotts Society of Edinburgh".

13. From the Rough Draft Minutes of the London Society, under date of July 9, 1751. Elisha Williams' proposal had been made at the preceding meeting, July 3rd. The moneys granted to Mrs. Sergeant were part of the action of the July 9th meeting. It is apparent from these records that the name of Elisha Williams carried weight and that approval of the new scheme he proposed amounted to a vote of confidence in him and a vote of gratitude to Mrs. Sergeant, for her husband's sake.

14. One such set of memoranda is labelled, "Account of Capt. Kelloggs Treatment of Mr. Hollis's Scholars" (Andover Collection). The jottings appear to have been made while the testimony was being listened to.

15. Dated Stockbridge, Feb. 24, 1752. From a copy in the Library of Lambeth Palace, London. The reply dated July 18, 1752, is also included. Joseph Paine explains his sending of the copy instead of the original thus:

"it is wrote in a hand hardly Legible".

He also adds apologetically,

"Permit me Sir farther to mention, that I do not Patronise his observation on the Episcopal Missionaries in New England, but, as that is part of his Letter, I could not avoid transcribing it with the rest".

16. The letter covers four folio pages (Andover Collection). In another letter to Andrew Oliver, Apr. 13, 1753, he states that the town has no chance of peace while Col. and Mrs. Dwight remain. The purport of this letter is to urge that Mrs. Dwight be denied the headmistressship of the girls' school. This denial will, he thinks, end the unrest.

17. It burned Feb. 8, 1753. Gideon Hawley's *Journal* has this entry relative to the fire (Vol. IV):

"There were many, & with considerable reason, who suspected the house to have been set on fire by some evil minded person and under the circumstance of a party who wished to demolish it".

Vol. IV of this Journal is in the form of a letter. The MS. is owned by the Congregational Library of Boston.

18. Dated Apr. 15, 1754 (Andover Collection).

19. Quoted in the *Journal* of Eli Forbes, of Brookfield, Mass. (*Mass. Hist. Soc. Proc.*, 1892, p. 384).

20. On an undated sheet (Yale Collection).

21. Undated; headed "Speech to the Mohawks" (Andover Collection).

22. He had been appointed missionary to the Iroquois in 1751. His early record provides much intimate detail for the Stockbridge years.

23. Owned by the Yale University Library. Various excerpts, selected by Josephine Fisher, were published together with critical comment, in the *New England Quarterly*, 1930, III, 297–315, under the title, "The Journal of Esther Burr".

24. Lucy Edwards to Mary Dwight, undated (Andover Collection).

25. *Journal* of Esther Burr, MS. (Yale Collection).

26. *Ibid.*

27. *Ibid.*

28. *Ibid.*

29. *Ibid.*

30. *Ibid.*

31. Dated Nov. 2, 1757 (Andover Collection); printed in Dwight, *Life*, 571–73, but not accurately.

32. Lucy Edwards to Mary Dwight, Aug. 20, 1754.

33. Written June 2, 1748, on occasion of her absence during Col. John Stoddard's last illness. She had gone to Boston to care for him. Another letter, a fragment (Andover Collection), ends thus:

> "I am your most affectionate Companion
> JONATHAN EDWARDS".

CHAPTER XIV, *"Life Passed through the Fire of Thought"*

1. *Works*, VII, 197.

2. *Ibid.*, p. 210.

3. *Ibid.*, p. 279.

4. Undated (Andover Collection).

5. The Rev. Israel Holly of Suffield, in reply to the Rev. Mr. Bartholomew, who had written "A Dissertation on the Qualifications necessary to the lawful profession and enjoyment of special ordinances". Holly's reply is quoted from in the *Historical Magazine*, 1867, p. 334.

6. His correspondence during the 1740's furnishes frequent evidence of his intention to write on this subject. For example, to Joseph Bellamy, Jan. 15, 1746/7 (Yale Collection); printed with five other letters by Stanley T. Williams, in the *New England Quarterly*, 1928, I, 226–42:

> "I have got so deep into this Controversy, that I am not willing to dismiss it, till I know the utmost of these matters. . . .
> "If you could Enquire of Dr. Johnson, or Mr Beach, or some other, & find me what is the best Book on the Arminian side, for the Defence of their notion of Free Will; & whether, there be any better & more fully than Whitby, I should be glad; provided you have convenient opportunity. I don't know but I shall publish something after a while on that Subject".

To John Erskine, Aug. 31, 1748:

"You would oblige me, if you would inform me what are the best Books that have lately been written in defence of Calvinism".

To Erskine, July 5, 1750 (Andover Collection; printed by Dwight, *Life*, pp. 405–13):

"An End is put for the Present by these Troubles to the studies I was before engaged in, and my Design of writing against Arminianism. I had made considerable Preparation, and was deeply engaged in the Prosecution of this Design, before I was rent off from it by these Difficulties, and if ever God should give me Opportunity, I will again resume that Affair".

7. *Winthrop's Short Story* contains a Catalogue of these errone- ous opinions. Included by Charles Francis Adams in *Antinomian- ism in the Colony of Massachusetts Bay, 1636–1638* (1894), p. 95.

8. *Works*, I, 153.

9. *Ibid.*, p. 355.

10. *Ibid.*, p. 410.

11. James Dana, *An Examination of the Late Reverend Presi- dent Edwards' "Enquiry on Freedom of Will": More Especially the Foundation Principles of his Book, with the Tendency and Consequences of the Reasoning therein Contained* (Boston, 1770). Cf. Preface, and also Appendix, pp. 128–40.

12. *An Examination of President Edwards' Inquiry on the Freedom of the Will* (New Haven, 1841). Cf. Introduction.

13. *Literary Diary*, III, 361, under date of July 26, 1789. The entry reads:

"Kept Sabbath at Oxford & preached all day for Rev⁴ Mr. Brownson. Mr. B. tells me his Class was the first yᵗ recited Edward⁸ on the Will— that Presᵗ Clap offered the Class to chuse the Book of Mor. Phil. they wished to recite, the Class chose Edwᵈˢ & appointed Dr. Huntington & himself to wait on the Presidᵗ with their Choice who approved it. Last recited 1775".

II, 349, under date of June 24, 1779:

"Yesterday I put the Senior Class into President Claps Ethics or Moral Philosophy. It was printed just before his death, and has been sometimes recited by the Classes. Afterwds President Edwᵈˢ on the Will was recited; this giving Offence was dropped".

14. From Dana's Preface.

15. Published in 1738.

16. *Works*, II, 349–50.

17. *Ibid.*, p. 336.

18. The full title is *A Winter's Conversation upon the Doctrine of Original Sin* (Boston, 1757). Webster was pastor at Salisbury, Mass.

19. For specific applications of Samuel Hopkins' teaching to

foreign missionary enterprise in the next century, see Oliver W. Elsbree, "Samuel Hopkins and His Doctrine of Benevolence", *New England Quarterly*, 1935, VIII, 534–50.

20. The nucleus of this idea was first presented in a series of sermons, preached as early as 1739. One volume of materials shaped toward this project was printed posthumously. It contains little promise of greatness (*Works*, Vol. V).

21. *God's Last End in Creation* (*Works*, I, 529).

22. *Ibid.*, p. 531.

CHAPTER XV, *Honor Too Late*

1. Originally printed by Samuel Hopkins, *Life and Character* (1765), and frequently reprinted. Cf. *Works*, I, 78–82.

2. Ezra Stiles, writing in his *Diary* twenty years later, May 24, 1779, evaluated Jonathan Edwards' abilities for the presidency thus (II, 337), under the heading,

"Presidents of Colleges with whom I have been personally acquainted":

"Mʳ Edwards succeeded him—a great Divine—a good Linguist especially in Hebrew—a good Scholar, but not equal to Mʳ Burr. He was well skilled in the Logic of Ramus & Burgersdisius, & the philosophy of Wendeline, but not in Mathematics & the Ratiocinia of the Newtonian Philosophy. A gᵗ Metaphysician! He was rather adapted to a recluse contemplative serious Life, than to the Labors & Activity of the Head of a College".

3. Andover Collection.

4. *Literary Diary*, II, 337, continuing the quotation cited above (note 2).

5. Dated May 6, 1752; the addressee is not named (Princeton University Library).

6. From Samuel Hopkins' account, *Life* (1765).

7. In a letter to Sarah Edwards dated Mar. 22, the day of Jonathan Edwards' death. The original is in the Andover Collection. Printed in Dwight, *Life*, 579–80. There is also another letter, written by John Ballantine Mar. 29th to Esther Hopkins of Springfield, but no new details are added (Andover Collection).

8. Andover Collection. On the same sheet, Susannah wrote a letter to one of her sisters. It is this letter which recounts the Stockbridge farewell. Printed in Dwight, *Life*, p. 581.

9. The grave of Esther Burr is not marked.

10. Dated Mar. 14, 1753. Northampton Court House. The will was printed in *Bibliotheca Sacra*, 1876, XXXIII, 438–47.

11. 1745–1801. Born in Northampton; was graduated from Princeton, 1765; after a brief pastorate at Bethlehem, Conn., accepted a tutorship at Princeton; after two years became pastor of White Haven church; married in the following year; was dismissed in 1795; went to Colebrook, Conn., and after two years accepted the presidency of Union College, Schenectady, N. Y.

He was orthodox in his views, and with certain important reservations continued the battle his father had begun. His chief contribution to theology was his forceful development of the idea that God is beneficent, not arbitrary, and his interpretation of the doctrine of the atonement was in line with this modified concept.

12. The *Boston Gazette* of Apr. 10th did better, printing the following eulogy, obviously of ministerial composition:

"On Wednesday, the 22nd of last month, died, by inoculation, at Nassau Hall, an eminent servant of God, the Rev. pious, Mr. Jonathan Edwards, President of the College of New Jersey; a gentleman of distinguished abilities, and an heavenly temper of mind; a most rational, generous, catholic and exemplary christian, admired by all who knew him, for his uncommon candour and disinterested benevolence; a pattern of temperance, meekness, patience and charity; always steady, calm and serene a very judicious and instructive preacher, and a most excellent divine. And as he lived, cheerfully resigned to the will of Heaven, so he died, or rather, as the Scriptures emphatically express it, with respect to good men, he *fell asleep in Jesus,* without the least appearance of pain".

13. As might have been expected, this publication called forth a reply by Samuel Webster. It was entitled, *The Winter Evening's Conversation Vindicated: Against the Remarks of the Rev. Mr. Peter Clark of Danvers.* Other pamphlets followed on both sides.

SELECTED BIBLIOGRAPHY

This bibliography includes only those materials which have been directly used in the preparation of the various chapters in this book. No attempt is made to list, in addition, the large body of background materials which contribute to the understanding of an eighteenth century American who was both churchman and thinker.

MANUSCRIPTS

I. THE EDWARDS MSS.*

Most of the extant Edwards MSS. are to be found in the Yale Collection (Yale University Library) and the Andover Collection (Andover-Harvard Theological Seminary Library). The more important items in these two collections are as follows:

Yale Collection

1. Sermons and Sermon Outlines (about 1,150 in all)

568 complete sermons in homemade and hand-sewed booklets, measuring 3⅞ by 4⅛ inches. The number of pages varies, one booklet sometimes containing the matter of several sermons intended to be preached in series. Sermons are fully written out, even to minute corrections and interpolations. All but 52 sermons (in larger booklets) are dated, and the place of preaching noted. The earliest date on any booklet is 1733. Texts from the New Testament predominate, although all books of the Bible are represented. Only about 50 of these sermons have been published.

About 350 sermon outlines, varying in length from three to six pages, and usually sewed together after the fashion of the sermon booklets. Most of these bear dates for the last decade of the Northampton pastorate, 1740–1750.

175 briefer outlines, belonging to the Stockbridge years, 1751–1757. Many of these outlines consist of a single page, and are written on mere scraps of paper of uneven size. All but 50 are on texts chosen from the New Testament.

2. Notebooks

Miscellaneous Observations. 8 vols., varying slightly in size but approximating to the folio (1,406 pp.). These volumes, really

---

* For an earlier description of these materials, see Franklin B. Dexter, "On the Manuscripts of Jonathan Edwards", *Massachusetts Historical Society Proceedings,* 2nd series, 1902, XV, 2-16.

commonplace books, contain notations of many sorts under numbered topics, 1 to 1360. The whole is carefully indexed and provided with an elaborate system of cross-reference. One volume, entitled *Types of the Messiah,* is separately indexed. A Supplement to this volume, which appears in another notebook, is bound with pieces of the *New York Mercury* for Aug. 23, 1756, suggesting that this inquiry was one of Jonathan Edwards' later interests. Selections from the materials in these volumes were first published under the editorship of John Erskine, with the titles, *Miscellaneous Observations on Important Theological Subjects,* Original and Collected (Edinburgh, 1793) and *Remarks on Important Theological Controversies* (Edinburgh, 1796). Both of these volumes were later included in the Worcester, Leeds, New York, and London editions of Edwards' collected works. The volume entitled *Types of the Messiah* was first published, in part, by Dwight in 1830, included in the Supplement to the Leeds edition in 1847, and in the subsequent reissues of the earlier editions. In their published form, these materials have been greatly altered, the result often amounting to a free translation of the original.

Commonplace book on Theological Controversy. 298 pages, folio.

Notes on the Bible. 3 quarto vols., containing annotations and comment under numbered texts and topics. Portions from these volumes were published by Dwight in 1830, and subsequently included in reissues of earlier editions. On the back cover of the second MS. volume, this note appears, in Jonathan Edwards' hand:

"If I live to make another Book of this sort to observe to cut the gashes for the Stitching in deeper & not so near to the Joinings of the Stitch that the Book may open more freely & fully. Let the sheets be divided into twice so small divisions & st[it]ch no paper in a paper Cover for that makes it weak & if that don't do try next stitching the Back of all the divisions of sheets to a Slip of the Leather & sew the Cover over the Leather."

Notes on Revelation. 197 pages, containing many excerpts from Boston and New York newspapers, 1747–1757. Next to the last item in Section I, p. 167, is taken from the *Connecticut Gazette* for Dec. 10, 1757, a little more than three months before Jonathan Edwards' death.

Shadows of Divine Things. Folio. Annotations and comment on numbered topics (Death Temporal, Lightning, The Tongue, etc.). Indexed both by subject and by Scripture texts noted. 23 pages.

Efficacious Grace. 3 volumes, containing 316 pages. Printed in part by Erskine in *Miscellaneous Observations* (Edinburgh, 1793) and included in later editions of Edwards' collected *Works.*

Faith. 51 pages. Printed in part as Chapter VII in Erskine's *Remarks on Important Theological Controversies* (Edinburgh, 1796). The cover is lined with a portion of a broadside elegy for William

Seward, companion in travel of Whitefield on the 1740 visit to America.

Harmony of the Genius, Spirit, Doctrines and Rules of the Old Testament and the New. 196 pages. A list of parallel texts from the Old and New Testaments, assembled under topics. The last entry is *Psalms* 149.

Catalogue. 43 pages stitched together and bound in heavy brown paper. The book measures 6⅜ by 8⅜ inches. 5½ pages at the end are blank. Perhaps the most important item in the whole collection. It contains a list of 600 titles of books read and to be read, with annotations. See pp. 119–22 and Note 9, Chap. VI, *supra*. On the last full page (p. 42) there is reference to a letter dated Jan. 13, '57. "in my Drawer". Jonathan Edwards died Mar. 22, 1757/8.

Notes on Natural Science. Cover page only.

Notes for Sermons. 6 quarto volumes of miscellaneous jottings intended as suggestions for sermons: texts for special occasions, timely themes, and reminders of parish needs. Some of these suggestions are mere hints; as, "Preach a sermon to Young People", "To Preach a sermon against Spiritual Pride"; others are sufficiently detailed to indicate the entire sermon development.

Notes on Old Testament History. 129 pages.

Notes on the History of the Early Church. 21 pages.

Signs of Godliness, 20 pages, folio.

Index to *The Mind.*

3. Other Items

Interleaved Bible. A book designed for the purpose, with blank pages alternating with pages of biblical text. The flyleaf bears the inscription:

Benjamin Pierpont
His Book A.D.
1728
Jonathan Edwards his Book 1748.

Almost every page has annotations, but few are filled. Several pages at the end contain records of the savings accounts of the Edwards children, with receipts, expenditures, borrowings, carefully itemized. The *verso* of the first flyleaf has a list of symbols used by Jonathan Edwards for cross-reference in his notebooks. Only the first two symbols are explained.

An early draft of the *Reply to Solomon Williams.* 2 quarto volumes, totaling 179 pages.

Portions of an early draft of the *Doctrine of Original Sin.*

Essay on the Trinity. 6 pages.

Notes on Free Will, Efficacious Grace, Truth of the Christian Religion, etc. 14 pages.

The Valedictory Oration, delivered in September, 1720.
A few personal letters and fragments of letters.
The *Journal of Esther Burr*, daughter of Jonathan Edwards, written in the form of letters addressed to Sally Prince of Boston. Entries date from Oct. 1, 1754, to Sept. 2, 1757, the day on which the fatal illness of Aaron Burr, husband of Esther, began.

Andover Collection

1. Sermons and Sermon Outlines

Five sermons and about fifty sermon outlines, belonging chiefly to the Stockbridge years.

2. Notebooks

Prophecies of the Messiah. 112 pages, folio. A continuation of the volume in the Yale collection.
The Fulfillment of the Prophecies. 143 pages.
Types of the Messiah. 16 pages, quarto. A continuation of the Yale notebook by the same title.
The Treatise on Grace. Copy. (Printed by Alexander B. Grosart in *Selections from the Unpublished Writings of Jonathan Edwards of America*, Edinburgh, 1865.)
Shadows of Divine Things. Copy.

3. Other Items

Originals of the early writings: *Of Being, The Soul, The Rainbow, Of Insects,* etc.
Testimony of the culprits and various other memoranda relating to the discipline case of 1744.
A Draft of the Letter to Benjamin Colman (printed as *A Faithful Narrative of the Surprizing Work of God*, Boston, 1737).
Family letters. The richest part of the collection. Letters written by Timothy Edwards to Esther, his wife, during Jonathan Edwards' childhood and student years.
Various letters written by Jonathan Edwards to his father and to his sister Mary during his college years.
Various letters written by Timothy Edwards to his daughters.
Many first drafts of letters and some originals written by Jonathan Edwards to the Boston Commissioners, to Joseph Bellamy, William Hobby, John Erskine, and other ministers, particularly during the Stockbridge years.
Papers belonging to the Clap controversy; some originals and some first drafts.
Memoranda concerning the Stockbridge Mission.
Rev. Timothy Edwards' Notices of his Father Rich. Edwards. Esq., a homemade notebook, measuring 6¾ by 4⅜ inches and numbering 86 pages. See note 28, Chap. I, *supra*.

Tributes to Jerusha Edwards by her sisters and by Timothy Edwards. See note 27, Chap. II, *supra.*

A few of Timothy Edwards' sermons and a small notebook with jottings from his reading.

Scattered Items in Other Collections

A few letters and various fugitive sheets in Jonathan Edwards' handwriting are to be found in the libraries of Princeton University, the Massachusetts Historical Society, the American Antiquarian Society, the Library of Congress, the New York Public Library, the Boston Athenaeum, the Congregational Libraries of Boston and London, and elsewhere. Much remains to be discovered, if indeed the lost manuscripts may ever be found. Alexander B. Grosart, who examined the entire manuscript collection preparatory to participating in a plan to publish a definitive edition of Edwards' works, remarked in the 1865 Preface to his volume, *Selections from the Unpublished Writings of Jonathan Edwards of America,* that he had then in his possession "priceless and hitherto unknown materials for a worthy biography". These materials, not otherwise described, have never come to light. John A. Stoughton, in his Preface to *"Windsor Farms",* 1883, quoted from a letter by Anne Grant, great-granddaughter of Anne Edwards, as follows:

"When I was a child there was a great heap of papers on the garret floor belonging to the Edwards estate; of these many were injured by the rain from the leaky roof until they crumbled to dust, and many others were given to various persons, who, anxious to obtain some memento of the family were allowed to help themselves from the collection."

Doubtless all of these, some of which might also have been "priceless", have now perished. Many of the more valuable originals from the collections of Sereno E. Dwight, now forming the Andover Collection, have been missing for many years.

II. OTHER MS. MATERIALS USED IN THIS STUDY

Adams, Hugh, "A Narrative of Remarkable instances of a particular faith, 1724–5." Massachusetts Historical Society.

Clap, Thomas, "Some Considerations tending to put an end to the Differences that have been about Singing by Rule." Yale University Library.

The Cleaveland Papers. Essex Institute.

The Colman Papers. Massachusetts Historical Society.

The Connecticut Archives. The wills of James Cole, Anne Cole, Richard Edwards of Hartford, Timothy Edwards, and various other papers relating to Richard Edwards.

Records of the Consistory Court of London. *Liber Vicarii Generales,* Vols. XII and XIII, for items relating to Richard Edwards of London and Anne, his wife, Somerset House, London.

Records of the Coopers' Company, Coopers' Hall, London.

The First Church Records, Northampton, Mass.

Flynt, Henry (Tutor), *Diary, 1724–1747*. Harvard College Library.

Hall, David, *Diary, 1740–1789*. Massachusetts Historical Society.

The Minutes of the Hampshire Association, Oct. 1731–Nov. 1756. Forbes Library, Northampton, Mass.

Hawley, Gideon, *Journal, 1754–57,* 4 vols. Congregational Library, Boston.

The (Joseph) Hawley Papers. New York Public Library.

The Judd MSS. Forbes Library, Northampton, Mass.

Liber Ordinationum, 1578–1628. St. Paul's Cathedral, London.

The Archives of Massachusetts, Vols. XIII and XXXII. Statehouse, Boston.

Munter, Henry and Julian, the wills of. Somerset House, London.

Northampton Town Records. Northampton, Mass.

"Papers relating to the American Colonies", No. 1123. Lambeth Palace Library, London.

Parish Registers: St. Botolph's (Aldgate): St. Mary's, Whitechapel; St. Dunstan's, Stepney. London.

Regulations concerning the Almeshouse at Ratcliffe. Sloane MS. 2177, British Museum.

Society for the Propagation of the Gospel in New England, MS. Journals of, No. 1124, Lambeth Palace Library, London, Rough draft Minutes for the 1750's. Entries concerning the Stockbridge mission. Under the title, *New England Company,* Archives kept at 26, Bloomsbury Square, London.

Wallington, Nehemiah, Letter-book entitled *Coppies of profitable and Comfortable Letters.* Sloane MS. 922, British Museum.

THE PUBLISHED WORKS OF JONATHAN EDWARDS

A complete bibliography of Jonathan Edwards' works, in all editions and reprints, is being prepared by James Thayer Gerould, Librarian of Princeton University. Such a list has long been needed, and its publication will answer many questions as to the continuing interest in the writings of Jonathan Edwards through the years. The present bibliography lists only the separate items published during his lifetime, and the collections of his complete works which have appeared since his death. Only one edition is noted for each item, chronologically by group. (See also the Bibliography prepared by John J. Cross, *Cambridge History of American Literature* [New York, 1917], I, 427–32.

WORKS PUBLISHED DURING JONATHAN EDWARDS' LIFETIME

God Glorified in the Work of Redemption, by the Greatness of Man's Dependence upon him in the Whole of it. Boston, 1731.

A Devine and Supernatural Light, Immediately imparted to the Soul by the Spirit of God, Shown to be both a Scriptural and Rational Doctrine [The Reality of Spiritual Light.] Boston, 1734.

Part of a Large Letter from the Rev. Mr. Edwards of Northampton giving an account of the Late Wonderful Work of God in those Parts, dated Nov. 6, 1736. Boston, 1736. (Appended to *The Duty and Interest of a People* by William Williams.) (A letter of Jonathan Edwards to Dr. Colman of Boston contradicts what he calls an erroneous impression as to his displeasure over the printing of this letter at the end of "Uncle Williams Sermon". He was not displeased, he says, but honored; it was Williams who was displeased. The letter is owned by the Massachusetts Historical Society.)

A Faithful Narrative of the Surprizing Work of God in the Conversion of many Hundred Souls in Northampton and the Neighboring Towns and Villages, in a Letter to the Rev. Dr. Benjamin Colman of Boston. Boston, 1737.

The Church's Marriage to her Sons, and to her God: A Sermon Preached at the Instalment of the Rev. Mr. Samuel Buel as Pastor . . . at East-Hampton on Long-Island, September 19, 1746. Boston, 1746.

True Saints when Absent from the Body are Present with the Lord: A Sermon preached at the Funeral of Mr. David Brainerd. Boston, 1747.

An Humble Attempt to promote Explicit Agreement and Visible Union of God's People in Extraordinary Prayer for the Revival of Religion and the Advancement of Christ's Kingdom on Earth. Boston, 1747.

A Strong Rod broken and withered: A Sermon Preached at Northampton, . . . June 26, 1748, On the Death of the Honourable John Stoddard, Esq. Boston, 1748.

An Account of the Life of the Late Reverend Mr. David Brainerd—chiefly taken from his own diary and other Private Writings, written for his own Use and now Published. Boston, 1749.

Christ the great Example of Gospel Ministers: A Sermon Preach'd at Portsmouth, at the Ordination of the Reverend Mr. Job Strong, . . . June 29, 1749. Boston, n.d.

An Humble Inquiry into the Rules of the Word of God, Concerning the Qualifications Requisite to a Compleat Standing and full Communion in the Visible Christian Church. Boston, 1749.

Preface to Joseph Bellamy's *True Religion Delineated.* Boston, 1750.

A Farewel-Sermon Preached at the first Precinct in Northampton After the People's publick Rejection of their Minister. . . . on June 22, 1750. Boston, 1751.

(See *Breck Case* under *Books and Periodicals.*)

Discourses on Various Important Subjects. Nearly concerning the great Affair of the Soul's Eternal Salvation. Boston, 1738.

The Distinguishing Marks of a Work of the Spirit of God, with a preface by the Rev. Mr. Cooper of Boston. Boston, 1741.

The Resort and Remedy of those that are bereaved by the Death of an Eminent Minister; A Sermon preached at Hatfield, Sept. 2, 1741. Being the Day of the Interment of the Reverend Mr. William Williams, the aged and venerable Pastor of that church. Boston, 1741.

Sinners in the Hands of an Angry God: A Sermon preached at Enfield, July 8th, 1741, at a Time of great Awakening. Boston, 1741.

Some Thoughts Concerning the Present Revival of Religion in New-England. Boston, 1742.

The Great Concern of a Watchman for Souls, In a Sermon Preach'd at the Ordination of the Reverend Mr. Jonathan Judd, June 8, 1743. Boston, 1743.

The True Excellency of a Minister of the Gospel: A Sermon preached at Pelham, Aug. 30, 1744 at the ordination of the Rev. Mr. Robert Abercrombie. Boston, 1744.

An Expostulatory Letter from the Rev. Mr. Edwards of Northampton to the Rev. Mr. Clap, Rector of Yale-College in New-Haven. Boston, 1745.

Copies of the Two Letters cited by Rev. Mr. Clap in his late printed Letter to a Friend in Boston. Boston, 1745.

A Treatise Concerning Religious Affections; in Three Parts. Boston, 1746.

Misrepresentations Corrected, and Truth Vindicated, In a Reply to the Rev. Mr. Solomon Williams' Book. Boston, 1752.

True Grace, Distinguished from the Experience of Devils: in a Sermon, Preached before the Synod of New-York, . . . Sept. 28, 1752. New York, 1753.

A Careful and Strict Enquiry into the Modern prevailing Notions of that Freedom of Will, which is supposed to be essential to Moral Agency, Vertue and Vice, Reward and Punishment, Praise and Blame. Boston, 1754.

Works Published Since His Death

The Great Christian Doctrine of Original Sin Defended. Boston, 1758.

The Life and Character of the late Reverend Learned and Pious Mr. Jonathan Edwards . . . together with a Number of his Sermons on Various Important Subjects, ed. by Samuel Hopkins. Boston, 1765.

Two Dissertations: I, Concerning the End for which God created the World; II, The Nature of True Virtue. Boston, 1765.

A History of the Work of Redemption, Containing the Outlines of a Body of Divinity. Edinburgh, 1774.

Sermons, ed. by Jonathan Edwards the younger. Hartford, 1780.

Christian Cautions, or, The Necessity of Self-Examination. Edinburgh, 1788.

Practical Sermons on Various Subjects. Edinburgh, 1789.

Miscellaneous Observations on Important Theological Subjects, ed. by John Erskine. Edinburgh, 1793.

Remarks on Important Theological Controversies. Edinburgh, 1796.

Practical Sermons never before published. Edinburgh, 1797.

Collected Works

Works, ed. by Sereno E. Dwight. 10 vols. (Vol. I containing a *Life* by Dwight), New York, 1829, 1830.

Works, ed. by E. Williams and E. Parsons. 8 vols., Leeds, 1806–1811; reissued in a new edition, London, 1817; reissued, with a two-volume Supplement, ed. by R. Ogle, Edinburgh, 1847.

Works, ed. by Samuel Austin. 8 vols., Worcester, 1808–9; reissued with additions, including the supplementary volumes edited by Ogle and an index, New York, 1847, and various times since.

Works, ed. by E. Hickman. 2 vols., London, 1833; reissued with an essay on the *Genius and Writings* of Edwards by H. Rogers and the *Memoir* by Dwight, London, 1834; reprinted in one volume, London, 1835; reprinted in 4 vols., New York, Boston, Philadelphia, 1843, 10. vols., Edinburgh, 1847.

Works not included in these editions:

Charity and its Fruits, ed. by Tryon Edwards. London, 1851.

Selections from the Unpublished Writings of Jonathan Edwards of America, ed. by Alexander B. Grosart. Edinburgh, 1865.

Observations concerning the Scripture Oeconomy of the Trinity and Covenant of Redemption by Jonathan Edwards, ed. by Egbert C. Smyth. New York, 1880.

An Unpublished Essay of Edwards on the Trinity, with Remarks on Edwards and his Theology, ed. by George P. Fisher. New York, 1903.

"Six Letters of Jonathan Edwards to Joseph Bellamy", ed. by Stanley T. Williams, *New England Quarterly,* 1928, I, 226–42.

Selected Works:

Selected Sermons of Jonathan Edwards, ed. by H. M. Gardiner. New York, 1904.

Benjamin Franklin and Jonathan Edwards: Selections from Their Writings, ed. with an Introduction by Carl Van Doren. New York, 1920.

Jonathan Edwards: Representative Selections (with Introduction, Bibliography, and Notes), ed. by Clarence H. Faust and Thomas H. Johnson. New York, 1935.

BOOKS AND PERIODICALS *

Adams, Charles Francis, *Antinomianism in the Colony of Massachusetts Bay, 1636–1638* (including the *Short Story* and other Documents). *The Publications of the Prince Society*, Vol. XXI, 1894.

Allen, Alexander V. G., *Jonathan Edwards.* Boston, 1889.

Alvord, Samuel Morgan, *A Historical Sketch of Bolton, Connecticut, for the Bolton Bicentennial Celebration, September 4, 1920.* Manchester, Conn., 1920.

The American Magazine and Historical Chronicle, Vols. I–III, Boston, 1743–1746.

Ames, William, *The Marrow of Sacred Divinity.* London, 1643.

[Andover] *Exercises Commemorating the Two-hundredth Anniversary of the Birth of Jonathan Edwards, Held at the Andover Theological Seminary, October 4 and 5, 1903.* Andover, 1904.

Andrews, Charles McLean, *The Beginnings of Connecticut, 1632–1662.* New Haven, 1934.

—— *The River Towns of Connecticut; A Study of Wethersfield, Hartford, and Windsor* (John Hopkins Studies in History and Political Science, 7th Series). Baltimore, 1889.

[Aspinwall] *A Volume relating to the Early History of Boston, Containing the Aspinwall Notarial Records from 1644 to 1651.* Boston, 1903.

Baxter, Joseph, *The Duty of a People to Pray and to Bless God for their Rulers: who are to promote peace and godliness, and honesty among them* (Election Sermon, May 31, 1727). Boston, 1727.

Bayley, Frank William, *Five Colonial Artists of New England.* Boston, 1929.

Beach, John, *A Sermon, Shewing that Eternal Life is God's Free Gift, And that Free Grace and Free Will Concur, in the Affair of Man's Salvation.* Newport, 1745.

Belden, Albert D., *George Whitefield, the Awakener: A Modern Study of the Evangelical Revival.* London, 1930.

The Belknap Papers (*Massachusetts Historical Society Collections*, 5th Series, 1877, Vols. II and III).

Bellamy, Joseph, *The Works of the Rev. Joseph Bellamy, D.D., late of Bethlehem, Conn.* 3 vols., New York, 1811–12.

* See also the Bibliographies by John J. Coss in *Cambridge History of American Literature*, I, 432–38 and Faust and Johnson in *Jonathan Edwards: Representative Selections*, pp. cxix–cxlii.

Bennett, Charles A. A., "An Approach to Mysticism", *Philosophical Review*, 1918, XXVII, 392–404.

—— *A Philosophical Study of Mysticism: An Essay*. New Haven, 1923.

Bennett, Joseph, Diary (*Massachusetts Historical Society Proceedings*, 1861, V, 115–17).

Bentley, William, *The Diary of William Bentley, D.D., 1784–1819*. 4 vols. Salem, 1904–5.

Birch, John Godfrey, *Limehouse Through Five Centuries*. London, 1930.

Blake, Leroy, *The Separates or Strict Congregationalists of New England*. Boston, 1902.

The Boston Weekly News-Letter, 1704–1754.

Breck, Robert, *An Account of the Council which Dismissed the Rev. Mr. Edwards*. Boston, 1750.

[Breck Case] *A Narrative and Defence of the Proceedings of the Ministers of Hampshire, who disapprov'd of Mr. Breck's Settlement at Springfield*. Boston, 1737. (Prepared by Jonathan Edwards.)

—— *A Letter to the Author of the Pamphlet called an answer to the Hampshire Narrative*. Boston, 1737. (Probably by Jonathan Edwards.)

Buckingham, Stephen, *The Unreasonableness and Danger of a People's Renouncing their Subjection to God*. (Election Sermon, May 10, 1711). Boston. 1711.

Burgess, Walter H., *The Pastor of the Pilgrims: A Biography of John Robinson*. London, 1920.

Burrage, Champlin, *The Early English Dissenters in the Light of Recent Research* (1550–1641). 2 vols., Cambridge, 1912.

Calvin, John, *Institutes of the Christian Religion*, translated by J. Allen. 2 vols., Philadelphia, n.d.

[Cambridge Platform] *A Platform of Church-Discipline; Gathered out of the Word of God; and Agreed upon by the Elders and Messengers of the churches assembled in the Synod at Cambridge, in N.E. 1648*. Boston, 1649; Reprinted, 1757.

Canby, Henry S., *Classic Americans*. New York, 1931.

Carpenter, Frederick I., "The Radicalism of Jonathan Edwards," *New England Quarterly*, 1931, IV, 629–44.

Chauncy, Charles, *Enthusiasm described and caution'd against, a sermon*. Boston, 1742.

—— *The late religious commotions in New-England considered: An answer to the Reverend Mr. Jonathan Edwards's sermon entitled, "The Distinguishing Marks of a Work of the Spirit of God . . ."* Boston, 1743.

—— *Seasonable Thoughts on the State of Religion in New England*. Boston, 1743.

Clap, Thomas, *The Annals or History of Yale-College. In New Haven, in the Colony of Connecticut, from the First Found-*

ing thereof, in the Year 1700, to the Year, 1766. New Haven, 1766.

Clap, Thomas, *A Brief History and Vindication of the Doctrines Received and Established in the Churches of New-England, with a Specimen of the New Scheme of Religion beginning to prevail.* New Haven, 1775.

———— *A Catalogue of the library of Yale-College in New-Haven.* New London, 1743; facsimile reprint, New Haven, 1931.

————*The Greatness and Difficulty of the Work of the Ministry, A Sermon Preached . . . Sept. 20, 1732.* Boston, 1732.

———— *A Letter from the Rev. Mr. Thomas Clap, Rector of Yale-College at New-Haven, to a Friend in Boston; . . . concerning what Mr. Edwards told him that Mr. Whitefield said . . . about turning out the generality of Ministers.* Boston, 1745.

———— *A Letter from the Rev. Mr. Clap, rector of Yale College in New-Haven, to the Rev. Mr. Edwards . . . expostulating with him for his injurious reflections in his late letter to a friend, and shewing, that Mr. Edwards, in contradicting the rector, plainly contradicts himself.* Boston, 1745.

Clapp, Ebenezer, *The Clapp Memorial: Records of the Clapp Family in America.* Boston, 1876.

Clark, Peter, *The Scripture-Doctrine of Original Sin, stated and defended, In a Summer-Morning's Conversation, between a Minister and a Neighbour.* Boston, 1758.

Clark, Solomon, *Antiquities, Historicals and Graduates of North-ampton, Mass.* Northampton, 1882.

———— *Historical Catalogue of the Northampton First Church.* Northampton, 1881.

Coffin, Joshua, *A Sketch of the History of Newbury, Newbury-port, and West Newbury, from 1635 to 1845.* Boston, 1845.

Cole, Frank T., *The Early Genealogies of the Cole Families in America.* Columbus, Ohio, 1887.

Colman, Benjamin, *Letter to the London Ministers.* London, 1742.

———— *Souls Flying to Jesus Christ pleasant and admirable to behold: A Sermon Preach'd . . . October 21, 1740.* Boston, 1740.

Colyer-Fergusson, Sir Thomas, ed., *The Marriage Registers of St. Dunstan's, Stepney, in the County of Middlesex,* Vol. I. Canterbury, 1898.

A Confession of Faith, Owned and Consented unto by the Elders and Messengers of the Churches Assembled at Boston in New-England, May 13, 1680. Reprinted, Boston, 1757.

The Congregationalist and Christian World, LXXXVIII, Oct. 3, 1903.

[Connecticut] *The Public Records of the Colony of Connecticut, 1636–1776.* 15 vols.; ed. by J. Hammond Trumbull (I–III) and C. J. Hoadly (IV–XV). Hartford, 1850–1890.

Dana, James, *An Examination of the late Reverend President Edwards's 'Enquiry on Freedom of Will'.* Boston, 1770.

—— *The 'Examination of the late Rev'd President Edwards's Enquiry on Freedom of Will' continued.* New Haven, 1773.

Day, Jeremiah, *An Examination of President Edwards's Inquiry on the Freedom of the Will.* New Haven, 1841.

Declaration of the Association of the County of New Haven, . . . Feb. 19, 1744/5. Concerning the Reverend Mr. George Whitefield, His Conduct, and the State of Religion at this Day, Boston, 1745.

The Declaration of the rector and tutors of Yale-College in New-Haven against the Reverend Mr. George Whitefield, his principles and designs, in a letter to him. Boston, 1745.

DeWitt, John, *Jonathan Edwards: A Study* (an address delivered at Stockbridge, Mass., Oct. 5, 1903). Reprinted from the *Princeton Theological Review,* Jan. 1904.

Dexter, Franklin Bowditch, ed., *Documentary History of Yale University, Under the original charter of the Collegiate School of Connecticut 1701–1745.* New Haven, 1916.

—— *A Selection from the Miscellaneous Papers of Fifty Years.* New Haven, 1918. (This collection includes the papers entitled, "The Founding of Yale College", "The Manuscripts of Jonathan Edwards", "The Removal of Yale College to New Haven in October, 1716".)

—— *A Sketch of the History of Yale University.* New York, 1887. [See also Stiles, Ezra, *infra.,* and note, p. 373, *supra.*]

Dexter, Henry Martyn, *The Congregationalism of the Last Three Hundred Years as Seen in Its Literature.* New York, 1880.

Dickinson, Jonathan, *Familiar Letters to a Gentleman upon a Variety of Seasonable and important Subjects in Religion.* Boston, 1745.

—— *The True Scripture-Doctrine Concerning Some Important Points of Christian Faith, particularly, eternal election, original sin, grace in conversion, justification by faith, and the saints' perseverance.* Boston, 1741.

Doddridge, Philip, *The Correspondence and Diary of Philip Doddridge,* ed. by John Doddridge Humphreys. 5 vols., London, 1829–31.

Dudley, Paul, "Diary". *New England Historical and Genealogical Register,* 1881, XXXV, 28–31.

Dwight, Sereno Edwards, *The Life of President Edwards* (Vol. I of *Works*). New York, 1829–1830.

Dwight, Timothy (1752–1817), *Travels in New-England and New-York.* 4 vols., London, 1823.

The Edwardean, Devoted to the History of Thought in America (a quarterly, ed. by William H. Squires, Clinton, N. Y.), 1903–4.

Edwards, William H., *Timothy and Rhoda Ogden Edwards of Stockbridge, Mass., and Their Descendants.* Cincinnati, 1903.

Elsbree, Oliver Windell, "Samuel Hopkins and His Doctrine of Benevolence". *New England Quarterly*, 1935, VIII, 534–50.

Emerson, Joseph, "A Journal of Rev. Joseph Emerson" (Aug. 1, 1743, to Apr. 9, 1749), *Massachusetts Historical Society Proceedings*, 1900, XLIV, 262–82.

Emerson, Ralph Waldo, *Works* (Riverside Ed.). Boston, 1904.

Everts, Louis H., *History of the Connecticut Valley in Massachusetts.* 2 vols., Philadelphia, 1879.

Faust, Clarence H., "Jonathan Edwards As a Scientist", *American Literature*, 1930, I, 393–404.

———— and Johnson, Thomas H., *Jonathan Edwards.* New York, 1935.

Firth, James F., *Historical Memoranda, Charters, Documents, and Extracts, from the Records of the Corporation and the Books of the Company* (The Coopers' Company). London, 1848.

Fisher, George Park, *History of Christian Doctrine.* New York, 1896.

———— "The Philosophy of Jonathan Edwards", *North American Review*, 1879, CXXVIII, 284–303.

———— *An Unpublished Essay of Edwards on the Trinity, with Remarks on Edwards and His Theology,* New York, 1903.

Fisher, Josephine, "The Journal of Esther Burr". *New England Quarterly*, 1930, III, 297–315.

Foster, Frank Hugh, "The Eschatology of the New England Divines", *Bibliotheca Sacra*, 1886, XLIII, 6-19.

———— *A Genetic History of the New England Theology,* Chicago, 1907.

Gardiner, H. Norman, "The Early Idealism of Jonathan Edwards", *Philosophical Review*, 1900, IX, 573–96.

———— *Jonathan Edwards; A Retrospect* (addresses delivered in connection with the unveiling of a memorial in the First Church in Northampton, Mass., on the 150th anniversary of his dismissal. Boston, 1901).

Gewehr, Wesley March, *The Great Awakening in Virginia, 1740–1790.* Durham, N. C., 1930.

Goodwin, Nathaniel, *Genealogical Notes, or Contributions to the Family History of Some of the First Settlers of Connecticut and Massachusetts.* Hartford, 1856.

Green, Joseph, "The Diary of Rev. Joseph Green, of Salem Village", *Essex Institute Historical Collections*, 1866, VIII; 1900, XXXVI.

Green, Mason Arnold, *Springfield, 1636–1686: History of Town and City.* Springfield, Mass., 1888.

Greenleaf, Jonathan, *A History of the Churches, of All Denominations, in the City of New York, from the First Settlement to the Year 1846.* New York, 1846.

Hall, Thomas Cuming, *The Religious Background of American Culture.* New York, 1930.

Haroutunian, Joseph, *Piety Versus Moralism: The Passing of the New England Theology.* New York, 1932.

Hart, William, *Remarks on President Edwards's Dissertation concerning the Nature of True Virtue; showing that he has given a wrong idea and definition of virtue, and is inconsistent with himself.* New Haven, 1771.

Hart, William, *A Sermon of a New Kind, Never preached, nor ever will be; Containing a Collection of Doctrines, Belonging to the Hopkintonian Scheme of Orthodoxy: Or the Marrow of the most Modern Divinity.* New York, 1769.

[Hartford] *Original Distribution of the Lands in Hartford, 1635–1716. Collections of the Connecticut Historical Society, 1912, XIV.*

———— *Hartford Town Votes, 1635–1716. Collections of the Connecticut Historical Society, 1897, VI.*

Hartley, W. M. B., *Hartford in the Olden Time.* Hartford, 1853.

Hempstead, Joshua, *The Diary of Joshua Hempstead of New London, 1711–1758. New London County Historical Society, I, 1901.*

Higginson, John, and Hubbard, William, *A testimony to the Order of the Gospel, in the Churches of New-England.* Boston, 1701.

Hill, George W., and Frere, Walter H., *Memorials of Stepney Parish, that is to say, the vestry minutes from 1579 to 1662 . . . To which is appended a reprint of Gasgoigne's map of the parish, 1703.* Guildford, 1890–91.

Hinman, Royal Ralph, *A Catalogue of the Names of the First Puritan Settlers of the Colony of Connecticut.* Hartford, 1846; enlarged, 1852.

Hoadly, C. J. *See* [Connecticut] *The Public Records . . .*

Hobby, William, *Vindication of the Protest against the Result of the Northampton Council,* Boston, 1751.

Holmes, Oliver Wendell, "Jonathan Edwards", *International Review,* 1880, IX, 1–28.

Holyoke, Edward A., *The Reverend President's Answer to the Things Charg'd upon him by the Reverend Mr. Whitefield, as Inconsistencies* (dated and signed, Feb. 20, 1744). Boston, 1745.

———— and Holyoke, John, *The Holyoke Diaries, 1709–1856.* Salem, 1911 (To 1748.)

Hopkins, Samuel (1693–1755), *Historical Memoirs, Relating to the Housatunnuk Indians, or An Account of the Methods used, and Pains taken, for the Propagation of the Gospel among that Heathenish-Tribe, and the Success thereof, under the Ministry of the Late Reverend Mr. John Sergeant.* Boston, 1753.

Hopkins, Samuel (1721–1803), *The Life and Character of the Late Reverend, Learned and Pious Mr. Jonathan Edwards, President of the College of New Jersey: Together with a Number of his Sermons on Various Important Subjects.* Boston, 1765.

———— *The Works of Samuel Hopkins, D.D.* (with a Memoir of His Life and Character, by Edwards A. Park). 3 vols., Boston, 1852. Memoir, vol. I.

Hornberger, Theodore, "The Effect of the New Science upon the Thought of Jonathan Edwards", *American Literature,* 1937, IX, 196–207.

———— "Samuel Johnson of Yale and King's College: A Note on the Relation of Science and Religion in Provincial America", *New England Quarterly,* 1935, VIII, 378–97.

Hosmer, Stephen, *A People's Living in Appearance and Dying in Reality Considered; a Sermon preached . . . May 12, 1720.* New London, 1720.

Howard, Daniel, *Glimpses of Ancient Windsor from 1633 to 1933* (Windsor Tercentenary Commission). Windsor, Conn., 1933.

———— *A New History of Old Windsor.* Windsor Locks, 1935.

Hubbard, William. *See* Higginson, *supra.*

Huntoon, Daniel T. V., *The History of the Town of Canton, Norfolk County, Mass.* Cambridge, 1893.

Jackson, John, *Notes on the History and Antiquities of the Worshipful Company of Coopers.* London, 1914.

James, William, *Varieties of Religious Experience; A Study in Human Nature.* New York, 1902.

Johnson, Samuel, *Samuel Johnson, President of King's College, His Career and Writings,* ed. by Herbert and Carol Schneider. 4 vols., New York, 1929.

———— *An Introduction to the Study of Philosophy, Exhibiting a General View of All the Arts and Sciences,* 2nd ed., enlarged. New London, 1743.

Johnson, Thomas H., "Jonathan Edwards' Background of Reading", *Publications of the Colonial Society of Massachusetts,* 1931, XXVIII, 193–222.

———— "Jonathan Edwards and the Young Folks' Bible", *New England Quarterly,* 1932, V, 37–54.

———— *See also* Faust, Clarence H., *supra.*

Jones, Adam Leroy, *Early American Philosophers.* New York, 1898.

Jones, Electra F., *Stockbridge, Past and Present, or Records of an Old Mission Station.* Springfield, 1854.

Kelly, John Frederick, *Early Domestic Architecture of Connecticut.* New Haven, 1933.

[Keough, Andrew] *Papers in Honor of Andrew Keogh, Librarian of Yale University,* by the Staff of the Library. New Haven, 1938.

Kingsley, William Lathrop, ed., *Yale College: A Sketch of Its History.* 2 vols., New York, 1879.

The Law Papers: Correspondence and Documents During Jonathan Law's Governorship of the Colony of Connecticut, 1741–1750 (Connecticut Historical Society Collections, 1907–14, 3 vols., XI, XIII, XV.)

Lechford, Thomas, *Notebook Kept by Thomas Lechford, Esq., Lawyer, in Boston, Massachusetts-Bay, from June 27, 1638, to July 29, 1641.* Cambridge, 1885.

Lee, Umphrey, *The Historical Backgrounds of Early Methodist Enthusiasm.* New York, 1931.

—— *John Wesley and Modern Religion.* Nashville, 1936.

Loring, Israel, *The Duty of an Apostatizing People to remember from whence they are fallen, and repent, and do their first works; a Sermon preached . . . May 25, 1737.* Boston, 1737.

Love, William DeLoss, *The Colonial History of Hartford* (gathered from the original records). Hartford, 1914.

Lydekker, John Wolfe, *The Faithful Mohawks.* New York, 1938.

Lynde, Benjamin (1721–1780), *Diaries of Benjamin Lynde and of Benjamin Lynde, Jr.* Boston, 1880.

Lyon, Georges, *L'Idéalisme en Angleterre au XVIII° Siècle.* Paris, 1888.

McCook, Henry C., "Jonathan Edwards As a Naturalist", *Presbyterian and Reformed Review,* 1890, I, 339-402.

MacCracken, John H., "The Sources of Jonathan Edward's Idealism", *Philosophical Review,* 1902, XI, 26-42.

McGiffert, Arthur Cushman, *Jonathan Edwards.* New York, 1932.

Maclean, John, *History of the College of New Jersey, from its origins in 1746 to the Commencement of 1854.* Philadelphia, 1877.

Manwaring, Charles William, *A Digest of the Early Connecticut Probate Records.* 3 vols., Hartford, 1904–06.

Mather, Cotton, *A family well-ordered, Or An Essay to render parents and children happy in one another.* Boston, 1699.

—— *The good old way . . . An essay tending to revive the languishing interests of genuine and practical Christianity.* Boston, 1708.

—— *Magnalia Christi Americana.* 2 vols., from the London edition of 1702, Hartford, 1820.

Mather, Increase, *A Dissertation, wherein the strange doctrine lately published in a sermon, the tendency of which, is to encourage unsanctified persons (while such) to approach the table of the Lord, is examined and confuted.* Boston, 1708.

—— *The First Principles of New-England, Concerning the Subject of Baptism & Communion of Churches.* Cambridge, 1675.

Mather, Increase, *Ichabod, or, A Discourse, Shewing what Cause there is to Fear that the Glory of the Lord is Departing from New-England*. Boston, 1702 (Preface dated 1701).

—— *The Judgment of Several Eminent Divines of the Congregational Way, Concerning a pastor's power*. Boston, 1693.

—— *The Order of the Gospel, Professed and Practised by the Churches of Christ in New-England Justified by the Scripture* . . . Boston, 1700.

—— *Pray for the Rising Generation, Or a Sermon Wherein Godly Parents are Encouraged to Pray and Believe for their Children*. Cambridge, 1678.

—— *Returning Unto God the Great Concernment of a Covenant People*. Boston, 1680.

Maxson, Charles Hartshorn, *The Great Awakening in the Middle Colonies*. Chicago, 1920.

Meadows-Cooper, Joseph, *Canterbury Marriage Licenses* (1st Series, 1568–1618). Canterbury, 1892.

Means, Oliver William, *A Sketch of the Strict Congregational Church of Enfield, Conn*. Hartford, 1899.

Miller, Perry, "The Halfway Covenant", *New England Quarterly*, 1933, 676-715.

—— "The Marrow of Puritan Divinity", *Publication of the Colonial Society of Massachusetts* (*Transactions*, 1933–37), XXXII, 247-300.

—— *Orthodoxy in Massachusetts, 1630–1650; A Genetic Study*. Cambridge, 1933.

Moffatt, R. Burnham, *Pierrepont Genealogies, From Norman Times to 1913*. New York, 1913.

More, Paul Elmer, "Edwards", *Cambridge History of American Literature* (New York, 1917), Vol. I, pp. 57-71.

Morgan, John Hill, *Early American Painters* (illustrated by examples in the collection of the New York Historical Society). New York, 1921.

Morison, Samuel Eliot, *Three Centuries of Harvard, 1636–1936*. Cambridge, 1936.

Morris, Henry (1636–1675), *Early History of Springfield: An Anniversary Address Delivered on the Two Hundredth Anniversary of the Burning of the Town by the Indians*. Springfield, 1876.

[New York] *Minutes of the Town Council of the City of New York, 1675–1776*. 8 vols., New York, 1905.

[Northampton] *Historical Localities in Northampton*, compiled by the Committee on Historical Localities for the celebration of the 250th Anniversary of the Settlement of the Town. Northampton, 1904.

Norton, John, *The Heart of New-England Rent, at the Blasphemies of the Present Generation*. Cambridge, 1659.

Oviatt, Edwin, *The Beginnings of Yale* (1701-1726). New Haven, 1916.

Paine, Solomon, *A Short View of the Difference between the Church of Christ, and the Churches in the Colony of Connecticut . . .* Newport, 1752.

Park, Edwards A., "Remarks of Edwards on the Trinity", *Bibliotheca Sacra*, 1881, Vol. XXXVIII, pp. 147-87; 333-69.

Parkes, Henry Pamford, *Jonathan Edwards, the Fiery Puritan.* New York, 1930.

———— "New England in the Seventeen-Thirties", *New England Quarterly*, 1930, III, 397-419.

Parkman, Ebenezer, *The Diary of Rev. Ebenezer Parkman, of Westborough, Mass., . . . 1737–1780*, ed. by Harriette M. Forbes. 1899.

Parrington, Vernon Louis, *The Main Currents in American Thought:* Vol. I, *The Colonial Mind, 1620–1800.* New York, 1927.

Porter, William S., *Hartford in 1640.* Hartford, 1843.

Post, John J., *Old Streets, Roads, Lanes, Piers and Wharves of New York,* New York, 1882.

Prince, Thomas, *An Account of the Revival of Religion in Boston, In the Years 1740–1–2–3.* Reprinted, Boston, 1823.

———— *The Christian History, containing accounts of the revival and propagation of religion in Great-Britain and America.* Published weekly, Mar. 5, 1743, to Feb. 23, 1744/5,

———— *The People of New-England Put in Mind of the Righteous Acts of the Lord to them and their Fathers, and Reasoned with concerning them* (Election sermon, May 27, 1730). Boston, 1730.

Quincy, Josiah, *The History of Harvard University.* 2 vols., Cambridge, 1860.

The Religious History of New England (King's Chapel Lectures). Cambridge, 1917.

Result of a Council of Nine Churches met at Northampton, June 22, 1750. N.p., n.d.

Riley, I. Woodbridge, *American Philosophy: The Early Schools.* New York, 1907.

Rolle, Richard (of Hampole), *The Fire of Love (Early English Text Society,* Original Series, Vol. CVI, 1896).

Russell, George William (Æ), *The Candle of Vision,* London, 1919.

Russell, Noahdiah, "Diary", *New England Historical and Genealogical Register,* 1853, VII. 53–59.

Russell, William, *The Decay of Love to God in Churches, Offensive and Dangerous* (Election Sermon, May 14, 1730). Hartford, 1730.

[Salem] *A Faithful Narrative of the Ecclesiastical Council Convened at Salem in 1734.* Boston, 1735.

[Saybrook Platform] *A Confession of Faith owned and consented to, by the Elders and Messengers of the Churches in the Colony of Connecticut in New-England, assembled by delegation at Saybrook, Sept. 9, 1708.* New London, 1710.

Schneider, Herbert Wallace, *The Puritan Mind*. New York, 1930.
———— *See also* Samuel Johnson, *supra*.

Scholes, Percy A., *The Puritans and Music in England and New England*. London, 1934.

Sergeant, John, *A Letter from the Rev'd Mr. Sergeant of Stockbridge to Dr. Colman, of Boston; containing Mr. Sergeant's Proposal of a more effectual Method for the Education of Indian children*. Boston, 1743.

Sewall, Samuel, *Diary of Samuel Sewall, 1674–1729 (Massachusetts Historical Society Collections, 1878–82, 5th Series, Vols. V-VII)*.

Seward, William, (Gent., Companion in Travel with the Rev. Mr. George Whitefield), *Journal of a Voyage from Savannah to Philadelphia, and from Philadelphia to England, 1740*. London, 1740.

Shipton, Clifford K., *Sibley's Harvard Graduates*. Vol. IV, 1690–1700, Cambridge, 1933.

[Smith, Josiah] *Some Observations on the Reverend Mr. Whitefield, and his Opposers*. Boston, 1740.

Smith, Rev. Thomas (1702–1795), *Journals of the Rev. Thomas Smith and the Rev. Samuel Deane, Pastor of the First Church in Portland*. Portland, 1849.

Smyth, Egbert C., "Jonathan Edwards' Idealism", *American Journal of Theology*, 1897, I, 950-64.

———— "Some Early Writings of Jonathan Edwards", *Proceedings of the American Antiquarian Society*, 1895, n.s. X, 212-47; 1896, XI, 251-52.

Sprague, William Buell, *Annals of the American Pulpit*. 9 vols., New York, 1859–69.

The State of Religion in New-England, Since the Reverend Mr. George Whitefield's Arrival there, by A. M. Glasgow, 1742.

Stiles, Ezra, *Extracts from the Itineraries and other Miscellanies of Ezra Stiles . . . 1755–1794*, ed. by Franklin B. Dexter, New Haven, 1916.

———— *The Literary Diary of Ezra Stiles, the President of Yale College, 1769–1795*, ed. by Franklin B. Dexter, 3 vols., New York, 1901.

Stiles, Henry Reed, *The History of Ancient Wethersfield, Connecticut*. 2 vols., Hartford, 1892; enlarged, New York, 1905.

———— *The History, Genealogies and Biographies of Ancient Windsor, Conn*. New York, 1891-92.

Stoddard, Charles and Elijah, *Anthony Stoddard & His Descendants*. Revised and enlarged, New York, 1865.

Stoddard, Solomon, *An Appeal to the Learned, being a vindication of the rights of visible Saints to the Lord's Supper*. Boston, 1709.

———— *The Defects of Preachers Reproved, in a sermon . . . May 19, 1723*. Boston, 1724.

Stoddard, Solomon, *The Doctrine of Instituted Churches, explained and proved from the word of God.* London, 1700.

―――― *The Efficacy of the Fear of Hell, to restrain Men from Sin, shewed in a sermon, Dec. 3, 1712.* Boston, 1713.

―――― *The Inexcusableness of Neglecting the Worship of God, under the pretence of being in an unconverted condition, shewed in a sermon . . . Dec. 17, 1708.* Boston, 1708.

―――― *The Safety of Appearing at the Day of Judgment in the Righteousness of Christ.* Boston, 1687.

Stoughton, John A., *"Windsor Farmes": A Glimpse of an Old Parish.* Hartford, 1883.

Suter, Rufus, "The Conception of Morality in the Philosophy of Jonathan Edwards", *Journal of Religion,* 1934, XIV, 265-72.

Sweet, William Warren, *The Story of Religions in America.* New York, 1930.

Swift, John, *A Sermon preach'd at Boston, Before that Great and General Assembly, May 31, 1732.* Boston, 1732.

Talcott, S. V., *Talcott Pedigrees in England and America.* Albany, 1876.

Tarbox, I. N., "Timothy Edwards and His Parishioners", *Congregational Quarterly,* 1871, XIII, 256-74.

―――― "The Theology of Edwards As Shown in His Treatise Concerning Religious Affections", *American Theological Review,* 1859, I, 199-220.

Testimony of a Number of New-England Ministers Met at Boston, Sept. 25, 1745, professing the ancient faith of these churches. Boston, 1745.

Testimony of the Pres., professors, tutors, and Hebrew instructor of Harvard College in Cambridge, Against the Reverend Mr. George Whitefield and his Conduct. Boston, 1744.

Todd, Charles Burr, *A General History of the Burr Family* (with a genealogical record for 1193 to 1891). New York, 1891.

Townsend, Harvey Gates, *Philosophical Ideas in the United States.* New York, 1934.

Tracy, Joseph, *The Great Awakening: A History of the Revival of Religion in the Time of Edwards and Whitefield.* Boston, 1843.

The Trial of Mr. Whitefield's Spirit, In some remarks on his fourth Journal. Boston, 1741.

Trumbull, Benjamin, *A Complete History of Connecticut, Civil and Ecclesiastical, 1630–1764.* 2 vols., New Haven, 1818.

Trumbull, James Russell, *History of Northampton, Mass., from Its Settlement in 1654.* 2 vols., Northampton, 1898–1902.

Tudor, John, *Deacon Tudor's Diary* (1732–1793). Boston, 1896.

Turell, E[benezer], *Mr. Turell's Dialogue Between a Minister and his Neighbour about the Times.* Boston, 1742.

Tuttle, George Frederick, *The Descendants of William and Elizabeth Tuttle.* Rutland, Vt., 1883.

Tyerman, Luke, *The Life and Times of Rev. John Wesley, A.M., Founder of the Methodists*. 3 vols., London, 1870.

———— *The Life of the Rev. George Whitefield*, 2 vols., London, 1876–77.

Underhill, Evelyn, *Mysticism*. New York, 1911.

Upham, William P., "On the Shorthand Notes of Jonathan Edwards", *Massachusetts Historical Society Proceedings*, 1902, 2nd Series, XV, 514-21.

Wadsworth, Daniel, *The Diary of Rev. Daniel Wadsworth*. Hartford, 1894.

Walker, George Leon, *Some Aspects of the Religious Life of New England*. Boston, 1897.

Walker, Timothy, *Diaries of Rev. Timothy Walker, . . . Nov. 18, 1730, to Sept. 1, 1732*. Concord, N. H., 1889.

Walker, Williston, *The Creeds and Platforms of Congregationalism*. New York, 1893.

———— *A History of the Christian Church*. New York, 1918.

———— *A History of the Congregational Churches in the United States*. New York, 1894.

Webster, Samuel, *A Winter Evening's Conversation upon the Doctrine of Original Sin, between a minister and three of his neighbors, accidentally met together*. New Haven, 1757.

———— *The Winter Evening's Conversation vindicated against the remarks of the Rev. Mr. Peter Clark of Danvers*. Boston, 1758.

Welde, Thomas, *An Answer to W. R., his Narration of the Opinions and Practices of the Churches lately erected in New-England*. London, 1644.

———— *A Brief Narration of the practices of the churches in New-England*. London, 1645.

Wesley, John, *The Doctrine of Original Sin, according to Scripture; reason, and Experience, in answer to Dr. Taylor*. New York, 1817.

———— *Journals of the Rev. John Wesley*, ed. by Nehemiah Curnock. 8 vols., London, 1909–16.

Whitefield, George, *The Works of George Whitefield*, 6 vols., London, 1771.

———— *Directions how to Hear Sermons, Preach'd by the Reverend Mr. George Whitefield*, 3rd ed., Boston, 1740.

———— *Journal of a Voyage from London to Savannah*. London, 1739.

———— *Journal of a Voyage from Gibraltar to Georgia*. Philadelphia, 1740.

———— *A Continuation of the Reverend Mr. Whitefield's Journal, From a few Days after his Return to Georgia to his Arrival at Falmouth on the 11th of March, 1741*. London, 1741.

———— *A Continuation of the Reverend Mr. Whitefield's Journal . . .* London, 1744.

Whitefield, George, *Letter to the Rev. President and Professors, Tutors, and Hebrew Instructor, of Harvard-College, in Cambridge.* Boston, 1745.

———— *Some Remarks on a Late Pamphlet entitled, The State of Religion in New England, since the Rev. Mr. George Whitefield's Arrival there* . . . Boston, 1743.

Wigglesworth, Samuel, *An Essay for Reviving Religion: A Sermon Delivered in Boston, May 30, 1733* (Election Sermon). Boston, 1733.

Willard, Samuel, *The Perils of the Times Displayed, Or the Danger of Men's taking up with a Form of Godliness, but Denying the Power of it.* Hartford, 1700.

Williams, Solomon, *The True State of the Question Concerning the Qualifications Necessary to Communion* . . . Boston, 1751.

Williams, Stephen West, *The Genealogy and History of the Family of Williams in America.* Greenfield, Mass., 1847.

The Willys Papers (Conn. Hist. Soc. Coll., 1924, XXI).

[Windsor] *Proceedings of the Dedication of the Memorial Gateway to Jonathan Edwards at the Old Burying Ground, South Windsor, 25 June, 1929, by the Connecticut Society of the Colonial Dames of America.* New Haven, 1929.

———— *A Record of the Services Held at the Congregational Church of Windsor, Connecticut, in Celebration of Its Two Hundredth and Fiftieth Anniversary, 1880.* Hartford, 1888.

Wise, Jeremiah, *Rulers the Ministers of God for the Good of their People: A sermon preached May 28, 1729* (Election sermon). Boston, 1729.

[Woodbridge, Jonathan Edwards] *The Memorial Volume of the Edwards Family Meeting at Stockbridge, Mass., September 6–7, A.D., 1870.* Boston, 1873.

Wright, Thomas Goddard, *Literary Culture in Early New England, 1620–1730.* New Haven, 1920.

Wright, W. J. P., "Whitefield and the Newspapers", *Congregational Historical Society Transactions*, 1927–29, X, 111-21.

INDEX

INDEX

365